Sacrifice and Cosmos

Yajña and the Eucharist in Dialogue

George Praseed, IMS

With a Foreword by
George Gispert-Sauch, S.J.

Decent Books
New Delhi

Cataloging in Publication Data — DK
[Courtesy: D.K. Agencies (P) Ltd. <docinfo@dkagencies.com>]

Praseed, George, 1962-

Sacrifice and cosmos : yajña and the eucharist in dialogue / George Praseed.

p. cm.

Originally presented as the author's thesis (doctoral) — Pontifical University of St. Anselm.

Includes bibliographical references (p.)

ISBN 8186921486

1. Yajña. 2. Lord's Supper — Sacrifice. 3. Sacrifice — Hinduism. 4. Sacrifice — Christianity. 5. Hindu cosmology. 6. Biblical cosmology. 7. Hinduism — Relations — Christianity. 8. Christianity and other religions — Hinduism. I. Title.

DDC 261.245 22

ISBN 81-86921-48-6
First published in India in 2009

Published and printed by:
Decent Books
D-36/A-1, Mohan Garden
Najafgarh Road
New Delhi - 110 059
Ph. (011) 2535 3435

Distributed by:
D.K. Printworld (P) Ltd.
Regd. Office: 'Sri Kunj', F-52, Bali Nagar
Ramesh Nagar Metro Station
New Delhi-110 015
Phones: (011) 2545 3975; 2546 6019; *Fax*: (011) 2546 5926
E-mail: dkprintworld@vsnl.net
Website: www.dkprintworld.com

To

My Parents

and to

Rev. Prof. Giuseppe Segalla

whose constant encouragement
is at the source of this research
and enabled me to publish the book

Foreword

This is a book I had been dreaming of writing for many years, and never put myself seriously to the task. It is a book that needed to be written. I would have never completed it, certainly not with the competence and wide reading with which Dr Praseed has enriched it. The theme is of importance because, first, the concept of sacrifice is both so important in religious thought and yet so ambiguous, and at the moment in danger of dying by asphyxiation. Both Hinduism and Christianity have lived for centuries with a deep understanding of this theme. *Yajña* is the very heart of Vedic thought and practice, is pervasive in many parts of the epics, features prominently in many Paurāṇic stories, and is transformed into an ethical, spiritual and even political value in modern Hinduism, from Tilak to Mahatma Gandhi.

Unlike Hinduism, Christianity had generally not spoken of God's creative activity as a sacrifice, but has from the beginning interpreted the mission of Jesus not merely in terms of a religious or ethical doctrine which he imparted to his disciples but as a true, though non-ritual sacrifice which resulted in the gift of salvation, or of God's own Spirit, to the world. Perhaps this is best symbolized in the way St John describes the last moment of Jesus: "Jesus said, 'It is completed,' and inclining his head he gave out the Spirit." The belief that the death of Jesus was not merely the supreme witness of a martyr to the truth he had spoken to the world, but also the moment when the death of a person was transformative for humankind, has been one of the prime, or rather the prime theme of the Christian understanding of the meaning of Jesus through the last twenty centuries.

In the Catholic stream of Christianity the historical sacrifice of Christ on the cross is made present symbolically in the sacrament of the Eucharist. The Eucharist is not merely a memorial service of thanksgiving to the Creator for the gift to us of life in Jesus, or to Jesus himself for his generous self-offering on Calvary. It rather makes that peak moment in the history of humanity mystically available to all generations so that the one sacrifice of Jesus Christ can be appropriated by every believer who is thus made a participant and not a mere passive recipient of the mystery of salvation that was enacted on Calvary. Not surprisingly therefore much of this thesis centres on the ritual re-presentation of the sacrifice of Jesus Christ rather than offering a new study of the theological meaning of the event on Golgotha.

Yet sacrifice has also had its critics not only from outside the fold of religion but also from inside, whenever the stress shifted from the cosmic order to the individual ethical concerns. Buddhism certainly represented one such criticism, and the criticism of the value of the sacrificial mentality and terminology has continued to our days. It is to be welcomed that the author of this research has dared to study the sources of both Hinduism and Christianity and has thrown light on the inner meaning that sacrifice had for both of them. Both seem to see it as the incandescent moment when the divine-human relation is made visibly manifest. In the process the author shows that the two traditions can only enrich themselves by a mutual dialogue wherein each listens to the other.

The book of Dr Praseed does not bear directly on a philosophy or theology of sacrifice in general, but studies concrete sacrificial institutions that use similar concepts and makes them look at one another. More creatively, he shows how the two traditions have related sacrifice to the reality of the whole cosmos, including the material universe. It is this ecological perspective that gives a special value and relevance to this research. For although the ecological concern is at the moment strong in the Christian churches it cannot be said that it is convincingly related to the core understanding of the Christian faith. It seems to remain marginal, a kind of ethical demand at best related to the Ten Commandments. This thesis could help placing the ecological concern close to the centre of the Christian vision of reality. While reading this book one is reminded of the powerful words of St Paul that "creation waits with eager longing for the revealing of the children of God; for the creation was subjected to futility, not of its own will but by the will of the one who subjected it, in the hope that creation itself will be set free from its bondage to decay and will obtain the freedom of the glory of the children of God" (Rom 8: 19-21).

Dr Praseed is a generous host. At the end of the rich fare provided for us in this book he offers a juicy dessert: he devotes a chapter to comment, somewhat briefly as desserts must be, on the *pañca-mahāyajña*s of the medieval tradition, in some way relating them to the devotional Catholic practice of a daily Eucharist. Scholars may question if these practices are related to the Vedic *yajña*s or the later *pūjā*s, and whether *yajña* and *pūjā* are in reality directly connected as the author seems to suggest. And one may or may not see the Eucharist as an intrinsic "daily" offering. But if one does, it is not futile to look at it from the perspective of the *pañca-mahāyajña*s no less than against the background of the Vedic sacrifice, as it has been done at times so far. Whatever the strength of these tentative *bandhutā*s (the "correlations" so dear to the Vedic philosophy) this serious study may encourage future researchers to do a more thorough study of this area of "sacrificial" life in our country.

It is left for me to congratulate the author for offering to us the fruit of a long research and to let the reader enjoy what comes after the foreword.

Vidyajyoti, Delhi **Dr George Gispert-Sauch, S.J.**
November 2, 2007

Preface

SACRIFICE has been the subject of study by many scholars, yet there is still no satisfactory answer to its relation to the cosmos/universe. What is sacrifice? How is it that the entire religious world is based on sacrifice? How does it relate to our ecological home? These are questions which still need to find satisfactory answers. This work is an attempt to understand the complexity of these above-mentioned issues and to bring to light that the overwhelming importance sacrifice has received in almost all the religions has its basis in its close relation to the cosmos/universe.

The Vedic sacrifice is the most global and paradoxical. It shows a way to answer the problems mentioned above because of its close cosmic dimension. For, in Vedism there is a close relation between God, sacrifice and the cosmos. The universe takes its birth from the divine sacrifice and it remains in existence thanks to sacrifice. This cosmic dimension is often not sufficiently stressed when we speak of the purpose of the Vedic sacrifice. It is too often treated as a means to gain one's selfish motives. It is time that we recognized the true nature and purpose of *yajña*.

Coming to the Eucharistic sacrifice, the Christian worship that celebrates the memorial of the death and resurrection of Jesus Christ, it too has a cosmic dimension. However, this dimension of the Eucharist is not given sufficient attention by the Western Church, whereas the Eastern Church sees it as an essential characteristic of its sacramental theology. Therefore, after discussing the sacrificial nature of the Eucharist this work will show the cosmic dimension of the Eucharist through a study of four scholars: Maximus the Confessor (580-662), Vladimir Lossky (1903-58), John D. Zizioulas (also known as Ioannes Zizioulas, Metropolitan of Pergam, 1931-), and Pierre Teilhard de Chardin (1881-1955).

We find that at the theological level the profound relation between creation and redemption comes to light in the sacrifice. Either in creation or in redemption there is a divine sacrifice in Vedism and in Christianity. If the Vedic view is the best example of creation through divine sacrifice, the cross can be taken as the best example of redemption through divine sacrifice. *Yajña* and the Eucharist thus put us not only in relation to God but also to the universe, our home. They tell us that we humans and nature are relatives because both of us have a common origin. We depend on each other, we sustain each other.

This study was originally made as a dissertation presented to the Institute of Pastoral Liturgy, Abbey of St. Justine, Padua — Incorporated into the Faculty of Sacred Theology of the Pontifical University of St. Anselm, Rome — for my Doctorate in theology under my old name George Padinjattukara Varkey.

I am deeply indebted to several persons and institutions who in different ways helped me do my studies in Padua, Italy. First of all my thanks go to Prof. Aldo Natale Terrin, my professor and moderator of the thesis for his help and inspiration. Then my thanks go to Prof. Giuseppe Segalla, the first censor as well as the person who inspired my doctoral research. The publication of this book would not have been made possible but for the help and constant encouragement given by Prof. Giuseppe Segalla. My thanks then go to Rt. Rev. Dr. Alceste Catella, Prof. Giorgio Bonaccorso, Prof. Andrea Grillo, and to all other Professors who taught me and encouraged me in my studies at the Institute of Pastoral Liturgy, Padua. I am indebted to the Mission Office of the Padua Diocese for the scholarship, to Rev. Fr. Innocenzo Agostino Negrato OSB, the Abbot of St. Justine's Abbey, to Fr. Francesco Trolese OSB, the Prior, and to Fr. Filippo Resta OSB, the Director of the Institute, for the hospitality during my studies. I remember with gratitude the families of Mr Vittorio Nizzero — Mrs Ivana Guderzo, late Mr Lucio Bortoli and his wife Mrs Patrizia Bolzonella Don Danilo Povolo and Don. I also remember with gratitude late Mrs Gina Dalsanto in Rizzolo, Don Danilo Povolo and Don Paolo Bicciato, the parishioners of Saints Mary and Zenon, Zugliano and Santa Maria Annunziata, Albignbasego. My thanks then go to Fr. Iswar Prasad IMS, Fr. Mahendra Paul IMS, and all those IMS members who encouraged me to go ahead with my studies. I also remember with gratitude all my teachers, professors, companions, students, friends and well-wishers who helped me and encouraged me in different ways. I express my sincere thanks to Prof. George Gispert-Sauch S.J., Vidyajyoti, Delhi, for writing the foreword of this book and also for the proof-reading and valuable suggestions. I also express my sincere thanks to late Mrs Monica Lang, Vienna, and to Mr N.T. Tomy, Nav Sadhana, Varanasi, for the proof-reading.

Parts of this book were published earlier. Chapters two and five were first published as thesis abstract and then appeared in two periodicals under my new name George Praseed (2002) and (2006b).

George Praseed

Contents

Abbreviations

AB	:	*Aitareya Brāhmaṇa*
AitUp	:	*Aitareya Upaniṣad*
AV	:	*Atharvaveda*
BG	:	*Bhagavad-Gītā*
BṛUp	:	*Bṛhadāraṇyaka Upaniṣad*
BŚS	:	*Baudhāyana Śrauta-Sūtra*
ChāUp	:	*Chāndogya Upaniṣad*
ff.	:	*Following*
GB	:	*Gopatha Brāhmaṇa*
ĪśaUp	:	*Īśa Upaniṣad*
JB	:	*Jaiminīya Brāhmaṇa*
KaṭhUp	:	*Kaṭha Upaniṣad*
KB	:	*Kauṣītaki Brāhmaṇa*
KauṣUp	:	*Kauṣītaki Upaniṣad*
KenaUp	:	*Kena Upaniṣad*
KS	:	*Kaṭha Saṁhitā*
KŚS	:	*Kātyāyaṇa Śrauta-Sūtra*
MaitrīUp	:	*Maitrī Upaniṣad*
MaitUp	:	*Maitrāyaṇī Upaniṣad*
MāṇḍUp	:	*Māṇḍūkya Upaniṣad*
Mbh	:	*Mahābhārata*

MS	:	*Maitrāyaṇī Saṁhitā*
MuṇḍUp	:	*Muṇḍaka Upaniṣad*
NT	:	New Testament
OT	:	Old Testament
PB	:	*Pañcaviṁśa Brāhmaṇa*
PGS	:	*Pāraskara Gṛhya-Sūtra*
PraśUp	:	*Praśna Upaniṣad*
RSV	:	Revised Standard Version (edition of the Bible)
ṚV	:	*Ṛgveda*
ŚB	:	*Śatapatha Brāhmaṇa*
SC	:	Sacrosanctum Concilium
ŚGS	:	*Śāṅkhāyana Gṛhya-Sūtra*
ss.	:	Seguenti (following)
ŚvetUp	:	*Śvetāśvatara Upaniṣad*
TA	:	*Taittirīya Āraṇyaka*
TaitUp	:	*Taittirīya Upaniṣad*
TB	:	*Taittirīya Brāhmaṇa*
Tr.	:	Translated
TS	:	*Taittirīya Saṁhitā*
YV	:	*Yajurveda*
v.	:	Verse

BOOKS OF THE BIBLE: OLD TESTAMENT

1 Chron	:	1 Chronicles
2 Chron	:	2 Chronicles
Dt	:	Deuteronomy
Ex	:	Exodus
Ezek	:	Ezekiel

Gen/Gn	:	Genesis
Hos	:	Hosia
Is	:	Isaiah
Jer	:	Jeremiah
Josh	:	Joshua
Lev/Lv	:	Leviticus
Neh	:	Nehemiah
Nu/Num	:	Numbers
Ps	:	Psalms
1 Sam	:	1 Samuel
2 Sam	:	2 Samuel

BOOKS OF THE BIBLE: NEW TESTAMENT

Acts	:	Acts of the Apostles
Col	:	Colossians
1 Cor	:	1 Corinthians
2 Cor	:	2 Corinthians
Eph	:	Ephesians
Gal	:	Galatians
Hb	:	Hebrews
Jn	:	John
Lk	:	Luke
Mk	:	Mark
Mt	:	Matthew
Phil	:	Philippians
Rev	:	Revelation
Rom	:	Romans

Note: All the biblical quotations are taken from the *Revised Standard Version*.

ABBREVIATIONS OF THE PERIODICALS

CBQ	:	*The Catholic Biblical Quarterly*
HR	:	*History of Religions*
JAOS	:	*Journal of the American Oriental Society*
JBL	:	*Journal of the Biblical Literature*
Vidyajyoti	:	*Vidyajyoti Journal of Theological Reflection*
VT	:	*Vetus Testamentum*
WZKS	:	*Wiener Zeitschrift für die Kunde Süd — und Ostasiens/Südasiens*
ZAW	:	*Zeitschrift für die Alttestamentliche Wissenschaft*
ZDMG	:	*Zeitschrift der Deutschen Morgenlandischen Gesellschaft*

ABBREVIATIONS OF THE BOOKS

AGNI	:	F. Staal (ed.), 2001, *Agni: The Vedic Ritual of the Fire Altar.* 2 vols, Delhi: Motilal Banarsidass [1983].
AOCF	:	E.A. Livingstone (ed.), 1997, *Athanasius and his Opponents, Cappadocian Fathers, Other Greek Writers after Nicaea.* Papers presented at the Twelfth International Conference on Patristic Studies held in Oxford 1995. Leuven: Peters (Studia Patristica 32).
BSSB	:	R.T. Beckwith and M.J. Selman (eds.), 1995, *Sacrifice in the Bible.* Carlisle (U.K.): Paternoster Press.
CDHA	:	P. Gilbert et al. (eds.), 1999, *Cur Deus Homo.* Atti del congresso anselmiano internazionale, Roma, 21-23 maggio 1998. Rome: Pontificio Ateneo S. Anselmo (Studia Anselmiana 128).

CFGA	:	E.A. Livingstone (ed.), 1993, *Cappadocian Fathers, Greek Authors after Nicaea, Augustine, Donatism and Pelagianism.* Papers presented at the Eleventh International Conference on Patristic Studies held in Oxford 1991, Leuven: Peeters (Studia Patristica 27).
CRSP	:	Associazione Biblica Italiana, 1976, *La Cristologia in San Paolo.* Atti della XXIII settimana biblica, Brescia. Paideia.
GGPU	:	T. Linders and G. Nordquist (eds.), 1987, *Gifts to the Gods.* Proceedings of the Uppsala symposium 1985, Uppsala: Boreas (Uppsala Studies in Ancient Mediterranean and Near Eastern Civilization 15).
LCCS	:	A.M. Triacca and A. Pistoia (eds.), 1998, *Liturgie et cosmos.* Conférences saint-Serge XLIV Semaine d'Études liturgiques, Paris, 1-4 juillet 1997, Rome: C.L.V. Edizioni liturgiche (B.E.L. Subsidia 98).
MCAS	:	F. Heinzer and C. Schönborn (eds.), 1982, *Maximus Confessor.* Acts du symposium sur Maxime le Confesseur, Fribourg, 2-5 septembre 1980. Fribourg Suisse: Éditions Universitaires Fribourg Suisse (Paradosis Études de littérature et de théologie anciennes 27).
PG	:	J.P. Migne (ed.), 1857, *Patrologie Cursus Completus.* Series Graeca, Paris.
PVE	:	R. Panikkar (ed.), 1977b, *The Vedic Experience, Mantramañjarī: An Anthology of the Vedas for Modern Man and Contemporary Celebration.* London/Darton: Longman and Todd.

SRDE : S.W. Sykes (ed.), 1991, *Sacrifice and Redemption: Durham Essays in Theology.* Cambridge: Cambridge University Press.

SBE : M.F. Müller (ed.), 1967, Sacred Books of the East, 50 vols, Delhi: Motilal Banarsidass, reprint [1894].

SEER : S. Ubbiali (ed.), 1998, *Il sacrificio: evento e rito.* Padua: Messaggero-Abbazia di S. Giustina (Caro Salutis Cardo. Contributi 15).

Introduction

Yajña and the Eucharist — two interesting and fascinating topics of the two major religions of the world — in my opinion, hold the keys to the Vedic and Christian religious concepts which give the possibility of the mutual understanding between the two great religions. I think that an experience of interdependence can be considered a vital element not only in Vedism but also in Eucharistic theology; even though there is a difference to the Eastern sacramental theology, the Western theology has not paid much attention to it. The intuitive approach of the totality vision of Vedism draws our attention to the hidden cosmic dimension of the Eucharist.

This topic enables us first to make a comparison between the Vedic and the Eucharistic sacrifice and second to bring to light the hidden cosmic dimension of the Eucharist. Thirdly, the selection of the topic was motivated by a pastoral concern, i.e. to investigate the relation between sacrifice and the cosmos in the day-to-day life of a Hindu and a Christian. In this we have found that *yajña* being the quintessence of Vedism, and the Eucharist being the summit and source of the Christian life can be the best topics to understand the actual story of a lived religious experience of a Vedic Hindu and a Christian.

In our research we intend to use the phenomenological, descriptive, and comparative methods, for we find that they are the best methods to study the religious experience of a different religion. By phenomenological method we hold what A.N. Terrin intends when he writes:

> *. . . a particular religious sensibility united to the capacity to recognize wider and wider horizons to the world of religions.* I call this capacity and sensibility "phenomenological method" in the study of the religions and I intend it . . . as the incorporation of the subject within the vests of history to participate in the designs of the religions and thus to contribute to redesigning the co-ordinates of the religions themselves.[1]

We intend to proceed in our research with *such sensibility to recognize wider and wider horizons to the religious experience* of Vedism and Christianity. In our opinion this approach can help us to understand the religious experience of a different faith and enter into a real religious dialogue without the pretension of being superior. But we do not limit ourselves with this phenomenological method alone. For, we find that no single method is sufficient to bring to light the many elements of the complex religious experience called sacrifice. The complexity of the religious experience calls for the use of different methods. For this reason we use phenomenological, descriptive, and comparative methods in our research. The phenomenological method helps us not only to accept the richness of the religious experience, but also to respect the religious experience of another which cannot be reduced to concepts. And the comparative method helps in our research to put side by side the convergences and the differences which exist between the *yajña* and the Eucharist. Even though "there is no one-to-one" relation or similarity,[2] such comparison can help one to go deep into the religious experience of another and to see the points of meeting and the distances in certain aspects.

For the sake of clarity we divide our work into three parts, and each part connects and completes the other two. The first part is devoted to a general enquiry of sacrifice and to the Vedic vision of sacrifice; the second part deals with the cosmic dynamism

---

1. A.N. Terrin (1997), p. 11. Translations and italics are mine.
2. Ibid., Also A.N. Terrin (1999b), p. 324.

of the Eucharistic sacrifice; and the third part is a dialogue between the Vedic sacrifice and the Eucharist on the basis of the cosmic perspectives which emerge from parts one and two.

In the first chapter we will make a short survey on the *status quaestionis* of the complex notion of sacrifice to illustrate the difficulties on the concept. Sacrifice means different things in different cultures, and it is not easy to reduce it to a single notion. Although the term sacrifice cannot be easily reduced to any single theory acceptable to all the religions of the world, the most pervading character is in its cosmic aspect.

In the second chapter we will show that the Vedic vision of sacrifice and the cosmos are interrelated, and that they form a cosmic metabolism. In our analysis we will see in which way sacrifice is seen as the source of all reality, and as the foundation of everything. Sacrifice is said to maintain the whole cosmos in order and to create the continuity of time. Our attempt will be to bring to light the cosmic function of the Vedic sacrifice.

In the third chapter we will discuss the interiorization of the Vedic sacrifice in the Upaniṣads and its effect in the emergence of the notion of *bhakti* in the *BG*. It is interesting to see how the sacrifice of the Brāhmaṇas gets subordinated to the notion of knowledge in the Upaniṣads, and again how it gets subordinated to *bhakti* in the *BG*. Sacrifice gets a new appearance in the Upaniṣads and in the *BG* but without losing its cosmic character. In the *BG* the cosmic welfare, the *lokasaṁgraha*, becomes the only valid motive for the sacrifice. And it becomes a loving action to a God of love.

After clarifying the cosmic function of the Vedic sacrifice, in the fourth chapter we will discuss the descending and the ascending dimensions of the Eucharistic sacrifice to bring to light the hidden cosmic dimensions found implicit in it. We will see that this hidden cosmic dimension of the Eucharist has to be sought in the sacramental dimension of the Eucharist. The Eucharist, as the sacrament of the sacrifice of the cross plays a role of mediation between God and creation: this is its cosmic function. However, in this chapter our attempt will be limited to the sacramental character of the Eucharist which forms the basis for the rediscovery of the cosmic aspect.

In the fifth chapter we will discuss in detail the cosmic dynamism of the Eucharist through a brief study of four theologians: Maximus the Confessor, Vladimir Lossky, John D. Zizioulas and Teilhard de Chardin. We will see that the cosmic function of the Eucharist, which is almost neglected by the Western Church, is one of the essential elements of the Eucharistic theology of the Eastern Church. This cosmic dimension of the Eucharist can be understood only against the background of the relation between creation, incarnation and redemption. The unity amongst these elements shows that Christ is the creator and redeemer of the whole cosmos, and not merely of the human race. Christ is the meeting point of God, humans and the cosmos, the centre of space and time.

Chapter six will be dedicated to a dialogue of *yajña* with the Eucharist to bring to light the convergences and the differences. In this chapter we will put side by side the Vedic and the Christian notions of sacrifice and see the points of convergences and differences. We will show that just as the myth of Puruṣa-Prajāpati holds the key to understanding the Vedic vision of sacrifice, so too, the Christ-Event forms the key to understanding the Eucharistic sacrifice. If Vedism stresses the sacrificial creation, Christianity stresses the sacrificial redemption. In both of them there exists a divine sacrifice for the sake of creation or redemption.

In the seventh chapter we will bring to light the similarities and the differences between the *pañca-mahāyajña*s (the five daily great sacrifices) with the Eucharistic sacrifice. In this chapter we will show that liturgical life should not be separated from the daily life of man. We will show how sacrifice can help man to go beyond one's limited experience of space and time by opening a wider horizon of divine-human-cosmic relationship. In this chapter we will show that the *pañca-mahāyajña*s and the Eucharist are complementary.

Thus, through the phenomenological, descriptive and comparative methods we intend to bring to light on the one hand the relation between the cosmos and sacrifice, and on the other the convergences and the differences between the Vedic and the Eucharistic sacrifice.

Part I
Sacrifice and the Cosmos in the Vedas

1

Status Quaestionis on Sacrifice

We find that sacrifice was the central ritual practice of most of the ancient religions; yet its origin and meaning are little understood and also vary from religion to religion, from culture to culture, from time to time. The variety and the complexity of this universal religious phenomenon make it almost impossible to propose a general theory which embraces the origin, nature and function of all the sacrifices in all the religions of the world, of the past and the present. In my opinion any such attempt is bound to fail. For, as Dan Sperber rightly holds, no single theory is able to describe adequately the notions of sacrifice in different religions such as the Hindu sacrifice, the Greek sacrifice, the Jewish sacrifice, the Egyptian sacrifice, the Roman sacrifice, the Nuer sacrifice, the Azetec sacrifice,[1] etc. The meaning of the term sacrifice may vary from a gift to a deity to ward off danger to a complex world-maintaining activity. No single classification is able to express the main aspects of all sacrifices. The variety and the complexity of sacrifice call us to make a survey of the different theories presented

1. D. Sperber (1984), p. 42; see also E.E. Evans-Pritchard (1956), pp. 272-86. The word sacrifice is used not only for ritual offerings but also for altruistic acts, patriotic death in war, renunciation of certain commodity for a greater good of the country, etc. On such uses see I. Strenski (1996), pp. 10-26. Here when we use the term sacrifice we mean the ritual sacrifice whether it consists in killing and offering a living being or in a mere vegetable offering. See also H. Hubert and M. Mauss (1981), pp. 12-13. On a general theory of sacrifice see A.M. di Nola (1973), Col. 649-77; T.P. van Baaren (1964), pp. 1-12; K.W. Bolle (1983-84), pp. 37-63; B. Chilton (1992), pp. 3-42.

by different scholars. Hence we make here a quick survey of *status quaestionis* on sacrifice.

In our survey we find that each religion propagates a theory on the nature and the meaning of sacrifice based on the world vision it advocates, and scholars have considered one or other as the main underlying theory. For Edward Burnett Tylor sacrifice meant offering a gift to the deities to get their favour or to placate them;[2] for Edward Oliver James it meant offering the life force to the deity,[3] for William Robertson Smith it meant communion with the deity,[4] for Henry Hubert and Marcel Mauss it meant a consecration and a communication between the sacred and the profane,[5] for René Girard it meant the ritual through which society replaced the violence against the "other," for its own survival,[6]

---

2. E.B. Tylor (1913), pp. 375ff.
3. E.O. James (1971), particularly pp. 32-34.
4. W.R. Smith (1894), p. 345.
5. H. Hubert and M. Mauss (1981), p. 97.
6. R. Girard (1986), pp. 14-15, 25, 36. See also R. Girard (1989), pp. 112-24; G. Praseed (2006a), pp. 269-86. Bruce Chilton, too, argues that the purpose of most of the sacrifices is to redirect the violence into generosity, see B. Chilton (1992), p. 31. This concern with the violence in sacrifice has almost led to heated contemporary public debates having to do with gender, poverty and Third World justice issues. Sacrifice is not an invention of contemporary people but of primitive people and it is as old as religion and culture. (The term "primitive" in this book is used not in a derogative sense but to express the ancient people's complicated and well advanced way of thinking.) As Strenski rightly argues, "much of what theorists say *about* ritual sacrifice seems rhetorically directed by a subtext of personal, moral and political commitments; much of what theorists say about ritual sacrifice is really being said *with* their revulsion to injustice at different levels. Concerns about public policy are thus used in subtle ways against what is argued about the nature of ritual sacrifice. Girard, for example, projects his own *moralistic* social ethic onto the ritual lives of traditional societies." See I. Strenski

→

for Edward Evans Evans-Pritchard it meant separation of God from the human world,[7] for authors like A.E. Jensen,[8] Mircea Eliade,[9] Bruce Lincoln,[10] Raimundo Panikkar,[11] and Luc de Heusch[12] it meant the ritual repetition of the creation of the world and a world-sustaining activity. This shows that the origin and the function of sacrifice vary from gifts to the gods to a complex world-maintaining activity. Any attempt to reduce them to a single theory is to lose sight of the variety and the complexity of the case. The main theories on sacrifice can be put under five theories, for each theory reveals an aspect of its origin and function in society.

Our basic question is not which is the oldest theory but which is the underlying factor common to most religions and theories mentioned. On the one hand the material performance of sacrifice has undergone a drastic change and in some cases it has been fully substituted with symbolic rituals and prayers; on the other hand even today sacrifice remains an important factor of the

---

→ (1996), p. 11. Therefore, some of the theories which have a predominantly sociological or psychological outlook have arisen from moral or political inspiration and in some way try to replicate it. In this way the entire enquiry of sacrifice has become something of an exercise in a projection of our own hang-ups about certain contemporary social problems and the moral concerns have become the starting point of their enquiry. This way of looking into sacrifice is reductive in nature. We cannot reduce the primitives' way of seeing the world and the ritual expression of their dependence on the divine in sacrifice into our own constructions of the world.

7. E.E. Evans-Pritchard (1956), p. 275.
8. A.E. Jensen (1963), pp. 162-90.
9. M. Eliade (1959a), pp. 51-73, 78-80.
10. B. Lincoln (1984), pp. 863-74; B. Lincoln (1975-76), pp. 121-45.
11. *PVE*, p. 353.
12. L. de Heusch (1985), p. 194.

religious experience. In my opinion *sacrifice has never lost fully its cosmic function*. The thesis that I consider most important is this that *the world-maintaining function of sacrifice is not only the most common factor underlying most religions but also that it is present in all the major theories on sacrifice.*

Sacrifice as Gift

Over the centuries the study of sacrifice has been dominated by one theory, the gift theory, though this is not the central theory. It was E.B. Tylor, a scholar of the primitive culture and civilizations, who first gave a detailed discussion of this theory. According to him, sacrifice was originally a gift that the primitives made to the spirits to secure their favour or to minimize their hostility, and only at a later time it did become a homage and a renunciation in which the sacrificer offered himself completely.[13] Tylor therefore saw the origin of sacrifice in the primitives' way of securing the protection of the deity or warding off their anger. According to this, in the last analysis sacrifice is a matter of gift-giving to the deities. Gradually gift-giving gave rise to complex sacrificial rites.

Seeing sacrifice as a gift in expectation of a counter-gift has given rise to a utilitarian explanation (*do ut des*). According to it, the principal motive behind such gifts is a desire of a counter-gift. In my opinion, however, gifts to the gods mean much more than a *do ut des* contract. For gifts to the gods are not always offered with an intention to ward off danger, war, famine, diseases, etc. but are also offered to create a relationship, to express dependence on the gods, and thanksgiving for gifts received. In the words of Walter Burkert, ". . . at an earlier stage, communication established by giving was as important as the exact counting of return."[14] Tylor, however, saw only one aspect of the sacrificial gift, that is, sacrifice as gift to the spirits to ward off danger and to minimize hostility.

---

13. E.B. Tylor (1913), pp. 375ff.
14. W. Burkert (1987), p. 49.

It is true that *do ut des* mentality is often found at the base of many sacrifices, but neither can we reduce all giving to the gods to this nor can we consider it as the starting point of ritual sacrifice. For according to Thomas P. van Baaren, even though it is not possible to project the phenomenological differences back into history and to speak of a development in a historical sense, yet sociological evidence suggests that this *do ut des* formula is probably a later development which came in when,

> the idea of community with its natural and spontaneous exchange has been replaced by the desire to obtain something by means of giving something. The exchange of gifts establishing a relation has been replaced here by the idea of performance and recompense, finally even of purchase-money and merchandize.[15]

The first thing in the gifts was relation, and the idea of counter-gift came in only at a later stage when the idea of community weakened. Gifts to the gods in sacrifice cannot be reduced to a *do ut des* formula. As Gerard van der Leeuw rightly says:

> In fact there is no doubt that *do-ut-des* often forms the basis of sacrifice. But giving does not mean to present arbitrarily an object with this or that particular intention. *Giving* is to put oneself in relation with another person through an object, that is, in reality not an object but a part, a piece of one's self. *Giving* means to bring to the unrelated existence something of oneself so that a strong relation may be established.[16]

Even when the gift received may demand a counter-gift it can be considered neither as the primary aim nor as a commercial dealing. Edmund Leach writes,

> Gods do not need presents from men; they require signs of submission. The material body of the sacrificial victim may well be a serious economic cost to the giver of the sacrifice, but, at the metaphysical level, economics is not the issue. What matters is

15. T.P. van Baaren (1964), p. 12.

16. G. van der Leeuw (1975), p. 277. (The translation is mine.)

> the act of sacrifice as such, which is indeed a symbol of gift giving, but gift giving as an expression of reciprocal relationship rather than material exchange.[17]

The gifts to the gods are, therefore, to be seen mainly as a means to creating a relationship with them and ratifying the existing relationship with them rather than as a means to have a counter-gift. To receive a gift is, in the first place, to accept the giver together with a certain obligation, and to reject a gift is to declare war, that is, to reject the friendship and the communion which is being offered. The gift in a certain manner creates friendship, sustains it, and strengthens it; while rejection is a sign of the refusal of the communion which is being offered.[18] Sacrifice to the gods is a gift that not only guarantees life but also creates a relation and communion between the gods and the sacrificers. Tylor's theory of the origin of the sacrifice from the primitives' way of warding off danger or the hostility of the gods is not fully acceptable. The primitives offered sacrifice not only to get favours but also to keep the cosmos going. As Van Baaren rightly says:

> In various cultures we find the conception that the making of the prescribed sacrifices according to the traditional rites is necessary to maintain the world order. The regular course of the cosmos would fall into confusion, or come to a standstill if the sacrifices were not made.[19]

And H. Oldenberg writes:

> Sacrifice is far more than a simple act on the part of man whereby he pays honour to gods. The gods themselves, too, practise this sacred function of life which upholds the order of the universe and keeps the individual self in harmony with it.[20]

---

17. E. Leach (1976), p. 139.
18. Sacrifice as gift to the gods is much more complicated than we think. For more details see G. van der Leeuw (1975), pp. 278-79.
19. T.P. van Baaren (1964), p. 12.
20. H. Oldenberg (1919), p. 150, as quoted by T.P. van Baaren (1964), p. 6.

Therefore the sacrificial gift to the gods had a cosmic function. The sacrificial gifts were offered to maintain the cosmos in order.

Sacrifice as Communion

If for Tylor the origin and the meaning of sacrifice were to be searched in the primitives' way of warding off danger and the hostility of the gods through gifts to them, for William Robertson Smith they are to be searched in the primitives' desire for mystical communion with the gods and their desire to establish strong bond among themselves. Smith argued against gift theory proposed by Tylor stating that the primitives did not have the concept of private property which is essential to the notion of sacrifice as gift.[21] In his opinion the idea of gift in the sacrificial offering came in only at a later stage. Further, the sacrificial gift of the primitives, when it is a totemic animal, cannot be considered as an inanimate thing but is itself a divine being. The totemic animal being a clan-god acts simultaneously as victim and as deity. For him the primitives offered the sacrifice to have a mystical communion with the deity and to strengthen the bond among themselves. This mystical union with the deity came in the ritual meal of the flesh of the victim.[22] The ritual consumption of the flesh of the animal sacrificed made the consumer one with the deity. Sacrifice, therefore, according to him, could not be considered as a gift, but rather as the primitives' way of having communion with the gods. It was a ritual meal by which they entered into a mystical communion not only with the deity but also with the members of their own group by sharing the divine energy contained in the animal-god (totemic animal) which was sacrificed. The sharing of the flesh of the totemic animal made the

---

21. W.R. Smith (1894), p. 395.

22. Ibid., p. 346.

flow of the divine energy into the participants possible.[23] In his views it was the primitives' desire for the mystical communion with the deity that gave rise to the rite of sacrifice, and not the gift theory of Tylor.

W.R. Smith was influenced by the theory of totemism and made use of the conclusions of his contemporaries to interpret the Semitic sacrifice without first verifying them.[24] The weakness of his theory consists exactly in this: he erroneously thought he had discovered in the Semitic religions traces of an ancient totemism and identified the totemic animal as the clan-god. He was a professor of Arabic at the University of Cambridge and was influenced by his Arabic studies in his interpretation of the Semitic sacrifice.[25] He wrongly interpreted the custom of the *Beduini* among the Arabs to offer a camel and eating its flesh as if it was a totemic animal. J. Chelhold argues against Smith's theory stating that none of the Arab sacrifices treated by our author can be interpreted as a sacrifice of communion in the manner in which he intends, for in none of them do the sacrificers treat the sacrificed animal as a clan-god.[26] Another drawback of his theory consists in his evolutionary presupposition. It reduces the whole system of sacrifice to a single theory of communion with the deity and argues that the notion of sacrifice as a gift was a later theory. This theory itself is today abandoned by scholars. For example, Evans-Pritchard argues that the communion aspect of sacrifice is not

---

23. If for W.R. Smith sacrifice meant a ritual meal through which the divine energy flows into the participants, for Edward Oliver James it meant just the opposite. It meant transmitting the power of life to the deity or the dead, through the pouring of blood. See E.O. James (1971), pp. 32-34.

24. He used the conclusions of J.F. Mac Lennan and J.G. Frazer. See A.M. di Nola (1973), col. 653. See also A. Colombo (1998), p. 73, fn. 3.

25. B. Chilton (1992), p. 8.

26. J. Chelhold (1955), p. 181; see also R.S. Hendel (1989), pp. 366-90.

found in Nuer sacrifices, and the function of the sacrifices in the Nuer religion is not union with God but separation from Him or from his Spirit.[27] He writes:

> The theory of communion which Robertson Smith defended . . . does not help us at all to understand better the sacrifices the Nuer make to a God . . . that what Georges Gusdorf says of religious sacrifice in general, that is, it is not only something to the gods but also against them, is very true of Nuer. . . . The ideas of purchase, redemption, indemnity, ransom, exchange, purchase and payment are very manifest in the Nuer sacrifices.[28]

Just as in Nuer sacrifices, so too, in Vedic sacrifice communion with the deity cannot be seen either as the origin or as the main scope of sacrifice.[29] Even though the Nuer and the Vedic sacrifices show the idea of mystical communion with the deity and strengthening the bond among the participants, this cannot be taken as the universal characteristic of all sacrifices nor as the main function of sacrifice. However, we cannot fully deny the communion aspect of it. The ritual sharing of the animal sacrificed certainly brings a mystical communion with the deity and a strengthening of bond among the participants.

Communion is also found in the sacrifice of the Eucharist. Such communion takes place in eating and drinking the bread

---

27. E.E. Evans-Pritchard (1956), p. 275. This may be because the Nuers consider the presence of God or Spirit as dangerous to their lives and sacrifices were to be performed to separate them from the humankind.

28. Ibid., pp. 272-76.

29. Even though the Vedic Soma sacrifice may have this mystical communion with the deity, the main function of the Vedic sacrifice is not the communion with the deity but the acquisition of immortality through ritual means. In other sacrifices the sharing of the part of the sacrificial offering was limited between the priests, sacrificer and the members of his family. There was no common sharing. It is only in the Āgamic (later non-Vedic sacrifices) this communion aspect with the sharing of the *prasāda* is evident. On this see, X. Irudayaraj (1978), pp. 305-15.

and wine consecrated through the *epiklesis* in the celebration. Unlike in primitive sacrifices, here there is no killing and cutting of a victim but a sharing of the consecrated bread and wine which have become the body and blood of Christ.

According to Aldo Natale Terrin, in Greece communion is not only fundamental but also the very foundation of the *polis* (city).[30] The *polis* is constituted at the moment when there takes place a communion sacrifice. In the feasts of *bufonie* in which the sacrifice of the cow took place, the ritual is mentioned as the factor that unites the community in a great communion that serves not only to strengthen the bond with the deity but also among the participants. Here the killing of a cow and eating its meat together give origin to a community out of which the *polis* comes into existence.[31] Therefore, the *polis* had its origin in the ritual communion through a sacrifice.

In my opinion even though Smith's starting point was wrong his theory of sacrifice as communion cannot be fully ignored. The sharing of the flesh of the sacrificial victim is a well-known practice, even though this cannot be taken as a universal factor. In such sharing a mystical communion is established between the sacrificer and the divinity to whom the sacrifice is offered. One of the aims of sacrifice is this communion with the divinity. In this communion there is a certain communication between the divine and the profane.

Sacrifice as Communication Between the Sacred and the Profane

In his research about the origins and the meaning of sacrifice Smith had limited himself to the study of a single religion but Henri Hubert and Marcel Mauss took a wider look at the phenomenon

30. A.N. Terrin (1998), p. 292.

31. This gave rise to a new theory of sacrifice as the correct means of consuming meat, or sacrifice as something that legitimises the consumption of meat. See C. Grottanelli (1993), pp. 15-23.

of sacrifice. They neither limited themselves to one religion, nor did they reduce the numerous forms of sacrifice to a single arbitrarily chosen principle. They made a comparative study of the Semitic and the ancient Hindu sacrifices and defined sacrifice thus: "Sacrifice is a religious act which, through the consecration of a victim, modifies the condition of the moral person who accomplishes it or that of certain objects with which he is concerned."[32] But towards the end of their book while they wrote about the main unifying character of sacrifice they shifted the importance from the consecration of the sacrificer or the objects to the procedure of communication. They wrote:

> But if sacrifice is so complex, whence comes its unity? It is because, fundamentally, beneath the diverse forms it takes, it always consists in one same procedure which may be used for the most differing purposes. *This procedure consists in establishing a means of communication between the sacred and the profane worlds through the mediation of a victim, that is, of a thing that in the course of the ceremony is destroyed.*[33]

For Hubert and Mauss sacrifice meant first a ritual act that modifies the condition of the sacrificer or the objects intended through the destruction of the victim, and secondly it meant a procedure that brought about communication with the sacred. The victim is important because it serves as a medium. As Victor Turner writes, "Visible can only communicate with invisible through a luminary object whose destruction or immolation opens a channel, as it were, between their domains."[34] This fact makes it necessary that a victim takes the place of the sacrificer himself. The victim plays simultaneously the roles of mediation and substitution in the ritual sacrifice, and in that it modifies the condition of the moral person who performs it or of the object with which he or she is concerned. Sacrifice, therefore, is a consecration and a communication with

32. H. Hubert and M. Mauss (1981), p. 13.

33. Ibid., p. 97.

34. V. Turner (1976-77), pp. 201-02.

the divine world through the medium of a victim. Even though these elements are present in the Vedic sacrifice, our authors did not bring out that for a Vedic person sacrifice was primarily a world-maintaining activity, and that consecration and communication was not the primary aim of sacrifice.[35]

Edmund Leach too maintains that sacrifice is a medium through which there occurs a communication between "this World" and the "Other World."[36] The sacrifice, therefore, serves as a bridge or as a channel of communication, through which the powers of the gods can be made available to human beings.[37]

In this case the sacrificial offering is a gift to the gods with an intention of reciprocity. The gods are obliged to give benefits in return. The animal has to be killed first to separate its metaphysical essence and transmit it to the "Other World." The gift has to be transmitted to the gods/souls of the dead through the same path they have trodden. In his opinion the communication and the economy cannot be separated. Hence he sees every act as a process of communication, whether it be an economic transaction or a ritual act.

Leach treats sacrifice as an element of culture, and culture communicates[38] because every phenomenon of culture is communication. The drawback of this theory is that the author treats the religious phenomenon of sacrifice on the same level as other cultural signs. He thinks that he can understand the religious meaning of sacrifice by just analysing its elements. Just as every phenomenon of culture has a system of signs, and is open to an analysis according to the conceptual categories of interpretation of the science of semiology, so too, the religious sacrifice is open to similar analysis. As a consequence he studies myths and rites as linguistic facts and not as a religious phenomenon. In my opinion

35. See in this chapter pp. 21-23, 26-28.
36. E. Leach (1976), pp. 136-37, 140; E. Leach (1981), p. 111.
37. Ibid., pp. 136-38, 140, 144; E. Leach (1981), p. 111.
38. E. Leach (1981), p. 14.

whatever meaning one may seek in a myth or in a rite, it has to be sought keeping in mind the religious sentiments of the believer. Otherwise one ends up reducing everything to semiotic categories which cannot include the faith dimension. An application of the semiotic or structuralistic method to the religious phenomenon of sacrifice does not help us much to know the religious motivation of the sacrificer. Sacrifice belongs to the symbolic behaviour of a religious person, and needs to be studied from the point of view of one's religious sentiments, not as a mere fact of semiology.

Sacrifice as Ritual Repetition of the Creation of the World

In my opinion the creation of a world from the body of a primordial being, through a self-immolation or through a sacrifice by gods or demons, found not only in many texts within the Indo-European group[39] but also among the Red-Indians of America and the Indonesians,[40] is the starting and the central point for any reflection on the complex religious phenomenon, the sacrifice by the primitives. Creation by sacrifice means that the first living being had to die for the sake of creation and the ritual sacrifice is nothing other than the ritual repetition of the creation of the world[41] or of the *civitas* or *polis,* through which the cosmos and society had to be renewed. In this light not only the Vedic *Aśvamedha* (horse sacrifice) and the *Agnicayana* (the construction of the fire altar) are the ritual repetition of the primordial sacrifice of Puruṣa-Prajāpati (*R̥V* 10.90) which gave origin to the cosmos and life,[42] but also every Greek sacrifice is the repetition of the gesture of Prometheus,[43] and every Zoroastrian sacrifice[44]

39. B. Lincoln (1975-76), p. 123; G. Bonfante (1959), p. 18.
40. G. Hatt (1951), pp. 853-914.
41. B. Lincoln (1975-76), pp. 140-41.
42. M. Eliade (1959), pp. 78-80.
43. C. Grottanelli et al. (1984), pp. 832-33.
44. M. Molé (1963), pp. 85-147; see also B. Lincoln (1984), pp. 870-71.

performed with the recitation of a cosmogony, and every Dogon[45] and annual human sacrifice of the Semnones in Germany[46] were the ritual repetition of the creation of the cosmos.[47]

Sacrifice as Ritual Action that Maintains the World

Sacrifice is the ritual actualization of the great sacrifice that gave birth to the primeval cosmos. It is the ritual through which the ancient culture not only called to mind its own origins but also accepted the role of the sacrifice in the maintenance of the cosmos. This ritual actualization was needed to maintain the cosmos. Every ritual killing re-establishes a new order in the world based on the primordial killing or sacrifice.[48] The ritual repetition of the first primordial act, therefore, not only reminds human beings of the

---

45. L. de Heusch (1985), p. 194.

46 The Semnones used to offer annually a human sacrifice to remember the primordial act. As Lincoln, quoting Tacitus, writes: "The Semnones consider themselves as the most ancient and noble among the Suebi. This belief is being celebrated through a religious ceremony of most ancient origin. At a fixed time all the people of the same blood used to gather together through their representatives in a forest consecrated through the sacred signs of cult of their fathers and with an ancient sacred fear. There they celebrate with barbarous rites the terrible and fearful origins through the sacrifice [*caeso*=dismemberment] of a man for the public good. . . . In that place the faith of all used to look back to the primordial past, as if that place were the origin of the race. There is god who reigns over all. . . ." B. Lincoln (1984), p. 867. However, this does not mean that the human sacrifice was offered only for the ritual repetition of the creation of the cosmos. It was also performed for the fertility of the land. On this see J.G. Frazer (1996), pp. 519-37.

47. C. Grottanelli (1980), pp. 207-35; C. Grottanelli (1981), pp. 173-96.

48. This is the main thesis of A. E. Jensen. For a good discussion on it see A.M. di Nola (1973), col. 663-65.

primordial act behind the creation of the world but also of the fact that the continued existence of creation depends on this daily or periodical dying for life. Life comes from death and can be maintained only through a continuous death. In this sense we may even consider not only sacrifice as a dying for life, but also every female initiation as a ritual dying for a new life.[49] Behind such primitive thinking we can see a certain parallelism between the primordial self-immolation (or the sacrifice by gods or demons) which caused the creation of the world and the growth and the continued existence of creation. To sacrifice at this stage is not only to become conscious of one's own origin and that of the cosmos but to ritually repeat it for the sake of the continued existence of the cosmos. Life and the cosmos need to be periodically renewed and revitalized by the means of sacrifice.

Just as the primordial sacrifice was the reason for the creation of the world, so too, every ritual actualization of it re-creates and maintains it in existence. Such ritual actualization of it became necessary not only to make creation grow as *Manu* 1.31 puts it, or to revitalize it but also to give energy or power to the divinity that it may be able to carry out its functions.[50] Lack of the performance of sacrifice may become dangerous not only to the gods, but also to the creation, for the latter depends on the former for its existence.[51] According to R. Turcan, the function of the

49. On the cosmic function of female initiation see B. Lincoln (1983).

50. According to E.O. James, sacrifices were meant to keep gods vigorous and to placate them of their anger. See E.O. James (1971), pp. 184-85. Even in this function of placating gods we can see a cosmic aspect. On this see T.P. van Baaren (1964), pp. 11-12.

51. According to the myth of Persephone, the goddess Demeter in her grief for the disappearance of her daughter Kore (Persephone) withheld rain from the earth so that nothing grew; men were in danger of starvation, and the gods themselves were threatened with similar fate since the altars lacked the life-giving sacrifices. See E.O. James (1971), p. 122. C. Grottanelli writes that according to a text of *Uccelli aristofanei,* the gods died because the rebellious →

traditional Roman sacrifice was to make grow, to strengthen, and to revitalize the gods.[52] Such concept gave rise to the theory of sacrifice as food for the gods.[53]

In my opinion the theory of sacrifice as food to the gods cannot be easily reduced to a primitive anthropocentric conception of the gods but rather has to be seen in the light of the cosmic function of sacrifice. The gods need food and strength to carry out their world-maintaining activity and they obtain strength from the sacrifices offered to them. Sacrifice therefore, has to be seen as an action in which humans help the gods to carry out their role to uphold the world. To sacrifice is to co-operate with the gods in carrying out their cosmic function. This concept is very clear in Mesopotamia where the offering of food to the gods used to be considered as offering of maintenance. And the gods, in return, granted favours to humans.[54]

In Egypt too the food to the gods had a world-maintaining function. Gertie Englund writes that the sacrificial offerings in Egypt consisted of 40 items (animals, fruit, vegetables) and were called the "eye of the Horus."[55] This eye of the Horus again

→ birds had blocked the smoke of sacrifice. See C. Grottanelli (1993), p. 27. According to a Zoroastrian myth, god Tištrya could not win the demon Apaoša who held all the water and threatened the destruction of the whole creation because men had ignored him in their rites. Ahura Mazda is then said to have venerated him offering him sacrifices and as a consequence he is said to have emerged victorious in the battle against the *daevas* and assured the earth the fertility. See M. Eliade (1979a), p. 326. In *Śatapatha Brāhmaṇa* the reconstitution of Prajāpati after his procreative emission is presented as the effect of *agnicayana* ritual (6.1.2, pp. 13ff). Prajāpati regains his strength through the *agnicayana* ritual by Agni.

52. R. Turcan (1980), pp. 361-62.
53. A.N. Terrin (1998), pp. 283-88.
54. Ibid., pp. 283.
55. G. Englund (1987), p. 57.

represented a cosmogonic myth in which the two antagonists, Horus and Seth, who represent the constructive and the destructive forces of the cosmos, fight with each other; the evil force, Seth, manages to capture the eye of Horus and this injured eye is healed thanks to the intervention of Thot, the god of Wisdom, and brought back to Horus, its owner.[56] However, in the myth of Osiris, Horus is said to have brought his eye to his dead father, who devours it as an offering meal, and is thereby recalled to life.[57] This healed eye is called the *wedjat-eye* and becomes the symbol for the re-establishment of ordered condition after disturbance. It is, therefore, seen as the "guarantee of life and of the regeneration of life. The fact that the offerings are called the eye of Horus thus indicates that they are considered to participate in the preservation of life."[58]

This preservation of life and the cosmos in sacrifice is also related to *Maat* (the right order) on which depends the whole universe. The king offered up this *Maat* and himself to the gods for two motives, first to maintain life and order, and second to confirm his divine status. Englund writes:

> The goddess Maat, the daughter of the creator, represents the order and structure of the creation on all levels: on the cosmic level in the form of the right and orderly rising and setting of sun, moon, and stars; on the earth in the form of the right and just functioning of the society, its laws and rules; and in the personal, human sphere in the form of right and truthful lives.[59]

Thus the sacrificial gifts to the gods in Egypt meant food items and right order on which depended the functioning of the universe. They were seen as the means to feed the gods and to strengthen the established order which were needed to preserve life on the

56. Ibid.
57. Ibid.
58. Ibid.
59. Ibid.

universe.[60] Through the sacrificial gifts the king strengthened the life of the gods who in turn bestowed gifts on him. "Reciprocal giving thus shows the interaction between the king and the god in the maintenance of the established order of life and cosmos."[61] Sacrifice, therefore, in Egypt was food to the gods with a view to helping them to maintain the cosmos in life and order.[62]

Like in Egypt, so too, in the *Bhagavad-Gītā* sacrifice is seen as food to sustain gods. In sacrifice consists the food to the gods and the food of humans comes from the gods. The *BG* says,

> With this shall ye sustain the gods so that the gods may sustain you [in return]. Sustaining one another [thus] ye shall achieve the highest good. For [so] sustained by sacrifice the gods will give you the food of your desire. Who so enjoys their gift yet gives nothing [in return] is a thief, no more no less.
>
> From food do [all] contingent beings derive and food derives from rain, rain derives from sacrifice and sacrifice from works.
>
> — *BG* 3. 11-13[63]

Therefore, in sacrifice humans sustain gods and they in return sustain the cosmos. There is a mutual sustaining function in sacrifice.

---

60. Ibid.
61. Ibid., p. 66
62. In Egypt the king is considered to be the officiating priest and all the sacrifices are offered in his name, and the performance of the sacrifice should never be hindered. The gift that he offers is himself, and a statue of the offering king, kneeling, prostrated or in some other position of devotion was placed in the temple so that he was present permanently in the temple and could assure the continuous offering to the gods for the preservation of the cosmos. Ibid., pp. 60-61.
63. The translations of the *BG* texts are taken from R.C. Zaehner (1969). When a different translation will be used, it will be specified.

Again, if in Egypt the cosmic order depended on *Maat*, in Vedic India it depended on *ṛta*, sacrificial order. *Ṛta* is the norm for the functioning of the universe, and for a Vedic person such norm rests neither on gods nor on any other ground but on sacrifice. In sacrifice gods and humans collaborate for the maintenance of the universe by promoting the established order. This order is nothing other than *satyam* (truth) and *dharma* (righteousness).[64] In this case we can find that the main function of the Vedic sacrifice is a world-maintaining activity through the promotion of truth and righteousness. It is the activity *par excellence*, for the existence of the universe depends on it.

This cosmic function of the Vedic sacrifice comes from the Vedic conception of cosmology. According to the Vedic person, the cosmos is a juxtaposition of five constitutive elements: space, air, fire, water and earth (*TaitUp* 2.1) which have a natural tendency to segregate and return to their natural state, bringing the whole cosmos to an end. Because of this, the main preoccupation of the Vedic person is not one's own personal survival but that of the *whole cosmos*. It is this that one seeks in sacrifice. One's personal interests are subordinated to the wider good of the cosmos. In this case sacrifice takes a wider function. It is a world-maintaining activity. As R. Panikkar rightly puts it:

> To perform the sacrifice is not to participate in a good act or to do good to the gods, to mankind, or to oneself: it is to live, to "make" one's own survival and that of the whole universe. It is the act by which the universe itself continues in existence.[65]

A text of the *Śatapatha Brāhmaṇa* goes to the extent of saying that the sun will not rise if the priest does not offer fire sacrifice (2.3.1.5). Commenting on this text R. Panikkar argues:

---

64. On the relation between the *ṛta* and *dharma* see S. Piano, (1993), pp. 7-22.

65. *PVE*, p. 353.

> This . . . is certainly not owing to some mysterious magical connection between Agnihotra and the sun, but to the the anthropocosmic link that maintains the whole of reality in truth and order, for Man is not simply a spectator in the cosmic display or an outsider set there just to exploit the earth for his own benefit.[66]

This shows that the Vedic person considered oneself part and parcel of the cosmos wherein one had a role to play, together with the deity, for its continued existence. The cosmos is not a finished product, it is in evolution and the ritual sacrifice is the means to help it evolve.

Like in Egypt and Vedic India, so too, in Rome we can find a world-maintaining function of sacrifice. Of course, this notion is very much related to the Roman concept of *civitas.*[67] In the views of Jaan Puhvel, the founding of Rome is quite literally a saga transposition of the act of creating the world, humans and society.[68] Remus can be seen as the totality from which the *civitas* took its origin. The existence of the *civita*s depended on the deity and on humans. Humans carried out their function by correctly performing the ritual sacrifice. This also shows not only the need for sacrifices for the good of the *civita*s but also the transition from the family sacrifices to the state sacrifice. On festival days sacrifices and prayers used to be offered to renew this relationship and it was also held that the lack of the celebration of the festivals

---

66. PVE, p. 361.
67. Scholars like W. Burkert, B. Lincoln and J. Puhvel consider the Roman legend of foundation, that is the killing and dismembering the body of Remus by senators, each one carrying away a piece of his body, to be a Roman adaptation of the proto Indo-European myth of creation. See W. Burkert (1962), pp. 356-76; B. Lincoln (1984), p. 865; B. Lincoln (1975-76), pp. 137-39; J. Puhvel (1975-76), pp. 146-57.
68. J. Puhvel (1975-76), p. 154.

could be dangerous for the *civitas*. As Jo-Ann Shelton writes:

> Failure to celebrate the festival meant that the gods would no longer be benevolent; they would be disinterested or even hostile. Therefore, although many families celebrated the festivals with private prayers and sacrifices, the state assumed the responsibility of public prayers and sacrifices to ensure that no deity whose goodwill was necessary for the survival of the state was neglected . . . the performance of the appropriate rites was left to state officials. Prayers and sacrifices took place outside the temple of the deity whose co-operation was being sought. . . .[69]

In Rome the performance of sacrifice not only meant seeking the benevolence of the deity for the survival of the state but the reaffirmation of the social hierarchy. For they thought that the *civitas* depended on the maintenance of the correct established social hierarchy and the ritual sacrifice was used periodically to reaffirm this social hierarchy. Perhaps for this reason in Rome the correct performance of sacrifice and the correct division and the distribution of the parts of the victim were considered to be most important.[70] In this way, in Rome too we can find that sacrifice had a wider function of strengthening the relationship between the deity and the human beings, and of fostering the unity and the bond among the members of the *civitas*.

The scholars of the Greek sacrifice are divided into two groups on the question of the cosmic character of the Greek sacrifice. According to J.P. Vernant, the Greek sacrifice not being a prototype cosmogonic sacrifice like the Vedic has no cosmic function.[71] But according to G.S. Kirk, J. Rudhart, and Cristiano Grottanelli, it is not possible to deny the cosmic character of Greek sacrifice even

---

69. J. Shelton (1988), p. 380.
70. On the division of the parts of the sacrificial victim in Rome see J. Scheid (1993), pp. 267-92; C. Santini (1993), pp. 293-302.
71. J.P. Vernant (1980), p. 12.

though it has predominantly a family function.[72] Unlike the Indo-European myths of creation, in Greece, humanity does not take birth from the victim sacrificed but from the murderers.[73] Here, like in Rome, sacrifice is related more to the origin of the *polis* than to the origin of the cosmos. However, according to Lincoln, this founding of the city can be seen in a real sense as an act of creation[74] and the ritual repetition of it in sacrifice is meant to revitalize the state.[75] What V. Turner writes while commenting on the functions of sacrifice in non-developed cultures like that of Ndembu and of higher cultures can be true of both Roman and Greek sacrifices, where sacrifice was performed to maintain order and structure at the level of state or *polis*.[76]

This world-maintaining activity is also present in the Zoroastrian ritual sacrifices. Just as the *Aśvamedha* (horse sacrifice) was a repetition of the creation with a scope to assure the continuity of the existence of the universe, so, too, in the Zoroastrian sacrifice by the Magi and in the *yasna* we can see a certain cosmic function of world renewal. In the sacrifice the sacrificer not only recreates the world but also restores it to its primordial situation.[77]

---

72. See C. Grottanelli (1993), pp. 29-30; see also C. Grottanelli (1999), pp. 35-38.
73. M. Detienne (1981), pp. 123-55.
74. B. Lincoln (1975-76), p. 138.
75. The sacrifice of the *bufonie* in Greece was considered to be necessary to establish the relation between the divinity and the *polis,* and the well-being of the latter was considered to depend on the good relation between the gods and the *polis*. It was for this reason the killing of the cow in the sacrifice of *bufonie* was tolerated.
76. V. Turner (1976-77), p. 202.
77. M. Eliade (1979a), p. 315.

According to Marijan Molé, the world-maintaining activity was the central character of Zoroastrian sacrifice.[78] It was not offered for one's own fortunes but for the good of all. Sacrifice, here, certainly had a wider meaning. And while the sacrifice was being offered, a Magi used to sing the theogony. Lincoln explains the relation of the sacrifice of the Magi and the theogony arguing that Zoroastrians did not have gods of human forms, and hence the elements mentioned in the cosmogony such as the sky, sun, moon, earth, were considered as gods and the song which narrates the birth of such gods was nothing other than a cosmogony.[79] Again the relation between the sacrifice of the Magi and the recreation of the world is seen in the cutting of the victim. For when the animal was cut into pieces the Magi was considered to be recreating the cosmos.[80]

Even though the eschatological renewal was more important in the *yasna* sacrifice, its cosmic function cannot be overlooked.[81] According to the Zoroastrian belief, the world was supposed to be renewed through the means of the creative power of the ritual sacrifice by the Zoroastrian priest. In this way the Zoroastrian priest anticipates the final sacrifice through which Saoshyant will accomplish the final renewal and as a consequence the priest is identified with Saoshyant and implicitly with Zarathustra.[82] Sacrifice is, therefore, a ritual action that not only recreates and renews creation thereby making its existence possible but also anticipates the final victory of the Zoroastrians over the *daevas*.

---

78. For the world-maintaining character of the Zoroastrian sacrifice by the Magi and the *yasna* sacrifice see M. Molé (1963), pp. 85-147; see also M. Eliade (1979a), pp. 309-33.

79. B. Lincoln (1984), p. 870.

80. Ibid., p. 871.

81. M. Eliade (1979a), pp. 327-28.

82. Ibid.

Coming to Judaism, even though the cosmic character of the Jewish sacrifices[83] is not that evident, we cannot fully ignore at least an initial cosmic function of the Jewish Passover. For, the Passover originally had some sort of cosmic function.[84]

Again we can also find a cosmic symbolism[85] of the Jerusalem temple whose structure was revealed to Moses directly from heaven (Ex 25: 9, 40). The temple is the centre of cosmos and the various decorations present in the temple represent the whole cosmos. In the following passage Flavius Josephus gives a cosmic interpretation of the temple decorations and the structure:

> The first portion, partitioned off at forty cubits, contained within it three most wonderful works of art, universally renowned: a lampstand, a table, and an altar of incense. The seven lamps (such being the number of the branches from the lampstand) represented the planets; the loaves on the table, twelve in number, the circle of the Zodiac and the year; while the altar of incense,

---

83. For recent detailed studies on the Jewish sacrifices see G.A. Anderson (1987), pp. 1-126; See also the different articles in R.T. Beckwith and M.J. Selman (1995).

84. A.J. Chupungco (1977), pp. 11-26. According to M. Eliade, the Jewish Passover was originally an autumn pastoral feast, an expression of the cosmic religiosity which was later historicized to commemorate the exodus from Egypt. See M. Eliade (1979a), p. 427. Just as the unleavened bread, so too, the Passover feast had a cosmic function. For, as A.J. Chupungco argues, ". . . the more widely accepted etymology of *Pesah* (to skip or pass over, spare) seems to indicate it was a rite originally celebrated by nomads as a protective measure against some malignant cosmic powers which menaced the shepherds and the flocks. In order to chase away these destructive forces, they marked the lintels of their tents with the blood of the lamb, and most likely, the sheep themselves, as Arabs also did." A.J. Chupungco (1977), p. 15.

85. For a detailed vision of cosmology in the Jewish and Christian Apocalyptics see A.Y. Collins (1996), pp. 1-217.

> by the thirteen fragrant spices from sea and from land, both desert and inhabited, with which it was replenished, signified that all things are of God and for God.[86]

The temple curtain also has a cosmic meaning:

> Before these hung a veil of equal length, of Babylonian tapestry, with embroidery of blue and fine linen, of scarlet also and purple, wrought with marvellous skill. Nor was this mixture of materials without its mystic meaning: it typified the universe. For the scarlet seemed emblematical of fire, the fine linen of the earth, the blue of the air, and purple of the sea; the comparison in two cases being suggested by their colour, and in that of the fine linen and purple by their origin, as the one is produced by the earth and the other by the sea. On this tapestry was portrayed a panorama of the heavens, the signs of the Zodiac excepted.[87]

Philo Judaeus of Alexandria, Egypt, a contemporary of Jesus and Paul, also holds a cosmic value to the temple decorations and the vestments of the Jewish high priest. According to him, the candlestick with three branches on each side and a central one represented the seven stars which are called seven planets.[88] On the cosmic value of the vestments of the high priest, Philo writes,

> Such, then, is the dress of the high priest. But we must not omit to mention the signification which it conceals beneath both in its whole and in its parts. In its whole it is a copy and representation of the world; and the parts are a representation of the separate parts of the world.
>
> — *On the Life of Moses,* II, XXIV (117)

> And we must begin with the long robe reaching down to the feet of the wearer. This tunic is wholly of the colour of a hyacinth, so

---

86. F. Josephus (1966a), pp. 216-18. On Flavius Josephus cosmic interpretation of the Jerusalem temple see also B. Chilton (1992), pp. 69-87.

87. F. Josephus (1966a), Book V, pp. 212-14.

88. C.D. Yonge (1993), p. 500.

as to be a representation of the air; for by nature the air is black, and in a measure it reaches down from the highest parts to the feet, being stretched from the parts about the moon, as far as the extremities of the earth, and being diffused everywhere. On which account also, the tunic reaches from the chest to the feet, and is spread over the whole body, and unto it there is attached a fringe of pomegranates round the ankles, and flowers, and bells. Now the flowers are an emblem of the earth; for it is from the earth that all flowers spring and bloom; but the pomegranates (*rhoiskoi*) are a symbol of water, since, indeed, they derive their name from the flowing (*rhysis*) of water, being very appropriately named; and the bells are the emblem of the concord and harmony that exist between these things; for neither is the earth without the water, nor the water without the earthly substance, sufficient for the production of anything; but that can only be effected by the meeting and combination of both.

— *On the Life of Moses,* II, XXIV (118-19)

. . . the two emeralds on the shoulder-blades, which are two round stones, are, in the opinion of some persons who have studied the subject, emblems of those stars which are the rulers of day and night, namely, the sun and moon; or rather, as one might argue with more correctness and a nearer approach to truth, they are the emblems of the two hemispheres; for, like those two stones, the portion below the earth and that over the earth are both equal, and neither of them is by nature adapted to be either increased or diminished like the moon. And the colour of the stars is an additional evidence in favour of my view; for to the glance of the eye the appearance of the heaven does resemble an emerald; and it follows necessarily that six names are engraved on each of the stones, because each of the hemispheres cuts the Zodiac in two parts, and in this way comprehends within itself six animals.

— *On the Life of Moses,* II, XXIV (122-23)

Then the twelve stones on the breast, which are not like one another in colour, and which are divided into four rows of three stones in each, what else can they be emblems of, except of the circle of the Zodiac? For that also is divided into four parts, each

> consisting of three animals, by which divisions it makes up the seasons of the year, spring, summer, autumn, and winter distinguishing the four changes, the two solstices, and the two equinoxes, each of which has its limit of three signs of this Zodiac, by the revolutions of the sun, according to that unchangeable, and most lasting, and really divine ratio which exists in numbers; on which account they attached it to that which is with great property called the logeum. For all the changes of the year and the seasons are arranged by well-defined, and stated, and firm reason; and, though this seems a most extraordinary and incredible thing, by their seasonable changes they display their undeviating and everlasting permanence and durability.
>
> — *On the Life of Moses,* II, XXIV (124-25)

> The high priest, then, being equipped in this way, is properly prepared for the performance of all sacred ceremonies, that, *whenever he enters the temple to offer up the prayers and sacrifices in use among his nation, all the world may likewise enter in with him, by means of the imitations of it which he bears about him,* the garment reaching to his feet, being the imitation of the air, the pomegranate of the water, the flowery hem of the earth, and the scarlet dye of his robe being the emblem of fire; also, the mantle over his shoulders being a representation of heaven itself; the two hemispheres being further indicated by the round emeralds on the shoulder-blades, on each of which were engraved six characters equivalent to six signs of the Zodiac; the twelve stones arranged on the breast in four rows of three stones each, namely the logeum, being also an emblem of that reason which holds together and regulates the universe.
>
> — *On the Life of Moses,* II, XXIV (133)[89]

This cosmic representation of the vestments of the high priest and the temple decorations can help us to understand that sacrifices in Israel cannot be reduced to a private affair. They had a wider meaning and purpose. They were considered as something that promoted the welfare of the community and Flavius Josephus

---

89. Ibid., pp. 501-02. Italics are mine.

invited the sacrificer to give precedence to the welfare of the community and the fellowship over the private interests of the sacrificer saying:

> Our sacrifices are occasions not for drunken self-indulgence — such practices are abhorrent to God — but for sobriety. At these sacrifices prayers for the welfare of the community must take precedence of those for ourselves; for we are born for fellowship, and he who sets its claims above his private interests is specialy acceptable to God.[90]

Hence in Judaism, too, sacrifice is much more than a private affair, it has a wider function. It is performed for the common good of the people.

In the views of R. Hayward in Ben Sira's writing we can find some sort of connection between the Torah, sacrifice and the cosmic order.[91] He argues that sacrifice, being part of the Torah, is part of the divine order of the universe and this sacrifice is performed in the temple. Further the priest offers sacrifice as the first human person and his ritual action to some extent is the earthly reflection of the divine order which permeates the universe and on which the creation stands.[92] A famous saying from a Mishnah clearly puts this relation between the temple, sacrifice and the cosmic order: "Upon three things the universe stands: upon the Torah, and upon the Temple service, and upon deeds of loving

---

90. F. Josephus (1966b), Book II, pp. 195-96; see also B.J. Malina (1996), p. 26.

91. R. Hayward (1991), pp. 22-32. According to John J. Collins, the wisdom, the human attribute of understanding has also a cosmic dimension in the Wisdom writings of Solomon for it is wisdom that holds all things together. See J.J. Collins (1977-78), pp. 121-42, particularly p. 125. The wisdom, Torah and the temple service are all interrelated and have some sort of cosmic function. C. Thoma, too, in one of his articles recognizes a cosmic function of the Jewish temple service. See C. Thoma (1978), p. 1423.

92. R. Hayward (1991), pp. 29-30.

kindness (M. Aboth 1: 2)."[93] Sacrifice in Judaism is, therefore, one of the three pillars that maintain the universe in its position.

In Christianity too this cosmic function of sacrifice is not absent, though it is not that explicit like in other religions as we have seen above. Jesus' sacrificial death is considered to have redeemed the whole created order, thus restoring to its former perfection (Col 2: 8-23; 2 Cor 5: 14-19). And the Eucharist, being the memorial of this sacrifice of Jesus which has redeemed not only humanity but also the whole of creation, too has a cosmic function.[94]

Conclusion

Our analysis of the main theories on the functions of sacrifice shows that each religion stresses a certain aspect on the basis of its particular world vision and its conception of God. However, according to me, even though we can find that in some cases all the five elements considered above are interwoven in some sacrifices, and in some cases only some of them, there are two basic elements in all the sacrifices we have analysed here: first, it is a ritual action that maintains the cosmos in order. To perform sacrifice is to make possible the survival of the cosmos. This world-maintaining function is at the basis of most of the sacrifices as we have seen above. Second, through the ritual sacrifice humans expressed their dependence on the deity for their survival. It is around these two functions that the ritual sacrifice developed as a great social and religious activity, as the activity *par excellence*. Sacrifice is a ritual to maintain the cosmos and this world-maintaining function is therfore to be considered as its main purpose.

---

93. R. Hayward (1991), p. 31.

94. This point we will see in detail in the fifth chapter of this book.

2

The Vedic Sacrifice and its Vision of the Cosmos

In our brief survey of the *status quaestionis* on sacrifice we found that even though the universal phenomenon of sacrifice cannot be reduced to a single theory applicable to all the religions of the world, the most basic character is that of world maintenance. This world-maintaining or cosmic aspect is the underlying function of the Vedic sacrifice which we will be discussing in this chapter. Even though over the centuries the Vedic sacrifice underwent a drastic change in its material performance and took on different practices and meanings, yet it maintained the cosmic function in the background. This makes it necessary for us to analyse the Vedic sacrifice and its vision of the cosmos which are not only correlated but are also dependent on each other. The Vedic *ṛṣi*s consider sacrifice as the source and foundation of everything in this world: creation, the cosmic order, the continued existence of the universe, the immortality of the gods and the human beings, the offspring, the material prosperity and even the popularity of an individual. These are all the result of sacrifice and dependent on it. Sacrifice is the beginning of everything and the means for anything.

In this chapter we will analyse the Vedic sacrifice and show its cosmic significance as the world-creating and maintaining. We will then study two famous sacrifices, the *Aśvamedha* and the *Agnicayana,* in detail so as to understand their world-maintaining function.

Creation as the Self-Sacrifice of Puruṣa

The fact that many scholars have chosen the creation myths as the chief approach to a foreign culture shows that they not only have religious and social significance, but also are the best means to enter into the primeval way of thinking.[1] This may be because the creation myths are not only a "sacred history"[2] that speaks of the sacred origin of a people with its religious and social systems, but also the primitive's vision of the cosmos and reality. The creation myths can, thus, be seen as the first attempt by the primitive person to define himself/herself in relation to the divine and the cosmos. And one such myth that clearly speaks of the origin of the cosmos, of the human race with its different social stratification and rituals is the Puruṣa-Sūkta of the *R̥V* 10.90 which has become the central myth for all subsequent Brāhmanic theories on sacrifice, rituals and *pūjā*, the contemporary worship.[3] In the words of Jan Gonda,

> Special attention must be paid to the Puruṣa-Sūkta (*R̥V* 10, 90) which, treating the act of creation as a sacrificial rite, was not

---

1. B. Lincoln (1975-76), p. 121. F.B.J. Kuiper considers that the key to an insight into the Vedic religion consists in its cosmogony: F.B.J. Kuiper (1975-76), p. 107.
2. F.B.J. Kuiper (1970-71), p. 91; M. Eliade (1969a), pp. 72-87. On myth as symbolic and metaphoric language see T. Manickam (1998), pp. 56-65.
3. Vedic sacrifices have become almost a relic of the past and *pūjā* has become more important in the daily and occasional worship of the Hindus. The standared type of *pūjā* consists of sixteen elements (*ṣoḍaśopacāra pūjā*): 1. invocation of the deity, 2. offering of a seat, 3. water for washing the feet, 4. water offered at the respectful reception of a guest (*arghya*), 5. water for sipping, 6. bath, 7. garments, 8. sacred thread, 9. sandalwood paste, 10. flowers, 11. incense, 12. lamp, 13. food, 14. mouth perfume, 15. hymn, and 16. circumambulation. At each service a verse from the Puruṣa-Sūkta is recited. There can be some differences in the list as can be seen in *ṣoḍaśopacāra pūjā* I & *ṣoḍaśopacāra pūjā* II. G. Bühnemann (1988), pp. 135-77.

> only to exert a powerful and permanent influence upon the speculative thought of the post-Ṛgvedic period but also to play an important part in a variety of rituals.[4]

Verses of this hymn are recited in various rituals,[5] even in the contemporary *pūjā*.

For the Vedic person the creation of the universe is a divine sacrifice[6] and it can survive only through a continued sacrifice. V.S Agrawala while commenting on the Vedic sacrifice argues that creation on the cosmic plane is a universal sacrifice in which the creator offers himself as the *āhuti* (offering).[7] Ugo Bianchi, too, has a similar view on the Vedic concept of creation for, while discussing various Vedic theories about the origins of god and the universe, he comes to a similar conclusion when he writes, ". . . Creation is a primordial sacrifice, done by the primordial being, or else done by gods, on a primordial being."[8] In the Vedas creation is not only associated with a divine sacrifice but also the first principle of all life. This idea is the central theme of the Puruṣa-

---

4. J. Gonda (1980), p. 222.
5. Ibid., pp. 222-23.
6. Creation as a sacrifice of a primordial being is found not only in Vedic texts but also in other religious texts belonging to the Indo-European group. For more details see B. Lincoln (1975-76), pp. 123ff. See also C. Grottanelli (1980), pp. 207-35. Creation of the cosmos from the sacrifice and dismemberment of a primordial being can be a sophisticated piece of speculation on the relation between the microcosm and the macrocosm, whereby a human being is understood to be the microcosmic image of the world and the world as the macrocosmic projection of human being. B. Lincoln (1975-76), 122. But what is interesting is that in the Vedic India this myth is interpreted not only to justify the different sacrifices and rituals but also to assign each member of a *varṇa* (colour, caste) a particular god, hymn, season, place, etc., in society. See B.K. Smith (1994), pp. 58-349.
7. V.S. Agrawala (1962), p. 7.
8. U. Bianchi (1960), p. 66.

Sūkta.[9]

This myth can be considered to be the key to the Brāhmanic theory of sacrifice, i.e. as the creative and world-maintaining activity[10] and its importance in the Vedic rituals is clear from the fact that it is recited during *Aśvamesdha*, *Agnicayana*, at the rites which are performed by those who long for the birth of a son, in the ceremonies for the foundation of a temple, in initiation rites, in the healing ritual (of physical illness), in the bathing ritual to ward off sins and evil or also in the expiation rites, in the funeral rites to help the soul in its transition, when a devotee is admitted into a religious community, in the *pūjā*, etc.[11]

---

9. For a detailed analysis of this myth see L. Malieckal (1989b), pp. 78-126.

10. The important Vedic cosmogonies are the following: creation through the dismemberment of *puruṣa* (*ṚV* 10.90), the Emergence of the Hiraṇyagarbha and subsequent breaking of its shells which form the heaven and earth (*ṚV* 10.121.1), Viśvakarman (*ṚV* 10.81), and the cosmogonic boar bringing some mud upward from the bottom of the Waters which then became the beginning of the earth (*MS* 1.6.3; *KS* 8.2; *TS* 7.1.5.1; see also *TB* 1.2.1.3 and *TA* 10.1.8), and the killing of Vṛtra by Indra and subsequent liberation of water (*ṚV* 1.32); creation through *vāc* by Prajāpati (*ŚB* 2.1.4.11-13); creation through *tapas* by Prajāpati (*ŚB* 11.5.8.1-4), etc. For the different Vedic passages on creation see R. Panikkar (1966), pp. 87-98. These myths show that the Vedic theories on creation cannot be reduced to a single theory. Creation is not the work of a single god but the result of different gods, who created in different ways. However, the most important Vedic theory of creation is *the creation through the dismemberment of puruṣa* which is the central myth for the subsequent Vedic theories on sacrifice and other rituals. For the cosmogonic myths of the *ṚV* in general see W.N. Brown (1965), pp. 23-24; W.N. Brown (1942), pp. 85-98; F.B.J. Kuiper (1983); and on the Puruṣa-Sūkta see W.N. Brown (1931), pp. 108-18; For the cosmogonic myths of Prajāpati in the Brāhmaṇas see the excellent work of B.K. Smith (1994), pp. 331-45.

11. J. Gonda (1977), pp. 97-98.

The close relation of this myth to a number of rites calls us to look briefly into the relation between the myth and the ritual. Starting with Robertson Smith,[12] the Cambridge Myth and Ritual School which began among the nineteenth century anthropologists, has explained this relation in terms of a priority of the rite over the myth.[13] According to this school, every myth has a direct reference to a rite and it is the latter that has given rise to the former.[14] Whatever position one may take on this matter depends on the definition we give to rite and myth. Given the complexity of the matter we limit ourselves to pointing out the intimate relation between myth and rite. Myths seem to be elaborated in the course of time to give credibility and authority

---

12. W.R. Smith (1894), pp. 13ff.

13. The theory of the dependence of the myth on the rite suggested by W.R. Smith was taken up by G. Frazer and many other followers of the Cambridge school like J. Harrison, S.H. Hooke, etc. For a detailed discussion on the scholars of this school who hold the priority of the rite over the myth see W. Burkert (1981), p. 41 and the foot notes 105-09; W. Burkert (1991), pp. 59-67; A.N. Terrin (1983), pp. 32-33; A.N. Terrin (1999a), pp. 315-16. However, according to U. Bianchi, the thesis of the *Myth and Ritual School,* that every myth has a direct reference to a rite, is only a hypothesis for work. U. Bianchi (1986), p. 150. W. Burkert, who follows a sociobiological approach to the study of the rituals, after having presented the views of the Cambridge school argues that myth and rite are very closely related but they need not be dependent on one another, and given the fact that rituals are found in the animal world, the rite can be seen as older than the myth. W. Burkert (1991), p. 92. In another work he argues that the myth is not necessarily a part of the ritual as the *Myth and Ritual School* holds. W. Burkert (1981), p. 42.

14. The scholars, like J. Fontenrose and Geoffrey S. Kirk, are against the view that rite is prior to the myth. Against W.R. Smith and Frazer see J. Fontenrose (1966), p. 54; G.S. Kirk (1993), pp. 233-36. According to Kirk, " . . . religious rituals are not often, in themselves, the prime causes of myths, nor are myths primarily 'aetiological' of religious rituals. . . . Some rituals depend on myths, rather →

to the rites.

If the myth is dependent on the rite, as the Myth and Ritual School holds, then we may say that the myth of the Puruṣa-Sūkta may be the result of the ritual practices in the Brāhmaṇas. It becomes, then, difficult to identify which original rite caused the formulation of this myth. Its importance can be seen from the fact that it forms the basis for the Brāhmanic theory on sacrifice, and for the time being we make a distinction between the myth and the rites which make use of this myth.[15]

We give here the *puruṣa* myth which speaks about creation as the divine sacrifice and is the basis for all later speculation on

---

→ than vice versa, and many myths . . . are devoid of ritual aspects except for what might be implied by heroic cults." G.S. Kirk (1972), pp. 90-94. Here our author opposes the thesis of the *Myth and Ritual School* by demonstrating that all narrations are myths and some of these myths have no rituals, or some of the rituals have no myths. Surely that all myths do not have rituals does not rule out that myths and rituals are closely connected. The complexity of the matter calls us to view the myth-ritual theory or study its developments from different perspectives. This is the new method that Robert Segal has adopted in his book on *The Myth and Ritual Theory*. See R.A. Segal (1998), pp. 357-467.

15. However, Frits Staal is against any such view that the Vedic rituals are related to the myths. He argues that the connection between the myth and rite is a Western concern and says: "The idea that rites and myths are closely connected is a typically Western idea. It is connected with the notion of 'orthodoxy,' which stress the importance of opinions and ideas. To the Indian Ritualist it is the activity that counts. As a mode of existence it is perfect in itself and does not stand in need of something else." *AGNI*, vol. 1, p. 12. Even though Frits Staal does not recognize any connection between the myths and rituals there are a number of passages which speak of the myths as the motive for the rituals, or myths are created to support the ritual. On the myths see the *Agnicayana* section. F. Staal himself seems to contradict what he has written later on when he affirms that the *Agnicayana* and *Puruṣamedha* are related to the Puruṣa-Sūkta. See ibid., pp. 115 and 124.

sacrifice in the Brāhmaṇas. First we will present the whole poem[16] and then we will analyse it to gather its meaning and implications for the Vedic theology on sacrifice. We follow the translation of Frits Staal.[17]

> *Puruṣa* has a thousand heads, a thousand eyes, a thousand feet. He pervades the earth everywhere and extends beyond for ten fingers' breadth ॥1 ॥
>
> *Puruṣa* himself is all this, whatever has been and whatever is to be. He is the lord of immortality and also lord of that which grows on food ॥2 ॥
>
> Such is his greatness, and *puruṣa* is yet greater than this. All creatures make up a quarter of him; three quarters are the immortal in heaven ॥3 ॥
>
> With three quarters *puruṣa* has risen above, and one quarter of him still remains here, whence he spread out everywhere, pervading that which eats and that which does not eat ॥4 ॥
>
> From him Virāja was born, from Virāja came *puruṣa* who having been born, ranged beyond the earth in the west and in the east ॥5 ॥
>
> When the gods performed the sacrifice, using *puruṣa* as the offering, spring was the clarified butter, summer the fuel, autumn the oblation ॥6 ॥
>
> They sprinkled *puruṣa,* the sacrifice, born at the beginning, upon the sacred grass. With him the gods, the *sādhyas*, and the sages sacrificed ॥7 ॥
>
> From that sacrifice in which everything was offered the clarified butter was obtained, and they made it into those beasts who live in the air, in the forest, and in villages ॥8 ॥
>
> From that sacrifice in which everything was offered the verses and chants were born, the meters were born, and the formulas were born ॥9 ॥

---

16. The fact that the entire myth has been reproduced in *AV* 19.6 and in *YV* 31.1-16 shows its importance in the Vedic religion.

17. *AGNI*, vol. 1, pp. 113-15.

Fom it horses were born, and those other animals that have a double set of incisors; cows were born from it, and goats and sheep were born from it ॥10॥

When they divided *puruṣa,* into how many parts did they disperse him? What became of his mouth, what of his arms, what were his two thighs and his two feet called? ॥11॥

His mouth was the Brahmin, his arms were made into the chieftains, his two thighs were the tribesmen, and from his feet the servants were born ॥12॥

The moon was born from his mind; the sun was born from his eye. From his mouth came Indra and Agni, and from his breath wind was born ॥13॥

From his navel the atmosphere was born; from his head the heaven appeared. From his two feet the earth, and the regions of the sky from his ears. Thus they fashioned the worlds ॥14॥

There were seven enclosing fire-sticks for him, and thrice seven fire-sticks when the gods, performing the sacrifice, bound down *puruṣa* as the sacrificial victim ॥15॥

With this sacrifice the gods sacrificed; these were the first *dharma.* And these powers reached the dome of heaven where dwell the ancient *sādhya*s and gods ॥16॥

According to this myth, the creation of the universe is the result of a dismemberment of the cosmic giant, *puruṣa* — later on identified with Prajāpati in the Brāhmaṇas[18] — by the gods. In the words of Jan Gonda the "*Puruṣa*-hymn can be said to be the

18. According to *ŚB* 6.1.1.5, "That same Person (*puruṣa*) became Prajāpati, the lord of generation." Hence the *puruṣa* of the *ṚV* not only becomes the main deity in the Brāhmaṇas but is also said to be the thirty-fourth and the summation of all the gods for he encompasses all beings. See B.K. Smith (1989), pp. 54-55. It is true that the name Prajāpati is more predominant in the Brāhmaṇas but that does not mean that he is the creation of the

→

first expression of the idea that the creation of the universe is the self-limitation of a transcendent Person 'who is this All,' manifesting himself in the realm of our experience."[19] Such an idea does not stop there, it goes further and affirms the Vedic doctrine of sacrifice. According to Jan Gonda, this myth affirms three points: the unity of all existence, the performance of a ritual indispensable in the process of creation, and the rite as an *opus operans* in itself.[20]

M. Biardeau's and C. Malamoud's comment on the Vedic theory of creation through the self-immolation of the creator can help us to understand the main thrust of the *puruṣa* hymn. In their words,

> This man/*puruṣa* is at once the sacrifice and the sacrificial victim, while he represents the totality of the spatio-temporal universe, of the domain mortal and immortal, visible and invisible . . . we have here clearly the first Brāhmanic philosophy: *the cosmos is the product of sacrifice, the sacrifice is in the beginning of everything.*[21]

The same idea can be also found in R. Panikkar when he writes that *puruṣa* stands for the total reality of which we are a reflection:

> The primordial Man is not simply another name for a heteronomous God, nor a mere euphemism for an autonomic individual Man, but the living expression of the ontonomic Man, that total reality of which we are a reflection, a reflection that

---

→ Brāhmaṇas for according to J. Gonda, ". . . there are sufficient data pointing to the existence of Prajāpati in a comparatively early period of Indian history as a 'popular deity,' worshipped by the common man, believed to meet his wishes, and mainly functioning in accordance with the literal meaning of his name." J. Gonda (1982-83), p. 147.

19. J. Gonda (1977), p. 95. J. Gonda (1996), p. 25.

20. Ibid., p. 96.

21. M. Biardeau and C. Malamoud (1976), p. 16. This translation is taken from L. Malieckal (1989b), pp. 83-84.

> contains the whole, indeed, but in a rather limited and all too often narrow way.[22]

As we have seen, this myth has 16 verses and the very selection of 16 verses indicates at the outset the totality,[23] which is the main theme of the first five verses. These verses give a description of the greatness and the all-inclusiveness of the *puruṣa* and the birth of *puruṣa* itself. For the Vedic people cosmogony is related to theogony. Verse 15 comes back to the theme of totality. Verses 6-16 describe the sacrifice of *puruṣa* and the gods, the birth of the sacrificial animals and the ritual *formulae*, the social stratification, etc. Hence, the main thrusts of the myth are twofold: first to affirm the *totality of puruṣa and the primordial unity he breaks to give form to creation,* and secondly to affirm *the creation as a divine sacrifice thereby bringing everything under 'sacrifice,'* the *nābhi* (navel) of the world (*R̥V* 1.164.35). The hymn speaks of a mysterious oneness, a symbolic correlation between the humans and nature.[24] In the words of Subhash Anand the hymn says, "Humans and the rest of creation are *bandhus* (relatives), and the bond (*bandha*) that binds us together is the belief that we all have our birth from a common parent."[25] The hymn can be divided into two sections, the first about the totality of *puruṣa* and the second about the sacrifice as the beginning of everything.

Puruṣa as "Thiss All" and the Meeting Point of History

The hymn is a masterpiece of the Vedic theology which progressively unveils the thinking pattern of Vedism. The first part describes *puruṣa* as the totality of this universe (vv. 1-5, 15), the meeting point of history and his immanent and transcendent characters. This theme of *puruṣa* as the totality of the *spatio-temporal*

22. *PVE,* p. 73.
23. J. Gonda (1977), p. 98.
24. See S. Anand (2002), p. 26.
25. Ibid., p. 27.

reality forms the background to the second part of the hymn which is dedicated to creation as the divine sacrifice.

The hymn begins with the affirmation of the totality, the all-inclusiveness of the *puruṣa* through the use of three epithets, thousand-headed, thousand-eyed and thousand-footed and through the phrase that he "extends beyond for ten fingers' breadth" (*ati atiṣṭhad daśāṅgulam*) (v. 1).[26] The word thousand in the Vedas means not so much a number as the totality, all-inclusiveness, and according to W.N. Brown it means the manifold nature of *puruṣa*.[27] In the words of L. Malieckal it means here the multiplicity and the infinity of *puruṣa*.[28] The word "thousand," therefore, comes to say that *puruṣa* pervades the earth on all sides and extends beyond it, he is everything that exists here, and more. The epithet "thousand eyed" which is given to Indra and Vāyu in *ṚV* 1.23.3 and to Agni in *ṚV* 1.79.12; *TS* 5.4.7.2 and to Viśvakarman in *ṚV* 10.81.3, is here given to *puruṣa* and it means his all-seeing capacity. This explains, on the one hand, that *puruṣa* is the totality of creation, and on the other, the interrelatedness between the creation and the creator which is a must for its continuity. For the Vedic person there is nothing in this universe which is not related to the Creator, for *puruṣa* is the totality of all that exists in this universe and beyond it. *Puruṣa* is whatever has been and whatever will be. *Puruṣa* is the meeting point between the past, present and the future, and hence he is not only the totality of space but also of time.

---

26. For a detailed discussion on this phrase see A.K. Coomaraswamy (1946), pp. 145-61. This verse (1) is recited while offering the first element of *pūjā*. See G. Bühnemann (1988), p. 136.

27. W.N. Brown (1931), p. 109.

28. L. Malieckal (1989b), p. 93. The *ŚB* while interpreting the symbolic meaning of the scattering of the thousand golden chips on the *Agnicayana* says that thousand means everything (8.7.4.9 and 11).

This *puruṣa* who is the totality of the universe in its *spatio-temporal dimensions* is the lord of immortality and the lord of that which grows on food (v. 2).[29] In this way the author puts *puruṣa* in relation to Agni, one of the important Vedic gods and the indispensable element in the sacrifice. *Puruṣa* is therefore related to *amr̥tattva* (immortality) and *anna* (food) just like Agni.[30] Sacrifice is thus put in relation to immortality, food and Agni who is considered to be the mouth of the gods, and the conveyor of the sacrifice to the gods.

Even though *puruṣa* is spoken of as the totality of space and time in the previous verses, the author is careful not to reduce *puruṣa* to this universe and exactly for this reason in verse three he says that *puruṣa* is more than the universe.[31] All creatures are only a quarter of him, three quarters are what is immortal in heaven.[32] He is immanent and transcendent; he is the creation and more than it. The myth of the *puruṣa* helps to maintain both the immanent and the transcendent characters of the creator without denying either of them.

---

29. In this translation the *puruṣa* is said to be the Lord of that which grows on food. According to me such a translation cancels the sacrificial connotation of *annena* that cannot be overlooked. This verse (2) is recited while offering the second element of *pūjā*. See G. Bühnemann (1988), p. 137.

30. See W.N. Brown (1931), pp. 110-11. See also W.N. Brown (1968), pp. 199-218.

31. These verses (3-4) are recited while offering the third and fourth elements of *pūjā*. See G. Bühnemann (1988), p. 138.

32. The number four is typical to the Vedic way of thinking. In *R̥V* 1.164.45 the *vāc* is fourfold of which only onefold is accessible to humans, just as only one fourth of *puruṣa* is accessible to humans in our above-mentioned verse. Again the Vedas are fourfold, the ends of life (*puruṣārtha*) are fourfold, the *yuga*s are fourfold, the stages of life are fourfold, and the castes are again fourfold. The number four means perfection. See L. Malieckal (1989b), pp. 98-101.

The birth of Virāja[33] from *puruṣa* and vice versa in verse five has also something to do with the theme of totality.[34] The mutual parenthood stands not only for the source of reality, but also the reality in all its manifested relationships.[35] We may interpret the mutual parenthood of *puruṣa* and Virāja to mean that *puruṣa* is not only the source of Reality but also the sum total of all realities.

The details of the ritual demarcation of space and time through the symbols of sacrificial sticks in verse 15,[36] too, have some cosmic and sacrificial connotations. The seven enclosing sticks of which our verse speaks are given a wider meaning, for they stand for the sacrificial nature of *puruṣa* in the cosmic context. It then speaks of thrice seven or 21 sacrificial sticks which may also have a cosmic significance. According to Sāyaṇa, it means 12 months + 5 seasons + 3 worlds + the sun = 21. Therefore, the 21 sacrificial sticks may

---

33. It is not that easy to pinpoint the exact nature of Virāja, for he/she is given multiple associations and identifications with the names of high divine powers as Indra, Agni, Prajāpati, Parameṣṭhin, and is given different interpretations by different scholars. *PVE*, p. 77, footnote 5. Etymologically Virāja means "to reign, to rule, to excel, to shine forth" and Panikkar calls it the "first uncreated emanation of the Supreme." Ibid., p. 75.

34. Even though this type of mutual parenthood may seem to be contradictory at the outset, it is not uncommon in the *R̥V*, for Dakṣa is said to be born of Aditi and Aditi of Dakṣa (10.72.4-5), Aditi is said to be simultaneously mother, father and son (1.89.10), Indra is said to beget his parents and vice versa (10.54.3). L. Malieckal (1989b), p. 12.

35. For L. Malieckal while commenting on this mutual parenthood of Aditi and her son argues that such mutual parentage stands to affirm her as the source of Reality in its manifested and non-manifested realms and he writes: "Now, Aditi is also father as well as son. So she is not only the source of Reality but Reality as well in all its manifested relationships." Ibid.

36. This verse (15) is recited while performing the circumambulation in *pūjā*. See G. Bühnemann (1988), p. 174.

mean that *puruṣa is the totality of space and time.*

The verse under discussion has: "They bound the *puruṣa* to the *yūpa*" (sacrificial post). This *yūpa* too has a cosmic significance because it serves as a means of communication between heaven and earth and, according to M. Eliade, it stands in close relationship with the cosmic tree:

> The installation and consecration of the sacrificial post constitutes a rite of the centre. Assimilated to the cosmic tree, the stake (*yūpa*) becomes in its turn the axis connecting the three cosmic regions. Communication between heaven and earth becomes possible by means of this pillar. He who makes the sacrifices does, indeed, go up to heaven, alone or with his wife, upon this post ritually transformed into the World Axis itself.[37]

Also according to H. Aguilar this *yūpa* is related to the cosmic tree[38] and is invoked to protect and bring home safe the sacrificer. In *R̥V* 3.53.20 the tree is implored not to abandon or injure the persons, but to bring home safe, to remove the bonds, and to give them freedom. However, Malieckal finds in this sacrificial post and cosmic tree a symbol of cosmic separation and re-union, for he writes:

> Thus the sacrificial post to which *puruṣa* as *paśu* (sacrificial animal) is said to be bound, through its association with the cosmic Tree (*skambha/vanaspati*) may be seen as referred to in this verse 15 as a great symbol of cosmic separation and re-union, manifestation and re-unification.[39]

---

37. M. Eliade (1961), p. 45. The *yūpa* is very much linked with the *skambha* (cosmic pillar that supports the whole cosmos: see *AV* 10.7) and to the cosmic tree standing in an inverted position. See *Kaṭha Upaniṣad* 6.1.
38. H. Aguilar (1976), pp. 125-47.
39. L. Malieckal (1989b), p. 115. See also W.N. Brown (1965), p. 28.

But in my opinion *yūpa* in this verse means not only this cosmic separation and reunion, manifestation and reunification, but also the very support of the cosmos, that is, none other than *puruṣa* himself in this context.

The first part of the myth is, therefore, dedicated to the all-inclusive character of *puruṣa,* which serves as a background to the second part which deals in detail the origin of everything from the sacrifice of *puruṣa*. We can find that the hymn follows a progressive disclosure of the characters of *puruṣa,* starting with his all-inclusive nature, his transcendence and immanence, as the meeting point of space and time, his relation to Agni, as the lord of immortality which grows on food, etc. Our hymn reveals all these elements without either giving the impression of pantheism, or denying non-dualism.

SACRIFICE AS THE STARTING POINT OF ALL REALITIES

After affirming *puruṣa* as the totality of creation and his transcendent and immanent characters in the first part, the hymn develops the theme of sacrifice as the origin of all that exists in this cosmos: the gods, the natural forces such as the sun, moon, the winds, the space, the time, the social divisions, the sacred scriptures, etc. all come from this primordial divine sacrifice, and sacrifice as the first *dharma*.

The second part of the hymn (vv. 6-14, and 16) clearly mentions how the One or this totality became many for the sake of creation. All that exists is the consequence of the dismemberment of the *puruṣa* by the gods.[40] The *yajña* is the starting point of all realities,

40. The presence of gods at the sacrifice of *puruṣa* creates some difficulties, because if everything was born from the self-sacrifice of *puruṣa* then how are we to account for the origin of gods, who appear to be there before this sacrifice takes place? In another account of creation it is said clearly that the gods came afterwards with the creation of this universe (*R̥V* 10.129.6). This apparent contradiction can be explained in the following way. In *R̥V* →

for all realities take their origin from the primordial sacrifice of *puruṣa*. In this section too, the hymn discloses the origin of the cosmic elements. Verses six and seven say that when the gods offered[41] *puruṣa* as *haviṣ* (oblation), the cosmic elements, spring, summer and autumn, constituted the sacrificial offering (butter, fuel, and the oblation). The gods' activity of spreading/anointing the *puruṣa*, tying him, and offering him in sacrifice show the sacrificial procedure in the animal sacrifice such as anointing the animal with the clarified butter, tying it to a *yūpa* (sacrificial post), killing it and offering it, etc.[42]

→ 10.121.7 the gods are spoken of as the breaths of Prajāpati. The *Jaiminīya Brāhmaṇa,* while explaining the *Agnihotra* sacrifice (fire-sacrifice), describes the life-breaths or vital powers (*prāṇaḥ)* of the sacrificer as gods (*devaḥ*) (1.1). Accordingly *puruṣa* having divided them threefold and having made them divine powers he keeps offering in them (for the rest of his life). Gods indeed are his divine (vital) powers (*devaḥ)*. These are *devaḥ* for him because he keeps offering in (and to) them (*JB* 1.1). The gods are, therefore, the vital breaths of Prajāpati the creator. It is through the help of his vital breaths that he self-immolates for the sake of the creation. For more details see J. Gonda (1983a), pp. 5-42.

41. These verses (6-7) are recited while offering material for bath, and the garments (the sixth and seventh) elements of *pūjā*. See G. Bühnemann (1988), pp. 141 & 155.

42. Sacrifice is depicted as a *tan* (weaving), spreading, stretching out to the world of gods and vice versa, or as a re-birth where the victim offered in sacrifice is said to be re-born in the celestial world. A text says that when Soma is pressed (killed) and spread out, it is re-born: ". . . Now when they press him, they slay him; and when they spread him, they cause him to be born. He is born in being spread along, he is born moving (*yan gāyate*) . . . " (*ŚB* 3.9.4.23). The translations from the *ŚB* are taken from J. Eggeling (1966), SBE vols., 12, 26, 41, 43 & 44. When a different translation is used it will be specified. This interpretation of sacrifice as weaving or stretching is in accordance with the *ṚV* 10.130.1-2 where sacrifice is clearly mentioned as weaving, and stretching out. The text says:

Everything in this cosmos comes from the primordial sacrifice of *puruṣa*, starting from the beasts of the air, forest, village, and the three Vedas: *R̥V*, *Yajur* and *Sāma* (vv. 8-9). In these verses we can also see a change in the subject of the action:[43] in the early verses gods were said to have offered *puruṣa* as *haviṣ* (oblation) but in these verses *puruṣa* itself is said to perform the primordial sacrifice for the sake of creation. Special mention is made of the sacrificial animals in verse ten,[44] for all the animals mentioned are the animals fit for sacrifice: horse, bull, sheep and goat. The ritual purpose of this myth should not be overlooked.

Even the origin of the *varṇa* (social division), exactly in parallel with the social function that the members of each group had in the Vedic society, is said to be the fruit of the primordial divine

---

→ a. Sacrifice (resembles) a loom with threads extended this way and that, composed of innumerable rituals. Behold now the Fathers weaving the fabric; seated on the outstretched loom. "Lengthwise! Crosswise!" they cry.

b. Behold now a Man who unwinds and sets the thread, a Man who unwinds it right up to the vault of heaven. Here are the pegs; they are fastened to the place of worship. The *sāman*-hymns are used for weaving shuttles.

Translation from *PVE*, pp. 356-57. Such weaving and stretching out into the world of gods and to that of humans mean a divine-human collaboration in sacrifice to keep this universe going smoothly. Therefore, sacrifice is not only a divine-human enterprise for the maintenance of the world but also a new-birth for when humans perform sacrifice they are born again.

43. These verses (8-9) are recited while offering the eighth and ninth elements of *pūjā*. See G. Bühnemann (1988), pp. 156 & 160.

44. This verse (10) is recited while offering flowers, the tenth element of *pūjā*. See ibid., p. 136.

sacrifice (vv. 11-12).[45] The powers of nature and the gods are said to be born from the sacrifice. The moon and sun are born from his mind and eyes respectively, the Vedic gods Indra and Agni from his mouth, Vāyu from his breath (v. 13).[46] This creation of the powers of nature can be seen as an attempt to dissociate from the belief that they are supernatural powers[47] and the creation of Indra, Agni, and Vāyu can be seen as an attempt to bring them under one creator God, Puruṣa-Prajāpati, the One that became many for the sake of creation. In this verse too the origin of a certain god is said to be in parallel to the function that god played in Vedic society: Agni is seen as the mouth of gods in which the oblations are offered and for this reason he is said to be born of the mouth of *puruṣa*, Vāyu is the god of the winds and is said to be born of the breath of *puruṣa*. Just as the division of the classes is the result of the sacrifice of *puruṣa*, so too, the universe is divided into four spheres of air, sky, earth and the quarters (v. 14).[48]

---

45. These verses (11-12) are recited while offering the eleventh and twelfth elements of *pūjā*. See ibid., pp. 163-64. The brāhmins main occupation was teaching and performing rituals which consisted of actions and the recitation of the *mantras*, hence they are said to be born of the mouth of *puruṣa*. The warriors came from the kṣatriyas and their main occupation was to defend the country from the attack of foreign invaders and hence they were said to be born of the arms of *puruṣa*. The vaiśyas were employed in agriculture, crafts and business, hence they are said to be born of the thighs of *puruṣa* and the śūdras were the servants and are said to be born of the feet of *puruṣa*.

46. This verse (13) is recited while offering the thirteenth element of *pūjā*. See ibid., p. 167.

47. H. Aguilar is against the naturalistic interpretation given to the Vedic gods, that is, the Vedic gods as the divinisations of natural forces. See H. Aguilar (1976), pp. 112-24.

48. Verse 14 is recited while prostrating in front of the deity, and verse 15 is recited while performing the circumambulation of the deity, the sixteenth element of *pūjā*. See G. Bühnemann (1988), pp. 173-74.

The last verse of the hymn can be seen as the climax wherein the whole intention of the hymn becomes clear, i.e. the trilogy of the sacrifice, sacrifice as the first *dharma*, and as the means for immortality. This trilogy of sacrifice[49] is seen in the phrase: "With this sacrifice the gods sacrificed. . . ." But this is not the literal translation of it and the literal translation should be "With the sacrifice the gods produced the sacrifice."[50] The new translation of Frits Staal does not keep in mind the trilogy of sacrifice, i.e. the identity between the sacrificer, the victim (sacrifice) and the divine receiver, which is an intrinsic aspect of later theories on Vedic sacrifice. According to J. Gonda the paradoxical statement, "With sacrifice the gods sacrificed to the sacrifice," should be taken to mean that *puruṣa* was both the victim and the divinity to whom the sacrifice was offered,[51] that is, he was both the subject and the object of the sacrifice. According to our author, this myth affirms

---

49. A text from the *ŚB* can help us to understand this paradoxical statement which explains this trilogy of sacrifice, oblation and receiver: " . . . And, indeed, there was no other (victim), meet [fit] for sacrifice, but that one (Prajāpati), and the gods set about offering him up in sacrifice. Wherefore it is with reference to this that the *ṛṣi* has said . . . "The gods offered up sacrifice by sacrifice" — for by sacrifice they did offer up him (Prajāpati), the sacrifice: "these were the first ordinances" for these laws were instituted first . . . " (10.2.2.1-2). Therefore, the gods began to offer him in sacrifice because there was no one else. But in the *Taittirīya Brāhmaṇa* it is said that the gods being desirous to perform a sacrifice, seized their father Prajāpati who then became a horse (3.9.22.1), and the horse resembles him most and for that reason it is offered to him. This may also explain the origin of *Aśvamedha* which we will be discussing later in this chapter.

50. W.N. Brown in his earlier article translated it more literally, i.e. "with sacrifice gods sacrificed to the sacrifice." W.N. Brown (1931), p. 118. But in his later article he translated as "With the sacrifice gods produced the sacrifice . . ." W.N. Brown (1965), p. 32.

51. J. Gonda (1983c), p. 9.

three aspects: the unity of all existence, that the performance of a ritual is indispensable in the process of creation, and that the rite is an *opus operans* in itself.[52] The trilogy of sacrifice, therefore, affirms the Vedic idea that sacrifice is self-sacrifice, and that the efficacy of the rite is an *opus operans*, for no deity is invoked in this sacrifice: "with sacrifice they sacrificed to the sacrifice." Again this verse affirms that sacrifice was the first *dharma* and the gods obtained immortality through it.

We find that this event which took place at the beginning of creation represents the transition of the One, the primeval Totality, into the plurality of the phenomenal universe. For the Vedic *ṛṣis*, sacrifice is the first creative act and of this first creative act every sacrifice is a repetition.[53] The *ṛṣis* consider creation as the self-sacrifice of the creator for the sake of creation. Such a view maintains on the one hand the totality of *puruṣa*, his all-inclusive character and on the other holds the sacrifice as the beginning of everything, and as the foundation of everything. In the words of L. Malieckal:

> It is an intuitive experience of the togetherness of *God-Man-World*. It means neither that the Ultimate is standing apart as the totally Other over against the finite realm of manifestation, nor that the Ultimate is the sum total of the contingent beings or finite existence.[54]

Therefore, in my opinion, the theory of creation through the self-immolation of the creator can be seen as an attempt made by the Vedic *ṛṣis* to explain the divine origin of everything and the supreme value of sacrifice itself. By this they not only explain the essential unity of the unmanifest and the manifest realms of the reality but also sacrifice as the origin and the means for everything,

52. J. Gonda (1977), p. 96.
53. J. Gonda (1983c), p. 8.
54. L. Malieckal (1989b), p. 1. See also L. Malieckal (1984), pp. 265-66.

even for the continued existence of the cosmos. We may say, therefore, that the *puruṣa* myth explains not only the origin of the cosmos but also its unity with the creator. Everything in this universe has a divine origin.

Sacrifice as Condition for the Existence of the World

This cosmos that had its origin from the divine sacrifice cannot exist except in and through sacrifice. Here we will see the relation between sacrifice and the existence of the world. Sacrifice is indispensable for humans and for creation because, according to the Vedic conception of Reality, what is immediately given is imperfect and only what is ritually made is perfect. The continued existence of this world depends on sacrifice. Sacrifice is the means to cure all the defects in the cosmos and is the condition for the continued existence of the world.

A text of the *Pañcaviṁśa Brāhmaṇa* says that by means of a long *Soma* sacrifice of twelve years Prajāpati was able to set the whole universe in motion (25.6.1ff). Therefore, those who follow his example become Prajāpati and acquire the same ability to keep moving the wheel of the cosmos. A text of the *Yajurveda* says:

> All power to our life through sacrifice!
> All power to our lungs through sacrifice!
> All power to our eyes through sacrifice!
> All power to our ears through sacrifice!
> All power to our backs through sacrifice!
> All power to sacrifice through sacrifice! (9.21).[55]

Thus, by means of sacrifice humans renew and strengthen the cosmos and make possible their survival and that of the cosmos at large.

The preoccupation for the continued existence of creation may arise because, as Verpoorten says, for a Vedic person the natural

---

55. This translation is taken from *PVE*, p. 346.

state of things is a juxtaposition of parts which have an intrinsic tendency to disintegrate and to separate into its constitutive elements.[56] Naturally the stability and the continuity of the cosmos became a major preoccupation of the Vedic people[57] who found in sacrifice the medicine for the natural tendency of the material and biological beings towards disintegration. Vedism considers sacrifice not only the world-creating principle but also the medicine that cures all the deficiencies of creation. It is sacrifice that gives strength and vitality to the parts and maintains everything in its proper position.

And the universe does not rest either in gods or on any other ground, but on sacrifice. It is the foundation of the world, which holds together the *dharma*, the order and the truth. As R. Panikkar says:

> To perform the sacrifice is not to participate in a good act or to do good to the gods, to mankind, or to oneself: it is to live, to "make" one's own survival and that of the whole universe. It is the act by which the universe itself continues in existence.[58]

In this sacrifice which maintains the world, gods and human beings collaborate with one another.[59] Therefore, to perform sacrifice is not to lose sight of the origin of life and the cosmos itself and we need to understand in this sense the text of the *ŚB* which says that the sun would not rise if the priest were not to make the morning *Agnihotra* (2.3.1.5). R. Panikkar commenting on this text says that it does not speak of a

> . . . mysterious magical connection between *Agnihotra* and the sun, but to the the anthropocosmic link that maintains the whole of reality in truth and order, for Man is not simply a spectator in

---

56. J.M. Verpoorten (1977), p. 62.
57. B.K. Smith (1985a), pp. 84-85.
58. *PVE*, p. 353.
59. G. Favaro (1993), p. 31.

> the cosmic display or an outsider set there just to exploit the earth for his own benefit.[60]

The one who sacrifices becomes Prajāpati himself and, as Heesterman says, the sacrificer "incorporates alone the whole universe, articulating by himself the cosmic process, like his prototype Prajāpati who is at the same time sacrificer, victim and recipient of the sacrifice."[61] Hence for the Vedic people to sacrifice means to fulfil their duty towards the maintenance of the world and there seems to be a parallelism between everything that takes place on the *vedī* (altar) and the universe, for creation is not a finished product but to be continually recreated and renewed.

INTERRELATION BETWEEN YAJÑA, ṚTA AND DHARMA

Ṛta, the cosmic order, is another central point of Vedic religion, and is correlated to sacrifice. It is not easy to explain the exact nature and meaning of *ṛta* — which is often translated as the cosmic order — for in the course of time it has been equated with *yajña*, the energy of sacrifice, *satyam* (truth), water, *dharma* (righteousness),[62] etc. We analyse some passages which identify *ṛta* with the above-mentioned terms to see its central meaning.

Ṛta as Yajña

Ṛta and *yajña* are synonymous terms in the Vedas; to say *ṛta* is to say *yajña*, the world-creating and maintaining principle, the *karman par excellence*. In *ṚV* 4.3.9 we can read this identification of

---

60. *PVE*, p. 361.

61. J.C. Heesterman (1987b), p. 30.

62. According to Stefano Piano, *ṛta* and *dharma* are substantially the same and are related to the microcosmic and macrocosmic level. The microcosm is the individual with all his ethical and theoretical problems and the macrocosm is the universe, and both of them are subordinated to that eternal law — *dharma* on the basis of which the celestial bodies move and is the norm of behaviour for human beings. S. Piano (1993), pp. 8-9.

ṛta as *yajña* when it says: "With *ṛta* I worship the immovable *ṛta*." Here *ṛta* means sacrifice and with sacrifice one worships the sacrifice. In yset another text of the same Veda the highest abode of *ṛta* is identified with the supreme abode of the sacrifice (1.43.9). In yet another text of the same Veda the *sukṛtasya loka* is identified with the *sukṛtasya yoni* (10.85.24), that is, the abode of sacrifice with the abode of *ṛta*. Again in the *AV* too we can find the identification of the abode of sacrifice with that of *ṛta*, for a text says: "may the sacrificial goats reach the world of the *sukṛtaḥ* situated across the great darkness in the third firmament" (9.5.1). Another text of the same Veda speaks of six pillars which uphold the earth all of which are sacrificial elements such as *satya, ṛta, dīkṣā, tapas, brahman* (prayer) and *yajña* (12.1.1).[63] From these passages we can see that for the Vedic people to say *ṛta* is to say sacrifice, the primordial source from which originates the cosmos.[64]

Ṛta as Satyam

Ṛta is sometimes identified with *satyam* (truth) and the latter is again identified with gods.[65] According to H. Lüders, *ṛta* should mean *satyam,* from which the gods are born, and the origin of the world has to be attributed to *ṛta* which again has nothing to do with sacrifice,[66] a theory that cannot be accepted as H. Aguilar has rightly shown.[67] We cannot accept the statement that *ṛta* has nothing to do with sacrifice for there is not only a direct connection between sacrifice and *ṛta,* but also the term *satyam* itself has to be

---

63. See also *MS* 1.10.12.
64. H. Aguilar (1976), p. 27. Such an identification of terms has led Aguilar to use both the terms together (*ṛta/yajña*) whenever he has to mention the term *yajña* in his book.
65. G. Gispert-Sauch (1977), pp. 40-43.
66. H. Lüders (1959), p. 26.
67. H. Aguilar (1976), pp. 18-32. For these subsections I depend mainly on the sources gathered by Aguilar.

seen in the sacrificial sense.[68] According to Aguilar, truth and sacrifice are not only related but also there is no *ṛta* without sacrifice because, "The Aryan Truth is undoubtedly to sacrifice, for without *yajña* no *ṛta* of any kind is possible in the eyes of the Vedic Indians."[69] For the truth is the sacrificial order and *ṛta* is nothing other than this sacrificial order that governs the cosmos. In this case too, the word *satyam* has to be seen in its sacrificial sense. For Vedic people sacrifice is the truth behind all reality.

Ṛta and the Primordial Waters

Ṛta is related to *āpaḥ* (waters), for *āpaḥ* are the primordial waters which are not only the birth place of all realities but also the foundation of all realities. In *ṚV* 10.121.7-8 the primordial waters are said to have conceived the cosmic egg (*hiraṇyagarbha*) as a germ.[70] The same idea is found in another hymn of the same Veda which says:

> That which the Waters first received, beyond the heavens, beyond
> the earth, beyond both Gods and demons —
>
> say, what was that, the first primeval germ,
> when all the assembled Gods, and they alone, were
> watching?

---

68. H. Aguilar shows that in Iran truth meant the cult of *asuras* and lie meant the cult of *daevas* and in India they meant just the opposite: truth meant the sacrifice and lie meant the non-sacrifice which was the character of *asuras*. Ibid., p. 26.

69. Ibid.

70. When came the mighty Waters, bringing with them
the universal Germ, whence sprang the Fire,
thence leapt the God's One Spirit into being.
What God shall we adore with our oblation?
This One who in his might surveyed the Waters
pregnant with vital forces, producing sacrifice,
he is the God of Gods and none beside him.
What God shall we adore with our oblation?
— *ṚV* 10.121.7-8

This translation is taken from *PVE*, p. 72.

He was the primal germ borne by the Waters,
wherein all the Gods were coalesced together;
at the navel of the Nonborn the One and Only is set,
he upon whom depend all created beings

— *R̥V* 10.82.5-6[71]

These verses say clearly that the waters bore the cosmic egg, hence the waters is the place from where the creation began. Another hymn goes a step further and says that in the beginning everything was unrecognizable water:

1. At first was neither Being nor Non-being.
There was not air nor yet sky beyond.
What was its wrapping? Where? In whose protection?
Was Water there, unfathomable and deep?

2. There was no death then, nor yet deathlessness;
of night or day there was not any sign.
The One breathed without breath, by its own impulse.
Other than that was nothing else at all.

3. Darkness was there, all wrapped around by darkness,
and all was Water indiscriminate. Then that which was hidden
by the Void, that One, emerging,
stirring, through power of Ardor, came to be

— *R̥V* 10.129.1-3[72]

Now a number of passages identify this primordial waters from which creation took place with the abode of *r̥ta* and such an identification forces us to think that the primordial waters are nothing other than *r̥ta* itself. In *R̥V* 9.86.25 we read: "To the bosom of the waters, to the bosom of *r̥ta*, the Āyus, the buffaloes, have sent off the seer."[73] Here the bosom of waters is the same as the bosom of *r̥ta*. Another hymn says: "Clarified the swift Indus have

71. Translation taken from ibid., p. 813.

72. Translation from ibid., p. 58.

73. This and the following translations from the *R̥V* and Upaniṣads in this section are taken from H. Aguilar (1976), p. 30.

gone cheerfully to the sea, to the bosom of *ṛta* (*ṚV* 9.64.17); "To the sea have gone the Indus, to the bosom of *ṛta*, like the milk-kine to their stable (*ṚV* 9.66.12). Here too the bosom of water is considered as the bosom of *ṛta*. If the bosom of *ṛta* is the same as that of the waters they may be one and the same principle but expressed in different terms in order to denote a certain function, and should not be considered as two distinct principles.

However, in the Upaniṣads the *Brahman*, the origin and the foundation of the whole universe, is identified with water. According to a text of the *Kauṣītaki Upaniṣad*, "Water indeed is this my world, the whole Brahmā-world, and it is thine" (1.7).[74] Such an identification of *Brahman* with the waters is also found in the *Bṛhadāraṇyaka Upaniṣad*, where it is said:

> Water indeed becomes that one seer, (water) without any duality: this is the Brahmā-world, O king." Thus did Yājñavalkya teach him. This (water) is his highest goal (the highest goal of the seer), this is his highest success, this is his highest world, this is his highest bliss. All other creatures live on a small portion of that bliss.
> — 4.3.32[75]

These identifications of *ṛta* with water show that the latter is closely related to the cosmogony,[76] and in the Vedas cosmogony is again closely related to *yajña*, the first principle of the universe. Therefore, the primordial water has to be taken first in its relation to cosmogony, i.e. as the birth place of all reality and secondly in its relation to *yajña*.

Ṛta and Dharma

The Vedic *ṛta* has also been identified with the later notion of *dharma* which includes a moral and ethical character. *Dharma*, the principle of social morality, is also intrinsically related to the

74. Translation from ibid., p. 215.
75. Translation from ibid.
76. F.B.J. Kuiper (1970-71), pp. 91-138.

cosmic order. This has led to the identification of *ṛta* with *dharma*, the righteousness or the ethical law that governs not only the human beings in their day-to-day life but also the functioning of the whole cosmos. According to Stefano Piano, even though *ṛta* and *dharma* are elaborated in different times they are substantially the same and are related to the microcosm and the macrocosm.[77] P.V. Kane too admits the moral character of *ṛta* in the triple aspect of it, viz. the course of nature or the regular order of the cosmos, the moral behaviour of humans, and the correct performance of sacrifice to the gods.[78] In my opinion this triple aspect of *ṛta* is not independent, but interconnected. Such connections are to be seen from the background that the cosmos cannot exist merely on physical or mathematical laws but also on the religious and ethical orders which influence the cosmic functioning. For as Panikkar rightly says:

> It is by *ṛta* also that Men are saved from their iniquities, for this concept does not refer only to cosmic order; it includes also the ethical sphere which is not separate and autonomous but is ontonomically linked with the state of the cosmos.[79]

Even though Mitra and Varuṇa are considered as the guardians of the *ṛta*, the latter had the closest relation to *ṛta* and is said to

---

77. According to S. Piano, ". . . the concepts of *ṛta* and *dharma*, which are substantially equivalent but were elaborated in different periods, put themselves in relation with the universe both in the microcosmic and the macrocosmic levels. The microcosm is the individual with all his ethical and theoretical problems, the macrocosm is the universe constituted substantially — at least according to the system of cosmology *par excellence* of India, the Sāṁkhya — by Nature. Both of them are placed under that same atemporal, eternal and unfailing norm, that is, *dharma*. It is on the basis of *dharma* the celestial bodies move, and it is always the *dharma* that dictates the rules of behaviour for man and for his journey on this earth." S. Piano (1993), pp. 8-9.
78. P.V. Kane (1941), vol. 4, pp. 2ff.
79. *PVE*, p. 509.

control and survey both the operation of the cosmic law and deeds of human beings. In *R̥V* 1.105.15 it is said that at Varuṇa's prayer *r̥ta*, the cosmic order, was born. Varuṇa is therefore, the originator and the guardian of cosmic law and the social morality and he stands above all other deities and punishes severely the sinners who break his ordinances and tell lies.[80] He is said to control the order of the world in its ethical and physical aspects and is being invoked by people in the time of peril and distress as the deliverer from sin, the merciful god as well as the one who punishes the sinners.[81] God Varuṇa punishes the breakers of laws or moral rules and binds them with his nooses (*MS* 2.33; *KB* 5.33; *ŚB* 5.2.4.2). It is again by means of sacrifice such beings are delivered. Prajāpati is said to have delivered the creatures from Varuṇa's noose by means of a sacrifice (*ŚB* 2.5.3.1; 2.6.3.4), he again healed them by means of another sacrifice (*ŚB* 2.5.2.3), and by a definite ritual technique he made them happy (ŚB 2.5.2.11; 4.1.3.14). In another text it is said that when the gods and the *asura*s were in conflict, Indra made Prajāpati to offer sacrifice for producing unanimity among the gods and the *asura*s (*TS* 2.2.11.5).

In the last analysis, the regular course of nature and the moral behaviour of humans are their sacrificial relation to the gods, for there is no ethical or natural law more important than the Vedic injunction to sacrifice. It is the law of the universe and of human behaviour. The flow of the rivers which fertilize the fields and rising and setting of the sun depend on this ethical behaviour which in the last analysis is nothing other than the sacrificial behaviour.

---

80. A. Macdonell (1995), pp. 22-28. See also *R̥V* 8.86.3-4 and *AV* 4.16.6.

81. In the *R̥V* different hymns are dedicated to Varuṇa, Agni, Soma, Rudra and to other gods in asking them pardon for the sins committed knowingly or unknowingly. For a collection of such passages see *PVE*, pp. 482-515.

THE COSMIC ORDER AS SACRIFICIAL ORDER

After having seen the relation of *ṛta* to *yajña, satyam,* the cosmic waters and *dharma,* here we will see its relation to sacrificial order. *Ṛta* is often translated as the cosmic order but this cosmic order should not be seen as something independent from sacrifice. As Panikkar rightly says:

> *Ṛta* is generally translated by "Cosmic Order," which is a valid translation provided one bears in mind that cosmic order is not a fixed physical or mathematical law, but a "sacrificial" order.[82]

A similar view can be found in V.M. Reddy when he writes,

> The universe is not governed by any fixed physical or mathematical laws; it is itself a sacrificial order. Being an act of Truth it is upheld by Truth. It is through Truth, *ṛta,* that the universe is established and governed. *Ṛta* is the ultimate foundation. From *ṛta* comes the Word, and from the Word are born the many worlds. *Ṛta* is the universal order "embodied in sacrifice"; it is the rhythm proper to sacrifice while it is sacrifice that brings into existence things as they are. By sacrifice, men and gods collaborate for mutual increase as also for the existence, sustenance and growth of the universe. It is by an inner necessity and structural rhythm that the cosmos is sustained. *Ṛta* constitutes this structural necessity and rhythm. It is out of this inbuilt contingency that the universe is what it is. This universe is a self-existent, self-sustaining and self-fulfilling act of sacrifice.[83]

Ṛta is the sacrificial order because sacrifice is not only the birth place of the cosmos but also the structure of the cosmos, that which keeps the cosmos in order and existence. And this *ṛta* is not to be considered as a substance or thing, but as the unifying force that might be seen as the very soul of sacrifice,[84] or the very

82. *PVE,* p. 350.
83. V.M. Reddy (1991), vol. 1, p. 77.
84. *PVE,* pp. 350-51.

dynamism of sacrifice. *Ṛta*, being the primordial dynamism that is inherent in everything as the soul of sacrifice, is even said to be superior to the gods.

According to P.V. Kane, *ṛta* in the *ṚV* denotes "the supreme transcendental law or the cosmic order with which the universe is governed and also the gods and that is intimately connected with sacrifice."[85] But Radhakrishnan considers the moral aspect of *ṛta* as its main meaning, for according to him it stands for the law in general and the immanence of justice which is very much related to the cosmic order:

> *Ṛta* literally means the "course of things." It stands for law in general and the immanence of justice. This conception must have originally been suggested by the regularity of the movement of the sun, moon and stars, the alternations of day and night, of the seasons. *Ṛta* denotes the order of the world. Everything that is ordered in the universe has *ṛta* for its principles. It corresponds to the *universalis* of Plato. The world of experience is a shadow or reflection of the *ṛta*, the permanent reality which remains unchanged in all the welter of mutation.[86]

However, Giancarlo Montesi gives a different interpretation of *ṛta*, for in his opinion *ṛta* means the interrelation between humans and the cosmos and has to be seen in opposition to chaos (*tamas*).[87] There is a tendency in the cosmos to return to the original state of chaos and this tendency is being corrected with the help of *ṛta*. Therefore, not only the succession of day and night, the course of sun, of plant life, rains, human life and the functioning of the civil and the religious institutions are maintained by *ṛta* but are also protected against the danger of returning to the primordial chaos.[88]

---

85. P.V. Kane (1941), vol. 4, pp. 2ff. See also S. Piano (1993), p. 12.
86. S. Radhakrishnan (1923), vol. 1, pp. 78-79. See *BG* 18.5 on the three principles (austerity, alms giving, and sacrifice) that should not be abandoned.
87. G. Montesi (1953-54), p. 126.
88. Ibid., pp. 121 and 126.

Ṛta sometimes appears to be an independent entity which is not only superior to the gods but is also considered to be their instrument.[89] It is said to abide in the highest plane: the fourth plane, at the top of the universe, and according to Aguilar, this highest plane coincides with the "omphalos," the navel of the world, the starting point of every reality[90] which is none other than sacrifice. Hence the highest has to be seen in the theological sense, i.e. as the source and foundation of all realities and not in the geographical sense. Later on in the Upaniṣads *ṛta,* the source and the foundation of reality, gets identified with *Brahman.*[91] Therefore, *ṛta* takes a wider meaning in the later Vedas and it is closely connected with the origin of all Reality, be it sacrifice, be it Brahmā, be it Puruṣa-Prajāpati.

For the Vedic person the cosmic order is not a fixed physical or mathematical law, but a sacrificial order and this cosmic order is maintained by sacrificial order that is *ṛta*[92] (*ṚV* 1.23.5; 5.68.4). *Ṛta* is, therefore, the very energy of the sacrifice. It is not only the dynamism of sacrifice, but also the very law of the universe. Hence the whole order of the universe comes from and is maintained by the dynamism of *ṛta.*[93] Sacrifice is *ṛta* and *satyam*

---

89. "By means of the sacrifice the Gods obtained that supreme authority which now they wield" (*ŚB* 3.1.4.3).

90. H. Aguilar (1976), pp. 28 and 32.

91. A passage of *Mahānārāyaṇa Upaniṣad* says: "This only is the *ṛta,* this only is the truth, they say — this only is the Supreme *Brahman* of the Kavis" (1.6). Such an identification is also found in the *Taittirīya Āraṇyaka.* A text of our above-mentioned *Āraṇyaka* says: "He should say: *bhūr, bhuvaḥ, svaḥ!*" "This is the *Brahman,* this is the Truth, this is the *ṛta*" (1.1.2).

92. See *PVE,* p. 350, footnote 132, where the author explains the etymology of the word *ṛta.* According to our author, the root is *ṛ-, ar-,* meaning to put into motion, to move; the Indo-European root *ar* means to fit, to arrange (the spokes in the wheel), so that *ṛta* would be that which is well arranged, the established norm "truth," order, etc. always with a dynamic connotation.

93. Ibid., p. 350.

(truth) — no less than what we would call violations of moral rules such as adultery (*ŚB* 2.5.2.20). Cosmic order, justice, moral rectitude, can all be considered to be the product of sacrifice. It is sacrifice that creates and preserves the universe in existence.

Aśvamedha for the Renewal of the Cosmos

We will now study the rites which are related to the Puruṣa-Sūkta[94] and one of such rites is the *Aśvamedha*,[95] the most important Vedic animal sacrifice that is considered to be the king of sacrifice. The importance of this sacrifice is so great that it is even said to be able to wipe out the sin of a brāhmin killer (*ŚB* 13.3.1.1), the worst sin that one could commit in one's life. In this section we will see the relation of the *Aśvamedha* with the renewal or the recreation of the world. In the *ŚB* the *Aśvamedha* is identified with Prajāpati and the one who performs this important sacrifice is said not only to make Prajāpati complete but also makes oneself complete. Making Prajāpati complete means here renewing and making possible the existence of the cosmos. Here we will discuss the *Aśvamedha* and its cosmic value.

The horse as a sacrificial victim represents the cosmogony, for it is considered to be associated with the primordial water,[96] the source, the mother of all creation whether animate or inanimate. The horse of the *Aśvamedha* also symbolizes the world for after the inaugural bath and consecration the priest identifies it with the world (*ŚB* 13.1.2.3).

---

94. The most important are the *Aśvamedha, Agnicayana* and the *Puruṣamedha* (the human sacrifice), and the *pūjā* of the present day. It is not sure whether there really existed the human sacrifice or it was a just mystic symbol of it. We will not be discussing this last one, but take the other two sacrifices in detail.

95. *Aśvamedha* is fully described in the *White Yajurveda, Śatapatha Brāhmaṇa* and in the *Taittirīya Brāhmaṇa.*

96. See C. D'Onofrio (1953-54), pp. 148ff.

In short, the *Aśvamedha* is performed by a victorious king who has actually been consecrated with the *Aindra Mahābhiṣeka*[97] on the 8th or 9th day of the bright half of the month of Phālguna (February-March). The rite lasts for a year.[98] The *Aśvamedha* begins with the selection of the horse and the initial ceremonies which last three days before it is let free. The horse is selected and is tied to a rope made of *darbha* grass (*poa cynosuroides*) while the Adhvaryu[99] tells the horse: "you are the world" (*ŚB* 13.1.2.3). Then the horse is

---

97. *AB* 8.12-13. In the *ŚB* 13.5.4.1-23 we get names of kings who had performed the *Aśvamedha*. The *Mahābhārata* and *Rāmāyaṇa* too speak of the *Aśvamedha* by Yudhiṣṭhira and Daśaratha respectively even though it was performed for two completely different purposes. Yudhiṣṭhira performed it to purify himself and his people from the sins committed in the Mahābhārata war, and Daśaratha performed it to have a child. The coins of Samudragupta bearing the legend of *Aśvamedha parākrama* show that they were probably issued after the performance of *Aśvamedha*. The last performance of it took place in the first half of the eighteenth century by Savai Jayasingh, king of Amber. For more details see N.N. Bhattacharyya (1996), pp. 1-2; G.P. Upadhyay (1979), pp. 73-75.

98. The actual performance of the sacrifice lasted for three days preceded by a year's preparation starting with the anointing and letting free of the horse and it might have taken another year to conclude. *PVE*, p. 376; C. D'Onofrio (1953-54), pp. 140-41. But according to a text of *Baudhāyana Śrauta-Sūtra, Aśvamedha* is performed in the period of three years (15.38). This might be an exception, usually it lasted for one year, though in some cases it lasted two years as mentioned.

99. In the *Aśvamedha* and *Agnicayana* like other solemn sacrifices there are four main priests accompanied by assistants. The names and the duties of the four main priests are Adhvaryu (the executor of various practical rites), the Hotṛ (who recites the chants or *mantras*), the Udgātar (who sings) and Brahman (the one who observes the performance and rectifies any eventual omission or ritual mistakes in time so that no undesired effect may take place).

given a ceremonial bath and a dog with four eyes is killed and is made to be stamped over[100] while the horse is still in the water. After that the horse is set free for a year and is allowed to wander freely that it may bring the whole kingdom in contact with the divine power inherent in it and also extend the rule and power of the king.[101] A group of 400 men belonging to different groups of soldiers and nobility have to follow it so that no king may deny it permission to wander in his territory and also to see that it does not mate with a female horse. If a king denies permission to the sacrificial horse to wander freely in his territory the soldiers have to defeat him or else the sacrifice has to be abandoned.[102] During this year several sacrifices are made day after day for the safety

---

100. This act of killing the dog with four eyes (with two spots over the eyes) and placing it under the legs of the horse is given different interpretations by different scholars and it is difficult to say which of the theories is correct. According to Dumont, it symbolizes the evil powers of the underworld. P.E. Dumont (1927), p. 27. Hence the dog symbolizes a danger for the sacrifice, and by killing it one overcomes such danger. According to M. Stutley and J. Stutley, it could also mean the taking away of the sins of the sacrificer or even the fight of Indra with Vṛtra. M. Stutley and J. Stutley (1980), p. 38. In this case the killing of the dog may be related to the cosmogony of Indra killing the Vṛtra, the hostile power that held the water, the cows and other elements for life. In this case even this action can be seen as related to the repetition of cosmogony, the killing of Vṛtra for the sake of creation. S.W. Jamison gives a new interpretation to it, for according to her, the act could be considered in relation to the prohibited sex, for the dog is killed by the son of a prostitute and not by any one of the low caste. S.W. Jamison (1996), p. 99. See also D.G. White (1988-89), pp. 283-303.
101. J. Gonda (1957), p. 135, see also p. 132.
102. Abandoning of the sacrifice after being initiated it is not a good thing for the king and for the people. It may be due to this reason that it is said that he who is weak and performs the *Aśvamedha* is crushed.

of the horse and the king and the priests have to recite the *pariplava* (revolving legends) regarding the mythical kings to whom he is compared.[103] After a year of the release of the horse the *dīkṣā*, initiation of the sacrificer, takes place and the whole rite lasts for 7 days and during these days a fire-altar is built and 21 sacrificial poles of 21 cubits long are erected (*ŚB* 13.4.4.5) to symbolize the 12 months of the year, 5 seasons, 3 worlds, and the sun, here identified with Prajāpati, the *Aśvamedha* (*ŚB* 13.4.4.11). Here too we can see not only a symbolic representation of time and the worlds in the horse sacrifice but also the erection of the sacrificial poles as a restoration of Prajāpati.

When the horse is returned the final series of sacrifices take place and the most important ones are of the last three days which consist of three of the seven forms of *Soma* sacrifices.[104] The ritual of the first day is called *agniṣṭoma* that which is performed every year in spring on the new moon and full moon[105] days, and the purpose of it is to make this world sure for the sacrificer (*ŚB* 13.5.1.2). On that day the 21 victims (horse and other 20 victims) are tied to the sacrificial posts.

The sacrifice of the second or the central day is called the *ukthya* sacrifice (*ŚB* 13.5.3.9) which is the same as the *ekaviṁśa* day[106]

---

103. Each day a passage was recited and a lute player sang in order to glorify the sacrificer and to identify him with the gods or mythical figures. The narrative circle consisted of ten days and was renewed every ten days during the year and for each day the king was identified with a certain god (*ŚB* 13.4.3.1-15). On each day the representatives of people or living-beings related to that god were to be present for the function.

104. The seven forms of *Soma* sacrifices are: *agniṣṭoma, atyagniṣṭoma, ukthya, ṣoḍaśin, vājapeya, atirātra* and *āptoryāma* (*Lāṭayāyana Gṛhya-Sūtra* 5.4.24; *Gautama Dharma-Sūtra* 8.20).

105. See N.N. Bhattacharyya (1996), p. 49, footnote 41.

106. J. Eggeling (1966), vol. 44, p. 331, footnote 1. Again this 21 versed hymn-form can also be seen as an allusion to Sun (*ŚB* 13.4.4.11) which is also identified with Agni and Prajāpati.

because on this day all *stotra*s are chanted in the *ekaviṁśa stoma,* i.e. 21 versed hymn-form and the purpose of it is to give the sacrificer a firm foundation (*ŚB* 13.5.1.5-7).[107] On this day the *hotṛ* recites the first 11 verses of the hymn of *ṚV* 1.162 and the horse is made to listen to such recitation. Then it is tied to a chariot of battle and the king dressed as if for battle together with the Adhvaryu leads the horse to the pond and it is made to enter into the water. Then a cloth with a piece of gold is brought and the horse is killed by suffocating with that piece of cloth while the *hotṛ* recites the Puruṣa-Sūkta. After the queen and the maidens have made a ceremonial mourning for the death of the horse, the chief queen (*mahiṣī*) lies with it under a cover and she urges the horse to lay seed (*ŚB* 13.5.2.2) while the priests and the other queens too engage in sexual dialogue.[108] Then the animal is cut

107. However, according to another text of the same Brāhmaṇa, the purpose seems to make the air-world prosper (*ŚB* 13.5.3.9).

108. The main queen's lying with the dead horse and the sexual dialogue between the other queens and the priest have led to different speculations among scholars. According to Bhattacharyya, the gesture of *mahiṣī* forms the central factor of *Aśvamedha,* and the *mantra*s of the *Vājasaneyī Saṁhitā* have to be taken as the original form of the *Aśvamedha*. N.N. Bhattacharyya (1996), pp. 26-27. M. Eliade seems to be of the opinion that at the *Aśvamedha* besides the animal victims, a man who was bought with a price of 1000 cows and 100 horses, after being left free for a year was also sacrificed and after that the queen used to lie with him. M. Eliade (1979a), p. 219. Here according to Eliade the human victim is killed and then the queen lies with him while according to Bhattacharyya there used to take place a ceremonial intercourse before killing him. It is not sure whether in the Vedic India *Puruṣamedha* used to take place. M. Eliade rightly notes that even though in many *Śrautasūtra*s the *Puruṣamedha* is mentioned, only the Sāṅkhāyana and the Vaitāna describe the real killing of the human being, and according to other texts the victim is let free at the last moment and in his place an animal is immolated. Ibid., 219. Therefore, the fact that *Puruṣamedha* is described only in a few of the ritual Sūtras has led the scholars to take different views on the existence of it and there is no →

into pieces and certain parts of it are cooked and eaten and the rest is burned in the fire altar.[109] On the same day several animals and birds are also sacrificed, some of them killed and others symbolically offered by taking them around the fire.[110]

The rituals of the third day are the same as those of the *atirātra* sacrifice[111] and the *stotras* (hymns of praise) on this day are chanted with all the *stomas* (way of recitation of a *stotra*) and the purpose of it is to obtain and secure everything for the sacrificer (*ŚB* 13.5.3.9). At the end of it when the king makes his purificatory bath, a leper, a bald headed person, or a lame man is picked up from the people present and is made to enter into the water and after having poured butter on his head, he is given 100 cows in gift and is sent away from the kingdom as the scapegoat. This man is called Gumbaka, and is identified with Varuṇa, and by pouring butter on his head, the sacrificer redeems himself from

---

→ consensus whether the *Puruṣamedha* is an imitation of the *Aśvamedha* or vice versa. For a detailed discussion of different views on it, see *AGNI*, vol. 1, pp. 117-21. According to S.W. Jamison, women are included in the rituals "to introduce sexual energy into the potentially sterile world of the orderly ritual." S.W. Jamison (1996), p. 53. This sexual act might have been a remaining part of a certain ancient fertility rite which might have been integrated into the *Aśvamedha* in its evolution.

109. According to Bhattacharyya, the *Aśvamedha* in the *ṚV* was originally a collective eating ritual meant to establish communion with the gods with a view to obtaining wealth of various kinds. But later on its purposes got changed in the Brāhmaṇas and in the Epics. N.N. Bhattacharyya (1996), p. 12.

110. On this day together with the horse 609 victims are offered, 349 of them are killed and the rest of them (the wild animals and birds) are only symbolically offered by taking them around the fire. Ibid., p. 11.

111. *Atirātra* is a *Soma* sacrifice which is to be performed before *agniṣṭoma* all through the night in four stages in which sacrificial cakes, animals, and cups of *soma* are to be offered to different deities especially to the Aśvins. Ibid., p. 49, footnote 51.

Varuṇa (*ŚB* 13.3.6.5). Then the king gets out of the water and gives *dakṣiṇās*[112] to the priests together with 12 measures of cooked rice (*ŚB* 13.3.6.6) or 12 *iṣṭis*, 1000 cows each with a certain quantity of gold to the priests and to the attendants.

In my opinion, the cosmic character of the horse and the participation of the whole society in the sacrifice show that it is a collective endeavour for the revitalization and reorganization of the whole of society. Thus the cosmogonic character of the horse and the participation of different members of society can help us to find out not only the cosmic character of *Aśvamedha* but also its social value. In it the members of different classes are represented and each one has a particular role to play. The priests belong to the brāhmaṇas, the king is the sacrificer and he is accompanied by his four wives and their maidservants; when the horse is let free for a year after the inaugural bath it is being accompanied by 100 sons of the king (or of the nobles), 100 soldiers with swords, 100 soldiers with spears, and 100 sons of officials (hence the ruling and the commercial classes), the dog with four eyes is being killed and put under the feet of the horse that it may trample it by the son of a prostitute (hence the representative of the sinful class). The participation of the members of different classes in the *Aśvamedha* may show the need of co-operation of all classes for the world-renewing sacrifice. It is the duty of every person to co-operate for the establishment of the cosmic order, for everyone has a part to play in the maintenance of the cosmos, the king and the priests being in the front line.

---

112. According to Heesterman, *dakṣiṇā* is meant to remove the sin of the sacrificer, for he writes: "The function of the Brāhmin officiant is to take over the death impurity of the patron by eating from the offerings and by accepting the *dakṣiṇās*. By gifts and food, evil and impurity are transferred and purity attained, especially if the donee is a brāhmin." J.C. Heesterman (1964), p. 3; see also J.C. Heesterman (1959), pp. 241-58. For a detailed discussion on the notions of gift in the Vedic India see also, J. Gonda (1964), pp. 9-33; J. Parry (1986), pp. 453-73; and T. Brekke (1998), pp. 287-320.

After having seen the ritual performance of the *Aśvamedha* now we are in a better position to discuss the meaning and the purposes of this complicated and costly sacrifice which only a few kings could afford. It is interesting to note that in this sacrifice no single deity is mentioned as the principal deity to which it is offered but all the important deities of the Vedas appear from time to time as the principal deity: Agni, Sarasvatī, Aśvins, Soma, Pūṣan, Sūrya (Sun), Yama, Tvaṣṭṛ, Vāyu, Indra, Viṣṇu, Prajāpati (*ŚB* 13.2.3-9,12-13, and Varuṇa (*ŚB* 13.3.6.5). This may be because in the cosmic renewal there is a need for the help of all gods.

Even though during the years the *Aśvamedha* has assumed various purposes such as fecundity,[113] purification,[114] and political supremacy,[115] its main purpose is to revitalize the whole cosmos and society. Now we should not isolate cosmogony, fertility rites and purificatory rituals for all these things are interconnected. As D'Onofrio rightly argues, for the primitives the cosmic character of water was also closely related to fecundity because the concepts

---

113. According to Bhattacharyya, *Aśvamedha* might have been developed out of the fusion of two different civilizations, namely the primitive vegetative and fertility rites of Harappa civilization and of the Ṛgvedic pastoralism. The queen's role in the *Aśvamedha* can be seen as a remnant of the Harappa civilization and the collective ritual eating mentioned in the *ṚV* 1.162 can be seen as the remnant of the pre-pastoral hunting stage of the Vedic Aryans N.N. Bhattacharyya (1996), pp. 22-26.

114. In the *ŚB* 13.5.4.1 it is said that the *Aśvamedha* purifies one from all sins including that of killing a brāhmaṇa. (See also Manusmṛti 75 and 83.) In the *Mahābhārata*, the main purpose of *Aśvamedha* is said to be not the political supremacy but that of purification from all sins, including that of killing people in the war.

115. This political supremacy, according to Bhattacharyya, seems to be the main purpose of *Aśvamedha* in the Brāhmaṇas (N.N. Bhattacharyya (1996), pp. 12). See also C. D'Onofrio (1953-54), pp. 151-53.

of cosmogony and fecundity are on the same level for the primitive's way of thinking, and every act of generation is the repetition of that first cosmogonic act and such ritual repetition of it in sacrifice is needed to maintain the cosmic order.[116] And the main purpose of the *Aśvamedha* is to establish the cosmic order.

The main purpose of *Aśvamedha* thus seems to be its cosmic function, very much related to cosmogony, and the annual repetition is meant to renew and strengthen the cosmic order.[117] The relation of the horse to the cosmic waters and its identification to Prajāpati show that its purpose is to renew the cosmos. Even the purification of sin has a cosmic value, for sins can bring the wrath of gods and are dangerous not only to the sinner but also to the whole cosmos. The performance of *Aśvamedha* gives fecundity and prosperity to the whole kingdom and the survival of a people depends on these factors.

According to M. Eliade, *Aśvamedha* was probably a New Year sacrifice[118] which was later changed into a year long complicated ceremony. The horse is identified with Prajāpati and its purpose is to reproduce the act of creation thereby to recreate and to re-establish the social classes and all the said duties in the better form.[119] As the following hymn expresses:

> O Brahman, in this kingdom may priests be born who shine brightly with sacred knowledge!

---

116. C. D'Onofrio (1953-54), pp. 150-51.

117. Ibid., p. 159.

118. M. Eliade (1979a), p. 218. The *Aśvamedha* as we have seen is celebrated in the spring, in the month of Phālguna and is very close to the Hindu New Year. This shows that M. Eliade could be right in his assumption. Again the ritual sacrifices of the first of the last three days consist of *agniṣṭoma* that is performed every year in spring on the new and full moon days.

119. Ibid.

> May here be born warriors of heroic stature, who are skilful shots, good marksmen, invincibile chariot fighters!
> May cows in this kingdom yield milk in plenty, our oxen be tireless, our horses swift, our housewives skilful!
> To him who offers this sacrifice may a hero-son be born, a champion, a mighty warrior, a persuasive speaker!
> May Heaven send us rain for our needs!
> May our fruit-bearing plants ripen in season!
> May joy and prosperity fall to our lot! — *YV* 22. 22[120]

It is through sacrifice that this world maintains itself alive, harmonious and fertile. Therefore, even the fecundity rite can have a cosmic value for the survival of a people depends on fertility at every level.

Agnicayana: Reconstruction of the Cosmos (Space and Time) through Sacrifice

In this section we will see the *Agnicayana,*[121] another important Vedic ritual which is again related to the Puruṣa-Sūkta,[122] and is meant to reconstruct the cosmos in space and time. In the course of our analysis, we will see that for the Vedic people the ritual sacrifice is not only the reproduction of the sacrifice of *puruṣa*

---

120. Translation from *PVE,* p. 379.

121. Probably the last solemn performance of this sacrifice was that which took place from 12 to 24 April 1975 at Pannal, Kerala, India at the request of Frits Staal and others, who participated in it and recorded everything. For more details on the actual performance of it see *AGNI,* vol. 1. But this *Agnicayana* was performed as an *Atirātra-Agnicayana* sacrifice and lasted only for 12 days and not one year. However, it gives a recent confirmation of a past rite which had become something of the past.

122. J. Eggeling and F. Staal consider that *Agnicayana* is related to the Puruṣa-Sūkta. For more details see J. Eggeling (1966), vol. 43, pp. XIV-XV; and *AGNI,* vol. 1, pp. 113-16. When the golden man who represents the Agni-Prajāpati and the *yajamāna* is buried under the first layer, the Puruṣa-Sūkta is sung.

which gave life to this universe and all that exists in it, but also the reconstitution of Puruṣa-Prajāpati which guarantees continuity of space and time. This continuity is seen as the result of sacrifice, for the creator has given it as the remedy to this first sacrifice[123] and one of such sacrifices is the year long *Agnicayana*.

Before considering the main purposes of *Agnicayana* both on the cosmic and the personal levels, let us see some of the passages which speak about the post-creative condition of Puruṣa-Prajāpati which is given as the motivation for the *Agnicayana* rite. According to the Brāhmaṇas after his creative sacrifice Prajāpati[124] is said to be totally spent, dissipated and needs to be restored back to completeness, and *Agnicayana* is nothing other than this sacrificial ritual in which the dispersed body of Prajāpati is reconstituted to its original unity to give it continuity of space and time. The texts depict him as exhausted (*TB* 1.2.6.1), diseased (*GB* 2.4.12) or disjointed, fallen to pieces (*TB* 2.3.6.1; *ŚB* 1.6.3.35,) and such a state is not only dangerous for creation but also for the creator god Prajāpati, for he is said to be in danger. At this stage he fears death (*ŚB* 10.4.2.2),[125] and his vital breaths (*prāṇa*) and luminous power (*tejas*) leave him (*ŚB* 6.1.2.12) as do the gods (*ŚB* 9.1.1.6) and cattle (*ŚB* 8.2.3.9). The texts therefore present the post-creative stage of Prajāpati as a chaotic stage and the way to escape from it is again another sacrifice. Here in these above-

---

123. C. Malamoud (1996), p. 31. R. de Smet speaking on the relation of the sacrifice and the continuity of time writes: "In the Vedas and in the Brāhmaṇas, the conception of time is intimately bound to the conception of causality." R. de Smet (1982), p. 119. In the words of G. Gispert-Sauch, in the Brāhmaṇas time is really conceived as the result of the activity, particularly of the sacrificial activity. G. Gispert-Sauch (1977), p. 18.

124. Cfr. *ŚB* 6.1.2.12.

125. In this way the Brāhmaṇas affirm that everything in this world is mortal. Only through the ritual one can attain immortality. To sacrifice is to redeem the creation from the chaotic stage of the post-creative Prajāpati and also to create an immortal self for the sacrificer.

mentioned passages we can see both cosmic and personal motives which are behind the *Agnicayana* sacrifice. In the cosmic level it reconstitutes Prajāpati, the lord of the creatures, and thereby makes possible the continuity of space and time, and at the personal level it gives immortality to the sacrificer. In the Vedic sacrifice there is always this dialectic between these two aspects.

When Prajāpati is disintegrated time is out of joint, because he is the year (*ŚB* 6.1.2.18-19), and his joints are the two junctions of day and night, of the waxing and waning of lunar half-months, and of the beginnings of the seasons. The texts say that after his procreative sacrifice he was unable to rise with his joints disjointed (*ŚB* 1.6.3.35-36) and he cried to Agni "Put me back together" and Agni did so by building him up piece by piece, just as the bird altar of the *Agnicayana* sacrifice is built-up brick by brick (*ŚB* 6.1.2.13 and 17).[126]

In another text of the *ŚB* the year is presented as death and gods were afraid of this Prajāpati, the Year, Death (10.4.3.1ff). They tried *Agnihotra*, the new and full moon sacrifices to escape from him (the death), but they were all ineffective. Then they tried out a fire-altar but it too did not work, until Prajāpati showed them just how to build it. These texts show on the one hand the supremacy of the *Agnicayana* rite and on the other the

---

126. This has given the mutual parenthood of Prajāpati and Agni. Agni is born from Prajāpati, hence he is the son of Prajāpati. At the same time it is Agni who restores Prajāpati hence he is said to be the father of Prajāpati. We have seen above that the redemption of Prajāpati to his original state is the work of a single god called Agni. But we can also see texts which say that the redemption of Prajāpati was the work of the gods; hence of more than one god. The *ŚB* 1.6.3.36 says that the gods with *agnihotra* (the twice-daily sacrifice) healed that joint of Prajāpati which are the two junctions of day and night. Again with the new and full moon sacrifices they healed that joint which is between the waxing and waning lunar half-months. And with the Cāturmāsyas they healed that joint which is the beginning of the seasons.

need to perform it in the correct way for any desired effect. In performing the *Agnicayana* one not only restores the disintegrated Prajāpati but also overcomes death. Such an idea shows the cyclical idea of death and rebirth.[127]

This rite of *Agnicayana*, part of the *Soma* sacrifice,[128] is itself a sacrifice whose sacrificial material consists of bricks which symbolize the year: the eternal circle of birth, death and new life. In this sacrifice the sacrificial material (*dravya*) is *iṣṭaka* (bricks)[129] and not animal or food material and is destined to Agni.[130] This use of *iṣṭaka* as the *dravya* (material fit for sacrificial oblation) is justified by a myth in the following words:

> In the fire the gods healed him by means of oblations; and whatever oblation they offered that became brick and passed into him. And because they were produced from what was offered (*iṣṭa*), therefore they are bricks (*iṣṭaka*). — *ŚB* 6.1.2.22

This construction of the fire-altar can be seen as the representation of Prajāpati as the sum total of space and time in this world, exactly in correspondence to the cosmic sacrifice of *puruṣa* which we have seen at the beginning of this chapter. The altar stands for a miniature representation of the visible universe for the layers of

---

127. We will see this in the next section of this chapter.

128. According to G. Gispert-Sauch, *Agnicayana* was originally an independent rite, but later made part of *Soma* ritual. G. Gispert-Sauch (1977), p. 25.

129. The Sanskrit word for brick, *iṣṭaka,* comes from *iṣṭi* that is oblation. Such a ritual use of bricks seems to point to a non-Aryan origin of this sacrifice. According to Hyla Stuntz Converse, the Aryan culture was not a brick-using culture and the Harappa culture which was destroyed by flood was a brick-using culture, and the measure of *Agnicayana* bricks (one foot long: see *ŚB* 8.7.2.7) is said to be the same as of the Harappa civilization. For more details on the non- Aryan origin of this complicated sacrificial ritual see H.S. Converse (1974-75), pp. 81-95.

130. However, this sacrifice also includes animal sacrifices and the offerings because it is combined with other *Soma* sacrifices.

the altar are arranged so as to represent earth, air and heaven, and the fire pan is again made in the miniature copy of the three worlds.[131] Prajāpati is also time, because he is the year, therefore the altar consists of five layers which represent the five seasons of the year. He is also the sum total of the social reality. Therefore, in this altar-building sacrifice different bricks are used and each type of brick stands for a certain category of person in the Vedic society. The first brick which is laid is called "unconquerable" (*asādha*) and it represents the entire terrestrial world and is made to the length of the feet of the sacrificer by the main wife of the sacrificer (*mahiṣī*),[132] the "special bricks" stand for the kṣatriyas (the nobles) and the "fillers of space" (*lokamprāṇa*) stand for the vaiśya,[133] the three naturally perforated bricks (stones) stand for the three spaces, etc.

Agnicayana is a brick altar to receive the *āhavanīya* fire, the most important of the three fires.[134] This sacrificial rite of building the fire-altar consists mainly in placing 10,800 bricks in five layers[135] with the recitation of certain *mantra*s accompanying each brick. The sacrificial rite begins with the *dīkṣā* of the sacrificer in which

---

131. J. Eggeling (1966), vol. 43, p. XIX.

132. In the Brāhmaṇas the sacrificer is identified with Prajāpati, the one who sacrifices for the sake of the world and this world is nothing other than Prajāpati. Hence the *asādha* brick stands for the terrestrial Prajāpati.

133. See C. Malamoud (1996), p. 41.

134. G. Gispert-Sauch (1977), p. 26.

135. Each layer has its specific bricks and the main categories of the bricks are *āpasyāḥ* (water bricks), *aśvinī* (medicine), *ṛtavyā* (seasonal), *prāṇabhṛt* (breath supports), *vṛṣṭisanī* (rain-winners), *vayasyā* (strengthening bricks=cattle), *mūrdhanvatī*, *svayamātṛṇṇā* stone (naturally perforated stone = atmosphere), *virāja* bricks, *stomabhāga*s (to create cattle), *diśyā* (quarters), *nākasad*, *codā viśvajyotis*, *saṁyānī*, *āditya*, *ghṛta*, *yaśodā*, *bhūyaskṛt*, *agnirūpā*, *draviṇodā*, *āyuṣyā*, etc. K.B. Sastri (2001), pp. 184-85. No broken bricks are used for fear of turning it into a failure (*ŚB* 8.7.2.16).

he takes the sacred fire into his own self (*ŚB* 10.4.2.29) and carries it for a year[136] before the actual performance takes place with the selection of the priests[137] and the demarcation of a circular sacred space, and the whole sacrificial rite lasts for a year. In the middle of the spot a lotus leaf is laid. On that then a golden man[138] is buried, together with a live tortoise and the heads of five sacrificial animals such as man, horse, ox, sheep, and goat.[139] When the golden man is laid, a part of the Puruṣa-Sūkta is chanted. The normal sacrifice consists in laying a stone or brick every night on the enclosure of the sacred space and laying a brick each day.

> Whenever he laid down an enclosing-stone he laid down a night, and along with that fifteen *muhūrtas*. . . . And whenever he laid down a brick with a formula (*yajuṣmatī*) he laid down a day, and along with that fifteen *muhūrtas*. . . . — *ŚB* 10.4.2.27

Thus, a day (night and day together) has 30 *muhūrtas* (an hour like division which consists of 48 minutes) and there are 360 days

---

136. See also *TS* 5.5.1.5-6. K.B. Sastri (2001), p. 186.

137. The solemn construction of the fire-altar requires four groups of priests such as Adhvaryu, Hotṛ, Udgātr, and Brahman each one assisted by four other priests, but the piling of the bricks has to be done solely by Adhvaryu at the appointed time in the appointed manner and sequence. See K.B. Sastri (2001), p. 189.

138. This stands for Agni-Prajāpati and the sacrificer.

139. The tortoise stands for Prajāpati for one of Prajāpati's animal manifestation is in the form of a tortoise and could also stand for the foundation of the world. The heads of the five victims stand for the five sacrificial animals. The presence of the human skull at the *Agnicayana* has given rise to the idea that at *Agnicayana* a human sacrifice was performed. However, the texts do not describe such sacrifice and it might have been that no real human sacrifice was performed but substitutes were used (of gold or clay). See J.C. Heesterman (1987b), pp. 22-43, especially pp. 30-42. The existence of *Puruṣamedha* in Vedic India is a disputed issue and it is probable that it never existed at least among the Āryans.

in a year, therefore one has to construct the *Agnicayana* altar with 10,800 (360130) bricks.[140] Each brick, therefore, stands for a *diś* (quarters) or for a *muhūrta*, a moment of the day or for a deity or for a class of persons in society and by ritually arranging it he joins space and time and in this way makes possible the continuity of space and time.

The following verses of the *ŚB* clearly say that when one builds up the fire-altar one reconstructs space and time, the body of Prajāpati. The space and time are the parts of the body of Prajāpati and when one arranges the five layers, one reconstitutes Prajāpati by his five bodily sections (*ŚB* 6.1.2.17). These five layers of the altar stand for the five seasonal joints (*ṛtu*) for there are five *ṛtus* (*ŚB* 6.1.2.18). Prajāpati is the year as well as the *diś*, the directions of space (*ŚB* 6.1.2.19). The fire which is laid on the altar is the sun, the Agni who restored Prajāpati (*ŚB* 6.1.2.20). The following verse of the *ŚB* tells clearly that the fire-altar is the year and that time, not being continuous, need to be constructed into a continuity.

> And, again, as to why he lays down seasonal (bricks), — this fire-altar is the year, and it is joined together by means of the seasonal (bricks): he thus makes the year continuous, and joins it together, by means of the seasons. . . . — *ŚB* 8.7.1 3 and 6

Another text of the *ŚB* while speaking about the motives for laying down the two dewy seasonal bricks identifies the fire-altar with the year and the year is this world. The text says:

> And as to why he now lays down these two; — this fire-altar is the year, and the year is these worlds; the fifth layer of this altar is the sky, and the dewy season of this (year) is the sky. . . .
>
> — 8.7.1.7

After having identified the fire-altar with the year and with the whole world the next verse of our Brāhmaṇa identifies Agni (fire-

140. R.V. de Smet (1982), pp. 129-30. However, the 1975 performance of *Atirātra-Agnicayana* at Pannal (Kerala) was done with 1000 bricks. For different types of *Agnicayana* see B. Sastri (2001), p. 183.

altar) with Prajāpati and Prajāpati with the year (*ŚB* 8.7.1.8). The fire-altar consists of five layers,[141] for Prajāpati is year and five are the seasons of the year and when one builds up the five layers he builds him up with five seasons (*ŚB* 6.1.2.18-19).

In this *Agnicayana* sacrifice too we can find a close relation to the cosmogony for not only the names of different gods involved in the cosmogony are mentioned but also different symbols related to the cosmogony are included into the sacrificial rite. In the foundation of the fire altar a lotus leaf is placed which stands for water, the womb from which Agni arose[142] and a text goes on to the extent of identifying the fifth layer of the altar with Viśvakarman who in turn is identified with Prajāpati.[143] All these show that in the Brāhmaṇas sacrifice is closely related to cosmogony and every sacrifice is the repetition of that first creative act for the continuity of the cosmos. As J. Eggeling rightly observes:

> Prajāpati, who here takes the place of the *puruṣa*, the world-man, or all-embracing Personality, is offered up anew in every sacrifice; and inasmuch as the very dismemberment of the Lord of Creatures, which took place at that archetypal sacrifice, was in itself the creation of the universe, so every sacrifice is also a repetition of that first creative act. Thus the periodical sacrifice is nothing else than a microcosmic representation of the ever-proceeding destruction and renewal of all cosmic life and matter.[144]

And in this destruction and renewal of the cosmic life depends the continuity of space and time, and the purpose of the *Agnicayana* rite is just to give this continuity to space and time.

---

141. However, in the *ŚB* 6.1.2.17 the five layers of the fire-altar are identified with five bodily parts of Prajāpati such as hair, skin, flesh, bone and marrow.

142. See *ŚB* 7.4.1.7-15.

143. *ŚB* 7.4.2.5.

144. J. Eggeling (1966), vol. 43, p. xv.

We may find a possible answer to this reconstitution of the creator in the sacrifice in the words of Panikkar,

> Creation is pictured . . . as the self-immolation of the Creator. It is only because Prajāpati sacrifices himself fully that he can give to creation his whole Self. It is only by the same sacrifice in the opposite direction, by the same sacrifice in which he has himself been offered as oblation, that Prajāpati is snatched back from death.[145]

Sacrifice, therefore, is seen as first dividing and then reintegrating into the original unity. As Coomaraswamy writes,

> And what is essential in the sacrifice? In the first place to divide, and in the second to reunite. He being One, becomes or is made into Many, and being Many becomes again or is put together again as One.[146]

Sacrifice is the means by which the Creator becomes many and also the means by which the cosmos becomes part of the Creator. This is the function of sacrifice, to put the creation in relation to the Creator. In doing so one performs a sacrifice in the reverse order of the primordial sacrifice thereby making possible the continued existence of the cosmos. The cosmos, therefore, returns to its Creator in and through sacrifice. The Creator, thus, gave sacrifice as the very *ṛta* or law of the universe.

THE AGNICAYANA AND THE OVERCOMING OF DEATH

The *Agnicayana,* which is the human imitation of the construction of the cosmic world of Prajāpati, restores on the cosmic level the space and time and on the personal level it creates an immortal self for the sacrificer.[147] These are the two functions of the *Agnicayana*. In this sub-section we will reflect on the personal aspect. If on the cosmic level the *Agnicayana* reconstructs and gives continuity to space and time, at the personal level it constructs an

---

145. *PVE*, p. 78.

146. A.K. Coomaraswamy (1941), p. 396.

147. See G. Gispert-Sauch (1977), pp. 26-37.

immortal self (*ātman*) to overcome death. Thus the *Agnicayana* sacrifice affirms not only the fleeting character of space and time which need to be ritually made continuous, but also the need for attaining a self (*ātman*) that is beyond the suffering and death. Again as we will see, the reason for this theory is based on the Puruṣa-Prajāpati myths.

Just as the disintegrated body of Prajāpati is made whole by the ritual acts of gods, so too, the *ātman* of the human being is to be made whole or perfected by the ritual activity.[148] Sacrifice is, therefore, the means to make one's self perfect so that one may attain immortality. The theology of Brāhmaṇas considers sacrifice as the means for immortality. Only through initiation into the Vedic study and sacrifice can one have a lasting *ātman*. The one who does not receive the initiation to the Vedic sacrifice and study and does not perform the prescribed sacrifice is considered not only as an imperfect being but also as a being without an immortal self. One of the purposes of *Agnicayana* is precisely to make an immortal self for the sacrificer and in such manner death is overcome through the means of sacrifice. As Heesterman says,

> The sacrifice is a cosmos which is violently broken up to be put together again. This is in accordance with the cyclical conception of the universe underlying the ritual literature: the constantly alternating movement between the two poles of disintegration and reintegration, death and birth, netherworld and upper world; an idea which found its clearest systematic expression in the building of the fire-altar conceived of as the restoration of the disintegrated cosmic man. The pivotal point, however, is that actual death and disintegration have been eliminated.[149]

According to the Brāhmaṇas, gods, *asura*s, and men are all born mortal and transcend this mortal stage with the help of sacrifice.[150]

148. We will examine this point in detail in pp. 101-09 of this chapter.

149. J.C. Heesterman (1987b), p. 24.

150. See *ŚB* 1.7.3.1-2; 2.2.2.8-14.

As Panikkar says, "Immortality is not the birthright of any being; it has to be acquired, conquered, merited, given."[151] And this is again the function of sacrifice and the *asuras* could not attain it because their sacrifice was considered to be imperfect. In the *ŚB* we read:

> (Once upon a time) the gods and the *asuras*, both of whom were offspring of Prajāpati, were striving between themselves. Both sides were destitute of spirit because they were mortal and he who is mortal has no spirit. Among these two groups of mortal beings one, Agni, was immortal and it was through him, the immortal, that they both had their being. Now, whichever of the gods was slain by the *asuras* was in very truth slain irrevocably. . . . Their [god's] gaze, then, fell upon the immortal sacred Agni. "Come," they said, "let us establish this immortality in our inmost self! When we have placed that immortality in our inmost self and have become immortal and unconquerable, we shall defeat our enemies who are neither immortal nor unconquerable.". . . So the gods established that Fire in their inmost self and, having established that immortality in their inmost self and became immortal and unconquerable, they defeated their mortal and conquerable enemies.
>
> — 2.2.2.8-10,14[152]

In another text it is said that it is through sacrifice that the gods proceeded to the heavenly realm (*ŚB* 1.7.3.1). *Taittirīya Saṁhitā* also has the same concept when it says:

> It was by the perfect accomplishment of the sacrifice that the gods proceeded to the heavenly realm, and it was by reason of the defective performance of the same that the *asuras* were conquered. — 1.6.10.2[153]

---

151. *PVE*, p. 365.

152. This translation is taken from ibid., p. 383.

153. Ibid., p. 385. However, according to the *Ṛ̥V*, gods and men attain immortality by drinking the *soma* (8.48.3), because *soma* was considered to be the drink of immortality.

Even the gods won immortality with the help of the sacrifice: the *asuras* could not attain it because their sacrifices were considered to be imperfect. Sacrifice is, therefore, the means for immortality.

Like the gods, human beings attain immortality through the ritual sacrifice. This *ātman* created in the sacrifices is that which gives immortality and the largest square of the fire-altar is considered to be the *ātman* of the sacrificer. The sacrifice transforms him and places him in the divine nature.[154] Through sacrifice one passes from the human world to the world of the gods (*ŚB* 1.1.1.4) and the *Agnicayana* is made in the form of a bird flying toward the east, the gate of heaven.[155] The sacrifice again procures for him a place in the heavenly world (*svargaloka*) and a divine self (*daiva ātman*) in that world after death.

---

154. B.K. Smith (1984-85), p. 292.

155. The purpose of the bird-shaped altar is not for carrying the sacrificer to heaven but to identify it with Prajāpati and his vital airs

> ". . . for what object is this fire (altar) built?" — "Having become a bird, he (Agni) shall bear me to the sky!" so say some; but let him not think so; for by assuming that form, the vital airs became Prajāpati; by assuming that form, Prajāpati creasted the gods; by assuming that form, the gods became immortal: and what thereby the vital airs, and Prajāpati, and the gods became, that indeed he (the Sacrificer) thereby becomes"
> —*ŚB* 6.1.2.36.

Here the bird-shaped altar is said to give immortality to the sacrificer in the same manner it gave to the gods and Prajāpati. However, in another text of the same Brāhmaṇa, Agni (the fire altar) is compared to an animal. The text says:

> "Now that Agni (the altar) is an animal, and (as such) he is even now made up whole and entire — those (bricks) which he lays down in front are his fore-feet, and those behind are his thighs; and those which he places in the middle are that body of his. He places these in the region of the two *retaḥsic* (bricks), for the *retaḥsic* are the ribs, and the ribs are the middle, and that body is in the middle (of the limbs). He places them all round, for that body extends all round"
> —*ŚB* 8.1.4.3.

This may also suggest that there were different shapes of *Agnicayana* altars, not the single bird-shaped one.

In sacrifice, the sacrificer ascends to the *svargaloka* with his *daiva ātman* and with the help of the "exit rites" descends from the sacred world.[156] Sacrifice plays the role of a vehicle in these ascending and descending processes of the sacrificer into the realm of heaven and back.[157] He cannot remain in heaven because his human body is an obstacle, but once he is assured of a divine body he descends to earth once more and purchases back from the gods his sacrificed body.[158] Only after his death will he be able to remain in heaven. Hence the journey to heaven in the sacrifice is considered to be a passing experience: the lasting experience will be after the death of the sacrificer. According to another text of *ŚB*, a man is born three times, first he is born from his mother and father, he is born a second time while performing the sacrifice and a third time when he dies and they place him on the pyre and he proceeds to a new existence and for this reason it is said that man is born three times (11.2.1.1). This second birth comes in the sacrifice and in it he offers his mortal body to the gods and receives in return an immortal body.

The *Agnicayana* has, therefore, both cosmic and personal functions: on the cosmic level it guarantees the continuity of space and time and on the personal level it gives immortality to the sacrificer. Sacrifice is thus the means to overcome death and to have an immortal self. None of these two functions should be overlooked, because every sacrifice moves in these two directions. We will see that when the latter aspect gets predominance over the former the sacrifice gets reduced to a ritual means to obtain personal benefits which the Upaniṣads and the *BG* will correct with their emphasis on the non-everlasting character of the world constructed in the sacrifice.

---

156. B.K. Smith (1984-85), p. 293.
157. For more details see ibid., pp. 292ff.
158. *PVE*, p. 389.

Sacrifice as Ātmayajña and the Substitute as the Counterpart of the Sacrificer

Creation by the sacrifice of the *puruṣa* can also be interpreted to show on the one hand that human life is a gift/debt and on the other that the divinity, the sacrificer, and the victim are "one." Just as creation is a divine sacrifice, so too, every human sacrifice is a self-sacrifice.

According to the Brāhmaṇas, human life is a free gift from the gods,[159] and like every gift, this too has to be acknowledged by counter-gifts. Such acknowledgement takes place in sacrifice. Sacrifice is then self-gift to the divinity who sacrificed himself for the sake of creation. It is self-sacrifice.[160] A.K. Coomaraswamy

---

159. The *ŚB* speaks of human life in terms of fourfold debts. According to a verse, when a man is born, whoever he may be, there is born simultaneously a debt to the gods, to the sages, to the ancestors, and to men (1.7.2.1). Human life is, therefore, seen in terms of a constitutive debt to all these persons. When a man offers a sacrifice he fulfils his duty towards all these beings to whom he owes his existence. He pays his debt to the gods by offering them sacrifices (*ŚB* 1.7.2.2), to the sages by reciting the Vedas (*ŚB* 1.7.2.3), to the ancestors by procreating (*ŚB* 1.7.2.4) so that the human life may continue on the earth. He then pays the debt to men by his hospitality to the guests (*ŚB* 1.7.2.5). This last verse says that the man who does all these things has performed a true work; he has obtained all, conquered all. The study of scriptures, the procreation, and a glass of water offered to a guest have the same value as a complicated ritual. And the highest liturgical act is the study of scriptures, because the sacrifice to *Brahman* consists of sacred study (*ŚB* 11.5.6.3). Thus, according to the *ŚB*, life is a gift and this gift has to be acknowledged through the performance of sacrifice, the means by which man expresses his gratitude towards the gods, and his ancestors.

160. S. Lévi (1898), pp. 32-33. On the identity between the victim and the sacrificer, see J.C. Heesterman (1987a), pp. 91-106. Here we are not discussing the suicidal sacrifices in times of war, or famine, or some other natural calamities. For such discussions see H.S. Versnel (1980), pp. 135-94.

says, "To sacrifice and to be sacrificed are essentially the same."[161] The self-sacrifice can be called the real sacrifice because anything else one offers is a substitute for oneself. As B.K. Smith argues, the least symbolic of all sacrifices is the suicidal human sacrifice, in which the symbol stands for itself[162] and that could be the end of sacrifice itself. Hence the Vedic ritualists have brought the theory of substitution in sacrifice to uphold both the theory that sacrifice is always self-sacrifice and the continued performance of it through the medium of substitution. Just as sacrifice is Prajāpati's *pratimā* (counterpart) so, too, what one offers in sacrifice is nothing other than one's counterpart.[163] And again in the victim what one offers is not something outside oneself but a part of oneself.

We have seen above that for the Vedic person creation is a divine sacrifice and according to J. Eggeling the reason for the identification of *puruṣa* with Prajāpati in the Brāhmaṇas is to show the identity between the Creator god, *puruṣa*, the sacrificer, and the sacrifice.[164] In this way to sacrifice is nothing other than to offer oneself as Prajāpati did and when one does so one recreates the cosmos. Thus as F. Staal writes: "The idea of self-sacrifice is basic to the Prajāpati cosmology and to the cyclical conquest of death through rebirth, which characterize the "*śrauta* ritual" in general and the *Agnicayana* in particular."[165] This self-sacrifice is done through the victim, or the offering which is identified simultaneously with Prajāpati and the sacrificer.

In a sacrifice substitute not only represents the sacrificer but also the invisible divine recipient. The victim by representing simultaneously two personalities plays the role of a double substitution. On account of this double substitution we can say

---

161. A.K. Coomaraswamy (1941), p. 359.
162. B.K. Smith and W. Doniger (1989), p. 191.
163. B.K. Smith (1989), p. 74.
164. J. Eggeling (1966), vol. 43, p. xv.
165. *AGNI*, vol. 1, p. 117.

that "every sacrifice is both an *Ersatz* self-sacrifice and a dramatization of a deicide"[166] due to the identity between the sacrificer, victim and the deity. However, as B.K. Smith and W. Doniger argue, sacrifice "is always an act of surrogation, an imitation of an ideal, a counterpart of an unrealizable prototype. . . . Sacrifice remains sacrifice only in so far as it substitutes for its own ideal form."[167] In this way the surrogate victim that stands in the place of the deity and the sacrificer not only saves the ritual killing from criminality but also makes possible the self-gift to the deity through the medium of a symbol. Violence[168] to the animal is not the intention of the sacrifice but self-gift to the divinity. But this self-gift is sometimes expressed through the medium of taking away life in order to show the offering of life to the deity.

After having seen the correlation between the sacrificer, the sacrifice, and the victim now we must see the Vedic theories of substitution which are again based on the identity between Prajāpati/sacrificer, sacrifice and the victim on the one hand[169] and on the principle of necessity on the other. In the *ŚB* we find that when the gods were going on offering to one another, Prajāpati gave himself to them as the sacrifice so that it became theirs and emitted from himself the counterpart (*pratimā*) of himself (11.1.8.2-

---

166. B.K. Smith and W. Doniger (1989), p. 190.

167. Ibid., p. 216.

168. It is true that violence is part of the animal sacrifice but it is a problem how to interpret this violence. R. Girard has emphasized the other side of sacrificial substitution, i.e. the displaced violence toward another. R. Girard (1986), pp. 101-03. According to him, society through the process of a double substitution transfers its own violence to a surrogate, i.e. to a scapegoat (a member of the community) and then to a ritual substitute to protect itself from the consequences of its own violence. Even though violence is part of animal sacrifice, Girard's position cannot be accepted for the displacement of violence is not the intention of religious sacrifice.

169. See *R̥V* 10.90.16. See also J.C. Heesterman (1987b), p. 30.

4). Therefore, to sacrifice is to offer oneself to the Creator, and in this sense sacrifice itself becomes a substitute for the primordial immolation and a surrogate for oneself. Further, creation can never be completely independent of the Creator (Prajāpati) because Prajāpati being the Totality (*sarvam*), embraces his creatures. The sacrificer and the victim form part of him. The victim, the sacrificer and the sacrifice are all his counterparts.

The sacrifice is not only the counterpart of Prajāpati but also of man, and through this identification of the sacrifice with man the *ŚB* tries to explain how man was considered to be the first sacrificial victim. For this, the above-mentioned Brāhmaṇa uses the hymn of the Puruṣa-Sūkta in a different context and it says:

> The sacrifice is man. It is man (who offers it) because it is man who spreads it out and because, in being spread out, it assumes exactly the nature and stature as man. For this reason, sacrifice is man.
> — 1.3.2.1[170]

As Panikkar says, "Sacrifice involves both immolation and new life — and so it is with Man also. He is born, dies and is reborn."[171] Sacrifice, therefore, functions as substitute for a daily dying to be reborn. The sacrificial victim dies in the place of the sacrificer and thereby protects the latter's life and at the same gives him a new birth. This is possible because the victim is his counterpart and what he offers is not something outside to oneself but a part of one's own self.

And the Vedas, basing themselves on the theory of resemblance, have created a chain of potential substitutes for man[172] so that the daily performance of sacrifice may not be

170. This translation is taken from *PVE*, p. 393.

171. Ibid., p. 388.

172. Man ranks first among the five animals fit for sacrifice. The order is as follows: man, horse, bull, ram and goat (*ŚB* 6.2.1.2-3). This order is not accidental but according to the relative excellence of each victim (*ŚB* 6.2.1.18).

obstructed. The Vedas hold that a sacrificial animal which most resembles the sacrificer stands as his prototype and in this manner the horse is the prototype of man, and the bull is the prototype of the horse, likewise the vegetable oblations as the prototype of lesser forms within the series of sacrificial animals. Also the baked cake is the counterpart of the sacrificial animal (*paśu*), and also the *pratimā* of the sacrificer (*TB* 3.2.8.8). As Smith and Doniger rightly say:

> The sacrificer and his oblation are in this way analogous of one another. And because of their affinity, the sacrificer is said to offer a form of himself when he offers clarified butter, the sacrificial cake, or an animal; for by virtue of the counterpart (*pratimāya*) it is the man.[173]

We also find that not all counterparts are created equal and therefore do not have equal ability to represent the prototype.[174] In any performance (where the optional injunctions are prescribed) the higher the choice the higher the fruit will be (*KŚS* 1.10). Hence the result depends also on the type of animal/ material offered to the deity. The one who gives more receives more, the one who gives the best of things receives the best of things.

We can also find a reversal of the hierarchical sacrificial order. This time the lowest on the scale, i.e. goat, is said to be the best victim and, therefore, the most used.[175] This might also explain the change from the bloody sacrifices to the use of the grains in sacrifice. A text says:

> The gods offered man as sacrificial victim. Then the sacrificial

---

173. B.K. Smith and W. Doniger (1989), pp. 198-99.

174. This explains why certain animals may be offered and not others and certain food and drinks and not others.

175. According to the *ŚB* 6.2.2.15, goat resembles man, horse, and bull, and when one offers goat, he offers all those *paśus* (animals fit for sacrifice).

> quality (*medhā*) passed out of the offered man. It entered the horse. Then the horse became fit for sacrifice and they dismissed him whose sacrificial quality had passed out of him. He (the former man, now devoid of the sacrificial quality) became a defective man (*kiṁpuruṣa*). They offered the horse, and the sacrificial quality passed out of the offered horse. It entered the cow. . . . They offered the cow. . . . The sacrificial quality entered the ram. . . . They offered the ram. The sacrificial quality entered the goat. . . . It (the sacrificial quality) stayed the longest in the goat, and it (the sacrificial quality) passed out of the goat. It entered this (earth), and therefore this (earth) became fit for sacrifice. . . . The *paśu*s whose sacrificial quality had passed out of them became unfit for sacrifice. Therefore, one should not eat them. They follow it (the sacrificial essence) into this (earth); it being followed, became rice. . . . When the rice cake (is offered), it is indeed a *paśu* which is offered up. Its stingy chaff, that is the hairs; its husk is the skin; the floor is the blood; the small grains are the flesh; whatever is the best part (of the grain) is the bone. He sacrifices with the sacrificial quality of all *paśu*s who sacrifices with the rice cake. — *AB* 2.8-9[176]

We have seen that the above-mentioned verses not only explain the reversal of the hierarchical sacrificial order but also the origin of the vegetable offerings. A myth was invented by the brāhmaṇa priests to convince the people that the vegetable offerings had the same value as the animal offerings. The transition of the sacrificial quality from one animal to another and finally to the grains was said to be the reason for the changes in the sacrifices. The vegetable offerings, therefore, substitute the animal sacrifices.

But the substitution of the animal sacrifices by the vegetable sacrifices has to be seen within the influence of Buddhism on the Vedic sacrifices.[177] For we know that under the influence of

---

176. This translation is taken from B.K. Smith and W. Doniger (1989), pp. 201-03.

177. Ibid., p. 214.

Buddhism the animal sacrifices of the Vedas underwent a drastic change. The doctrine of *ahiṁsā* (non-violence) became an important factor in the worship and the bloody animal sacrifices were slowly replaced by vegetable offerings, fruits, flowers, leaves, etc. To justify such changes in the sacrifices the Vedic ritualists invented the theory that the vegetable offerings possess as much potency as all the sacrificed *paśu*s would have. Thus, a ritual rethinking takes place, and the old is given a new form. The vegetable offering is, thus, considered to have the same effect of the animal sacrifice.

The phenomenon of the inaccessibility can be considered as another reason for the substitution.[178] As we know, inaccessibility necessitates a substitution for the uninterrupted performance of sacrifice for the maintenance of the world, to prevent the cosmos from disintegration. The *pūtīka* plant was offered in the place of *soma* plant because the latter was inaccessible (*TB* 1.4.7.5ff.; *JB* 1.354). The dialogue between the king Janaka of Videha and Yājñavalkya, the sage, on the material to be used for the *Agnihotra* sacrifice affirms that a substitute could be used in case of the inaccessibility of the original. Our text has it:

> Janaka of Videha once asked Yājñavalkya, "What is used for the *Agnihotra*, Yājñavalkya? Can you tell me?"
> "I can, O king," he replied.
> "What is it, then?"
> "Milk," he said.
> "If there were no milk, what would you use for the offering?"
> "Rice and barley."
> "And if there were no rice and barley, what would you use?"
> "Some other herbs."
> "And if there were no other herbs, what would you use?"
> "I would use wild herbs," he said.
> "And if there were no wild herbs, what would you use?"
> "Some fruit."
> "And if there were no fruit, what would you use?"

178. Ibid., p. 204.

"I would use water," he said.
"And if there were no water, what would you use?"
"Then indeed," he replied, "there would be nothing at all, and yet an offering could be made — truth with faith."

— *ŚB* 11.3.1.2-4[179]

From this above-mentioned dialogue we can see that the substitutes become the counterparts of inaccessible substances and therefore allow the continued performance of sacrifice on which stands the cosmic order and the continued existence of the world. The important thing, however, is that sacrifice needs to be performed without interruption and for this reason the texts declare that *nitya* or obligatory sacrifices may be performed with any number of substitutions, as long as they are done (*BŚS* 28.13). The substitutes allow an uninterrupted performance of the obligatory sacrifices in times of distress, war or when one is away on a journey (*BŚS* 29.8), and in this way guarantee the smooth running of the universe.[180]

We can also find in the Brāhmaṇas an interesting theory of the substitution of certain types of sacrifice by some other. In Vedic rituals on account of their all-encompassing nature certain sacrifices are said to be most perfect and thereby substitute all others. *Aitareya Brāhmaṇa* tells that the *soma* sacrifice contains within it all other sacrifices (4.40-41). *ŚB* presents the *Rājasūya* sacrifice as the all-encompassing sacrifice and by offering it one envelops all sacrificial rituals (5.2.3.9); but in another text the *Agnicayana* is presented as the most important sacrifice and it says that one

---

179. This translation is taken from *PVE*, p. 400.

180. However, even when the substitutes are used in sacrifice they are to be treated as if original, and the preparatory rites and the *mantras* recited for the original remain unchanged when there is a substitute. References in the prescribed verse to the original (e.g. *soma* or "goat") are kept even when a substitute is being used. Substitution is then for the practical purposes and for the continued performance of the sacrifice. B.K. Smith and W. Doniger (1989), p. 204.

obtains all the sacrifices with the *Agnicayana* (10.1.5.1-3). Here one sacrifice substitutes another by virtue of its superiority. Later on even the simple recitation of the Veda was regarded as the simplified equivalent of the actual performance of a Vedic sacrifice.[181] We can find, therefore, a continuous change in the practice and conception of sacrifice taking always new meanings without leaving aside its cosmic functions.

Sacrifice Gives Order and Form to the Formless Creation

Another important function of the Vedic sacrifice is that it gives order and form to the formless creation of Prajāpati and thereby not only heals the inherent deficiencies of the creation, but also assigns everything a proper place in the universe and in society[182] by giving it *nāma-rūpa*, name and form. Like creation, so too, the production of a cosmos takes place in sacrifice, for what is immediately given is not only chaotic but also discontinuous and needs to be made perfect in ritual sacrifice and only what is ritually produced is real.[183] As Smith puts it, "cosmogony, the production of an ordered universe out of a generated potential, is a secondary act in the Prajāpati myths"[184] and this is because,

> . . . the natural is the chaotic, the disorganized, the unformed. In cosmological terms, what is merely procreated by the Creator God is not cosmos or a universal whole made up of ordered parts. The origins of true cosmos are found not in this primary

---

181. Ibid., p. 208.
182. See B.K. Smith (1994), pp. 26-349; B.K. Smith (1989), pp. 46-119. I am indebted to B.K. Smith for the ideas treated in this and the following section.
183. L. Silburn (1955), p. 1. In the contemporary *pūjā*, as well as in some of the sacraments, the Puruṣa-Sūkta is sung. See G. Bühnemann (1988), pp. 135-76. As we have already mentioned, at the *dīkṣā*, at the healing ceremony, at the expiation rites, at the funeral ceremony, etc. this hymn is sung. J. Gonda (1977), p. 98.
184. B.K. Smith (1985a), p. 75; B.K. Smith (1989), p. 62.

> generative act but rather in a secondary operation — a ritual act that lends structure and order to a chaotic creation.[185]

J. Gonda too has a similar view when he writes: "Prajāpati's creation is described as imperfect as long as he has not completed it by some ritual means."[186] The Brāhmaṇas, therefore, consider the creation of Prajāpati as formless as long as he did not give form to it through the sacrifice. The function of sacrifice is not only to create but also to give order and form and to make perfect the imperfect creation of Prajāpati. Here below we will see the reasons for such imperfections in the Prajāpati's creation which are given as the motives for the sacrifices.

According to *Taittirīya Brāhmaṇa*, Prajāpati emitted creatures who were formless by virtue of their excessive cohesiveness or indistinguishable features: they were too much alike and clasped together, indistinct and thus chaotic (*TB* 2.2.7.1). A text of another Brāhmaṇa says that these undifferentiated creatures were at odds with one another and ate each other (*PB* 24.11.2). This excessive resemblance is explained by the term *jāmi*[187] and the opposite of it

---

185. B.K. Smith (1989), p. 50.

186. J. Gonda (1983c), p. 14.

187. *Jāmi* means an excess of resemblance which becomes an unproductive condition of homogeneity or redundancy. In the rituals it means the rites that are fruitlessly replicative within a ritual sequence, are non-productive (*AB* 3.47 and 48). For example, there is a *jāmi* when in sacrifice the same verses are recited as offering verses on the same day more than once. Hence to avoid such repetitions the *mantra* at the morning pressing of *soma* is different from that of the afternoon and evening pressing. *Jāmi* can also mean the homosexual union which is again considered to be unproductive because of its excessive resemblance (*JB* 1.300 and 1.330). For more details see B.K. Smith (1989), pp. 52-53; B.K. Smith (1985a), pp. 72-77. *Jāmi* is also one of the Sanskrit terms for sister and may mean one who cannot be a *mithuna*, i.e. a sexual partner because of the close connection to the brother. C. Malamoud (1992), pp. 46-47.

is *pṛthak*, which means the excessive differentiation.[188] Due to the excessive differentiation the creatures claim radical independence from the Creator and resist the superiority of Prajāpati which too has to be rectified. This is again the function of sacrifice and ritual in the Vedas. Hence for the Vedic people the natural is chaotic and imperfect due to the extreme resemblance and differentiation and has to be rectified through the means of sacrifice.

According to the Vedic *ṛṣis*, the production of an ordered universe occurs only when the creation is divided into its constituents. Excessive resemblance or *jāmi* is regulated by the introduction of form (*rūpa*) and difference through the sacrifice. Creatures who were clasped together due to excessive cohesiveness were made distinct when Prajāpati entered them with form (*rūpa*) (*TB* 2.2.7.1). Again with the help of the forty-nine-day sacrifice he separated every living being into its distinctive form and only then this creation became separated; cows became really cows, horses became really horses, and men became really men (*PB* 24.11.2). Hence in the words of Smith "here the origins of universal form and order are specifically said to be effected by the morphological power of ritual, subsequent to counteracting the creative emission."[189] Sacrifice not only creates but also gives form and shape to all beings. As Smith writes,

> Between procreation on the one hand and cosmogony and anthropogony on the other is inserted a set of *constructive* activities, that is, a set of *rituals*. Between Prajāpati's creation and the origin of cosmos are divine sacrificial acts which give

---

188. If *jāmi* means excessive resemblance and non-productive action, *pṛthak* means the opposite which is again non-productive due to its excessive differentiation and independency. The reality to be functional should be between these extremes. The role of sacrifice is to bring such differentiation in the cosmic and personal levels through sacrifices and sacraments. See B.K. Smith (1989), pp. 52-60; B.K. Smith (1985a), p. 73.

189. B.K. Smith (1985a), p. 75.

> form to a formless emission. Between creation of the individual and the origin of the human being are also ritual acts which fabricate a true human being out of a humanoid. Cosmogony and anthropogony are *activated* and *actualized* by sacrifice (*yajña*), by ritual action (*karman*). . . .[190]

According to the Brāhmaṇas, it is sacrifice that gives form to the naturally formless and brings order, and it is the function of sacrificial ritual to give form to creation by ritually recreating it and assigning it its proper place in the cosmos and human society. In such case, as Smith rightly puts it,

> The creation of true cosmos, otherwise put, is not simply a matter of the One becoming many but also and necessarily of the reintegration of the many into a new whole.[191]

Sacrifice, therefore, not only creates but also gives form and order to the formless creation of Prajāpati which has its correspondence in the Hindu *saṁskāra*s which we will see below.

SACRIFICE CREATES HUMAN BEING FROM THE HUMANOID

We have seen above that according to the Vedic conception what is immediately given is inherently defective and only what is subsequently formed through the ritual action is the ontologically real, both at the cosmic and individual level. As Smith puts it,

> If, in Vedic cosmological theory, creation is not cosmos but only a flawed precondition for the ritual task of construction, so, too, at the level of human beginnings procreation is not the bringing into existence of an ontologically sound human being.[192]

From this logic the Vedic sacrifices and *saṁskāra*s (sacraments) gain the function of giving form to the inherently defective human being and the one who does not receive the *saṁskāra*s is considered to be a defective being.

190. Ibid., p. 72. See also B.K. Smith (1989), p. 51.
191. B.K. Smith (1989), p. 62.
192. Ibid., p. 82.

Just as it is difficult to differentiate between the Vedic sacrifices and rituals, so, too, it is not that easy to distinguish between sacrifices and *saṁskāra*s, for both of them merge into one another.[193] However, every human being is born defective and needs to be ritually made complete and this is again the function of the *saṁskāra*s. The term *saṁskāra* is derived from the Sanskrit root *kṛ* = to make, with the integrate prefix *sam* = whole. The *saṁskāra*s are, therefore, the rituals which literally "make whole," "construct" or "perfect."[194] As Smith says:

> From conception to birth, and from birth to the "second birth" out of the Veda (*upanayana*) and marriage, the life of the boy is punctuated by these rituals of healing (eliminating the defects of the ungenerate and counteracting the natural defectiveness

---

193. In my opinion, in the Vedic ritualistic language to say sacrifice is to say ritual or *saṁskāra* even though all these terms have specific meanings and etymologies. Jan Heesterman in his chapter on ritual, after making an affirmation that it was ritual that brought about the definitive collapse of the world of ritual argues,

> "After all, sacrifice is a privileged occasion for elaborate and highly profiled ritual, and it seems all but impossible to distinguish between sacrifice and its ritual. Who says *sacrifice*, says *ritual*. It is in the first and the last place that the ritual of any event makes it possible to discern whether that event is a sacrifice and not, say, a simple killing or butchery." —J.C. Heesterman (1993), p. 45.

Such closeness between sacrifice and ritual even makes one to use them as terms synonymous as in the case of B.K. Smith when he writes:

> "Sacrifice, for them, was not primarily an honorific gift-giving exchange between gods and humans. Neither was it regarded as a symbolic representation of an already concretized reality. The brāhmaṇa ritualists themselves certainly did not understand the sacrifice to be meaningless activity done for its own sake or as a ritualized realm of anti-reality. Rather the ritual was the workshop in which all reality was forged." —B.K. Smith (1989), p. 50.

194. B.K. Smith (1989), pp. 86-87; B.K. Smith (1985a), p. 79. See also J. Gonda (1980), p. 364; R.B. Pandey (1998), pp. 15ff.

> of mere creation) and of construction (collecting together and ordering elements into viable and fit entities).[195]

In this case just as creation is not cosmos, so too, the birth should not be taken to mean the birth of a human being but of a humanoid, i.e. of a mere potential human being. As Smith writes,

> . . . birth and anthropogony are, like creation and cosmogony, regarded as two separate moments, distinguished by the absence or presence of ritual reclamation. The bringing into existence of a viable human being is, the ritualists proclaimed a matter of ritual rather than merely biological labour.[196]

He argues again:

> Human life is a process of ritually constructing and refining a self, an *ātman*, out of the raw materials of aboriginal creation, just as the *ātman* of Prajāpati is reconstituted (literally "remembered") by the post-creation rituals of the gods.[197]

The *saṁskāra*s, therefore, perfect a human being out of the raw materials of "aboriginal" creation, and to compose the *ātman* (the self). According to the *Aitareya Brāhmaṇa*, the sacrificer fashions his own self in a rhythmical way through the ritual chants (6.27). The *ŚB* too has a similar view when it holds that the heavenly body of a sacrificer is made complete by sacrifice; this new heavenly body is made complete (*saṁskriyate*) by that (sacrifice) (11.2.6.13).

We may say that for a Vedic person the procreative act of Prajāpati becomes the model for all ritual acts and just as the chaotic state of Prajāpati's creation was rectified through the means of various sacrifices, so, too, the natural state of a human being is in a kind of defective condition and need to be rectified in sacrifice

---

195. B.K. Smith (1985a), p. 79. On the initiation rite as a new birth and on the passages which speak of it see, J. Gonda (1979), p. 258. See also *PVE*, pp. 246-52.

196. B.K. Smith (1989), p. 82.

197. Ibid.

and *saṁskāras*. Therefore, any uninitiated child (to the study of Vedas and sacrifice) is considered to be incomplete, irresponsible and is on a level with the śūdras, and is excluded form the Vedic sacrifices. It is only his second birth, i.e. when brought into relation with the sacrifice that he is freed from his ontologically defective state. Like the śūdras, a member of a brāhmaṇa, kṣatriya or vaiśya is also born defective, but the members of the higher classes pass out of this defective condition when brought into relation with the sacrifice.[198] However, a member of the higher classes could also fall into that ontological deficiency through negligence. The texts say:

> If a Brahmin passes his sixteenth year without undergoing initiation, if a Kṣatriya his twenty-second or a Vaiśya his twenty-fourth, they become *patita-sāvitrīkas*, those who have lost their right to learn the Veda and to sacrifice.
>
> — *SGS* 2.1.9; *PGS* 2.5.39[199]

Another text says:

> No one should initiate such men, nor teach them, nor perform sacrifices for them, nor have intercourse with them. . . . A person whose ancestors through three generations have been *patita-sāvitrīkas* is permanently excluded from the *saṁskāra* (of initiation) and from being taught the Veda. — *PGS* 2.5.40,42[200]

In these above-mentioned verses we can see how the Vedas stressed the need for the initiation to the Vedic sacrifice and to the study of the Vedic scriptures prescribed for the three upper castes. Those who did not do such initiations were thus not only excluded from the religious life of the community but also considered to be defective creatures in line with the śūdras.

---

198. B.K. Smith (1985a), pp. 81-82.
199. This translation is taken from ibid., p. 82.
200. This translation is taken from ibid.

The Brāhmaṇas also consider the sick person as one without a firm foundation (*PB* 16.13.4) and such a person is seen in level with the post-procreative state of Prajāpati. He needs to be made firm with the ritual activity just like Prajāpati was made to regain his vigour through the *Agnicayana* sacrifice. In the case of a sick person the performance of the strong *Soma* rite may serve to block up, to rectify the rupture. A brāhmaṇa says that he should perform it for the one who is ill in any way (*PB* 18.5.9-11). The sacrifice is therefore prescribed as the medicine for the sick persons.

Just as a human being is ritually made perfect so, too, certain rituals have to be performed for the dead for his new existence in the other world. In the words of Panikkar,

> . . . the last rites, the blessings for the journey, and the climatic moment of death are of capital importance. They condition the new form of human existence. They open up the gates of the other world. It is for this reason that the various rituals are so important.[201]

This new existence depends on the rituals, for according to D.R. Shastri, at the death of a man the spirit (*preta*) does not immediately join the group of the ancestors, the spirit (*preta*) has to be ritually made over into an ancestor (*pitṛ*), just as the embryo and infant are constructed into a human being by ritual means.[202] Just as Prajāpati after his procreative emission is said to have fallen into pieces, so, too, the *preta,* the departed spirit is also said to be dangerously fragmented before its reunification and transformation into an ancestor.[203] Smith summarizes the functions of the Vedic sacrificial rituals in the following sentences:

> The child, the śūdra, the *patita-sāvitrīka,* the sick man, and the newly dead, all these states are similar regressions to the original

---

201. *PVE,* p. 541.

202. D.R. Shastri (1963), p. 62. See also B.K. Smith (1985a), p. 83; B.K. Smith (1989), p. 90.

203. B.K. Smith (1985a), p. 84.

> human condition of defectiveness. The remedy for illness, ritual reconstruction and reintegration, is but a special case of the remedy applied to all faulty beings. *Sacrifice is in Vedism the ontological medicine for all deficient creations*, and thus also the means for repairing debilitated forms. And rituals must be regularly repeated to protect against the natural inclination of structured entities to deconstruct into their atomistic constituents.[204]

In this way sacrifice is the cure for all inborn defects of creation itself. Just like creation is not cosmos so, too, the biological birth is not human birth: the person has to be sacrificially made perfect into a human being.

Fidelity to the Rules and the Validity of Sacrifice

Another important factor concerned with the Vedic sacrifice and with the Puruṣa-Sūkta in particular is to be found in the *śraddhā*, the absolute faith in the efficacy of the well-performed sacrificial ritual. According to J. Gonda, one of the purposes of the Puruṣa-Sūkta is to affirm the efficacy of rite in itself, for while speaking about the purposes of it he holds:

> In the third place: the *puruṣa* is no object of adoration; he is not invoked, he does not receive offerings. The rite is an *opus operans* in itself. It is a technique which, once started, goes on automatically and achieves its object automatically.[205]

Thus, our myth not only speaks about sacrifice as the means for everything but also as efficient in itself to produce the desired effect.

According to Ugo Bianchi, the doctrine of creation through sacrifice is a Brāhmanic invention to establish the efficacy of the sacrifice in itself, irrespective of the will of gods.[206] Hence, the

---

204. Ibid. The italics are mine.

205. J. Gonda (1977), p. 96.

206. U. Bianchi (1960), p. 66.

sacrificial ritual became an end in itself and the gods were put in a secondary place. A ritual performed correctly was supposed to bring its desired effect without the intervention of any gods. As Jose Thachil writes,

> Consequently the gods were relegated to a relatively unimportant position and sacrifice was now exalted to occupy their position. Though in each sacrifice certain gods were invoked, they were regarded merely as instruments in bringing about the sacrifice. Sacrifice is regarded as possessing a mystical potency superior even to the gods.[207]

And when the gods were pushed to the secondary level, the priests were raised to the status of gods and the *dakṣiṇā* became an important factor of every sacrifice.[208] A text of the *ŚB* says:

> Verily, there are two kinds of gods; for, indeed, the gods are the gods; and the Brahmans who have studied and teach sacred lore are the human gods. The sacrifice of these is divided into two kinds: oblations constitute the sacrifice to the gods; and gifts to the priests, that to the human gods, the Brahmans who have studied and teach sacred lore. . . . Both these kinds of gods, when gratified, place him in a state of bliss (*sudhā*). — 2.2.2.6[209]

---

207. J. Thachil (1985), p. 23.

208. We can also find that since the result of the sacrifice presupposed the correct performance of it, *dakṣiṇā* (the sacrificial fee), became an important factor in all the sacrifices. The *ŚB* goes to the extent of saying that there should be no offering without *dakṣiṇā* (1.2.3.4). It is seen as the means of invigorating the sacrifice (*ŚB* 2.2.2.2). With *dakṣiṇā* the sacrifice becomes more complete and successful (*ŚB* 4.3.4.2). Immortality and one's place in heaven depend on the *dakṣiṇā*s. Those who give large *dakṣiṇā*s stand high in heaven as stars, those who donate horses go into the company of the sun, and those who donate gold become immortal. Sacrifice and large donations were the means, therefore, to obtain the highest place in the heaven. But the *dakṣiṇā* can also stand for the sin of the sacrificer and by accepting it the priests take on themselves the sin of the sacrificer. J.C. Heesterman (1964), pp. 3ff.

209. See also *ŚB* 4.3.4.4.

The brāhmaṇa priests, therefore, become important because on the one hand the efficacy of the sacrifices depends on them and they are the only ones who are able to perform the sacrifices without mistakes, thereby bringing down the desired effects on the other.

The Pūrva-Mīmāṁsā, the Vedic school on ritual hermeneutic, therefore, stressed that the efficacy of a sacrifice depends on the correct performance of the sacrifice as given by the Vedas[210] and not on anything external to it. Here gods are not something external to sacrifice but part of it. Sacrifice, the guarantee for the cosmic harmony and the good social order is recommended by the Vedas for the maintenance of the world and it has an inner force that can bring the effect desired for, if performed correctly. Jaimini even goes to the extreme point that in the sacrifice the offering is the principal matter, while the *devatā* (the divinity) is to be reached relying on the offering.[211] Hence we find that the Vedic sacrifice, the world renewing and maintaining activity, becomes an end in itself, and is able to produce the desired effects even without the intervention of any god if performed exactly and at the right time given by the Vedas.

Such views have given rise to two extreme positions, first that the efficacy of sacrifice does not depend on the divinity to whom it is performed but on the correct performance of it, hence on the priests, and second, that it is the fear about the possible mistakes in sacrifice that has given rise to many expiatory sacrifices. Any ritual lapses or redundance could be dangerous for the sacrificer.[212] It is possible that such views were propagated to keep

---

210. G. Magi (1998), p. 17.

211. J. Thachil (1985), pp. 63-64.

212. J. Gonda (1983b), pp. 1-34. According to *Aitareya Brāhmaṇa*, if a priest omits a syllable in the sacrifice he is making a hole in the sacrifice (3.11), hence wasting it. In another Brāhmaṇa the sacrifice is compared to a heaven-bound ship which could be made to sink even through the presence of a single blameworthy

away the non-observing brāhmaṇa priests and the ordinary men from venturing into the institution of solemn sacrifices which was considered to be the only means for acquiring heaven and immortality. Whatever may be the motive, brāhmaṇas became the priests who maintained the cosmos in order through their ritual activity. Sacrifice needs to be performed with extreme care and faith in its efficacy.

The pre-occupation with the exactitude and the expiatory rites for errors is still present even today whenever Vedic sacrifices are offered. Frits Staal, who witnessed an *Agnicayana* sacrifice, writes, "The *Agnicayana* performance of 1975 was followed by a long series of expiation rites for mistakes that were or might have been committed."[213] However, Staal is against those who hold

---

→ priest hence the recommendation to keep away such priests from every sacrifice (*ŚB* 4.2.5.10). Another text of the same Brāhmaṇa says:

> "If he who draws near the sacrifice were to make an improper utterance he would waste the sacrifice, just as he might waste water by spilling it from a full vessel. Where the priests perform sacrifice as described with perfect mutual understanding, however, there everything takes place properly and no trouble appears. Therefore it is in this fashion that sacrifices should be carefully cherished" (*ŚB* 1.5.2.15).

This translation is taken from *PVE,* p. 400.

Even a mistake in the pronunciation may lead to an opposite effect to the one intented. Such an obsession with the rules not only makes the sacrifice complicated and difficult but also creates unnecessary anxiety during the whole duration of sacrifice. This is all because the efficacy of the world-maintaining and *ātman*-constructing Vedic sacrifices do not depend on a higher thing or person other than itself.

Again the means to repair eventual ritual mistakes is to recite the Puruṣa-Sūkta or to recite the three words through which Prajāpati created this universe: *bhūr, bhuvaḥ* and *svaḥ* (*AB* 5.32). See B.K. Smith (1994), pp. 63-64.

213. *AGNI,* vol. 1, p. 15; F. Staal (1979), p. 12.

that there exists an anxiety in the Vedic performance of rituals, for he holds that no such anxiety was found.[214] Such pre-occupation with the ritual exactitude is also found in the contemporary *pūjā*. Hence we find that sacrifice, the world-maintaining activity is not an easy task, it is a dangerous endeavour and it could bring success or disaster and again the ritual mistakes are healed by reciting the prescribed formulas, and one such formula is the Puruṣa-Sūkta.

Every sacrifice being the ritual repetition of the primordial sacrifice of *puruṣa* that gave birth to the cosmos or the reconstruction of the body of Puruṣa-Prajāpati, is at the same time a world creating principle and an expression of the world-becoming which does not depend on anyone because it is put in motion by the primordial sacrifice of the *puruṣa*. Sacrifice has its own internal laws and it functions in an automatic way and is, therefore, independent of external forces.[215] The Brāhmanic theory of creation through the primordial sacrifice performed by a primordial being or by gods on a primordial being also shares the theory of the efficacy of sacrifice in itself.

Conclusion

In this chapter we were trying to get a glimpse of the Vedic sacrifice and its vision of cosmos. This vision shows the two realities are not only closely interrelated, but are also dependent on each other. Such interdependence is justified by the fact that at the origin of cosmos and its continued existence there lies the primordial sacrifice of *puruṣa*, the life-producing and life-maintaining principle. Thus creation by the sacrifice of the *puruṣa* forms not only the basis for the Vedic vision of cosmos but also for the subsequent theories on sacrifice and rituals. Every sacrifice is the ritual repetition of the primordial life-producing sacrifice for the

214. Ibid.

215. G. Magi (1998), p. 21.

continued existence of the cosmos and for the ritual reconstruction of the dispersed body of Prajāpati to its primordial unity.

Sacrifice is the beginning of all realities, and to sacrifice is to make sure the survival of oneself and of the whole cosmos. For the Creator has given it as the medicine against the natural tendency of the cosmic elements to fall into decay and degradation. Further the cosmic order is sacrificial order, to sacrifice is to make possible the survival of the cosmos by maintaining its primordial god-given order.

For the Vedic people creation was not cosmos, it was only after certain ritual sacrifices that it became an ordered cosmos. Likewise humans are born imperfect, it is the ritual rebirth in sacrifice that makes them perfect.

Just as at the beginning of everything there is the self-sacrifice of the *puruṣa,* so too, sacrifice involves a self-sacrifice. To sacrifice is to offer oneself through the medium of a victim or some other *dravya* (sacrificial material) following the primordial sacrifice of *puruṣa*. In this way what one offers is not something external to oneself but a part of oneself. Further when sacrifice became a means to fulfil the wishes, it lost its cosmic concern and as a result the world created in sacrifice became the object of attack by the mystics of the Upaniṣads and the *Bhagavad-Gītā.*

3

The Interiorization of the Vedic Sacrifice and its Effect in the Emergence of the Notion of Bhakti

IN the last chapter we have seen that sacrifice is at the beginning of all realities, even of the gods themselves and the cosmic order is a sacrificial order. Nevertheless this vision is remarkably transformed in the Upaniṣads.[1] Even though the Upaniṣads

---

1. The Upaniṣads constitute the last part of the Vedas and their number varies from 108-12 to 200-35. But the most important or canonical ones (those commented on by Śaṅkarācārya or from which he has quoted in his commentary) are only 13. Two of them are ascribed the pre-Buddhist period of 700-550 BCE. The Upaniṣads contain profound philosophic reflections on God, humans and the world and can be considered to be an effort to grasp the nature of the universe and our place in cosmos. In the opening word of the *Śvetāśvatara Upaniṣad* we can find the main purpose of the Upaniṣads:

   "What is the cause? Brahmā? Whence are we born?
   Whereby do we live? And on what are we established?
   Overruled by whom, in pains and pleasures,
   Do we live our various conditions, O ye theologians . . .?"
   — 1.1

   This quest for the knowledge of the Ultimate Truth was led by the desire for immortality as a verse of one of the most important and earliest Upaniṣads expresses:

   "From the unreal (*asat*) lead me to the real (*sat*)!
   From darkness lead me to light!
   From death lead me to immortality!" — *BṛUp* 1.3.28

   For a detailed study on this prayer see G. Gispert-Sauch (1988), →

prolong the liturgical preoccupation of the Brāhmaṇas, they aim at a revalourization and spiritualization of the ritual.[2] The interiorization of the religious experience leads the sages not only to give less importance to the all-powerful sacrifice of the Brāhmaṇas, but to found the interior principle of all realities in the ground of the self, in the *ātman*. This is very new and the search for the ground and origin of all things in the Upaniṣads leads to the mystical apprehension of the oneness of all things in *Brahman*. The contemplation of this oneness of the *ātman-Brahman* within a person becomes the main thrust of the Upaniṣads.

Taking for granted that the Upaniṣads and the *BG* are closely connected[3] and the latter is considered to be the continuation of the former in the interiorization and the symbolic interpretations of sacrifice, we will discuss the two in the same chapter, even though there are many differences between the Upaniṣads and the *BG*. We will see, specifically, that the *BG* perfects the process of spiritualization and interiorization of the sacrifice advocated by the Upaniṣads and brings them under the devotion of a personal God. Thus, in the *BG* there takes place a fusion of the *Brahman* theory of the Upaniṣads with the belief in a personal being, Kṛṣṇa or Viṣṇu.[4] This is not a little variation. It changes the perspective: how to combine the personal vision of God with the cosmic vision

---

→ pp. 179-213. The translations of the thirteen principal Upaniṣads are taken from R.E. Hume (1949). When a different translation is used, it will be specified.

It is not easy to summarize all the concepts of the Upaniṣads on the Vedic sacrifice, hence here we limit ourselves to pointing out the main trends in the principal thirteen Upaniṣads which are considered to be canonical with regard to the interiorization and spiritualization of sacrifice.

2. G. Gispert-Sauch (1977), p. 25.
3. F. Edgerton (1952), vol. 2, p. 6.
4. *Gītā* owes much of its materials to the Upaniṣads and the *Bhāgavata* literature, and it is wrong to hold that the Upaniṣads is its only source. See M. Hiriyanna (1958), p. 131.

of the sacrifice, where *puruṣa* was not a god among the gods, but the unique principle of the world as sacrificer and victim. We will proceed by different steps and we will keep in mind the shift which occurs in the Upaniṣads.

The Subordination of Sacrifice to the Knowledge of the Ātman-Brahman in the Upaniṣads

We will begin our analysis of the interiorization of sacrifice in the Upaniṣads starting with its devaluation and subordination to the knowledge[5] of the *ātman-Brahman.* We can find that in the Upaniṣads the all powerful sacrifice of the Brāhmaṇas gets not

5. According to the Upaniṣads, knowledge can be divided into two categories: empirical or lower knowledge and metaphysical or higher knowledge. The empirical knowledge (*vyavahārika*) is the result of *avidyā* (ignorance) and aims at pleasure whereas the metaphysical knowledge (*paramārtha*) aims at the liberation, i.e. union with *Brahman*. See *KaṭhUp* 2.1-6; *MuṇḍUp* 1.2.8-10; *MaitrīUp* 7.9. Following this distinction Śaṅkara speaks of two ways of perceiving the *Brahman*: *saguṇa Brahman*, i.e. *Brahman* with qualities or Īśvara, a personal God through its association with the *māyā* (here the unreal principle), and *nirguṇa Brahman* that is *Brahman* without qualities or attributes. *Brahman* is beyond the human categories and all that can be spoken of Him is *neti, neti* (not this, not this). A.B. Keith (1925), part 2, pp. 515-16; G. Thibaut (1966b), p. xxx. But in *MaitrīUp* (6.15) the two forms of *Brahman* are spoken of in terms of time and timelessness. But for Rāmānuja the higher knowledge does not consist in considering *Brahman* as without qualities as held by Śaṅkara but in the *dhyāna* and *upāsanā*, and is called the direct knowledge which springs from the concentrated meditation. The second type of knowledge is called the indirect knowledge which one acquires from the study of the Śāstras and is considered to be the prerequisite for the direct knowledge. F. Vadakethala (1977), p. 50. Thus Rāmānuja does not consider two types of *Brahman* depending on the higher and lower knowledge. He considers *Brahman* as personal God, the all-powerful and all-wise ruler of a real world permeated and animated by his spirit. G. Thibaut (1966b), p. xxx. However, knowledge does not mean theoretical but intuitive knowledge of the Ultimate Reality behind all existence. It is the →

only an inferior position[6] but also is made needless through the allegorical interpretation of the cosmos and human life. As a result Prajāpati, the highest god of the Brāhmaṇas, together with Indra is made a doorkeeper of the abode of the *Brahman* in one of the Upaniṣads (*KauṣUp* 1.5).

This subordination of sacrifice to the knowledge of the *ātman-Brahman* may be the result of a gradual change of attitude towards the function of sacrifice itself and due to the growing mysticism in the Upaniṣads.[7] Unlike the Brāhmaṇas, sacrifice is not seen as the world-maintaining principle and *Brahman*[8] and the *ātman* are not the result of sacrifice but part and parcel of every living being. Sacrifice can lead one only to the world of fathers from where one will have to be reborn once the merits of sacrifices are over. For the mystics of the Upaniṣads all sacrifices fall within the domain of relative existence[9] and hence have no lasting effect on humans other than preparing the mind for the reception of the

---

→ soteriological knowledge of the identity of the *ātman-Brahman*. See S. Radhakrishnan (1957), p. 71; F. Edgerton (1952), vol. 2, p. 25.

6. Hiriyanna speaks of opposition or hostile position of the Upaniṣads to the Vedic sacrifices whereas according to Keith the general opinion that the Upaniṣads are against sacrifice is not right and it may be better to speak not of opposition but that sacrifice is given an inferior position. M. Hiriyanna (1958), p. 48; A.B. Keith (1925), part 2, p. 514.

7. The Upaniṣads contain the mystical secret doctrine imparted by a teacher to a student. See M. Hiriyanna (1958), p. 50. The central teachings of the Upaniṣads can be summarized in the phrases which show this identity of the *Ātman-Brahman*: *tat tvam asi* (That thou art *ChāUp* 6.8.7.), and *aham brahmāsmi* (I am *Brahman*, *BṛUp* 1.4.10).

8. A.B. Keith (1925), part 2, p. 447.

9. Śaṅkarācārya (1975), p. 4.

knowledge.[10] Such a change of attitude in the Upaniṣads has led the authors to consider sacrifice as something inferior to the knowledge of the *ātman-Brahman.*

The antagonism of the Upaniṣads towards the ritual is to some extent due to thesir belief in the identity of the *ātman-Brahman,* for in sacrifice one sees the divinity as distinct from oneself and the Upaniṣads do not accept such a distinction. The self is one with the Cosmic Self[11] and sacrifice is too narrow according to the mysticism and idealism of the Upaniṣads. According to A.B. Keith, the cult of the personal deity leads to this distinction between the world and the *ātman-Brahman,* a conception which the Upaniṣads could not accept. As Keith writes,

> It is this fact of universalism that gives the mysticism of the Upaniṣads in its purest form its chief appeal to many minds, which find in the cult of a personal deity too narrow an outlook and too selfish a destiny for man. To such spirits as these the ideal of merger in the absolute presents an effective antidote to the narrowness of traditional religion, and thus the philosophy of the Upaniṣads has for them the same attraction as systems of absolute idealism have had for many types of Western mind.[12]

For the mystics of the Upaniṣads, sacrifice, therefore, belongs to the realm of ignorance (*avidyā*) where the Absolute is seen as distinct from the individual self and the self is considered as distinct from the divinity. A text of the *BṛUp,* after affirming that the gods became *Brahman* through the knowledge of their identity with *Brahman,* argues:

---

10. According to Śaṅkara, the actions enjoined by scripture, such as sacrifices and a certain conduct are, however, required as conducive to the rise of knowledge in the mind. G. Thibaut (1966b), p. Lxxv.
11. According to the Upaniṣads, the Self is one reality with the *Brahman,* and he who knows such an identity becomes *Brahman.* See *BṛUp* 1.4.10; *MuṇḍUp* 3.2.9; cf. *ChāUp* 6.8.13
12. A.B. Keith (1925), part 2, p. 600.

> So whoever worships another divinity [than his Self], thinking "He is one and I another," he knows not. He is like a sacrificial animal for the gods. Verily, indeed, as many animals would be of service to man, even so each single person is of service to the gods. If even one animal is taken away, it is not pleasant. What, then, if many? Therefore it is not pleasing to those [gods] that men should know this. —1.4.10

Thus, sacrifice not only belongs to the realm of ignorance but also makes a sacrificer an animal, a victim of the gods. For the one who sacrifices to a divinity other than the self is called a *sacrificial animal* of the gods. In this way, the gods are not happy when human beings acquire knowledge because that would be the end of the sacrificial system. The two positions are in competition: interiorization and exteriorization, the inner view and the outer view. Thus, in the words of Hume, the rituals were considered to be a stupendous fraud by those who acquired the metaphysical knowledge for,

> No longer is worship or sacrifice or good conduct the requisite of religion in this life, or of salvation in the next. Knowledge secures the latter and disapproves of the former. The whole religious doctrine of different gods and of the necessity of sacrificing to the gods is seen to be a stupendous fraud by the man who has acquired metaphysical knowledge of the monistic unity of self and of the world in *Brahman* or *ātman*.[13]

Thus, the spirit of the Upaniṣads is opposed to sacrifice even though that does not mean a complete rejection of ritual system.

In the later Upaniṣads, however, there can be seen a tendency to return to the sacrificial performances as taught in the Brāhmaṇas,[14] and *MaitrīUp* holds that sacrifices are indispensable to the knowledge of the self (4.3). This could be because the reform was not radical and there was a constant tendency to return to

---

13. R.E. Hume (1949), p. 53.
14. M. Hiriyanna (1958), p. 54. *ŚvetUp* 2. 6-7; *MaitrīUp* 4.3.

the sacrificial practices.[15] Even when sacrifices were performed they did not have the same importance as they had earlier in the Brāhmaṇas.

When the Upaniṣads argue against the practice of sacrifice it is also to bring to light the limited power of sacrifice itself for sacrifice is not considered to be all-powerful. This may be because at the time of the Upaniṣads, the notions of *karma* and *saṁsāra* began to develop their meaningfulness and they conditioned the way of looking at the sacrifice itself. According to M. Eliade, the spiritual crisis that breaks in the Upaniṣads seems to be caused by the meditation on the powers of sacrifice, for once the merits of it are over one has to be re-born:[16] sacrifice has a limited power.

---

15. According to Keith, there was a constant tendency to restore the honour that sacrifice had lost. A.B. Keith (1925), part 2, pp. 514-15. Thus it is difficult to pinpoint whether the Upaniṣads are completely against the performance of sacrifice or against those who consider sacrifice as the means of salvation, and heaven as the ultimate goal of humans. *Bṛhadāraṇyaka* and *Chāndogya* Upaniṣads are clearly against sacrifices and they give only a symbolic interpretation of sacrifice. The other Upaniṣads seem to be not so radical in their rejection of sacrifice.

16. M. Eliade (1979a), p. 239. A passage of the *ChāUp* clearly says that those who sacrifice in the villages will have to be reborn again. It says:

> "Those who worship in the village, concentrating on sacrifices and good works and charity, they are born into the smoke, and from the smoke into the night, and from the night into the other fortnight, and from the other fortnight into the six months when the sun moves south. They do not reach the year. From these months they go to the world of the fathers, and from the world of the fathers to space, and from space to the moon. . . . When they have dwelt there for as long as there is a remnant [of their merit], they return along that very same road that they came along, back into space; but from space they go to wind, and when one has become wind he becomes smoke, and when he has become smoke he becomes mist; when he has become mist, he becomes a cloud, and when he has become a cloud, he rains. These are then born here as rice, barley, plants, trees, sesame plants, and

→

Thus, the notion of *karma* and *saṁsāra* made the Upaniṣadic scholars consider the merits of sacrifice as something transitory and not eternal and only knowledge was able to give eternal happiness to the *ātman* liberating it from the chain of rebirth. As Thibaut writes:

> Compliance with the injunctions of the *karmakāṇḍa* does not lead outside the *saṁsāra*; but he who, assisted by the grace of the Lord, cognizes — and meditates on — him in the way prescribed by the Upaniṣads reaches at his death final emancipation, i.e. he passes through the different stages of the path of the gods up to the world of *Brahman* and there enjoys an everlasting blissful existence from which there is no return into the sphere of transmigration.[17]

Sacrifices are still valid, however, for the attainment of heaven but the heaven acquired through it is not a place of everlasting bliss. For example, a text of the *BṛUp* tells that there are three worlds (of men, fathers and gods) and those who sacrifice go only to the world of the fathers but the best is the world of the gods which can be acquired only through knowledge (1.5.16).[18] Thus, only knowledge is able to lead one to the world of gods from which one will not have to be reborn. The way of sacrifice is not enough; it has to be followed by asceticism and mystical knowledge and it is auxiliary to the attainment of knowledge.

This new scope of sacrifice can be seen in one of the verses which is chanted during the purificatory rite after the performance of sacrifice: "From the unreal (*asat*) lead me to the real (*sat*). From darkness lead me to light. From death lead me to immortality"

→ beans. It is difficult to move forth out of this condition; but if someone eats him as food and then emit him as semen, he becomes that creature's semen and is born" —*ChāUp* 5.10.3-6.

This translation is taken from B.K. Smith (1989), pp. 206-07.

17. G. Thibaut (1966b), pp. xxix-xxx.

18. T.G. Goman and R.S. Laura (1972), p. 60. See also *BṛUp* 3.8.10; 6.2.15-16; *TaitUp* 2.5.

(*BṛUp* 1.3.28). The same verse then comments that unreal (*asat*), darkness (*tamas*), and death (*mṛtyam*) mean death and real (*sat*) and light mean immortality. Hence what one seeks in sacrifice is neither the fulfilment of one's desires nor the heaven but the immortality from the chain of rebirth.

The Upaniṣads, in their attempt to give a spiritual and interior meaning to the sacrifice consider the knowledge of the rite[19] not only as a prerequisite but at times even better than the performance of sacrifice itself and this can be seen as a way to accommodate the old within a new context. The knowledge of a rite is considered to be equal to its performance and is able to give the same effect of a rite. As Franklin Edgerton puts it: "If you know it, you have as good as performed it; that is, you can be sure of the benefits which are promised to the performer. . . ."[20]

---

19. However, we can also find passages in the *ChāUp* which speak of the performance of sacrifice. A text while explaining the difference between the sacrifice performed with and without knowledge says that the one who knows and the one who does not know perform sacrifice, but the difference is in their effect for only the sacrifice performed with knowledge, faith, and mystical doctrine is really efficient (1.1.10). Another passage of the same Upaniṣad argues that the performance of sacrifice without knowledge is useless, for the one who performs the *Agnihotra* without knowledge pours it on the ashes after removing the burning coal (5.24.1). We can also find passages which consider the performance of sacrifice with knowledge as not only valid for all the creatures and for all worlds but even as able to cancel the sins of the sacrificer (*ChāUp* 5.24.2-3). Another text says that the performance of the sacrifice without knowledge can be dangerous for he who performs the sacrifice without knowledge can have his head cut off (*ChāUp* 1.10.9-11; 1.11.4-9). Hence one should not venture into the performance of sacrifice without the proper knowledge for it can not only be counterproductive but even dangerous.
20. F. Edgerton (1929), p. 99. However, Edgerton considers the knowledge as the way to satisfy all desires in the Upaniṣads, as a short-cut to control of every cosmic power. Ibid., pp. 112 and 118.

In such a case the performance of sacrifice becomes unnecessary, and the knowledge is said to give the same effect of complicated ritual. Thus we can find that in the Upaniṣads the mystical knowledge is considered to be able to give the desired effect of the sacrifice[21] going beyond the power of the sacrifice self.

However, according to Goman and Laura, sacrifice is not rejected in the Upaniṣads but only that its place is redefined.[22] B.K. Smith, too, holds a similar view when he writes that the Upaniṣads do not reject sacrifice but the concept of sacrifice.[23] He argues further:

> In the Upaniṣads the *yajña* was transformed and redefined but nevertheless preserved as new religious practices — meditation, yoga, and contemplation on the ultimate nature of the self — were equated to it.[24]

In this way the Upaniṣads re-define its nature and scope[25] of sacrifice and anything that leads to the realization of the knowledge of the identity of the *ātman-Brahman* is given the name sacrifice. There is a real change of the meaning of "sacrifice" due to meditation and ultimately to the idealism and Advaita (non dualism) of the Upaniṣads. Thus, sacrifice which was an end in itself in the Brāhmaṇas becomes a means for the attainment of knowledge in the Upaniṣads: nothing more.

---

21. Ibid., pp. 108-09. However, here what is meant is the mystical identifications of the ritual elements and not the soteriological knowledge, the knowledge of the identity of the *ātman-Brahman*.
22. T. Goman and R.S. Laura (1972), p. 60.
23. B.K. Smith (1989), p. 210.
24. Ibid.
25. According to Heesterman, the institution of *saṁnyāsa* itself can be seen as an attempt to redefine sacrifice and the individualization of sacrifice need not necessarily be anti-Brāhmanical and the interiorization was meant to fuse into one person of patron and officiant. See J. Heesterman (1964), p. 27.

The Mystics of the Upaniṣads still continue to use ritual terms to explain the working of the cosmos and the human life and they continue to place the knowledge of the identity of the *ātman-Brahman* above the sacrifices giving *allegorical and symbolic interpretation to sacrifice*. Not only the sacrifice of the one who knows the mystical identity of the cosmic elements and the *ātman-Brahman* becomes effective, but also his whole life is considered to be a continuous sacrifice. Thus, even in the Upaniṣads sacrifice is still the object of speculation but not considered to be all in all[26] as was the case with the Brāhmaṇas. It is interiorized and spiritualized and its performance becomes almost needless. For example, a meditation on the *Aśvamedha* is said to have the same effect of actual performance[27] and the singing of the verses is said to have the same effect of an actual performance of it. All these may be because on the one hand the Upaniṣads do not want the place of knowledge to be questioned in any way, and on the other hand they make a compromise with those who hold that the performance of sacrifice is still a duty of every twice-born male. Conclusively, to some extent they replace the sacrifice with knowledge[28] and the purpose of the sacrifice should not be heaven but the acquisition of knowledge that leads to immortality.

The Ongoing Cosmic Sacrifice and the Background of Natural Mythology

In the Upaniṣads — as we have discussed — there is a drastic change with regard to the nature and purpose of the Vedic sacrifice. On the one hand the Upaniṣads uphold the validity of sacrifice for those who wish to obtain heaven, but on the other it subordinates it to the knowledge of the *ātman-Brahman*. Knowledge illuminates a human being not only to become aware

---

26. A.B Keith (1925), part 2, p. 442.
27. J. Thachil (1985), pp. 78-79.
28. F.X. Clooney (1985), p. 366.

of the identity of oneself and the Cosmic Self but also to recognize the ongoing sacrifice in the cosmos and within oneself. In such a process sacrifice gets more and more spiritualized and interiorized and becomes a *symbolic meditation on the working of the cosmos* itself. However, according to the Upaniṣads this cosmos is nothing other than the *ātman* or *Brhaman*[29] and the *AitUp* defines the *ātman* not only as Brahmā, Prajāpati, Indra, and all gods, but also as the five great elements — earth, air, space, water and fire (5.3.3). And the meditation of the horse sacrifice is considered to produce the same result in those who are not entitled to it.[30]

We have seen in the last chapter that from Prajāpati's self-immolation the cosmos, space and time were born and the main purpose of sacrifice was to recreate the cosmos. Now, even in the Upaniṣads the cosmos is not a finished product but is in a dynamic process of recreation and that takes place in the ongoing cosmic sacrifice and Prajāpati is spoken of as creating the cosmos through *tapas*.[31] A text of the *ChāUp* considers the cosmos as five great

---

29. *BṛUp* 1.4.10-17; *AitUp* 1.1.1-4.
30. Śaṅkarācārya (1975), p. 4.
31. On this Kaelber writes:

> "Prajāpati remains a major cosmogonic figure in the Upaniṣads, but not actually in his own right. He is frequently equated with or designated as a manifestation of the *ātman* or *Brahman*. He becomes a mythological or personified way of speaking about the *ātman* which in its unknowable, unalterable, impersonal, and ultimate nature would not be susceptible to description. By "retaining" Prajāpati as a cipher for the *ātman*, the Upaniṣads may speak mythically of things which, strictly speaking, transcend the mythical world and rest in the ultimate ground of existence accessible only through silence. Prajāpati as *ātman* thus continues to manifest many of his previous characteristics, but these are now seen to occur in a more cognitive, "unmoving," "unchanging," light in keeping with the character of the *ātman* which he portrays."
>
> —W.O. Kaelber (1975-76), p. 372.

sacrificial fires in which the gods[32] make a series of offerings; they offer faith (*śraddhā*) in the "heaven fire" to produce *soma*, then *soma* in the *parjanya* fire to produce rain, then rain in the "earth fire" to produce food, then food in the "man fire" to produce semen, and finally semen in the "woman fire" to produce an embryo (5.4.1-5.9.2).[33] This text also upholds the relation between the food and the ongoing sacrifice. Just as in the Brāhmaṇas the food is seen as the gift of the gods in return for the sacrifice offered by man, so too, our above-mentioned text of the Upaniṣad argues that the rain and the food are the results of the continuous cosmic sacrifice offered by the gods with the cosmic elements.

Thus, the Upaniṣads take distance from the Brāhmaṇas with their sacrificial description of the various cosmic elements and place the substitution of actual performance of sacrifice by the allegorical interpretation of it. The *BṛUp* begins with an allegoric description of a cosmic *Aśvamedha* and describes the world as a sacrificial horse:

> *Oṁ*! Verily, the dawn is the head of the sacrificial horse; the sun, his eye; the wind, his breath; universal fire (Agni Vaiśvānara), his open mouth. The year is the body (*ātman*) of the sacrificial horse; the sky, his back; the atmosphere, his belly; the earth, the underpart of his belly; the quarters, his flanks; the intermediate quarters, his ribs; the seasons, his limbs; the months and half-months, his joints; days and nights, his feet; the stars, his bones; the clouds, his flesh. Sand is the food in his stomach; rivers are his entrails. His liver and lungs are the mountains; plants and

32. However, these gods have no independent character as in the Brāhmaṇas, but are brought under the *ātman-Brahman*, and are a mythical way of speaking about the ultimate ground of existence while Prajāpati and Brahmā become the personified form of the Impersonal *Brahman*. See A. Hiltebeitel (1984-85), p. 3; S.G. Deodikar (1992), p. 21.
33. See D.M. Knipe (1972-73), pp. 28-41, especially p. 28.

> trees, his hair. The orient is his fore-part; the occident, his hind part. When he yawns, then it lightens. When he shakes himself, then it thunders. When he urinates, then it rains. Voice, indeed, is his voice.
>
> Verily, the day arose for the horse as the sacrificial vessel which stands before. Its place is the eastern sea.
>
> Verily, the night arose for him as the sacrificial vessel which stands behind. Its place is the western sea. Verily, these two arose on both sides of the horse as the two sacrificial vessels.
>
> — 1.1.1-2

Another Upaniṣad begins with the mental *Agnicayana* and speaks of a cosmic *Agnicayana* going on in the cosmos (*MaitrīUp* 1.1 and 6.33).[34] It describes the cosmic *Agnicayana* as follows:

> Verily, this [Gārhapatya] sacrificial fire with its five bricks is the year. For that [fire] the bricks are these: spring, summer, the rains, autumn, winter. So it has a head, two wings, a back, and a tail. In the case of one who knows the Person this sacrificial fire is the earth, Prajāpati's first sacrificial pile. With its hands it raises the sacrificer up to the atmosphere and offers him to Vāyu (the Wind). Verily, the wind is breath. — 6.33

Here we can find the cosmos itself is described as a sacrificial horse and various elements of the cosmos correspond to the various parts of the sacrificial horse and the Bay of Bengal and the Arabian Sea are seen as the two vessels in the *Aśvamedha*.[35] The cosmic forces, thus, offer a continuous self-immolation for the maintenance of the cosmos. Sacrifice, therefore, becomes a symbolic meditation on the sacrificial elements or on the cosmos itself which is identified with the *ātman* or *Brahman*.

---

34. H.W. Bodewitz (1973), pp. 278-83, 322. But according to Frits Staal these passages speak of actual *Agnicayana* and he argues that Bodewitz is mistaken in considering these passages as *prāṇāgnihotra* or speculation on *Agnicayana*. *AGNI*, vol. 1, pp. 68-70

35. R.E. Hume (1949), p. 73, footnote 3.

Reflections on Resemblance between Cosmos and Human Body

> *"Whether Waking or Sleeping, one is Sacrificing Continuously, Uninterruptedly"*
> — *KauṣUp* 2.5

We can find that just as there is an ongoing cosmic sacrifice, so too, in humans there is an ongoing sacrifice.[36] As Panikkar rightly holds, humans are considered to be deeply involved and ontologically committed to the ongoing cosmic sacrifice that they become part and parcel of the cosmic sacrifice itself.[37] According to our author, these new trends in sacrifice demonstrate:

> the centrality of Man and his body to the whole concept of sacrifice. The body here is the microcosm, the mirror and representative of the whole universe; it is not, however, the body alone or body independent of the mind which matters, but the whole Man. The *ātman*, the Self, is the sacrificer. Sacrifice is the integral human act and each act of life is a sacrificial act.[38]

A text of the *Kauṣītaki Upaniṣad,* mentioned above, while explaining "Inner *Agnihotra* sacrifice" and the perpetual sacrifice in humans, says:

> As long, verily, as a person is speaking, he is not able to breathe. Then he is sacrificing breath (*prāṇa*) in speech.
>
> As long, verily, as a person is breathing, he is not able to speak. Then he is sacrificing speech (*vāc*) in breath.
>
> These two are unending, immortal oblations; whether waking or sleeping, one is sacrificing continuously, uninterruptedly. Now, whatever other oblations there are, they are limited, for they consist of works (*karma-maya*). Knowing this very thing, verily, indeed, the ancients did not sacrifice the Agnihotra sacrifice.
> — 2.5

Thus there is a continuous sacrifice going on in us just like that of the cosmos. When we unite our "daily sacrifices" with that of the

---

36. X. Irudayaraj (1978), p. 308.
37. *PVE,* p. 405.
38. Ibid., p. 409.

ongoing cosmic sacrifice our own life becomes part of the ongoing cosmic sacrifice.

This ongoing sacrifice humans offer with their bodies and in their bodies with the vital breaths:[39] *prāṇa, apāna, vyāna, udāna,* and *samāna* to the *ātman* dwelling within themselves. The correlation between the vital breaths and the sacrifice[40] is very

39. The five vital breaths are as follows: *prāṇa, apāna, vyāna, udāna,* and *samāna.* A.H. Ewing summarizes the functions of them as follows:

   a. *Prāṇa* is the breath which moves upward from the navel or heart and includes both in-breathing and out-breathing. It is found in all the seven apertures of the head.

   b. *Apāna* is a term of varying signification. It means (1) The breath in the anus and scrotum. (2) The lower intestine. (3) The navel. (4) The "seizer of food," including both digestion and the carrying away of excrement.

   c. *Vyāna* is the breath which pervades the members of the body, and in which *prāṇa* and *apāna* inhere.

   d. *Udāna* is in part etymologically interpreted and refers (1) To eructation. (2) To the breath which carries the soul up to the skull in the state of *samādhi,* and on out in death. It is not only supposed to move in a great vein which extends from the centre of the body to the top of the head, but is identified with this vein.

   e. *Samāna* is located in the abdomen and is said to bring about the digestion of food. A.H. Ewing (1901), p. 277. These vital breaths are located in the heart, bowel, navel-region, throat, and in all the members respectively. Ibid., p. 265. These vital breaths also have a sacrificial meaning, for according to Ewing, *prāṇa* is related to Vāyu, the wind because it is said to have been produced from the breath of *puruṣa* (*ṚV* 10.90.13), and is related to Agni. Ibid., p. 251.

40. According to *MaitrīUp* 2.6, Prajāpati transformed himself into wind (*vāyu*) for the sake of creation and entered into the lifeless creatures to animate them. Singly he (Prajāpati-vāyu) could not do it, so he divided himself into five parts; becoming *prāṇa, apāna, samāna, udāna,* and *vyāna*. Therefore, the vital breaths have the same function in creation as the sacrifice in the Saṁhitās and in the Brāhmaṇas. Vital breaths, too, are a means of creation.

clear in a text of *PraśnaUp* 4.3-4 where *apāna* becomes the *gārhapatya* fire (western), *vyāna* the *anvāhāryapacana* fire (southern), *prāṇa* the *āhavanīya* fire (eastern) of the solemn sacrifice, and *samāna* becomes the one who distributes equally the two oblations — exhalations and inhalations — and the *udāna* becomes the fruit of the sacrifice (*iṣṭaphalam*) which carries the sacrificer to *Brahman* day-by-day (4.3-4).[41] Thus, we find that *udāna* performs the same function for the *ātman* of the ascetic, as the priest does for the performer of the ritual sacrifice. Hence the vital breaths are correlated to the Vedic sacrifice, and offering the vital breaths becomes a sacrifice. An ascetic performs his daily sacrifice with his vital breaths.

Again describing the continuous sacrificial process going on in humans the *Chāndogya Upaniṣad* considers eating, drinking, rejoicing, and procreation as part of this interior sacrifice (3.17.1-5). However, the eating and drinking are done in silence by restraining the speech and preceded by the purification of them and followed by the meditation of the self present in oneself.[42] All that an ascetic, who has acquired the supreme knowledge, eats is a sacrifice to the self-dwelling within. As A.H. Ewing writes: "All he needs to do is to say with the first mouthful of food, *prāṇāya svāhā*, and with the others in turn *vyānāya*, *apānāya*, *samānāya* and *udānāya svāhā*."[43] Hence the eating by an ascetic, who has acquired the supreme knowledge of the identity of the *ātman-Brahman*, not only becomes a sacrifice, but everything in the universe is said to take part in it (*ChāUp* 3.18-23).

The human body is, therefore, considered to be the sacrificial arena[44] wherein one offers one's continuous sacrifice to one's own inner self. A text of the *ChāUp* says,

41. A.H. Ewing (1901), p. 273.
42. See *MaitrīUp* 6.9 for the rite before eating.
43. A.H. Ewing (1901), p. 289.
44. The same view of the sacrifice with the body is clearly elaborated in two later Upaniṣads such as *Prāṇāgnihotra Upaniṣad*, pp. 33ff and *Mahānārāyaṇa Upaniṣad*, p. 543.

> Man, Gautama, is a fire. Speech is his fuel, breath his smoke, the tongue his flame, the eye his coals, the ear his sparks.
>
> — 5.7.1

> The sacrificial site (*vedī*) is indeed his breast, the sacrificial grass is his hair. The *gārhapatya* fire is his heart, the *dakṣiṇa* fire is his mind, the *āhavanīya* fire is his mouth. — 5.18.2[45]

In this the human body is considered as the altar and one offers one's sacrifice with one's body, in the three sacrificial fires *gārhapatya, dakṣiṇa,* and *āhavanīya* which are situated in one's heart, mind and mouth respectively.

The vital breaths also mean the cosmic elements, therefore, to offer the vital elements means to offer sacrifice with the cosmic elements. In *ChāUp* 5.19-23 we can find cosmological co-relations between the vital elements and the cosmic elements: *prāṇa* is the sun, *apāna* is the fire, *vyāna* is the moon, *samāna* is the rain, *udāna* is the sky (space). According to Carlo Della Casa, the three above-mentioned fires correspond to the three cosmic elements: *gārhapatya* corresponds to earth, *āhavanīya* to heaven (sky), and *anvāhāryapacana* to the atmosphere.[46] In a text of *ChāUp* the vital breaths are identified with the five *diśa*s: *prāṇa* corresponds to east, *vyāna* to south, *apāna* to west, *samāna* to north, and *udāna* to upper region (3.13).[47]

The sacrificial interpretation of human life also raised the different stages of human life into a sacrifice. From birth to death all that one does becomes a continuous sacrifice in the Upaniṣads.

---

45. This translation is taken from B.K. Smith (1989), p. 205.

46. C. della Casa (1976), p. 391, footnote 21.

47. In the *ŚB* 11.8.3.6 the various *diśā*s (spaces) are represented as putting their corresponding vital breath into the dead sacrificial victim: the eastern quarter puts in the *prāṇa,* the southern quarter the *vyāna,* the western quarter the *apāna,* the northern quarter the *udāna* and the upper quarter the *samāna* respectively. See also A.H. Ewing (1901), p. 274.

Just as creation is the self-sacrifice of Puruṣa-Prajāpati in the Saṁhitās and in the Brāhmaṇas, so too, in the Upaniṣads the human procreation is seen as a sacrifice. A text says:

> Woman, Gautama, is a sacrificial fire. The vagina is her fuel, foreplay her smoke, the womb her flame, the penetration her coals, and pleasure her sparks. Into this fire the gods make an offering of semen, and from that oblation the embryo is born.
>
> — *ChāUp* 5.8.1-2[48]

The same Upaniṣad considers not only the procreation as a sacrifice, but also the various stages of human life as a kind of *Soma* sacrifice, with its three periods of *brahmacarya, gṛahasta* and *saṁnyāsa-vānaprasta*[49] corresponding to the three *soma* pressings in the morning, midday, and evening. A text while speaking on *brahmacarya* in sacrificial terms says:

> What people call "sacrifice" (*yajña*) is really *brahmacarya,* for only through *brahmacarya* does he who is knower (*yo jñātā)* find that [knowledge]. And what people call "a sacrificial oblation"

48. Translation from B.K. Smith (1989), pp. 205-06.

49. Ancient Hinduism had divided the human life into four stages, namely, *brahmacarya, gṛhastha, vānaprastha* and *saṁnyāsa.* The first twenty-four years of a person is called the *brahmacarya* or the period of celibacy where one dedicates oneself to the study of the Vedas and the sacrifices. For a brief study on the four stages of life in the ancient Hinduism see R. Panikkar (1975), pp. 110-29. The sacrificial interpretation of the different stages of human life is already present in the *ŚB* for a text of the same Brāhmaṇa considers the *brahmacarya* as sacrifice in the following words: "He who enters upon *brahmacarya* enters into a long sacrificial session (*dīrgha-sattra*). The stick of fuel he places on the fire is the opening offering; and that [which he places on the fire] when he is about to bathe is the concluding offering; and what [sticks of fuel] there are [placed on the fire] between these, are his [offerings] of the sacrificial session." (11.3.3.2). Translation from B.K. Smith (1989), p. 207. On the relation between the *upanayana* and the *dīkṣā* (the initiation into the sacrifice) see J. Gonda (1985), pp. 315-412.

> (*iṣṭa*) is really *brahmacarya*, for only after having searched (*īṣṭvā*) through *brahmacarya* does one find the *ātman*. And what people call the "protracted sacrificial session" (*sattrāyaṇa*) is really *brahmacarya*, for only through *brahmacarya* does one find the protection (*trāṇa*) of the real (*sat*) *ātman*. — *ChāUp* 8.5.1.2.[50]

In this spiritualistic view of life human hunger and thirst are seen as the initiation sacrifice (*ChāUp* 3.17.1-3), death as the ablution after the ceremony (*ChāUp* 3.17.5), and asceticism, almsgiving, moral integrity, non-violence, truthfulness are all seen as the gifts for the priests (*ChāUp* 3.17.4). The above-mentioned Upaniṣad identifies sacrifice, the sacrificial offering (8.5.1), the long course of sacrifice (8.5.2), the practice of silence (8.5.2), and the solitude (8.5.3) to the self-disciplined life of a *brahmacārin* or student of sacred knowledge.

Not only the life of the *brahmacārin* is seen as a sacrifice but also the human life is seen in terms of sacrifice in the *ChāUp*:

> Man, in truth, is himself a sacrifice. His first twenty-four years correspond to the morning libation. The Gāyatrī[51] has twenty-

---

50. B.K. Smith (1989), pp. 207-08.

51. General morning hymn consisting of twenty-four syllables. It is the most sacred *mantra* of the Veda:

    Oṁ tat savitur vareṇyam ।
    bhargo devasya dhīmahi ।
    dhiyo yo naḥ pracodayāt oṁ ॥

    Oṁ We meditate upon the glorious splendour ।
    of the Vivifier divine ।
    May he himself illumine our minds! *Oṁ* । — *ṚV* 3.62.10

    According to me, even in these morning, midday and evening prayers, which begin and end with the mystical syllable *oṁ*, we can find an allusion to the cosmogonic myth where the creation is depicted through the word/sound. According to Marius Schneider, "the whole world subsists and maintains itself with the help of the prolonged mystical sound *oṁ*." M. Schneider (1969), p. 280. Schneider, again while writing on the Vedic doctrine of the origin of the world, holds: "The sound comes out →

> four syllables and the morning libation is offered with the Gāyatrī. With this the Vasus[52] are related. Now the vital breaths are the Vasus, because they cause everything to continue in existence. If he should be afflicted by sickness at this period of life, he should say: "O vital breaths who are the Vasus, let my morning offering be extended till the midday offering. Let me, who am the sacrifice, not perish in the midst of the vital breaths, the Vasus. . . ." His next twenty-four years[53] correspond to the midday libation. The Triṣṭubh[54] has forty-eight syllables and the midday libation is offered with the Triṣṭubh. . . . His next forty-eight years[55] correspond to the third libation. The Jagatī[56] has forty-eight syllables and the third libation is offered with the Jagatī.
>
> — *ChāUp* 3.16.1-3,5[57]

Just as the human procreation, the various stages of his life are sacrifice, so too, *death is also a sacrifice*; it is the final sacrifice that one offers in the funeral fire.[58] In this way the cosmogonic sacrificial dispersion of the body of Puruṣa-Prajāpati is not only repeated in the final sacrifice of a person in the funeral fire, but also the

---

→ from a sacrifice and is itself a sacrifice whose continuous production creates and maintains everything in existence in the universe." Ibid., p. 295. In this way even the prayers of the one who knows has the same effect as the actual sacrifice of the Brāhmaṇas in the Upaniṣads.

52. Etymologically *vas* means "to dwell, to live." It is also the name of a class of Vedic gods whose leader is Indra.
53. The period of *gṛhastha* or family life where one is called to fulfil a certain number of duties towards the gods, ancestors and to the society.
54. *Triṣṭubh* is the midday prayer consisting of forty-eight syllables.
55. Periods of *vānaprastha* and *saṁnyāsa* when one withdraws to the forest for a complete renunciation and meditation.
56. Vedic metre constituting of four feet (*pāda*) with twelve syllables each.
57. This translation is taken from *PVE*, pp. 410-11.
58. *ChāUp* 3.17.5 considers death as the final bath after the sacrifice.

elements of the human body are sacrificially reintegrated into the cosmos.[59] A text of the *BṛUp* says:

> . . . the voice of a dead man goes into fire, his breath into wind, his eye into the sun, his mind into the moon, his hearing into the quarters of heaven, his body into the earth, his soul (*ātman*) into space, the hairs of his head into plants, the hairs of his body into trees, and his blood and semen are placed in water. . . .
>
> — 3.2.13

In this way the whole human life is a continuous sacrifice. Whether one is awake or asleep one is performing a continuous sacrifice and one's final sacrifice is one's dissolution at death where one performs one's final sacrifice with one's body by offering it to the fire to be consumed. Again one offers sacrifice with one's body to the Self living within oneself and in this way the interiorization of sacrifice fuses the patron and the officiant into one person.

TAPAS AS SACRIFICE: THE METAPHORICS OF THE ASCETICISM

The interiorization of sacrifice in the Upaniṣads has led to the sacrificial interpretation of cosmos and human life so that all what one does to attain the illumination of the knowledge is raised to the realm of sacrifice. In this section we will see that *tapas* (ascetic austerity),[60] which consists in the self-discipline of body and mind

---

59. See B.K. Smith (1989), p. 206.

60. *Tapas* means "warmth, heat, pain, suffering, religious austerity, bodily mortification, penance, severe meditation," etc. M. Monier-Williams (1970), p. 437. According to W.O. Kaelber, it has also a sexual connotation and means sexual heat or brooding heat. W.O. Kaelber (1975-76), pp. 343-50. M. Stutley and J. Stutley consider it as an exterior sign of a profound spirituality. M. Stutley and J. Stutley (1980), p. 436. The notion of *tapas* is not the creation of the Upaniṣads, it was already present in the Saṁhitās and in the Brāhmaṇas. In *ṚV* 10.129.3 the creation is set in motion through *tapas*, and in the *AV* 11.5.19 the gods are said to have obtained immortality through the *tapas* (see also *ṚV* 10.167.1), →

is equivalent to sacrifice[61] and is even said to be better than sacrifice.

As we have seen above, in the course of time the faith in the power of sacrifice decreased and the knowledge of *Brahman* took its place. Later on *tapas,* which seems to be extra Āryan[62] in origin, is made into sacrifice according to M. Eliade[63] and B.K. Smith[64] to make place for the ascetics to remain within the realm of the sacrifice of the Brāhmaṇas.[65] Eliade writes:

> For *tapas,* too, is a "sacrifice." If, in Vedic sacrifice, the gods are offered *soma,* melted butter, and the sacred fire, in the practice of asceticism they are offered an "inner sacrifice," in which physiological functions take the place of libations and ritual objects. . . . The concept of this "inner sacrifice" is a fertile one, which will permit even the most autonomous ascetics and mystics to remain within the fold of Brāhmanism and later of Hinduism.[66]

→ and in the *ŚB* Prajāpati is said to have overcome death, the evil, through the means of *tapas* (10.4.4.1ff). In the Brāhmaṇas it was considered to be an ancillary to the actual performance of sacrifice but in the Upaniṣads it becomes more important or almost independent or substitute of the actual performance of sacrifice. For more details see H. Chakraborti (1973), particularly pp. 3-49.

61. M. Eliade (1969b), p. 113.

62. It is probable that *tapas* was taken over by the Vedic *ṛṣis* from the Indus Valley Civilization. See H. Chakraborti (1973), pp. 3 and 11.

63. M. Eliade (1969b), pp. 113-14.

64. B.K. Smith (1989), p. 210.

65. However, according to Haripada Chakraborti, *tapas* seems to have been initiated by the dissenters of Vedic ritualism and the fourth stage (*saṁnyāsa*) was subsequently added to the three existing stages of life (*āśramas*) to make place for these dissenters. H. Chakraborti (1973), pp. 12ff.

66. M. Eliade (1969b), pp. 111-12.

B.K. Smith, too, holds a similar view when he writes:

> The Upaniṣadic redefinition of the "true sacrifice" might be best seen not as the logical outcome of Vedic ritual thinking but rather as a valuable *objet trouvé* useful to assimilate the foreign to the traditional.[67]

Whatever the origin of *tapas* may be, the Upaniṣads consider the *tapas*[68] as true sacrifice. In this way the *tapas* helps on the one hand to redefine the true sacrifice and on the other not to abandon completely the notion of sacrifice.

This notion of *tapas* was slowly introduced by the Upaniṣadic *ṛṣis* who subordinated sacrifice to the knowledge of the identity of the *ātman-Brahman* and who considered the world gained by sacrifice as temporary. Liberation from rebirth could be attained only through the knowledge which required the proper disciplining of body and mind so that the mind might become fit for higher truths. We can find, thus, passages which consider austerity as a means to arrive at knowledge which liberates humans from the circle of rebirth. According to *TaitUp* (3.1-6), it is through the practice of asceticism that Bhṛgu comes to the knowledge that *Brahman* is food, vital breath, thought, knowledge, bliss, etc. The same idea is also found in the *MuṇḍUp* 3.1.8 where it is said that the ascetic through knowledge arrives at the Supreme *Brahman*. In another passage of the same Upaniṣad *Brahman* is known through asceticism (1.1.8.9), and the one who knows the *Brahman* becomes *Brahman* (3.2.9). The same Upaniṣad forbids the imparting

---

67. B.K. Smith (1989), p. 210.

68. In the *ŚB tapas* also means the meditation on ritual performance of the sacrifice. In *ŚB* 10.4.4.1-3 it is said that Prajāpati overcame Death, the evil, through the practice of 1000 years *tapas*. Converse, while commenting on this above-mentioned verse, argues: ". . . asceticism, which is the suppression or "death" of the experience of this world is never a direct way to immortality but relates to ritual performance whose ends are worldly as well as otherworldly." H.S. Converse (1974-75), p. 94.

knowledge of *Brahman* to the one who does not engage in *tapas* (3.2.10). In the *PraśnaUp* (1.2) Pippalāda asks his questioners, who want to know about the nature of *Brahman*, to dwell with him for a year or more with austerity, chastity and to ask questions about *Brahman* later. The practice of *tapas*, thus, becomes a necessity to acquire the knowledge of *Brahman* which is able to liberate a human person from rebirth. Again in *ŚvetUp* it is said that the *ātman* can be apprehended only in *tapas* and self-knowledge (1.15-16).

However, in the course of time asceticism which was a means for knowledge[69] becomes an independent way to salvation. Gradually the ascetic life which was a stepping-stone for the attainment of knowledge[70] became an outward sign of the attainment of the supreme knowledge and was considered to be greater than sacrifice.

Tapas becomes not only equal to sacrifice but greater than sacrifice because it is able to liberate human beings from the circle of rebirth.[71] Those who rely on the material sacrifice not only live in ignorance but will also have to be reborn. The *MuṇḍUp* while upholding *tapas* as greater than sacrifice says that sacrifices are unsafe boats and those who rely on the power of sacrifice live in ignorance, and argues:

---

69. This does not mean that through asceticism one can automatically arrive at the knowledge of the identity of the *ātman-Brahman* that liberates. According to *MuṇḍUp* 3.2.3 and *KaṭhUp* 2.23, the *ātman* reveals his own person to the one whom he chooses. Hence it is a gift and not a mere fruit of one's own effort. In *ŚvetUp* 6.21 the realization of *Brahman* is attributed to the efficacy of his austerity and the grace of God.

70. H. Chakraborti (1973), p. 21. We can also find a different idea that states asceticism as a result of the knowledge of *Brahman*. When one finds *Brahman* he leaves everything and leads an ascetic life (*BṛUp* 4.4.22).

71. A later Upaniṣad argues that neither through rites, nor through progeny, nor through wealth but through renunciation one can attain immortality (*Mahānārāyaṇa Upaniṣad* 10.5; 12.3.3).

> Unsafe boats, however, are these sacrificial forms,
> The eighteen, in which is expressed the lower work.
> The fools who approve that as the better,
> Go again to old age and death.
> Those abiding in the midst of ignorance,
> Self-wise, thinking themselves learned,
> Hard smitten, go around deluded,
> Like blind men led by one who is himself blind.
> Manifoldly living in ignorance,
> They think to themselves, childishly: "We have accomplished our aim!"
> Since doers of deeds (*karman*) do not understand, because of passion (*rāga*),
> Therefore, when their worlds are exhausted, they sink down wretched.
> Thinking sacrifice and merit is the chiefest thing,
> Naught better do they know — deluded!
> Having had enjoyment on the top of the heaven won by good works,
> They re-enter this world, or a lower. — 1.2.7-10

After having termed the eighteen forms of sacrifice as inferior forms of action and those who rely on the merit of sacrifice as ignorant persons our above-mentioned Upaniṣad argues that asceticism is better because it liberates one from the chain of rebirth. It says,

> They who practise austerity (*tapas*) and faith (*śraddhā*) in the forest,
> The peaceful (*śānta*) knowers who live on alms,
> Depart passionless (*virāga*) through the door of the sun,
> To where is that immortal Person (*puruṣa*), e'en the imperishable Spirit (*ātman*). — 1.2.11

The way of sacrifice is inferior to that of asceticism because once the merits of sacrifices are over the person will have to be reborn, but those who practise austerities will not have to be reborn.

Sacrifice, thus, belongs to the lower realm of life and those who rely on its power will have to be reborn but those who practise penance will not have to be reborn.[72] A text of the *MuṇḍUp* goes to the extent of saying that a brāhmaṇa who contemplates on the heaven created through sacrifice will be in despair and the remedy is to seek advice from a learned master (1.2.12). Like the above-mentioned Upaniṣads, the *PraśnaUp*, too, holds austerity as greater than sacrifice because the latter can lead only to the world of moon, and only through asceticism and knowledge can one attain the world of sun from which one will not be reborn (1.9-10). We find that *tapas* becomes not only a sacrifice but even greater than it.

In the *BṛUp*, one of the earliest Upaniṣads, asceticism was a means to knowledge and it had no independent role; because of its role in preparing the mind for the knowledge of the *ātman-Brahman* it was raised to the realm of sacrifice itself. Thus in the Upaniṣads the sacrifice is first subordinated to the knowledge of the identity of *ātman-Brahman* and then *tapas* is raised to be sacrifice because it leads to the knowledge of the identity of the *ātman-Brahman*.

SACRIFICE OF THE SELF AS SURRENDER TO THE COSMIC SELF

We have seen above that the main question in the Upaniṣads is not sacrifice or rejection of sacrifice, but rather what is true sacrifice and what is the scope of sacrifice. Such a redefinition of true sacrifice and the scope of sacrifice with the help of mystical knowledge led

---

72. However we can also find a passage in the *BṛUp* which considers both sacrifice and asceticism without knowledge as the same thing for both of them will have to be reborn:

> "He who, O Gārgī, in this world offers sacrifice or practises asceticism for many, even for a thousand years, and yet does not know that Imperishable, all his efforts will be in vain. And he, O Gārgī, who departs from this world without having known it is wretched. But he, O Gārgī, who departs from this world having known that Imperishable is a knower of *Brahman*." —3.8.10.

This translation is taken from *PVE*, p. 676.

to the discovery that true sacrifice cannot be the offering of a victim outside oneself, but of one's internal self to the cosmic self.[73] In this way even in the Upaniṣads we can find the idea that sacrifice is self-sacrifice. The true sacrifice is the sacrifice of the self to the Universal Self and the scope of it is to overcome the circle of death and rebirth.

This sacrifice of the self to the Universal Self is possible only after overcoming duality through the acquisition of real knowledge through an ascetic life. When one obtains knowledge one realizes that duality is the creation of ignorance or lack of knowledge of the real nature of one's self. It purifies one's mind of all desires and from the false concept of duality between the *ātman* and the Supreme Self. This is possible only by purifying and sacrificing the mind to the Supreme Self where the intellect becomes the sacrificer. As Panikkar writes: "Now the mental sacrifice becomes not only the sacrifice imagined or thought, that is, performed by the mind, but the sacrifice of the mind itself."[74] The mind is the officiating priest and the victim as Panikkar says:

> What is cast into the fire is no longer either material things or the thought of them, but thinking itself and all that is contained in the cave of the heart, in that hidden recess where all coalesces in a silence of mind and in an explosion of love.[75]

The sacrifice of the mind not only calls for the purification of the mind but also to a surrender of the self to the Supreme Self. The *Kaṭha Upaniṣad* says:

> The wise man should surrender his words to his mind;
> and this he should surrender to the Knowing Self;
> The Knowing Self he should surrender to the Great Self;

73. Panikkar considers this sacrifice of the Self to the Universal Self as the sacrifice of the mind. *PVE*, p. 417.

74. Ibid.

75. Ibid.

and that he should surrender to the Peaceful Self.

— 3.13[76]

Now we should also keep in mind that in the Upaniṣadic discussions *Brahman* is not seen as an entity to whom the sacrifice is offered. He "is neither the object of the sacrifice nor an object of knowledge. He is the knower, the sacrificer, and not the known, the sacrificed."[77] It is here the purification of the mind is required and in such purification of the mind consists of one's own liberation. As *Maitrī Upaniṣad* says:

> The bliss that arises in the state of highest absorption, when the pure mind has come to rest in the Self, can never be expressed by words! One must experience it directly, one's own self, in one's inner being. If a man's mind is merged in the Self, then he is completely released, just as water is not distinguishable in Water, or fire in Fire, or air in Air. The mind alone is man's cause of bondage or release: it leads to bondage when attached to the sense objects, and to release when freed from them.
>
> — 6.34.9-11[78]

Thus we find that according to the Upaniṣads the mind firmly established in *Brahman* becomes the perfect sacrifice and means of liberation.

The Vedic sacrifices, thus, without losing their cosmic dimension get changed in the Upaniṣads and for the mystics of Upaniṣads the sacrifices get subordinated to the knowledge of the identity of the *ātman-Brahman*. The knowledge of such identity helps us first to recognize the ongoing cosmic sacrifice, and secondly our life as a continuous sacrifice to the self living within. In such perspective sacrifice gets interiorized, and paves the way for a personal concept of God.

---

76. This translation is taken from *PVE*, p. 421.
77. Ibid., p. 419.
78. This translation is taken from *PVE*, p. 423.

Sacrifice as Cosmic Harmony and Welfare (Lokasaṁgraha) in the Bhagavad-Gītā

The *BG* continues the metaphoric interpretation of the concept of *yajña* started by the Upaniṣads[79] and like the latter it also gives a wider meaning to the Vedic sacrifice. On the one hand it holds the need for the performance of sacrifice and to support such practice it presents sacrifice as the law of life given by the Lord of creatures (Prajāpati) for fulfilling every desire (*BG* 3.10),[80] and on the other hand, it holds sometimes that a sacrifice, when performed with the desire for its effect, can become a bondage and can give rise to rebirth according to the doctrine of the *guṇas*. Such an action even binds the cosmos in bondage, because *karma* has a cosmic effect and every selfish *karma* pollutes the cosmos by disseminating selfishness.[81] In this sense the complexity of the doctrine about the sacrifice in the *BG* fully emerges and creates difficulties for our research. Although the concept of sacrifice is not at all easy to interpret in the *BG*, and even though the *BG* is not a treatise on sacrifice like the Brāhmaṇas, yet it has become the most important source and inspiration for the modern Hindu religious practices and worship on the background of the idea of sacrifice. Sacrifice is viewed step by step from the standpoint of the spiritualized vision of human life and from the point of view of love in its several features. Our task is to examine the progressive differentiation of this multiple concept of sacrifice.

---

79. See I. Vempeny (1988), p. 205.

80. The *puruṣa* of the *R̥V* 10.90 in the course of time gets identified with *Brahman*, Viṣṇu-Kr̥ṣṇa and the Mandasore inscription of CE 404 identifies the thousand-headed *puruṣa* as Viṣṇu-Nārāyaṇa. For more details on the relation between the Puruṣa-Prajāpati of the *R̥V* 10.90 and Viṣṇu-Kr̥ṣṇa see J. Gonda (1977), pp. 105-11. On the identity of *puruṣa* and Viṣṇu and the interpretation of the Puruṣa-Sūkta see also *Mudgala Upaniṣad* chapter 1. The quotations from the *BG* are taken from R.C. Zaehner (1969). When a different translation is used it will be specified.

81. F.X. D'Sa (1980), p. 335.

It is necessary to say, however, that the importance of the *BG*'s concept of sacrifice in modern Hinduism is not only attributed to its capacity to synthesize the various schools of thought on sacrifice and other religious beliefs without rejecting any of them, but also on the fact that it can be seen as the connecting link between the Vedic sacrifice and the *pūjā*[82] of modern Hinduism, connecting the past with the religious present. Its influence on the religious life of modern Hinduism is clear from the fact that it is the only Smṛti text to be raised to the realm of Śruti and has become in the course of time one of the canonical texts and the most important sacred book which is read.[83] Thus herebelow we intend to bring to light the cosmic as well as the love in a personal God in the *BG*'s approach to the notion of sacrifice.

Finally, the importance of the *BG* can be seen on the one hand in its synthetic approach with greater emphasis on the cosmic harmony and welfare and, on the other, it introduces a renewed notion of sacrifice by bringing it under the personal God. Sacrifice gets purified of its selfishness and the notion of *bhakti* makes it an offering to the Lord of Love in love and devotion. Sacrifices are to be performed under the dominant drive of love and, therefore, without the desire for its results. In this perspective any action done for the Lord's sake becomes itself a sacrifice.

SACRIFICE AS THE LAW OF LIFE

In its treatment of the Vedic sacrifice the *BG* maintains both the traditional Vedic concept of sacrifice and the Upaniṣadic

---

82. *Pūjā* is the contemporary term used for worship and offerings in Hinduism and is considered to be non-Aryan (Draviḍic) in origin. For more details on *pūjā* see G. Bühnemann (1988), pp. 29-190; J. Gonda (1993), pp. 8-9; K. Luke (1975a), pp. 345-65; G. Favaro (1993), pp. 31-66.

83. M. Dhavamony (1982), pp. 5-29. According to Zaehner, the *Gītā* is "the most influential Hindu scripture of all time . . . and its theological influence is greater even than that of the Upaniṣads themselves." R.C. Zaehner (1972) 167.

spiritualization and interiorization of it. The notions of sacrifice in the *BG* vary from the traditional Vedic ritual to the symbolic and such as the practices of austerities, *yoga*, the disinterested performance of one's duty (*niṣkāma karma*) and *bhakti*. In the *BG* sacrifice is seen as the law of life[84] in its various expressions.

In chapter 3.10-16 the *BG* clearly speaks about the traditional Vedic sacrifices and their cosmic function. Sacrifice is the divine norm for the well-being of all, for Prajāpati, the Lord of Creatures, has given it as the means for the fulfilment of any desires. For example it says:

> Of old the Lord of Creatures said, emitting creatures and with them sacrifice: By this shall ye prolong your lineage, let this be to you the cow that yields the milk of all that ye desire. — 3.10

In this verse Prajāpati, the Lord of the Creatures is said to be the originator of the sacrifice. By this it holds the Brāhmaṇas' vision of Prajāpati as the first sacrificer and sacrifice as the means for fulfilling all desires.

After affirming the divine origin the next two verses maintain the Vedic vision of sacrifice as a means to sustain the gods. Sacrifice is seen as the food for the gods[85] and our food is the return gift of the gods.

> With this shall ye sustain the gods so that the gods may sustain you [in return]. Sustaining one another [thus] ye shall achieve the highest good.[86] For, [so] sustained by sacrifice the gods will

---

84. S. Radhakrishnan (2004), pp. 137, 168.

85. In the *Śatapatha Brāhmaṇa* sacrifice is said to be the food of the gods (11.1.8.2-13). And our food depends on the gods who send rain from heaven. Hence there is a continuous mutual sustaining going on in sacrifice.

86. The phrase, "Sustaining one another [thus] ye shall achieve the highest good," while maintaining the mutual sustaining character of sacrifice, introduces a new element, that is, "the highest good" (*śreyaḥ param*), a phrase which is not only differently interpreted by different scholars but it could also →

> give you the food of your desire. Whosoever enjoys their gift yet gives nothing [in return] is a thief, no more nor less.
>
> From food do [all] contingent beings derive and food derives from rain; rain derives from sacrifice and sacrifice from works.
>
> — 3.11-12, 14

In these verses the *BG* affirms a close relation between sacrifice and the food of the living beings. Sacrifice is food to the gods and the gods pleased with the sacrifice send rain from which we get our food. Thus the *BG* affirms a mutual dependence of sacrifice and the well-being of humans.

Sacrifice being the law of life, the *BG* not only encourages the performance of it, but also calls those who do not sacrifice thieves.[87]

→ show a shift in the purpose of sacrifice itself. See R.C. Zaehner (1969), p. 165. According to Śaṅkarācārya, "The "supreme good" here spoken of may be either the knowledge of *Brahman* or *svarga.* The result depends upon the motives of the aspirant, according as he desires salvation or worldly enjoyment. In the former case, the sacrifice leads to purity of heart in this or a subsequent birth and ultimately leads to knowledge, whereas in the latter case it leads directly to *svarga.*" See Śaṅkarācārya (1995), pp. 98-99. Rāmānuja gives a different interpretation to the above-mentioned phrase and according to him it means liberation. Zaehner accepts the interpretation of Śaṅkarācārya as more correct because it is in keeping with the rest of the teaching of the *BG.* He rightly points out that according to the *BG* the worship of the gods (or sacrifice to the gods) does not lead to final liberation, because the gods can merely satisfy humans' worldly desires. See R.C. Zaehner (1969), p. 165. See also *BG* 7.20-22. Even in Śaṅkarācārya's view of "the highest good" as the knowledge of *Brahman* we can see an allusion to liberation because the knowledge of *Brahman* liberates. Hence the *BG* in the above-mentioned verse while maintaining the Vedic vision of sacrifice as a mutual sustaining principle between the gods and the human beings introduces a new element, that is, liberation form the circle of rebirth.

87. See *BG* 3.12.

Śaṅkarācārya explains the above-mentioned verse in the following way:

> He who enjoys what is given by gods, i.e. he who gratifies the cravings of his own body and senses without discharging the debt due to the gods, is a thief indeed, a robber of the property of the gods. . . .[88]

He further explains the phrase "gratifying the cravings of the body and senses" as feeding one's own body and senses without satisfying the gods, the *ṛṣis* and the *pitṛs*, by sacrifice, study of the sacred scriptures, and by offspring respectively.[89]

Like the Brāhmaṇas, the *BG*, too, considers sacrifice as the food of immortality and neither this world nor the other world belongs to the one who does not perform sacrifice. The *BG* says:

> Eating of the leavings of the sacrifice, the food of immortality, they come to primeval *Brahman*. This world is not for him who performs no sacrifice much less the other (world). — 4.31

We find that the scholars give different opinions on this above-mentioned verse. For example, Zaehner sees in this verse an equation of sacrifice with the official cult.[90] Radhakrishnan says that sacrifice is the law of this world and the one who violates this law cannot attain any spiritual dominion neither in this world nor in the next world.[91]

Sacrifice then brings the remission of sins, for the *BG* says: "Good men who eat the leavings of the sacrifice are freed from every taint, but evil are they and evil do they eat who cook [only] for their own sakes (3.13)." Śaṅkarācārya translates this verse as

---

88. Śaṅkarācārya (1995), p. 99.
89. Ibid., See also *ŚB* 2.7.2.1; 1.7.2.2-5 where human life is spoken of in terms of fourfold debts. We will see in detail in chapter 7 of this book on the five great daily sacrifices.
90. R.C. Zaehner (1969), p. 194.
91. S. Radhakrishnan (2004), p. 168.

follows: "The righteous, who eat the remnant of the sacrifice, are freed from all sins; but sin do the impious who eat and cook for their own sakes." According to Śaṅkarācārya, the phrase "freed from all sins" means the sins committed at the five places such as fire-place, the water-pot, the cutting, grinding and sweeping apparatus, the five places of animal slaughter where sins are committed from those involuntary acts of injury and other causes.[92] The offering of food to the gods and to the living beings before eating one's own food saves one from such sins committed against the living beings during the day.

Just as in the Puruṣa-Sūkta the *puruṣa* is said to be the cause behind the creation of everything in this cosmos, so too, in the *BG Brahman* is considered to be the source of everything and penetrates everything in this universe.[93] A verse explains the relation between *Brahman* and the sacrificial elements in the following way:

> The offering is *Brahman*, *Brahman* the [sacrificial] ghee offered by *Brahman* in *Brahman*'s fire: who sinks himself in this [sacrificial] act is *Brahman*, to *Brahman* must he thereby go. —4.24

Hence *Brahman* is not only everything connected with sacrifice but also he is sacrifice just as Prajāpati is said to be everything related with the sacrifice in *R̥V* 10.90.16. The same unity between the sacrificer, the oblation, the instrument, the sacrificial fire, and the receiver is mentioned in the above-given verse of the *BG*. *Brahman* is the link between the sacrificial action (*karman*) on the one hand and the Imperishable on the other hand (*BG* 3.15), the link between the eternal and the temporal, hence its presence

---

92. Śaṅkarācārya (1995), p. 100.

93. Aurobindo says, "The gospel of the *Gītā* reposes upon this fundamental Vedāntic truth that all being is the one *Brahman* and all existence the wheel of *Brahman*, a divine movement opening out from God and returning to God." Aurobindo (1974), p. 117.

"penetrating everywhere." In the same chapter three we can find a verse which affirms *Brahman* as the source of everything:

> From *Brahman* work arise, know this, and *Brahman* is born from the Imperishable; therefore is *Brahman*, penetrating everywhere, forever based on sacrifice. — 3.15[94]

The above-mentioned verses show that the *BG* does not reject the formal sacrifices, rather it upholds the necessity of sacrifice and calls it a duty. Those who do not sacrifice are called thieves, who profit from the things of gods without paying homage in sacrifice, and immortality is denied to them. Sacrifice is seen as the means for gaining the desires and as the means to sustain the gods, yet later on the *BG* will say that one needs to overcome the selfish performance of sacrifice following the example of God who works selflessly for the good of the cosmos.

---

94. In this verse the noun *Brahman* is used three times but it does not have the same significance, for the noun *Brahman* besides meaning the Absolute, can also mean the Veda, and the material Nature and the *akṣara* (Imperishable). It can also mean the syllable *oṁ*. Śaṅkarācārya takes *Brahman* to mean the Veda and the *akṣara Brahman* for he translates *tasmāt sarvagatam brahma nityam yajñe pratiṣṭhitam* as "therefore, the all-pervading *Brahman* ever rests in sacrifice." Śaṅkarācārya (1995), pp. 100-01. The purpose of such translation is to avoid saying "*Brahman* rests on (based on) sacrifice" because that would mean that sacrifice is the foundation or base of *Brahman*. According to Zaehner, *Brahman* rests in sacrifice can mean that he is present in the sacrifice: "Therefore is *Brahman*, penetrating everywhere, forever based on sacrifice" can mean "either that the Veda depends on the sacrifice, presumably because if sacrifice were to cease it would no longer be recited or that material nature depends for its continued existence on the sacrifice, since sacrifice and the world process are one and the same thing." R.C. Zaehner (1969), p. 167. Our author's translation of *pritiṣṭhitam* as "based on" is more literal but not in line with the Upaniṣadic and the *BG*'s teachings. Even though Śaṅkarācārya's translation is not literal, it is more in keeping with the teaching of the Upaniṣads and the *BG*.

SACRIFICE PERFORMED AGAINST THE COSMIC WELFARE (LOKASAṀGRAHA) IS IMPURE SACRIFICE

In the *BG* the motives for the performance of sacrifice become the deciding factors and they determine the nature of sacrifice. Thus even though it maintains the validity of the sacrifices, and speaks of it as the law of life, yet when it speaks of *yajña* it does not have the same Vedic ceremonial concept of sacrifice. In the *BG* the true sacrifice is an unselfish ritual action and any sacrifice performed with a desire for effect in an individualistic manner is considered to belong to the lower realms of *guṇas*.[95] A sacrifice that belongs to the lower realms of the *guṇas* (*rājasika* and *tāmasika*) cannot be considered a pure sacrifice because it has lost its cosmic principle and has become a means to have one's own desires fulfilled and as such has become a means of bondage and rebirth. Depending on the predominance of one or other *guṇa* every sacrifice can be classified as *sāttvika, rājasika* or *tāmasika.* The lesser the cosmic good is desired, the lower it becomes in the category. Let us see them one by one.

Only a sacrifice performed in accordance with the prescriptions of the scriptures without any desire for its fruit is called the *sāttvika* (goodness, pure) sacrifice. By this the *BG* denies any spiritual value

95. The *guṇas* are the three constituents of nature (*prakṛti*) which were first developed by the Sāṁkhya philosophy. They are the three tendencies of *prakṛti* (the female principle of reality) developed in proximity with the *puruṣa* (the male principle of reality). The three *guṇas* are *sattva, rajas* and *tamas. Sattva* is the radiant aspect of being, the light of consciousness in every being. *Rajas* is the purposeful activity, the aspect of wilfulness in man. *Tamas* is the aspect of darkness in the human being. Just as there are three *guṃas* so too there are three kinds of persons, sacrifices, actions, faith, food, penances, and alms giving — all depending on the predominance of one or other type of *guṇa.* See *BG* 14.9; 17.2-22. Zaehner translates the words *sāttvika, rājasika,* and *tāmasika* as goodness, passion, and darkness respectively. See R.C. Zaehner (1969), p. 101.

to the sacrifice performed with a desire for its effect and in this way purifies the Vedic sacrifice from its worldly scope. A text says:

> The sacrifice approved by [sacred] ordinance and offered up by men who would not taste its fruits, who concentrate their minds on this [alone]: "In sacrifice lies duty": [such sacrifice] belongs to goodness. —17.11

A *sāttvika* sacrifice is that which is offered as a duty not for any selfish desire to enjoy its fruits. Hence it is most cosmic. Further only a selfless performance of the sacrifice can open the way of *jñāna* which will lead the self to liberation. The inner disposition while performing a sacrifice is not only important but is the yardstick with which every sacrifice is judged. The motive for any sacrifice should be the harmony of all, the very cosmic good.

The second type of sacrifice is called *rājasika* sacrifice and is that which is performed with the desire for its effects, hence less cosmic. We can find that in the Vedic times sacrifice had become an element of display for attaining popularity thereby reducing the sacrifice as an exhibition of one's money and generosity. But the *BG* does not uphold such practices and condemns such a selfish attitude and argues:

> But the sacrifice that is offered up by men who bear its fruits in mind or simply for vain display, know that [such sacrifice] belongs to Passion. —17.12

Like the Upaniṣads, the *BG* too attacks the performance of sacrifice with the desire for heaven and argues:

> The essence of soul is will, [but the souls] of men who cling to pleasure and to power, seduced by flowery words, are not attuned to ecstasy. Such men give vent to flowery words, lacking discernment, delighting in the Veda's lore, saying there is naught else. Desire is their essence, paradise their goal, their words preach [re-]birth as the fruit of works and expatiate about the niceties of ritual by which pleasure and power can be achieved.

> [All Nature is made up of] the three "constituents": these are the Veda's goal. Have done with them, Arjuna: have done with [all] dualities, stand ever firm on Goodness. Think not of gain or keeping the things gained, but be yourself! — 2.42-45

Here we find a strong attack on the Vedic sacrifices by the *BG* because they belong to the realm of the *guṇa*s and Arjuna is told to rise above the individualistic view of Vedic sacrifice. Sacrifice performed with the desire for its effect belongs to the realm of passion and such sacrifices are not considered authentic sacrifices. As Radhakrishnan says:

> The teacher distinguishes true *karma* from ritualistic piety. Vedic sacrifices are directed to the acquisition of material rewards but the *Gītā* asks us to renounce all selfish desire and work, making all life a sacrifice, offered with true devotion.[96]

We can say that a *rājasika* sacrifice is impure because it is done for a selfish motive and such a sacrifice cannot take a sacrificer beyond Indra's heaven from where one will have to be reborn once the merits are over. In this way the *BG* attacks the selfish performance of the sacrifice because it has lost its cosmic purpose.

The third type of sacrifice is called the *tāmasika* sacrifice and is the lowest type of sacrifice, because it neither takes into consideration the cosmic good, nor the correct ritual procedure. As such it belongs to the realms of darkness, carelessness, and faithlessness.[97] A text says clearly:

> The sacrifice in which no proper rite is followed, no food distributed, no sacred words recited, no priests' fees paid-up, no faith enshrined, [such sacrifice] belongs to Darkness.
>
> — *BG* 17.13

However it does not say that an ill-performed sacrifice could bring danger to the sacrificer as the brāhmaṇas did.

96. S. Radhakrishnan (2004), p. 117.

97. On different types of faith (intellectual and ritual) in the *BG*, see P. Hacker (1963), pp. 151-89.

We have seen above that only a *sāttvika* sacrifice is considered a pure sacrifice and the other two sacrifices were seen as impure or as belonging to the realms of passion and darkness. But in chapter 2 the *guṇa*s are said to be belonging to the realm of Vedas and those who follow the Vedic religion are said to lack real wisdom (v. 45). As Surendranath Dasgupta writes, "The *Gītā* distinguishes between two kinds of motives for the performance of sacrifices. The first motive is that of greed and self-interest, and the second is a sense of duty."[98] Humans are, therefore, called to transcend the realm of selfish performance of sacrifice and to look for the cosmic welfare. Only the unselfish performance of the sacrifice is seen as real sacrifice, while the selfish performers of the Vedic sacrifice are people without vision. In such manner the *BG* corrects the Vedic sacrifices of selfish interests and restores their cosmic function as the determining factor in sacrifice. Humans need to overcome their selfish motives, because their every activity has a cosmic dimension.

The Symbolic Interpretation of Sacrifice in the BG

Keeping in mind that the *BG* is a synthesis of all the Vedas and closely follows the Upaniṣads, we can say that it too considers the whole human life as sacrifice. When the whole human life is a sacrifice, all what one does for the union with the *ātman-Brahman* or with a personal God becomes a sacrifice. Such a view has given rise to a symbolic interpretation of *yajña*. In the words of Tilak,

> This idea of symbolically extending the original meaning of the word *yajña* namely "a sacrifice of various materials," and making it include religious austerities (*tapas*), renunciation (*saṁnyāsa*), mental absorption (*samādhi*), control of the *prāṇa* or breath (*prāṇāyāma*), and other means of getting merged into the Blessed Lord, has not been mentioned by the *Gītā* for the first time.[99]

---

98. S. Dasgupta (1957), vol. 2, p. 484.

99. B.G. Tilak (1975), p. 957.

Sacrifice, therefore, does not mean merely ritualistic worship performed by offering material things, but it includes all kinds of spiritual activities. The giving up of desires, control of senses and of the breath, muttering of mystic syllables, are all considered as sacrifices (*BG* 4: 25-30; 10: 25). In fact, according to the *BG*, sacrifice includes all acts whatsoever done unselfishly. So any act done without selfishness can be regarded as a sacrifice.

Thus the *BG* continues the symbolic interpretation of the sacrifice started by the Upaniṣads, and completes it by introducing the element of love (*bhakti*). In this manner it goes further than the Upaniṣads. Herebelow we will analyse some of the verses which clearly speak of this symbolic interpretation of sacrifice.

SELF-DISCIPLINE AS YAJÑA

The *BG*, following closely the symbolic interpretation of *yajña* started by the Upaniṣads, gives a wider meaning to it. All that a person does for overcoming one's lower instincts and for the sake of the higher discipline become sacrifice. However, in the Upaniṣads the *tapas* was practised for the sake of preparing the mind for receiving the knowledge of the identity of the *ātman-Brahman*, but in the *BG* the purpose is not self-realization but God-realization.[100]

Like the Upaniṣads, in the *BG*, too, the ascetic life of a monk is considered to be a sacrifice.[101] A verse says:

> Some adepts offer sacrifice to the gods as their sole object; in the fire of *Brahman* others offer sacrifice as sacrifice [which has merit in itself].
> — 4.25

Śaṅkarācārya gives a different translation to this above-mentioned verse and puts it: "Other *yogins* resort to sacrifices to Gods; in the

100. M. Hiriyanna (1958), p. 126.

101. Just as there are three kinds of sacrifices depending on the *guṇas*, so too, there are three kinds of *tapas*: *sāttvika*, *rājasika* and *tāmasika* (*BG* 17.17-19). Again the austerity is divided into physical, of speech, and mental (*BG* 17.14-16).

fire of *Brahman* others offer the Self by the Self."[102] He translates the word *yajña* as Self and he further explains this verse saying:

> The oblation (*āhuti*) in his latter sacrifice is *yajña*, the Self, — for *yajña*, is enumerated among the terms synonymous with *ātman* — who is in reality one with *Brahman*, who is conditioned by the *upādhis* (such as *buddhi*) with all their attributes superimposed upon Him. This oblation of the Self is poured by the Self into *Brahman*, — here termed fire, the place into which that oblation is poured.[103]

The *Brahman* is the innermost self of all (*BṛUp* 3.2.1) and to know this identity of the *Brahman* and the self is in itself a sacrifice, even in the *BG*. As Śaṅkarācārya says:

> To know the conditioned Self as identical with the unconditioned *Brahman* is to sacrifice the Self in *Brahman*. This is the sacrifice which is performed by those who, having renounced all action, are ever steady in their knowledge of the identity of the Self with *Brahman*.[104]

The above-mentioned verses of the *BG* are in line with the Upaniṣadic teaching where the offering of the self was considered to be the real and daily sacrifice to be performed. The *BG* in this way brings sacrifice in relation to the self-offering to a personal God, for Kṛṣṇa is the manifestation of *Brahman*.

The offering of senses, life breaths and the self-control too become sacrifice. For the *BG* says:

> Yet others offer the senses — hearing and the rest — in the fires of self-restraint; others the senses' proper objects — sounds and the like — in the fires of the senses. Others offer up all works of sense and works of vital breath in the fire of the spiritual exercise of self-control kindled by wisdom. — 4.26-27

---

102. Śaṅkarācārya (1995), p. 144.

103. Ibid.

104. Ibid.

Just as in the Upaniṣads the *tapas* and yogic practices became sacrifices so, too, in the *BG tapas* becomes a sacrifice. In the above-mentioned verses we find that the offering of senses and the life-breaths, and the self-control take the significance of sacrifice.

Radhakrishnan while explaining the above-mentioned verse holds that every self-control or self-discipline is a sacrifice because in it we strive to penetrate into our innermost being. He says:

> A right enjoyment of sense objects is compared to a sacrifice in which the objects are the offering and the senses the sacrificial fires. Every form of self-control, where we surrender the egoistic enjoyment for the higher delight, where we give up lower impulses, is said to be a sacrifice.[105]

The self limitation, therefore, becomes the essence of all the sacrifices and hence all sacrifices can become means to spiritual maturation. Thus in a sacrificial interpretation of human life everything that a person does for a higher or noble purpose takes a sacrificial meaning. In such a vision nothing is lost when offered to God.

The offering of wealth, the hard penances, the spiritual exercises, the study of scripture, etc. all become sacrifice, for:

> Some offer up their wealth, some their hard penances, some spiritual exercise, and some again make study and knowledge [of scripture] their sacrifice — religious men whose vows are strict. — 4.28

Radhakrishnan translates the *dravyayajña* as material sacrifice and is the literal translation of it. But scholars like Śaṅkarācārya, J. Mascaró, R. Gnoli, and R.C. Zaehner translate it as "sacrifice of wealth."[106] Śaṅkarācārya sees in the sacrifice of the wealth "giving away wealth to the deserving,"[107] hence it can be taken to mean charity as sacrifice.

---

105. S. Radhakrishnan (2004), p. 167.
106. See their respective translations of the *BG* (4.28) as mentioned in the bibliography.
107. Śaṅkarācārya (1995), p. 146.

The breath offering and the breath-control, i.e. one of the eight limbs of the classical *yoga* too become sacrifices. For

> Some offer the in-breath in the out-breath, likewise the out-breath in the in-breath, checking the flow of both, on breath-control intent. Others restrict their food and offer up breaths in breaths. All these know the [meaning of] sacrifice, and by sacrifice [all] their defilements are made away. — 4.29-30

Verse 27 had already mentioned the offering of vital breath as sacrifice. Again in verses 29-30 the author takes up once again the breath offering. Zaehner identifies the offering of the vital breath with the offering of the self and sees in it an allusion to the allegorical interpretation of the *Agnihotra* or fire sacrifice which is described in *ChāUp* 5.19-24.[108] According to it a person offers a constant sacrifice to *Brahman* in surrendering oneself to *Brahman* in breathing — in and out. The breathing in surrenders itself to the breathing out and the latter then surrenders itself to the former. This is the constant sacrifice that man offers to *Brahman* when one offers one's life breaths to *Brahman* and such sacrifice is said to purify one from one's sins.

We find that the author of the *BG* after affirming the various kinds of sacrifices in verse 32 affirm that all the sacrifices are spread out through the mouth of *Brahman* and all of them involve work or action. It says:

> So many and various are the sacrifices spread out athwart the mouth of *Brahman*.[109] They spring from work, all of them: be sure

---

108. R.C. Zaehner (1969), p. 193.

109. There is no agreement among scholars about the interpretation of this verse. Śaṅkarācārya interprets the noun *Brahman* in the phrase "spread out athwart the mouth of *Brahman*" as Veda. Śaṅkarācārya (1995) p. 147. But Zaehner does not accept the interpretation of Śaṅkarācārya and suggests that the phrase could equally mean "offered in the presence of *Brahman*." R.C. Zaehner (1969), p. 195. Even Zaehner's view does not fully explain the verse because already in the 4.24 the *Brahman* was →

> of this; for once you know this, you will win release.
> — 4.32

Here the *BG* too speaks like the Puruṣa-Sūkta on the unity of sacrifice. The mouth of *Brahman* here means not only the presence of *Brahman* as Zaehner holds but also the unity between the sacrificer, the offering and the divinity and such a knowledge frees one from the bondage.

In the next verse the sacrifice of wisdom is considered to be superior to the sacrifice of the material things. It says:

> Better than the sacrifice of wealth is the sacrifice of wisdom. All works without exception in wisdom find their consummation.
> — 4.33

But Śaṅkarācārya gives a different translation to this verse. He puts it as:

> Superior is wisdom — sacrifice to the sacrifice with objects, O harasser of thy foes. All action, without exception, O son of Pṛthā, is comprehended in wisdom.[110]

Śaṅkarācārya further explains this verse saying that the sacrifice offered with material objects produces material effects, whereas wisdom sacrifice does not do so and is superior to the former for it is the means to liberation and comprehends all actions.[111] According to Zaehner, the wisdom sacrifice mentioned here can mean either the sacrifice of study and knowledge of scripture mentioned in 4.28 or the sacrifice that consists in wisdom, that is a sacrifice that does not have any earthly goal as its object.[112] To

---

→ identified with all that matters with sacrifice, the offering, the oblation, the instrument, the sacrificer and the receiver of the sacrifice. Again in chapter 9 Kṛṣṇa identifies himself as the rite, sacrifice, offering for the dead, healing herbs, sacred formula and the sacrificial fire, etc. (vv.16-17).

110. Śaṅkarācārya (1995), p. 148.

111. Ibid.

112. R.C. Zaehner (1969), p. 195.

me the second meaning seems to be more correct because immediately after this verse the following stanzas are dedicated to the explanation of the transcendent wisdom. Hence after affirming the various kinds of sacrifice the author is trying to show that sacrifice should be performed with right knowledge and only such knowledge can raise the human action into a sacrifice.

Therefore, the one who offers sacrifice in the wisdom of the *Brahman* must go into *Brahman* because he sees a fundamental unity between him and the transcendent *Brahman*. Everything in this world including the sacrificer belongs to *Brahman*, and to sacrifice is to offer back to him what belongs to him. The aims of *tapas* and self-offering can be nothing other than the union with *Brahman* through the self-control and purification of oneself of all desires.

NIṢKĀMA-KARMA AS SACRIFICE: THE TRUE CONCEPT OF DHARMA

According to the *BG*, sacrifice includes all acts whatsoever, done unselfishly (*niṣkāma-karma*)[113] for the main idea in a sacrifice is the offering of something to the deity. Scholars like Tilak[114] and Aurobindo[115] hold that the invariable and constant in the *BG* of the concept of *yajña* is this selflessness in the performance of an action. The *BG*, thus, by advocating it not only raises the whole life into sacrifice but also recommends the unselfish performance of every action or caste duty as a sacrifice. According to Panikkar, this may be a moving away from the traditional view to a larger concept of life as sacrifice,

---

113. This word is not found in the *BG*. However, this is the word traditionally used by the scholars of the Indian philosophy to mean the disinterested action taught by the *BG*. Some use the word *naiṣkarmya* to mean the same concept. In terms of Vedic theology, *niṣkāma-karma* looks a contradiction, for sacrifices are offered to obtain benefits and to satisfy one's desire (*kāma*). The *BG* is asking the sacrificer to go beyond this theology.
114. B.G. Tilak (1975), p. 407.
115. Sri Aurobindo (1974), pp. 164-65.

> a process of secularization away from the Vedic Brāhmaṇic conception of the sacrifice to the general conception of life itself as a sacrifice, maintained no longer by a specific *yajña* but by the karmic action of Men.[116]

The *BG* after devaluating the Vedic religion as selfish in 2.42-45, recommends surrendering of the fruits of action in verse 47 of the same chapter. In this verse Arjuna is told that work alone is his duty and not the fruit of it.[117] Through such a teaching it raises the unselfish or disinterested performance of action[118] or caste duty (*svadharma*)[119] as sacrifice and as the means of liberation from the

---

116. *PVE*, pp. 540-41. In this sacrificial interpretation of the whole of human life of the *BG* we can see a gradual moving away from the exaggerated ritualisms of the Brāhmaṇas and a return to the original Vedic experience of *karman* as sacrifice and in this way not only recommends the performance of action but also shows a way of liberation.

117. "[But] work alone is *your* proper business, never the fruits [it may produce]: let not your motive be the fruit of works nor your attachment to [mere] worklessness."

118. See 18.23; 4.23-25,32; 9.10ff; 18.46; 3.9; 3.14. According to L. Malieckal, the pure action as sacrifice also has its parallel in the Indo-European languages such as Greek and Latin, for the terms Greek *erdain/poiein* and the Latin *agere/facere* were used in a sacrificial context and he writes: ". . . words denoting "doing" or action pure and simple in these languages were originally used in the sense of sacred action, religious action, sacrifice." L. Malieckal (1989b), p. 34.

119. Zaehner comments on the above-mentioned verse by saying: "All work is or should be a sacrifice (3.10-16) and Arjuna's business is war, and war is the sacrificial fire of which the warriors are the priests (*Mbh* 5.139.29ff.): but whatever he does he must do it in a spirit of detachment. This is drummed in again and again throughout the *Gītā*." R.C. Zaehner (1969), p. 145.

effects of *karman.*[120] This disinterested performance of action needs the control of the senses (3.7) and various yogic techniques (6.1ff). In another text it holds the renunciation of the fruits of all actions (*sarva-karma-phala-tyāga*) (12.11) which might have even influenced the later performance of sacrifices where one is made to renounce the effect of action.[121]

In an attempt to advocate the disinterested action the *BG* calls the doer to follow the example of God, the selfless worker (3.22). The *BG* clearly advocates that non-action is impossible and that could be disastrous for the cosmos itself and what one should seek in this action is the *lokasaṁgraha,* the welfare of all (3.24-25). Thus, like the early Vedic sacrifices, the *BG,* too, admits a cosmic function of sacrifice when it speaks of acting for the welfare of all. The only motive for the performance of action should be the welfare of all and such an action does not bind. And to do everything for the moral imperative of duty is to transcend the ego to the Supreme Self identifying one's own will to the cosmic will of the Lord who is the protector of the eternal *dharma* and by doing so what one offers is not the material objects but the human will, the human desire. According to the *BG* an action done as a

120. The word *karman* comes from the root *kr-* whose primary meaning is "to do, make, perform, accomplish" appearing in *Ṛgveda* mainly. Then it has also a secondary meaning which means "to worship, sacrifice." See L. Malieckal (1989b), pp. 45-46. In the course of time it took a third meaning, that of the law of causality or the theory of transmigration and the *BG* uses the term in all these senses. According to G. Lanithottam, originally it meant simply action or sacrifice. G. Lanithottam (1993), p. 332. Panikkar, too, had a similar view and he wrote that its third meaning as the doctrine of causality or transmigration was only a later addition. He writes. "The term *karman* occurs almost forty times in the *Ṛgveda,* but never in the sense of the later theories on transmigration. It means simply works, deeds, and, especially sacred actions. *Karman* is directly related to the central idea of sacrifice." *PVE,* p. 539.

121. H.W. Bodewitz (1990), pp. 8ff.

duty is a sacrifice.[122] *Niṣkāma-karma* is, therefore, not the renunciation of action but the "renunciation in action" because neither the action nor its fruits belong to man. As Panikkar says,

> In fact any appropriation of fruits of the action by the individual agent would damage the cosmic interrelationship among all the elements of the sacrifice; it would endanger the action itself, and indeed so prevent it as to excommunicate it from the cosmic web of real actions which sustain the world. Disinterested action is required not only for the sake of individual moral purity, but because the maintenance and welfare of the world cannot be realized otherwise.[123]

Niṣkāma-karma means two things: first an unselfish action, done as mere duty not for any personal gain, secondly it means surrendering or offering back to God what belongs to him.

According to the *BG* any action which is not a sacrifice, i.e. not surrendered to God as an offering, is a means for bondage as a text says:

> This world is bound by bonds of work save where that work is done for sacrifice. Work to this end, then Arjuna, from [all] attachment gone. — 3.9

The scholars give different meanings to this verse. Śaṅkarācārya interprets the word "sacrifice" as Viṣṇu and adds that this world is not bound by action done for Lord's sake.[124] Action done for sacrifice then means action done for God's sake; such a view can also be found in Radhakrishnan where he says that every action should be done in the spirit of sacrifice, for the sake of the divine, as a religious duty.[125] Mascaró too gives a spiritualized interpretation of action in his translation of the above-mentioned

---

122. Sri Aurobindo (1974), pp. 103-04; Śaṅkarācārya (1995), p. 476.
123. *PVE*, p. 427.
124. Śaṅkarācārya (1995), p. 98.
125. S. Radhakrishnan (2004), p. 135.

verse: "This world is in the bonds of action, unless the action is consecration. Let thy actions then be pure, free from the bonds of desire."[126] All the actions which are done for a selfish motive bind because they are not done as sacrifice, and only an unselfish action which is done as sacrifice and is offered to God does not bind the soul. The interpretations of the different scholars mentioned above agree on the point that an action done for God's sake does not bind for such an action is a sacrifice because it is done in the spirit of sacrifice, that is, as a consecration.

In the next verse Kṛṣṇa invites Arjuna to offer everything to him and to fight without fear. Here we can say that an unselfish doing of one's caste duty is sacrifice. Arjuna is kṣatriya by caste and the duty of a kṣatriya is to fight. But he should not fight for selfish motives, led by likes or dislikes, but to fulfil his caste duty to uphold the *dharma*. Here according to F.X. D'Sa,

> The *Gītā* corrects the absolutization of the *kula-dharma*s and *jāti-dharma*s by pointing to a genuine experience of *Dharma* (singular) and asking Arjuna to give up all the (*kula-* and *jāti-*) *Dharma*s (pl).[127]

Kṛṣṇa says:

> Cast all your works on Me, your thoughts [withdrawn] in what appertains to self; have neither hope nor thought that "This is mine": cast off this fever! Fight! — 3.30

The phrase "cast all your works on Me" is an invitation to offer back to God whatever one does. It is to do one's duty as a sacrifice, as an offering to God. Commenting on the above-mentioned verse Zaehner says:

> This is what is meant when action (*karma*) is identified with sacrifice (3.9): you offer back to God the actions which seem to

---

126. J. Mascaró (1980), p. 57.

127. F.X. D'Sa (1980), p. 338.

> be your own but which are really initiated by God consorting with material Nature which is his. — 4.6[128]

Hence God is seen as the agent and source of every action, humans only co-operate with God in the action. If God is both the agent and source of action neither the action nor its fruit belongs to humans, but an ignorant person caught up in selfishness thinks oneself as the agent and desires for its fruit. Therefore, Arjuna is told to offer, or surrender all actions to God, the origin and source of every action, and such self-surrender in the *BG* takes the name "sacrifice."

In this way a work done as a duty becomes a sacrifice, because it is not done for any personal interest but to uphold the cosmic welfare, the *lokasaṁgraha*. In a disinterested action (*niṣkāma-karma)* we have the culmination of sacrifice because "the inner giving up of works and yet physical doing of them is the culmination of sacrifice."[129] In it we sacrifice our desires, hence it is the sacrifice of the human will. As Zaehner says,

> Work should be regarded as essentially a sacrifice, but unlike the routine sacrifices to the gods which are designed to produce material benefits, this sacrifice is a true sacrifice of the human will, and the goal of it is to have done once for all with the *bondage* that purposeful work entails.[130]

One who offers such sacrifice will not have to be re-born because what it teaches is not the sacrifice of the material objects but the sacrifice of the desire, the sacrifice of the ego[131] and in this way on the one hand it upholds the vision of the Upaniṣads and on the other raises the human life as sacrifice without the need for abandoning the village to lead an ascetic life.

---

128. R.C. Zaehner (1969), p. 172.
129. Sri Aurobindo (1974), p. 112.
130. R.C. Zaehner (1969), pp. 18-19.
131. A. Elenjimittam (1996), p. 77.

SACRIFICE AS OFFERING OF ONESELF TO THE LORD IN BHAKTI

The doctrine of *niṣkāma-karma* which we discussed above can have its meaning only if it is offered to a personal God in *bhakti*[132] (ardent love) and here in this concluding section of this chapter we will see that the interiorization of the sacrifice started by the Upaniṣads reaches its climax[133] in the *BG* with the introduction of a personal God who is able to enter into a love relationship[134] with the devotee who dedicates his/her whole life in search of him.

132. *Bhakti* comes from the root *bhaj* which means to divide, to distribute, to share with, to bestow, to serve, to adore, etc. M. Monier-Williams (1970), p. 743. For the different uses of this term in the *BG* see I. Vempeny (1988), pp. 212-13. Rāmānuja is the greatest promoter of this movement and according to Radhakrishnan the distinction between the creature and Creator is the ontological basis of this *bhakti*.

133. According to F. Edgerton, the climax of the *BG* is the relation of God to human salvation. He begins the chapter IX (the way of devotion to God) of his commentary on the *BG* in the following words:

> "It has required something like a *tour de force* to reserve for this place a treatment of the revelation of God to human salvation in the teachings of the *Gītā*. For in a sense it has involved temporarily ignoring the most cardinal doctrine of the poem. Yet the poem itself affords a precedent for approximately such an arrangement. The *Gītā* does not begin with this subject; and references to it in the early chapters are few and scattering. In the middle chapters of the work it gradually becomes more prominent, until it finally occupies the centre of the stage, with the climax in the eleventh chapter, in which the mystic vision of God's supernal form is revealed to Arjuna. After this, somewhat anti-climactically, the *Gītā* gradually drops into other themes again, to return to the theme of salvation thru God towards the end of its final, summary chapter (the eighteenth)."

F. Edgerton (1925), vol. 2, p. 70. On the divine manifestation of Kṛṣṇa to Arjuna after giving him a celestial eye, and on Arjuna's adoration of Kṛṣṇa see *BG* 11. 5-31.

134. Even though the notion *bhakti* is not developed in the Upaniṣads it is not completely absent. *ŚvetUp* concludes by stating that with highest devotion (*para bhakti*) for God and for one's spiritual →

If in the Upaniṣads sacrifice was subordinated to the knowledge of the *ātman-Brahman,* in the *BG* it reaches its climax where it is not seen as an offering which the individual self makes to the Cosmic Self but to a personal God who is able to enter into communion with the devotee.[135] Such a personal God is Kṛṣṇa on whom this cosmos exists[136] and he, in whom subsists all beings has to be won by love and worship (*BG* 8.22). And the one who through love and loyalty comes to know him enters into him (*BG* 18.55) and those who trust him will be saved by his grace (*BG* 18.56). Thus, sacrifice which had become a meditation or the intellectual activity in the Upaniṣads becomes an offering to a personal God who promises to save those who trust in him. In the words of Panikkar, in the *BG* sacrifice becomes a loving activity because,

> Worship, sacrifice, is above all an essentially loving activity, the loftiest activity in which Man can be engaged: that which employs his whole range of feeling powers, that personal love that makes of human existence a real sacrifice.[137]

In this context love becomes the measuring stick for every sacrifice. Any offering without love is not a sacrifice and when love becomes

→ teacher all things will become clear (6.23). However, this Upaniṣad is considered to be theistic in nature and belongs to the Śaivite group.

135. In the *BG bhakti* means the personal relationship between God and man. According to *BG* 7.16, this *bhakti* relationship are of four kinds: *artha* (the one who is in distress), of *jijñāsu* (the seeker of wisdom), of *arthārthī* (the one who seeks for wealth or strives for gain), and of *jñānī* (the man of wisdom). This last type is considered to be the best and Rāmānuja calls them those who have the devotion to a single person alone, *ekabhakti.* S. Radhakrishnan (2004), p. 219.

136. *BG* 9.16-19.

137. *PVE,* p. 424.

the motive for offering it is not important what one offers but with what motivation one offers. As Kṛṣṇa says:

> Be it a leaf or flower or fruit or water that a zealous soul may offer Me with love's devotion, that do I [willingly] accept, for it was love that made the offering. — 9.26

Commenting on this verse Radhakrishnan says that however poor the offering may be if it is offered with pure intention and with love it is acceptable to the Lord.[138] Therefore we find that in a spiritualized notion of sacrifice what is important is not what one offers but out of what motivation one offers. The only requirement of sacrifice is devotion and the only motivation should be love of God.

When love for God becomes the motive for sacrifice what one offers is not something external to oneself. As Kṛṣṇa says:

> Whatever you do, whatever you eat, whatever you offer in sacrifice or give away in alms, whatever penance you may perform, offer it up to Me. — 9.27

> Give in thought to Me all that you do, make Me your goal: relying on the integration of the soul, think on Me constantly. — 18.57

Thus in the *BG* sacrifice is primarily a loving activity and the only motivation of sacrifice should be love for God. Sacrifice becomes surrender to the personal God in the *BG* and such surrender also requires the need to control one's mind by constant practice of spiritual exercises and meditation.[139] Thus *bhakti* could also include the asceticism and the meditation of the Upaniṣads because it is performed for the sake of communion with God. It is not a mere sentimental love, it is something by which one participates in the divine nature of a personal God who manifests out of His grace.

---

138. S. Radhakrishnan (2004), pp. 249-300. Śaṅkarācārya and R.C. Zaehner are unusually silent on this verse.

139. J. Gonda (1977), p. 107.

As we have seen above the *BG* continues the metaphoric interpretation of the sacrifice started by the Upaniṣads and completes such a process with the introduction of the notion of *bhakti* to a personal God. In such case what one looks for in sacrifice is love and the cosmic well-being (*lokasaṁgraha*), and anything short of such ideals is considered to be impure because it goes against the norm of the cosmic good. By maintaining the divine origin of sacrifice it holds on the one hand sacrifice as the law of life, and on the other it purifies the intention through introducing the notion of *niṣkāma-karma*. In this way it gives back to sacrifice its cosmic function.

Conclusion

In our analysis of the interiorization and spiritualization of sacrifice in the Upaniṣads and in the *BG* we have seen that sacrifice gets a broader meaning in both of them. They consider the sacrifice of the brāhmaṇas as inferior for they can lead only to the heaven of Indra from where one has to be reborn once the merits of the sacrifices are over.

We can find that according to the Upaniṣads the mind firmly established in *Brahman* becomes the perfect sacrifice and means of liberation. The main question in the Upaniṣads is not sacrifice or rejection of sacrifice, but rather what is true sacrifice and what is the scope of sacrifice. True sacrifice cannot be the offering of a victim outside oneself, but of one's internal self to the cosmic self. In this way like the Brāhmaṇas, the Upaniṣads too, consider sacrifice as self-sacrifice but from a different perspective. The true sacrifice is the sacrifice of the Self to the Universal Self and the scope of it is to overcome such circles of death and rebirth. The *BG* too continues such a question of what is a true sacrifice, and it considers the Vedic sacrifices which were performed with a personal desire as belonging to the realm of *guṇa*s which binds one to the circle of death and rebirth. True sacrifice is any action performed without any desire for personal good (*niṣkāma-karma*) other than the cosmic welfare (*lokasaṁgraha*).

Both the Upaniṣads and the *BG* redefine the Vedic sacrifice and give an advanced spiritual meaning to it. The Upaniṣads present them under the knowledge of the identity of the *ātman-Brahman* and the *BG* presents it under the notions of *niṣkāma-karma* and *bhakti*. In such an attempt to redefine the Vedic sacrifice the Upaniṣads consider the *tapas* as not only greater than sacrifice but also as the means to arrive at the *jñāna* of the *Brahman* that liberates humans from bondage, and the *BG* brings the notions of *niṣkāma-karma* and *bhakti* as the means for liberation. Both the Upaniṣads and the *BG* in their interiorization of sacrifice raise the human life as sacrifice, and what one offers is oneself and not an external thing.

However, the *BG* goes further than the Upaniṣads and its importance today in modern Hinduism is due to this fact. It goes further and brings it under the *bhakti* of a personal God and raises not only the unselfish performance of *svadharma* into the realm of sacrifice but also as the duty of every person. But the motivation of it becomes the determining factor. The communion with a personal God or the contribution to the *lokasaṁgraha* (welfare of all) should be the only motives.

Again if in the Upaniṣads the knowledge of the identity of the *ātman-Brahman* was considered to be the means to obtain the liberation from rebirth, in the *BG* it is the personal God who liberates the soul of the one who offers himself in love to him. The *BG* first purifies the mind of the selfishness and then introduces the notion of *bhakti* as the motive for sacrifice. Sacrifice is, first of all, the self-surrender to God in love. And the external offerings should manifest the inner surrender to the personal God in love. In such a vision all selfless giving even of a leaf or a flower or a glass of water to God becomes a sacrifice. Every human act, therefore, when offered to God in love becomes a sacrifice and every self-surrender to God in love is equal or even greater than the costly Vedic sacrifice.

Part II
The Eucharistic Sacrifice and its Cosmic Dynamism

4

The Descending and Ascending Dimensions of the Eucharistic Sacrifice

THE almost self-evident cosmic dimension of the Vedic sacrifice which we have seen above urges us to bring to light the hidden cosmic dimensions of the Eucharistic sacrifice. This is our main task if we want to make a true comparison between the Vedic and the Eucharistic sacrifice. At the outset we should confess that it is not going to be an easy task, firstly due to the long controversies on the sacrificial nature of the Eucharist, particularly on the part of the Catholic and the Protestant theologians,[1] and secondly because of a lack of cosmic vision in the Eucharistic theology. Our attempt is at first to reconcile the long controversies on the sacrificial nature of the Eucharist in the sacramental order, i.e. in its mediation of the signs of bread and wine,[2] with an aim

---

1. The relation between the Eucharist and the cosmos is almost neglected by the Catholic and the Protestant theologians, and those who have treated this theme are the Orthodox theologians. We will see their positions in detail in the next chapter. Here in this chapter we try to demonstrate that the sacrificial nature of the Eucharist has to be sought in its sacramental character which again forms the basis for its cosmic dimension which we will see in detail in the next chapter.

2. The contemporary scholars, after a long discussion on the sacrificial nature of the Eucharist, seem to have come to an agreement on the point that it is sacrifice in the sacramental order. See C. Giraudo (1989b), pp. 606ff. We do not intend to make an elaborate study on the various theories on the Eucharistic sacrifice, but we limit ourselves to the sacramental character of the Eucharist to discover its cosmic role. On the

→

to rediscover the cosmic dimension of it.

If the Eucharist is the sacrament of the sacrifice of the cross that has redeemed not only human beings but the whole cosmos,[3] then it should surely have sacrificial and cosmic characters. And the Church as the Body of Christ cannot forget its cosmic dimension, for it is through the Church that the cosmos comes in contact with Christ, from whom it had its beginning and in whom it exists. Here the role of the Eucharist as the sacrament of the sacrifice of Christ becomes vital because it becomes not only the meeting place of God and the cosmos through Christ but also the means through which the cosmos enters into the fullness of Christ. As Josef Ernst writes: "The point at which this meeting of Church and cosmos, order of creation and order of redemption, takes place even now, is in the celebration of the Eucharist."[4] Thus, the Eucharist as sacrament of the sacrifice of the cross plays a role of mediation between God and the creation in which consists its cosmic function.

But before we proceed with our search into the Eucharistic sacrifice, the union of the divine and the cosmos, we should clarify certain points on the actual situation on the research on the sacrificial character of the Eucharist. This sacrificial character of the Eucharist, which has been the topic of heated discussions between Protestants and Catholics from the time of the Protestant reformation in spite of showing signs of consensus,[5] still remains one of the topics, not only between Protestants and Catholics but

---

→ relation of the sign, symbol, and the sacrament see G. Segalla (1977), pp. 17-44; S. Schneiders (1977), pp. 221-35; L.-M. Chauvet (1990), pp. 11-305; L.-M. Chauvet (1988), pp. 17-78.

3. See Col 1: 15-20. On the relation between Christ and the cosmos in Col 1: 15-20 see the different articles in Associazione Biblica Italiana (1976).

4. J. Ernst (1968), p. 55.

5. A. Gelston (1991), p. 118.

also among the Catholics themselves, where there seems to be little agreement among the scholars.[6]

Even though there are signs of a possible reconciliation of the Catholic and the Protestant views on the sacrificial nature of the Eucharist based on the biblical notion of the *anamnesis* and on its sacramental character, there is still no satisfactory explanation of the problem. Due to the inability to reconcile the different positions, there still remains certain reluctance on the part of the theologians to study it further. For example, C. Vagaggini after saying that from 1947 (i.e. from the *Mediator Dei*), it seems that on the sacrificial character of the Eucharist we have come to a dead end, asks whether it is worth re-trying the matter again.[7] Only recently Christian theologians started asking seriously the question of sacrifice because of the book of René Girard on the sacrificial mimesis.[8] The decline in the sacrificial aspect of the Mass in recent years of theological studies has brought impoverishment even in the very meal character of it.

E. Quarello considers that the decline in the study of the sacrificial character of the Eucharist is due to three reasons:[9] first, in the Mass, the whole life of Christ was present and not merely

---

6. For example, the Evangelical Lutherans and Methodists even today prefer to avoid the term sacrifice in connection with the Eucharist. See D.N. Power (1987), p. 2. The Lutherans and the Calvinists do not accept any sacrificial interpretation of the Eucharist. See also S.W. Sykes (1991b), p. 2. On the Catholic theologians' views on the Eucharistic sacrifice see E. Quarello (1970).
7. C. Vagaggini (1969), p. 179.
8. R. Girard (1986). According to A.N. Terrin, already in the 1980s a strong interest in the study of the sacrifice began to take place with the publication of the work of W. Burkert (1981). See A.N. Terrin (1998), pp. 263-64. This interest then widened with the publication of the work of R. Girard.
9. E. Quarello (1970), pp. 79-80.

of his sacrifice. Secondly, the growing ecumenical sensibility does not want to re-open the past disputes by treating it, and thirdly, the often disputed verdicts by authorities in the Catholic Church discouraged any new research in the field and gave the impression that the question was closed once and for all.

Even though from the first century the Christians considered the Eucharist as their sacrifice, today there is no unanimity over it.[10] This makes not only a general theory of the Eucharistic sacrifice difficult but also gives rise to the view that Christianity is an anti-sacrificial religion.[11] The result of such a view is that the Christian sacrifice is merely spiritual and not ritual. *Our attempt is to show the opposite, that the Christian sacrifice is not merely spiritual but ritual and, only as ritual, can it have a true cosmic value.* For Christ at his Last Supper commanded the disciples to "do this in memory of me," so that the Christians of all times could ritually celebrate his self-giving sacrifice to the Father for the salvation of humanity. The Eucharist, thus, being the ritual celebration of Christ's sacrifice has a cosmic value, and any attempt to reduce it to a spiritual sacrifice is to deny not only the fact that Christ himself made use of an existing rite, the Passover meal, to express symbolically his sacrificial self-giving to the Father and to the humanity on the cross, but also to deprive it of its sacramental and cosmic functions.

---

10. Ibid., pp. 111-12.

11. See R.J. Daly (1997), pp. 231-43; P.B. Duff (1997), pp. 245-48. In my opinion we cannot easily accept the theory that Christianity is an anti-sacrificial religion without accepting the mimetic theory of René Girard. The purpose of the whole issue of the above-mentioned periodical seems to re-affirm the thesis of R. Girard and his anti-sacrificial reading of Christianity. Hence according to me the starting point of the issue is mistaken, and any conclusion drawn from a wrong supposition cannot be easily accepted. For a recent critique of Girards' position see A. Colombo (1999), pp. 23-98; G. Bonaccorso (1998), pp. 181-202. See also L.-M. Chauvet (1990), pp. 209-12.

Any attempt to reduce the ritual sacrifice to the ethical or spiritual vision is not to take into serious consideration the sacramental character of the Eucharistic sacrifice.[12] Any effort to reduce it to a spiritual sacrifice[13] is to reject its role of mediation as sacrament, and thereby to reject its cosmic aspect as well. The way to come out of this problem may be to re-suggest the idea of A. Grillo to reintegrate the rite as a pre- and necessary condition of fundamental theology.[14] That would mean that we try to rediscover the original tension between the rite and its inner meaning, and not to accept easily the superiority of the ethics to the rite. Those who consider the ethics as superior to the rite soon fall into the negation of the latter[15] and impoverish our corporal dimension. As corporal beings, we need the sacrament to express our inner offering to God.

---

12. On an evaluation of the contemporary theologians who reduce the ritual sacrifice to an ethical vision, see A. Grillo (1998), pp. 203-43.

13. A spiritual sacrifice can be anything offered to God. According to the Reformers, the Mass can be considered only as a thanksgiving or a spiritual sacrifice which is an offering of prayers and good works done in faith in Jesus Christ. See D.N. Power (1987), p. 59. Commenting on the Protestant conception of the Eucharist as sacrifice E.O. James says: ". . . in the majority of the Protestant communities the idea of sacrifice has now almost lapsed except as a purely subjective offering of a pure heart, and vocal thanksgiving which is sometimes connected with the symbols of the death of Christ." E.O. James (1971), pp. 288-89. Such a conception does not take into consideration the ritual aspect of the Eucharist. E.O. James argues further that in every country where the Mass has been decentralized the institutionalized religion is in a process of collapse. The break-up of the ritual order is one of the most important causes of the collapse of the institutionalized religion, because the history of the ritual is the history of the religion. Ibid.

14. A. Grillo (1998), p. 207.

15. See ibid., pp. 210 and 219.

To avoid any reductionistic approach to the Eucharistic sacrifice we intend to approach the sacrificial character of the Eucharist in its wholeness, i.e. from the descending (God offering to humans in sacrifice), and ascending points (humans offering themselves to God in the Eucharist).[16] This descending sacrifice that was first revealed in the sacrifice of the cross makes possible our sacrifice and becomes the basis of any future reflection on the sacrifice of the Eucharist. Herebelow we begin our detailed analysis with the sacrificial nature of the Last Supper and the sacrificial death of Jesus on the cross.

The Sacrificial Character of the Last Supper and Jesus' Sacrificial Self-Giving to the Father on the Cross

The sacrificial nature of the Eucharist is to a large extent dependent on the sacrificial understanding of the Last Supper itself, because the double elements of the Last Supper, i.e. the words and gestures of Jesus over the bread and the wine reveal a sacrificial character. This makes it necessary that we begin our study starting with the Last Supper as the sacrament of the sacrifice of Christ and by analysing both the words and the gestures of Jesus at it without forgetting that Jesus' actions and words at the Last Supper cannot be separated from a series of his meals with his disciples.

THE LAST SUPPER AS THE SACRAMENT OF THE SACRIFICE OF CHRIST

In our attempt to rediscover the sacrificial nature of the Eucharist in its intrinsic relation to the cross and as its ritual celebration we do not intend primarily to proceed from the relation of the Last Supper to the Passover meal,[17] but from the words of Jesus himself

---

16. See E. Quarello (1970), p. 11.
17. There is no unanimity on the date of the Last Supper, because there are two different views on the date of it. According to the Synoptics, it takes place on the first day of of Unleavened Bread,

over the bread and wine. For, in my opinion the words of Jesus over the bread and wine and his actions over them give us the starting points on the analysis of the sacrificial nature of the Last Supper in relation to the cross.[18] Further this Supper, which was the sacrament of the sacrifice,[19] provides not only the essential link between Jesus' sacrificial death on the cross, but also the link with the Eucharist. These aspects make it necessary that we begin our discussion on the Eucharistic sacrifice starting from the relation between the Last Supper and Jesus' death on the cross.[20] Without this, in my opinion, it is not only difficult to grasp the sacrificial meanings of the words of Jesus at the Last Supper, but also it is

---

→ hence on the 15 of Nisan, but according to John it takes place "before the feast of the Passover (Jn 13: 1), that is, on the 14 of Nisan." The Synoptics' date seems to be impossible when we take into consideration the events described in connection with the trials and crucifixion with the Jewish observance of the feast day. Further the Synoptics' date contradicts with the warning of the Sanhedrin against taking action during the festival — "not on the Feast Day, lest there be a riot" (Mk 14: 2; Mt 26: 5). For a more detailed study on it see J. Jeremias (1987), pp. 15-84.

18. On the relation between the Christ-Event and the Christian sacrifice, see A. Catella (1998), pp. 312-29.

19. We do not make any net separation between the sacrifice and sacrament as the Council of Trent and most of the Post-Tridentine manuals on the Eucharist have done. We are aware of the unity between both of them and we separate them only to show the indivisible double elements of the Eucharistic sacrifice. On the unity of the sacrifice and sacrament, see A. Gerken (1977), p. 163. On the vast list of the manuals on the Eucharist which treat the Eucharistic sacrifice in separation from the sacrament, see C. Giraudo (1989b), pp. 4-6.

20. In this section we limit ourselves to the sacrificial nature of the Last Supper and the words of Jesus on the bread and wine, and in the next section we see in detail the sacramental character of the Last Supper when we will be discussing the memorial aspect of the Eucharist.

difficult to understand the very sacrificial nature of the Eucharist as a rite given by Christ himself.

Recent studies on the Eucharist have brought to light both the sacrificial and the sacramental characters of the Last Supper. This Last Supper, according to C. Vagaggini,[21] is the sacrament of the future sacrifice of Christ, the bread broken symbolized his body which will be broken for humankind, and the wine poured into the chalice meant the blood of Christ which was to be shed for the remission of sins. R. Daly, too, holds a similar view years later when he writes: "The evangelists also seem to present the Last Supper as a prophecy-in-act anticipation of Christ's sacrificial death."[22] Christ in the Last Supper gives himself sacramentally to his disciples in the forms of bread and wine.

The Synoptics and the Johannine[23] separation of body/flesh and blood under the species of bread and wine at the Last supper/ in the discourse on Jesus the bread of life (Jn 6:22-59) symbolically make present the sacrifice of the cross at the Last Supper. For according to J. Jeremias, the flesh and blood[24] which are often found in the sacrificial language mean the constituent parts of the animal sacrificed, which are separated through the killing.[25] Max Thurian, too, has a similar view when he holds that the bread and wine symbolize the gift of Christ in sacrifice.[26] For Jesus' identification of bread and wine with his body and blood, thus, represent the separated body and blood of the animal sacrificed, and in this case his body and blood which will be sacrificed in the near future for them. Again the body and blood in the Eucharistic

---

21. C. Vagaggini (1969), p. 185.
22. R.J. Daly (1978b), p. 128.
23. On Johannine Eucharist see discourse see 194-99.
24. Of course these are the Johannine use and not the Synoptics.
25. J. Jeremias (1987), pp. 221-22; A. Gerken (1977), p. 28.
26. M. Thurian (1961), pp. 51-52.

sacrifice stand for the double elements of the sacrifice of Christ, and in this way they make sacramentally present the sacrifice of Christ.[27] We will now see in detail the sacrificial elements of the Last Supper[28] from which the Eucharist gets its own sacrificial character.

"MY BODY GIVEN FOR YOU"

The words of Jesus at the Last Supper over the bread "my body given for you,"[29] and his gestures: taking the bread, giving thanks, breaking it and giving it to the disciples, evoke that the bread broken and given to the disciples is the symbol of his giving himself to them.[30] But this giving himself is a sacrificial giving, an aspect which seems to have been almost forgotten. For, Jesus identifies the bread with himself[31] and by breaking it and giving it to the disciples he alludes to his sacrificial self-giving death on the cross to the Father for the salvation of the world.[32] Jesus seems to be alluding: just as this bread is broken that you may take part of it, so too, my body will be broken on the cross that you may take part of the fruits of redemption by entering into communion with me.

The symbolism of the bread, which is identified with the body of Jesus broken and given for the disciples, has meaning only in a sacrificial understanding of the death of Jesus. Jesus himself saw his death as a sacrifice for others. Thus Jesus' gestures and words

27. Ibid., p. 55.
28. We leave aside all the biblical discussions about the Passover meal.
29. Lk 22: 19, parallels and 1Cor 11: 23-24. For an exegetic analysis of the words and the gestures of Jesus over the bread see C. Giraudo (1989b), pp. 189-224. See also J. Jeremias (1972), pp. 196-203.
30. See X. Léon-Dufour (1987), p. 62. See also H. Schürmann (1983), pp. 98-100.
31. See R. Daly (1981), pp. 24-25.
32. See C. Vagaggini (1969), p. 185.

at the Last Supper over the bread, identifying it with his body, breaking it, passing it and the invitation to eat it, have meaning only in relation to his life of service and his imminent sacrificial death on the cross for our sake. And to express such a sacrificial gift he made use of a sacrament, that is the Passover meal in which the bread and wine had a wider meaning, i.e. God's presence and faithfulness.

"MY BLOOD . . . SHED FOR MANY/FOR YOU"

Another indication of the sacrificial character of the Last Supper is given in the words of Jesus over the cup which identify the content of it with his blood.[33] Just as Jesus' words over the bread, so too, his words over the chalice "my blood of the covenant shed for many for the forgiveness of sins" (Mt 26: 28) evoke not only the gift of his life for humankind, that leads to the point of shedding his blood, but also the sacrificial character of it. The content of the cup is his blood shed, or to be shed, i.e. his very life given up unto death for the forgiveness of the sins "for many" according to Mt 26: 28, Mk 14: 24, and "for you" according to Luke 22: 20. Again the phrase "shed for many" expresses clearly the idea of vicarious,[34] universal atonement affecting Israel in the sacrificial death of Jesus on the cross. It is clear, therefore, that the words of Jesus over the cup refer to his death for the sake of many. As R. Pesch writes: "Jesus' words of interpretation signify first of all his death. The giving of the cup is the proleptic giving of the saving power of his death."[35]

---

33. Mt 26: 28, parallels, and 1Cor 11: 25. For an exegetic study over them see C. Giraudo (1989b), pp. 225-43.

34. H. Schürmann (1983), pp. 74-75; S. Lyonnet and L. Sabourin (1970), pp. 253-61.

35. R. Pesch (1978), p. 100. See also R. Daly (1981).

JESUS' BLOOD AS BLOOD OF THE NEW COVENANT

B. Cooke considers the synoptic presentation of the Eucharist as a covenant sacrifice,[36] but for H. Gese the Lord's Supper was a *todah* meal,[37] a view that is strongly rejected by P.F. Bradshaw in one of his recent articles on the ground that there is nothing which suggests that the supper was intended by Jesus as *todah* meal.[38] Rather Jesus' words over the chalice show that his blood is the blood of the covenant, for it evokes Ex 24: 8: "Behold the blood of the covenant which the Lord has made with you. . . . "[39] Max Thurian even sees in the narrative of the Sinai covenant (Ex 24: 4-8) the pre-Christian liturgy.[40] But even though there are similarities, it is not clear whether the early Church developed its liturgy based on the pattern of the Sinai covenant.

Just as the OT sacrifices can be understood only against the

---

36. B. Cooke (1960), pp. 1-44. Just as the OT theology of sacrifice is based on its notion of covenantal relation with Yahweh so too, the NT notion of Christian sacrifice is again based on the new covenantal relation with God in Jesus' death. His blood is the blood of the new covenant. For the relation between the OT theology of sacrifice and the covenant, see G.J. Wenham (1995), pp. 75-87, particularly pp. 84-85.

37. H. Gese (1981), pp. 137-38. Even though the communion aspect is fundamental to the Hebrew sacrifices and the Christian Eucharistic sacrifice, from the words of Jesus over the bread and wine *the Covenant aspect appears more fundamental*. Eating the body and drinking the blood surely have a communion aspect but this does not mean that the Last Supper was primarily a communion meal. It was rather a Passover meal in which Jesus gave himself as the victim of the new Covenant.

38. P.F. Bradshaw (1991), pp. 249-53.

39. A. Gerken (1977), p. 121. See also R.S. Hendel (1989), pp. 366-90; C.K. Barrett (1954-55), 210-18; B. Cooke (1960), 1-44; R. de Zan (1991), p. 583; A. Vanhoye (1992), pp. 118-32.

40. M. Thurian (1961), p. 54.

background of the Sinai covenant,[41] so too, the Eucharist, the Christian sacrifice can be understood only in the new covenantal relation of the new people of God with God the Father in the sacrificial death of Jesus on the cross. God in Jesus' blood has made a new and everlasting covenant with humankind and the Eucharist is the sacrifice of the new covenant. Generally a covenant

---

41. The OT sacrifices are expressions of the election of Israel and the covenantal relation to God. When the covenantal relation is broken through disobedience to the law, sacrifice is given as the means to re-establish the relation with the God of covenant on the one hand and the removal of the impurity on the other. According to Gordon J. Wenham, each time when an animal, wheat or oil is selected for sacrifice this covenantal election is manifested:

> "First, God's choice of Israel is recalled every time an animal, or wheat, or wine, was picked to be offered. Second, God's demand to be holy, to keep the commandment and so on was recalled in every sacrifice. . . . Leviticus 26 and Deuteronomy 28 contain lengthy descriptions of the terrible judgements that Israel's sin may provoke including famine, disease, death and loss of the land of promise. God the giver of life may take it away from his people if they fail to live by his commandments. This message is underlined in every sacrifice, in that the animal representing the Israelite is condemned to death. Its shed blood declares that the wages of sin is death. . . . But the very institution of sacrifice signals the irrepressible hope built into the covenant, that however much Israel sins, restoration and new life are possible if she repents (Lv. 26: 40-45; Dt. 30: 1-10): the animal dies so that the Israelite may live. Life in its fullness is God's ultimate plan for Israel, indeed as Gn. 8: 21 (cf. Gn. 12: 3) says, for the whole world, and every sacrifice declares the gospel of hope, that the God who so hates sin that he contemplates destroying all mankind has through sacrifice provided a way of salvation. And these great truths were reaffirmed, not just by individuals when they needed to offer sacrifice for themselves or their families, but by the priests who day by day offered the full range of sacrifices on behalf of the whole nation (Nu. 28-29)."

G.J. Wenham (1995), pp. 84-85. Thus the OT sacrifice expresses and re-establishes the covenantal relation with God and gives the irrepressible hope built into the covenant, that however much

→

between God and humankind was ratified in the blood and while concluding a covenant, a sacrifice used to be offered and a common meal used to be eaten, and a family relation was created through

---

→ Israel sins, restoration and new life are possible if she repents. In this way the sacrifice declares the gospel of hope, for God through sacrifice provides a way of salvation. Jesus' words at the Last Supper again proclaim the same gospel of hope that his death is for our sake.

The peculiarity of the OT sacrifice is that it has value only if it is followed by proper covenant statutes. The former cannot be the substitute for the latter. Rather it is the latter that gives meaning to the former even though the sacrificial system can function for some time for the rectification of the covenant violations. The prophets' criticism of the sacrificial system has to be understood in this perspective and not as against the system itself. Just as the efficacy of Vedic sacrifice became the object of harsh criticism by the illuminated Upaniṣadic sages, so too, the value of OT sacrifice became the object of criticism by the prophets at the time of moral and religious degradation. If for the Upaniṣadic scholars knowledge became more important than sacrifice, for the OT prophets the right way of life according to the covenant principles became the necessary condition for the divine acceptance of any sacrifice. This position was misunderstood and it is wrong to hold that the prophets are against the sacrificial system. The scholars who do consider the prophets as against the sacrifice see the moral fellowship between God and humans as the basis of Israelite religion and consider the sacrifice as irrelevant. A recent study of the sacrifice in the Prophets by E.C. Lucas show that such a view was criticised from the late 1930s onwards and in the 1960s Von Rad categorically denied such a view by saying: "We have also abandoned the whole idea of a religion of the prophets as a religion of the spirit opposed to the cultic religion of the priests." E.C. Lucas (1995), p. 59. See also G. von Rad (1965), vol. 2, p. 4. Thus, the prophets are not against the sacrifice or cult but against the dissociation of the cult from life, that is, from the ethical aspect. Where the cult was taken as sufficient without the practice of justice, mercy and a right way of life, the prophets like Hosea, Jeremiah, Amos, Isaiah, and the Psalmists came forward to →

all these.[42] Jesus in his Last Supper uses the OT sacrificial terminology of the covenant and combines all these three elements, the blood of the covenant, the offering of his life on the cross as covenant sacrifice, and the meal as the common meal which used to be held after ratifying the covenant, and the creation of a family tie with his blood.[43] The covenant sacrifice, therefore, brought communion with God and the participants,[44] and among the participants themselves. Jesus by giving his blood to be drunk wanted to establish this new covenant with humanity. His blood becomes the blood of the covenant that creates a new blood relationship with God.

Usually the blood was not allowed to be drunk (Dt 12: 23), because life was in the blood and it belonged to God alone but this blood of the new covenant is to be drunk because it is the covenant which would be written in the heart of people according to the prophecy of Jeremiah (31: 31-34) and the subsequent breaking of it will not bring death or exile but forgiveness. R. de Zan sees in Jesus' invitation to drink his blood an invitation to direct involvement in the acceptance of the salvation.[45] But

---

→ denounce such practices saying that God did not want sacrifice but a right way of life (Hos 6.6 = Mt 9: 13; 12: 7; Jer 22: 16-17; 2: 21-23; Amos 5: 22-25; Is 1: 10-13; I Sam 15: 22; Ps 40: 7; 50: 8-13; 51: 18; 69: 31-32). Hence the prophets should not be taken to mean as against the ritual sacrifice but against the dissociation of the ritual from the practice of justice, love and mercy. For more details see E.C. Lucas (1995), pp. 59-74.

42. Gen 31: 46, 54; 26: 28-31; Josh 9: 14; 2 Sam 8: 20.

43. See B. Cooke (1960), p. 26.

44. There are also attempts to show the relation of the Eucharist to the communion sacrifice of the OT, especially to that of *zebah todah*. According to Hermut Gese, the Lord's Supper was a *todah* meal. But such a relation can be attributed more to the origin of the Eucharistic prayers than to the Eucharistic meal.

45. R. de Zan (1991), p. 586.

according to B. Cooke, the sharing of the blood meant the constitution of a common brotherhood and the sharing of his mission.[46] He writes: ". . . His act of sharing this blood means that He is sharing His soul, His spirit, that He is establishing a brotherhood based upon community of intention."[47] These two views need not be seen as opposing ones, but complementary. For the acceptance of the blood of Jesus involves both the acceptance of his mission of redeemer and the gift of salvation itself. The blood of Christ, thus, means on the one hand Jesus' total gift to us and drinking it means the acceptance of this gift. All those who accept this gift enter into a new relationship with him and participate in his mission.

Jesus' blood *is not simply the blood of the covenant, but the blood of the new covenant* (Paul and Luke). It is here that the words take a new meaning. Paul in his letter to the Galatians says that the Old Testament covenant could only make slaves (4: 22-31) for it was based on law and given human fragility humans were not in a position to observe it without failure. The old covenant, therefore, created fear in front of God and never trust and love, for humans were always at fault with God. But Jesus in his sacrificial death on the cross, makes a new and everlasting covenant which is not based on law but on love. This covenant is not written on the tables of rock but on the hearts, and it may be for this reason that the blood which was forbidden to be drunk has to be drunk here. And our relationship depends not on our ability to observe the law without failure, but on his love and mercy. In the new covenant we approach God not as slaves or as criminals in front of a cruel judge but like a son or a daughter in front of a loving and forgiving father.

---

46. B. Cooke (1960), pp. 27-28.

47. Ibid., p. 28.

JESUS' BLOOD AS BLOOD OF THE NEW COVENANT FOR THE FORGIVENESS OF SINS

The phrase "my blood of the new covenant for the remission of sins" (Mt 26: 28) makes obscure the value of Jesus' blood as blood of the covenant. For the covenant blood was not initially given any expiatory character,[48] but according to Daly it later took an

---

48. The expiatory role of the sacrificial blood in the OT is closely related to its vision of sacrifice as the means to remove the sin and impurity acquired by the breaking of a covenantal relationship with God. For God has given it as the means to overcome the disorder created in the community with the breaking of the covenantal relationship. From this the OT sacrifice gets the role of removing the impurity from the life of the individual and the nation as a whole. Such an expiatory role of the sacrifice is related to the OT conception of God and holiness. God is holy and impurity is incompatible with holiness. If God has to dwell in the Tabernacle at the centre of the camp holiness is a necessity (Ex 25: 8); just as God is holy, so too, Israel has to be holy (Lev 11: 45; 19: 2; 20: 7), and when this holiness is destroyed, the sacrifice is given as a means to re-establish it so that the world order or the equilibrium may not be affected.

    According to Jenson:

    > "sacrifice can initiate a state of affairs (e.g. priestly status, Lev 8-9), it can correct a state of affairs (e.g. sin, impurity), and it can maintain and strengthen a relationship (the peace offering). It can be argued that the central concern of the priestly writings is the creation, maintenance and restoration of an ordered world. The concern with purity and impurity is in part a concern for maintaining boundaries which must not be transgressed. Otherwise, there will be descent into chaos, disaster and death. From this perspective, sacrifice has a crucial role in maintaining order and restoring the equilibrium when that order is disturbed. Both sin and impurity can be understood as generating disorder, a broad category which can apply to personal and the impersonal, the unavoidable and the deliberate, the individual and corporate."
    >
    > —P.P. Jenson (1995), p. 32.

    Jesus' blood here re-establishes the covenantal relation with God and such a relation will never be broken from God's part because it is the everlasting new covenant.

atoning character.[49] He holds that the phrase "my blood of the new covenant" alludes directly to the Mosaic covenant sacrifice of Ex 24: 8 which seems to have been interpreted at that time (e.g. of the targums) as also having an atoning significance."[50]

This forgiveness of sins in Jesus' death should not be taken to mean that it wiped away the wrath of God. Shedding of blood is an indispensable factor in any covenant and in the remission of sins, because without blood no covenant could be ratified and no remission of sins could be obtained. In the Leviticus we read: "For the life of the flesh is in the blood; and I have given it for you upon the altar to make atonement for your souls; for it is the blood that makes atonement, by reason of the life" (17: 11). For this reason the Rabbinic tradition held that there was no reconciliation without blood,[51] and the letter to the Hebrews will go to the extent of saying that without the shedding of blood there is no forgiveness of sins (9.22).[52] Therefore, the shedding of blood becomes necessary for the forgiveness of sins. R. de Zan

---

49. R. Daly (1981), p. 25.

50. Ibid.

51. C. Giraudo (1989b), pp. 97-98; R. de Zan (1991), p. 584.

52. Jesus' understanding of his death as an atoning sacrifice was soon taken up by the NT writers. Right from the early Church the Christian faith and theology were concerned not just with Jesus' death but with his death *for us* (1C or 15: 3-4). Jesus' death *for us*, therefore, became the centre of the Christian Gospel and proclamation. Among the NT writers Paul is the one who developed this theme in detail.

    In Romans 3: 24b-25 we find a clause which speaks of Jesus' death in terms of expiation. It says: "Christ Jesus, whom God put forward as an expiation by his blood." The phrase *hilasterion* (propitiation/expiation) *en to(i) aimati* (by his blood) gives an explicit sacrificial vision of Jesus' death. According to Dunn, the word *hilasterion* is used several times in the LXX for the lid of the ark, the mercy seat and therefore it should be understood as expiation and not as propitiation. J.D.G. Dunn (1991), p. 41. He →

argues that sin weakens the life, and blood which is life comes to

---

→ argues further saying that in Rom 3: 25 God is presented as the agent who brings about the expiation. Ibid. Therefore, Christ's death as sacrifice cannot be taken to mean an expiation paid to an angry God, for it is God who expiates the sins of the world in the blood of his beloved Son.

In another text Paul says: "For God has done what the law, weakened by the flesh, could not do; sending his own Son in the likeness of sinful flesh and for sin, he condemned sin in the flesh" (Rm 8: 3). The words "for sin" can mean also sinful offering. The RSV Bible adds a footnote to the above-mentioned words as indicating "sin offering." Dunn considers the New English Bible translation of the phrase *peri hamartias* as a sacrifice for sin as more correct and he argues that such a translation is justified because *peri hamartias* is regularly used in LXX to translate the Hebrew *hatta'th* (sin offering e.g. Lev 5: 6-7, 11; 16: 3, 5, 9; Num 6: 16; 7: 16; 2Cor 29: 23-24; Neh 10: 33; Ezek 42: 13; 43: 19) Ibid., p. 42. Again in 2Cor 5.21 Paul says: "For our sake he made him to be sin who knew no sin, so that in him we might become the righteousness of God." Here again Christ is the unblemished victim and again it is God who makes Jesus to expiate our sins. See also S. Lyonnet and L. Sabourin (1970), pp. 245-61.

However, those who start the discussion of the atoning character of the death of Jesus from the Letter to the Hebrews come to a different conclusion. Chester in one of his studies argues that the New Testament presentation of Jesus' death as atonement sacrifice should be taken in its Jewish religious background and the early Christian historical situation. For, according to Chester, the writer of the Hebrews was concerned with the immediate historical and the religious situation of his community. He discusses the themes such as priesthood and cult in a view to interpret Christ's death as the atoning sacrifice thereby mainly to solve the "urgent and the threatening issues" which arose in his community. For in Israel the temple cult was seen as the only means of attaining atonement for sins and the Aaronic priesthood as directly mediating the divine rule and thus the status of the temple and role of the Aaronic priesthood created problems for the Jewish Christians. A.N. Chester (1991), pp. 57-59. To solve such problems the author of the Hebrews

meet the weakness of life due to sin.[53] As a result "that which expiates is not therefore the death of a victim, but the "life" obtained through the death, given the fact that the blood cannot be obtained without an immolation or a killing."[54] The New Testament writers then associated to this vision of immolation-sacrifice the idea of vicariousness following Jesus' allusion to the suffering servant (Is 53) in his words over the chalice as the blood "shed for many" (Mk 14: 24; Mt 26: 28).[55]

The expiatory value of the blood of Jesus is intimately related to Jesus' own words at the Last Supper. But P. Fiedler does not accept the atoning value of Jesus' death on the ground that his teaching of the Kingdom of God is incompatible with the concept of his atoning sacrificial death.[56] Antwi tries to approach the

---

→ made recourse to the Jewish concept of atonement and demonstrated Jesus' death as the perfect sacrifice that obtained once and for all the atonement for all humanity. Jesus' priesthood and his sacrifice are termed as superior to the Jewish priesthood and sacrifice. But the problem is whether the superiority of Christ's sacrifice and his priesthood make invalid the sacrificial language in Christianity. This cannot be so because the NT writings use such language not only to express the soteriological aspect of Jesus' death for us, but also to express the celebration of the Eucharist.

53. R. de Zan (1991), p. 585.

54. N. Füglister (1976), p. 90.

55. J. Jeremias (1987), pp. 225-31. However, according to A. Vanhoye, the blood of Jesus can also mean his immense generosity. In this case the blood of Christ means Jesus' immense love for God and for us. His death is then the supreme testimony of his love. For Jesus said: "Greater love has no man than this, that a man lay down his life for his friends" (Jn 15: 13). Jesus' death therefore reveals not only his love for us but also God's love for us. A. Vanhoye (1992), p. 128.

56. P. Fiedler (1974), pp. 1440-49. But according to R. Pesch the atoning death of Jesus does not conflict with his preaching. R. Pesch (1977), p. 75.

question from a different point of view, i.e. by examining Jesus' own attitude to the sacrificial cult as an institution for atonement.[57] Whatever the case may be, Jesus' words at the Last Supper clearly demonstrates that his blood has an expiatory character, for it is shed for the remission of sins and for the redemption of humankind.

If Jesus' words over the cup were an expression of his own understanding of his sacrificial death, then by giving the cup to the disciples Jesus wanted to anticipate the effects of his sacrificial death, that is the forgiveness of sins. Only in this way can we understand his words over the cup and his invitation to drink from it. Max Thurian too has a similar view when he writes:

---

57. D.J. Antwi (1991), p. 18. Jesus' respect for the sacrificial system is clear in his words after healing the leper. In Mark 1: 44 we read: "See that you say nothing to any one; but go, show yourself to the priest, and offer for your cleansing what Moses commanded, for a proof to the people." The Greek has instead of "for a proof to the people," "for a proof to them." Contrary to Lohmeyer who considers this text not as a recognition from the part of Jesus respect for the sacrificial system but as a picture of conflict between the healing power of Jesus and the priestly sacrificial system, Antwi considers this phrase as decisive for Jesus' intention because in every instance the phrase occurs in the Gospels, it relates to the mission and message of Jesus. Another passage which Antwi shows as a proof for Jesus' respect for the sacrificial system is Matthew 5: 23-24 which reads: "So if you are offering your gift at the altar, and there remember that your brother has something against you, leave your gift there before the altar and go; first be reconciled to your brother, and then come and offer your gift." Here we find that Jesus considers that a proper relationship with one's brother an absolutely necessary part of any proper relationship with God, and a sacrifice without reconciliation with the brother is discouraged. Hence this should not be taken to mean the reconciliation is greater than sacrifice, but a proper relationship with one's brother is essential for effective cultic worship. Ibid., pp. 19-20.

> The Last Supper conveyed in advance the effects of the new covenant to the disciples: unity with God regained in the pardon and remission of sins.[58]

And this effect which was revealed to the disciples in the Last Supper is given to us in the Eucharist. For

> The Eucharist conveys the same effects of the new covenant to us at the present day: we are renewed in the union with God, who looks upon the blood of the covenant presented by us to Him and pardons our fault, remembering our offences no more.[59]

In the Last Supper Jesus anticipated to the disciples the effects of his sacrificial death, i.e. the forgiveness of sins, and to us also he gives the same effect in his Body and Blood, for his blood is the blood of the covenant shed for the forgiveness of sins. As Max Thurian writes,

> The new covenant with God, reconciliation and union, these are the fruits of the remission of sins through the blood shed on the cross, the sacrament of which was distributed to the disciples at the Last Supper. The Eucharist, since it is the sacrament of the sacrifice of the cross, renews us in the covenant with God, in reconciliation and the union with the Father, through the blood of Christ therein conveyed for the remission of sin. The cross alone *has established* the new covenant with God by the blood of Christ shed for the remission of sins, but the Eucharist at the present day *confirms* us in that covenant and re-establishes us in union with God by securing the remission of sins for us now.[60]

Thus the words of Jesus over the bread and wine at the Last Supper indicate the sacrificial and the sacramental character of it. And the sacrifice foreseen through the sacrament is again dependent on this understanding of Jesus' blood as blood of the new covenant for the remission of sins. In John we can find a

---

58. M. Thurian (1961), p. 56.
59. Ibid.
60. Ibid., p. 56.

widening of this sacrificial and sacramental significance of Jesus' flesh, because it is given for the life of world. This aspect we will see below.

"The Bread which I Shall Give for the Life of the World is My Flesh" —Jn 6: 51c

Even though John does not narrate the entire context of the institution of the Eucharist[61] at the Last Supper, the scholars like J. Jeremias[62] and G. Segalla[63] consider John 6: 51c "The bread which I shall give for the life of the world is my flesh" as the earliest formula of the consecration. Reymond E. Brown, too, considers the above-mentioned verse as the Johannine form of the words of institution.[64] The fact that J. Jeremias treats this verse as equivalent to the Pauline and Synoptic Jesus' words over the bread shows that it can be seen as the Johannine words of institution,[65]

---

61. We limit ourselves to pointing at the sacrificial and the sacramental dimensions of John 6. For a detailed study on it see G. Segalla (1976), pp. 9-114; R.E. Brown (1966), pp. 231-303. R. Schnackenburg (1977), pp. 25-159. According to J.M. Perry, John's community celebrated the Eucharist merely as the remembrance of the resurrection without the mention of the passion narrative. It was only at a later stage when the Jews were sent off the Temple that they started mentioning the passion narrative. See J.M. Perry (1993), pp. 22-35. B. Chilton, in an attempt to develop a different perspective on the origin of the Eucharist, adopts a similar view of the existence of the Eucharist without reference to the passion of our Lord when he writes that the Eucharist as mentioned in the Didaché and in the Liturgy of Serapion came from Jesus' fellowship at meals without connection to his death. See B. Chilton (1994), p. 3. But we do not know how reliable these hypotheses are because the unity of the death and resurrection formed the centre of the Apostolic Church's preaching and worship.
62. See the tables in J. Jeremias (1987), pp. 165, 199.
63. G. Segalla (1999), p. 259; G. Segalla (1976), pp. 99-100.
64. R.E. Brown (1966), p. 285.
65. J. Jeremias (1987), pp. 165, 199.

and the starting point for the analysis of Jesus' actions and words at the Last Supper. Still further, the verse alludes to the sacrificial death of Jesus and has to be understood in line with his crucifixion. For according to Craig R. Koester,

> The use of the future tense "I shall give" points to the act of self-giving that Jesus would perform on the cross. The comment that his gift would be given "for" (*hypèr*) the life of the world alludes to its sacrificial character, as do later references to the good shepherd laying down his life "for" the sheep and Jesus dying "for" the people. — 10: 11, 15; 11: 50[66]

C.K. Barrett goes even to the extent of saying that John is more interested in the Eucharist than the Synoptic Gospels because his programme is to identify Jesus himself with the bread to root it in the sacramental fact of the incarnation.[67] This sacrificial and the sacramental character of the Johannine Eucharistic theology, deeply rooted in the incarnation[68] and the redemption, gives us the starting points of our study to discover the cosmic dimension of the Eucharist.

Any study on the Eucharistic words of Jesus in John (6) needs to be done in the perspective of the whole chapter, especially against the background of the multiplication of the loaves (Jn 6: 1-15).[69] This is a must because the whole chapter of John (6) puts the Eucharistic bread and wine in relation to the incarnation and the redemption. Thus we begin our analysis of the Last Supper as the sacrament of the sacrifice of cross starting from John's Eucharistic treatment of the multiplication of the loaves and the Eucharistic words of Jesus, the bread of life descended from heaven for the life of the world.

---

66. C.R. Koester (1995), p. 98. See also X. Léon-Dufour (1987), pp. 266-72.
67. C.K. Barret (1960), p. 42; see also B. Chilton (1994), p. 137.
68. For a detailed study on the incarnation in the prologue of John see G. Segalla (1997), pp. 14-47.
69. G. Segalla (1999), p. 257.

The fact that the majority of the exegetes[70] consider the Eucharistic character of the multiplication of the loaves shows that in John the multiplication of the bread is also the anticipation of the Eucharistic bread and it has an Eucharistic connotation. Jesus' actions over the bread and wine at the Last Supper are identical to his actions over the loaves and the fish. He takes the loaves, gives thanks, breaks them and gives them to the disciples. Breaking the bread and asking the disciples to gather the parts left over that nothing may be perished (Jn 6: 13) leads to an Eucharistic interpretation of the multiplication of the loaves.[71] Again in John the multiplication of the bread takes place not to remove the hunger of the people as the Synoptics tell us but essentially to reveal Jesus.[72] Thus in John, more than the Synoptics, the multiplication of the loaves is an anticipation of the Eucharistic bread and action of Jesus at the Last Supper.

But the multiplication of the loaves which was meant to reveal Jesus was not properly understood by the people. They wanted to take him by force and make him king. From this context arises Jesus' further clarification of himself as the bread of life descended from heaven for the life of the world. There exist two types of bread, the one which perishes and the other which does not perish (Jn 6: 27). The people search for Jesus not because they desire to have this bread of eternal life[73] but because they want the bread

---

70. The scholars are divided into two groups about the Eucharistic character of the multiplication of the loaves in Jn 6: 1-15. However, the majority of the scholars do accept that the multiplication of the loaves not only in John but also in the Synoptics have an Eucharistic meaning. For more details see S.-A. Panimolle (1977), pp. 73-77; G. Segalla (1976), pp. 68-77; G. Segalla (1977), pp. 32-35.
71. S.-A. Panimolle (1977), pp. 87-88.
72. G. Segalla (1976), p. 74.
73. Jesus is the bread that gives people eternal life, i.e. a relationship with God that begins in faith and continues beyond the grave into eternity. C.R. Koester (1995), p. 96.

that perishes. Here comes the revelation that Jesus is superior to Moses because he is able to give the bread that does not perish, and he is able to do this because he has come down from heaven.

In Jn (6: 51) Jesus says: "I am the living bread which came down from heaven; if any one eats of this bread, he will live for ever; and the bread which I shall give for the life of the world is my flesh." This verse puts in evidence three aspects: first, Jesus is the living bread which came down from heaven, hence his incarnation which was already announced in the preceding verse.[74] Secondly, those who eat this bread will live for ever, hence Jesus, the bread of eternal life, has to be eaten sacramentally to have the effect.[75] Thirdly, the bread which Jesus gives is his flesh for the life of the world. Here again he identifies his flesh with himself, and the role of this food is not limited to Israel but to the world.[76] Hence there is a widening of the mission of Jesus to the world. This verse, therefore, reassumes the Johannine Eucharistic theology in relation to the mystery of incarnation, his sacrificial death for the life of the world, the sacramental eating of his body, and the new covenant in such sacramental eating.

This last aspect of covenant is very clear in Jn (6: 56) where Jesus says: "He who eats my flesh and drinks my blood abides in me, and I in him." According to G. Segalla, the background to

---

74. Already the preceding verse has mentioned this theme: "This is the bread which comes down from heaven, that a man may eat of it and not die" (Jn 6: 50).

75. But those who do not accept the sacramental character of the Johannine narration do not accept eating the body of Jesus and drinking the blood as an invitation to sacramental communion. They consider the eating as equivalent to believing, and such a theory impoverishes the sacramental theology of the Gospel of John. C.R. Koester, for example, does not give any sacramental reading of John and considers the faith as synonym of eating. See C.R. Koester (1995), pp. 260, 262.

76. Jn 6: 33. See also Ibid., p. 96.

understand the Eucharistic discourse in John (6) is the new covenant, for John (6: 56) is a *Christological interiorization of the formula of covenant, "I will be your God and you will be my people."*[77] Just as there is a mutual immanence of Jesus and the Father, so too, those who receive his body and drink his blood will have a mutual immanence which will grant them eternal life. In this sense in John the sacrifice of Christ appears more mystic, and only at a second moment does it reveal its sacrificial theme.

The phrase "my flesh for the life of the world" recalls the mystery of incarnation that is at the centre of the prologue (Jn 1: 14a) "And the Word made flesh and lived among us."[78] The flesh, therefore, stands for the person of Jesus, in his human condition of the incarnate Word. The future giving directs to the gift of the Eucharist in the death and resurrection of Jesus.[79] Historically it is the event of death and resurrection that makes possible his return into the heavenly glory and the giving of his flesh, the source of immortality. That which was promised as a future gift takes place in the Last Supper when Jesus by taking the bread and chalice identifies himself with the bread and the content of the chalice.

The whole chapter 6 of John, thus, has to be read in the Christological-Eucharistic perspectives,[80] i.e. in close relation to the incarnation and the redemption, in the descending and ascending dimensions. The Eucharistic bread and wine are nothing other than the flesh and blood of Jesus who descended from heaven to give life not merely to Israel as the *manna* of the desert, but to the world. Unlike in the Synoptics, in John the world, the cosmos, is the object of God's love even though it is also the entity that

77. G. Segalla (1976), pp. 59-60, 102; G. Segalla (1999), pp. 261-63.
78. Ibid., p. 99.
79. Ibid.
80. This is the perspective which G. Segalla follows in his book, G. Segalla (1976), pp. 68-115.

hates God.[81] His flesh is given for (*hypèr*) the life of the world, and this takes place at his sacrificial death on the cross. Thus, in John (6) we can find a theology of Eucharist which is closely related to the mystery of incarnation, redemption and the life of the cosmos.

Jesus' Command "do this in Memory of me" and the Eucharist as the Memorial of the "Once and for all" Sacrificial Self-giving Death of Jesus

The inseparable sacrificial and sacramental characters of the Last Supper which we analysed above call us to understand the Eucharist in the same perspectives, i.e. not in separation from the sacrifice of the cross. And a correct understanding of the sacramental character of the sacrifice of Christ is a must to avoid further difficulties and to rediscover the cosmic dimension of the Eucharist. For the sacrificial character of the Eucharist which has been the object of heated discussion between Catholics and Protestants from the sixteenth century onwards has its root in the failure to understand the sacramental character of the memorial of Jesus' sacrificial death.[82] Unlike the Catholics, the Protestants did not stress the sacramental aspect of the Eucharist and hence their position was less cosmic. The Catholic position which stresses the sacramental aspect of the sacrifice of Christ is more helpful in rediscovering the cosmic dimension of the Eucharist.

---

81. C.R. Koester (1995), p. 249.

82. Here we do not intend to go into any detailed study on the Catholic and Protestant controversies on the Eucharistic sacrifice and practice in the middle ages. Such a study would require a detailed analysis of all the texts of the Council and the counterattacks. We limit ourselves in concentrating on a few points which in our opinion is the way to come out of the dead end. For a detailed study on the Eucharistic sacrifice in the Council of Trent and in the middle ages, see D.N. Power (1987), pp. 27-133; L.-M. Chauvet (1998), pp. 20-51; P.J. Fitzpatrick (1991), pp. 129-53; J.F. McHugh (1991), pp. 157-80.

On the one hand, the Catholics failed to explain clearly this sacramental character of the Eucharist and that it was a representation of "the once and for all" sacrifice of Christ on the cross;[83] and on the other hand the Protestants failed to grasp the sacramental character of the Eucharistic sacrifice, the memorial of "the once and for all" sacrifice of Christ. In the words of J.M.R. Tillard, "the concept of *memorial* allows us to bring together two views of the "eucharistic sacrifice" which would formerly have been thought irreconcilable."[84] It is this sacramental aspect of the sacrifice of Christ that helps us to rediscover the cosmic dimension of the Eucharist which we will see in detail in the next chapter but here we limit ourselves to the discussion of the relation between the sacrifice of the cross and the Eucharist.

THE UNIQUE SACRIFICE OF THE CROSS AND THE SACRIFICE OF THE EUCHARIST

The sacrificial nature of the Eucharist can be rightly understood only by clarifying the relation between the historical sacrifice of Jesus on the cross, accomplished once and for all, and its ritual commemoration in the Eucharist. This ritual commemoration is primarily a sacrament which the Protestants failed to understand in the controversy against the Catholic position on the Eucharist as sacrifice. Only by rediscovering the sacramental aspect of the ritual memorial of "the once and for all sacrifice of Christ" are we able to overcome the conflict between the Catholics and the Protestants from the time of the Protestant reformation. We should not deny either the centrality of the sacrifice of Christ, or the sacrificial nature of the Eucharist.

Both Catholics and Protestants seem to have overlooked the sacramental nature of the ritual memorial of the sacrifice of Christ in their attempt to safeguard the sacrificial character on the one

---

83. See Hb 7: 27; 9: 12; and 10: 10.

84. J.M.R. Tillard (1981), p. 306.

hand and the uniqueness of the sacrifice of Christ on the other. According to J.M.R. Tillard,

> In the West two interpretations of the words "Do this in memory of me" came up against each other, sometimes in a polemical way. Both interpretations indeed agreed in general terms in recognizing in the Lord's command the will that his unique Sacrifice should be *represented* in the Church. But the Roman Catholic tradition put the main emphasis on *"represent,"* in the sense "present *again*," "renew," "repeat." . . . In opposition to this, the traditions which sprang from the Reformation placed their chief emphasis on the verb "represent" or "present," vigorously rejecting any allusion to a re, to an again, to any addition to the sacrificial value of the Cross.[85]

From this it is clear that even though both Catholics and Protestants accepted the uniqueness of the historical sacrifice on the cross, they did not have the same concept with regard to its ritual commemoration, for they overlooked the sacramental aspect of it. The Catholic tradition emphasized that the sacrifice of the Mass was the representation or the renewal of the sacrifice of the cross and such an emphasis gave an impression that something was added on to the historical sacrifice of the cross.[86] But the Protestants laid the emphasis on the fact that the Mass not being the representation or renewal of the sacrifice of the cross did not have any value in addition to that of the cross. The sacrifice of the cross was sufficient and nothing must be added to obscure its efficacy.[87] Here we can find that both Catholics and Protestants put aside the question of the sacramental characters of the Mass and they went on to stress the efficacy or the non-efficacy of Mass based on its sacrificial or non-sacrificial nature.

But according to Gerken, the problem between the Catholics and the Protestants lies in another aspect, that is, the Council of

85. Ibid.

86. Ibid.

87. Ibid.

Trent did not make any distinction between the actual presence and the commemorative presence of the death of Christ.[88] The Council was unaware of the real symbol and said that symbol was inadequate to express the Eucharist as sacrifice.[89] As a result the Council went on presenting the Eucharistic sacrifice as the representation or renewal of the sacrifice of the cross and based the nature of the Eucharistic sacrifice in the representation or renewal of the sacrifice of the cross. The Eucharist is a sacrifice because in it Christ is immolated in unbloody manner,[90] and the Council based the sacrificial character of the Mass on the offering of body and blood of Christ under the species of bread and wine.[91]

The Council, then, had to defend itself against the Protestant reformers' attack[92] on the celebration of the Mass for the remission of the sins of the dead which had become a regular practice from the time of St. Augustine.[93] The Eucharist is the sacrifice for the remission of sins because in it the same Christ who was immolated in a bloody manner on the cross is immolated again in an unbloody manner.[94] Such a view without doubt gave the impression that the Eucharist was a new sacrifice in addition to that of the cross, a view which according to the Protestants could not be held without questioning the centrality of the sacrifice of the cross. It is here, in my opinion, that the problem lies. This widened the misunderstanding between Catholics and Protestants on the sacrificial nature of the Eucharist.

Now both Catholics and Protestants accept that there is only one historical, unrepeatable sacrifice, offered once and for all by

88. A. Gerken (1977), p. 159.

89. Ibid., p. 164.

90. C. Giraudo (1989b), pp. 520-76.

91. A. Gerken (1977), p. 160.

92. See P.J. Fitzpatrick (1991), pp. 129-53.

93. See G. Bonner (1991), pp. 104-11.

94. See A. Gerken (1977), p. 158; C. Giraudo (1989b), pp. 573-76.

Christ and accepted once and for all by the Father. And the Eucharistic sacrifice does not obscure the efficacy of the sacrifice of the cross, rather it points to "the once and for all sacrifice of the cross." The problem can be solved if we understand the once and for all sacrifice not in a static sense but in a dynamic sense as Max Thurian suggests,

> The term "once for all" should not therefore be understood to have a static meaning relating only to the past. The word rather signifies the absolute, complete and everlasting character of Christ's sacrifice; it does not imply a unique moment with no effects under different modes which recall it and make it present.[95]

He further clarifies the perpetual nature of the sacrifice of Christ in heaven for our sake till the *parousia*:

> The sacrifice of the cross, qualified in this way, appears as an act which is unique, not in the sense that it will not appear again in any form but as the origin and source of a continual work which is the remission in Christ of the sins of all those who approach God through Him. The sacrifice of the cross is thus extended in the heavenly intercession of Christ until the Parousia. The uniqueness of Christ's sacrifice does not imply an isolated act in past history but an historical act with a continuing efficacy which is extended in the intercession of the Son of God: the unique sacrifice of Christ on the cross is an everlasting sacrifice which gathers together all the sacrifices, prayers and deeds of the people of God in the unity of His present and living intercession.[96]

The singleness of the sacrifice of Christ, thus, depends not much on the non-repeatable character of it but on the perpetual value of it. Hence the historically once and for all character of the sacrifice of Christ does not make invalid the sacrifice of the Mass, for the same Christ makes present the effects of his sacrificial death for

---

95. M. Thurian (1961), p. 8.

96. Ibid., p. 9.

the remission of sins. This surely takes place through the sacrament of the sacrifice of Christ.

In this sacrament of the sacrifice of Christ the presence of the same Christ who offered himself to the Father on the cross for the sake of the humanity, giving himself in the form of the Eucharistic bread and wine to the sinful community, has become one of the points on which some of the contemporary theologians base the sacrificial character of the Eucharist without denying the centrality of "the once and for all sacrifice of Christ." Quarello seems to move in this line of thought when he holds more than once:

> Just as Christ gives himself on the Cross, offering himself to his crucifier so, too, in every Mass Christ who is present gives himself to the members of his Church, who appears in the course of the history contaminated by sin. It is the same gift, under different forms.[97]

He writes again,

> The Eucharistic sacrifice perpetuates the sacrifice of the Cross in the sense that the same Christ sacramentally present on the altar offers himself sacramentally to his Church, in which there still exists the opposition of the sin, already present in the sacrifice of the Cross. The sacrificial aspect of the offering of Christ in the Church may base itself on the fact that his gift is a gift that directly concerns men still sinners as it were, even if to some extent different from that condemned him to death on the Cross. The sacrifice of the Cross and of the Eucharist is always a gift of the same Offerer to the sinful men, who want to be presented to the Father at the end of time "without spot or wrinkle." — Eph 5: 27[98]

Thus, it is the same Christ who offered himself on the cross and who offers himself to us in the Eucharistic sacrifice, and in this regard there cannot be two sacrifices, but one.

---

97. E. Quarello (1970), pp. 108-89.

98 Ibid., p. 121.

C. Vagaggini considers the perpetual nature of the sacrifice of Christ from another point of view, that is, from the formal and the material aspects. By the formal aspect he means the interior disposition and by the material aspect he means the exterior actualization of it. In Christ even now this formal aspect remains, for he writes,

> The formal aspect of that sacrifice which constituted its soul by giving to the external acts the proper value of sacrifice of an infinite value existed not only before the Calvary, but from the first instance of the incarnation, and with the death of Christ it continues in eternity, in heaven, in extension of that which was on the earth.[99]

The difference, for him, is in the material and the formal aspect, and both these elements are essential to the sacrament as well. The Eucharist as the sacrament of the sacrifice of the cross makes sacramentally present Christ who is now in heaven with the same disposition of his soul offered uninterruptedly to God the Father.[100] In this case the sacrifice becomes the external expression of the internal act. This position seems to be too spiritualistic and does not base the sacrificial nature of the Eucharist on the sacramental character of it but on the heavenly sacrifice of Christ.

THE EUCHARIST AS THE VISIBLE SACRIFICE OF THE CHURCH

The Eucharist as the sacrament of the sacrifice of Christ cannot be reduced to a spiritual sacrifice for it is a ritual commemoration. Those who consider the inner attitude of obedience and self-surrender as superior to the exterior dimension of its real actualization tend to devaluate the place of the ritual and sacrifice

---

99. C. Vagaggini (1969), p. 184.

100. Ibid., pp. 186-87. Such a view does not take into serious consideration the sacramental character of the sacrifice and gives an impression that the author reduces the sacrifice to an internal disposition. See also C. Vagaggini (1958), pp. 204-09.

in the life of the Church.[101] Such a view is often based on the false assumption that what is important is the inner attitude and not the exterior actualization of it through the rituals. Humans as corporal beings need rituals to express their religious and cosmic dimensions.

According to Rahner and Häussling, in Christ's death on the cross we can find that both the inner attitude and the exterior actualization of it,[102] hence we should consider the latter as constituent elements and not as two accidental elements. They write:

> Christ's death as an external visible event is the constitutive sign (the real symbol) under which and in which the inner intention and attitude of Christ is carried into effect and without which it would not be what it is. It was only in this actual death that Christ's obedience until death could be what it was to be by the will of the Father. In this death Christ's interior sacrificial attitude found expression. Yet the inner attitude is not the sacrifice itself. The sacrifice as such must become visible in what happened externally, which has to be recognizably a sacrifice. For sacrifice is essentially an external, visible ritual action.[103]

Rahner and Häussling, therefore, consider the sacrifice as essentially an external, visible ritual action. The same idea is also found in the Council of Trent when it calls the Mass "the visible sacrifice."[104] Thus, for the Council the visible ritual action itself is a sacrifice. Concretely this visible action consists in the offering of the body and blood of Christ under the species of bread and

---

101. Most of the Protestant Reformers move in this line. Also the contemporary Catholic theologians like Neusch, Chauvet, Power, etc. move in this line. See A. Grillo (1998), pp. 203-43.

102. K. Rahner and A. Häussling (1968), p. 15.

103. Ibid.

104. J. Neuner and J. Dupuis (1992), pp. 1548ff.

wine.[105] But according to K. Rahner and A. Häussling this does not mean:

> that under or behind the visible ritual proceeding which is not itself a sacrifice (a mere meal, for example, or a celebration of the mysteries), something is present in a hidden way, and this is what can be called sacrifice. A correct interpretation of the doctrine of the Council of Trent regarding the *sacrificium visibile* of the Mass must maintain that the sacrificial character of the Mass is to be sought on the plane of the visible liturgical action.[106]

If the sacrificial character of the rite itself belongs to the visible elements of the rite, then as Rahner and Häussling hold, "the sacrificial character of the Mass must therefore be visible in the liturgical rite itself,"[107] and not in the mere interior attitude of Christ. As sacrifice it has to be an externally perceptible act.

It is clear that Christ does not perform any new sacrifice, and hence the Mass cannot be taken as a new sacrifice even though the same Christ who gave himself in anticipation to the disciples at the Last Supper, is giving himself to us in the Eucharist under the double elements of his body and blood. What is new with regard to the Eucharistic sacrifice in relation to the sacrifice of the cross is that it is the sacrifice of the Church, the Body of Christ. As Rahner and Häussling write:

> What is posited in the sacrifice of the Mass as a new sacrificial act repeated in each instance, lies on the side of the Church. Obedient to our Lord's anamnesis command, the Church offers in a repeated liturgical celebration the sacrificial action of the

105. A. Gerken (1977), p. 160.

106. K. Rahner and A. Häussling (1968), p. 18. On the contrary for St. Augustine every visible sacrifice is the symbol of the invisible offering (*De Civitate Dei* 10.9), for the visible sacrifice is the sacrament, the sacred sign, of the invisible sacrifice (*De Civitate Dei* 10.5). See also G. Bonner (1991), pp. 102 and 106; A. Grillo (1998), pp. 203-43.

107. K. Rahner and A. Häussling (1968), p. 20.

> Mass. To the extent (but only to the extent) that this action is a visible sign, it is on each occasion the Church's own new celebration of the sacrifice.[108]

In this the double elements of the Mass, which like in every sacrament, prevent it from becoming a new sacrifice become clear. For:

> One lies on the place of liturgical rite which is performed by the Church in the name and the command of Christ. As such it constitutes a sacrifice precisely on this visible level and shows forth the sacrifice of the Cross. The other aspect lies on the plane of what is announced and made really present in this visible liturgical sacrificial rite. But what is rendered present is simply and solely the one sacrificial action of Christ, the sacrifice of the Cross. It is not some action distinct from this performed by the glorified Lord at the right hand of the Father.[109]

Thus, the sacrificial character of the Mass consists in the visible liturgical rite and as visible liturgical rite it is the act of the Church. Through the efforts of A. Vonier,[110] O. Casel,[111] K. Rahner and A. Häussling,[112] etc. the disputed sacrificial character of the Eucharist has become closer and closer in recent years through the discovery of its sacramental character.

The *unity between the sacrament and the sacrifice* shows that the sacrificial character of the Eucharist had to be sought in the visible aspect of the sacrament and not in any invisible offering of Christ by the Church under the forms of bread and wine. It is not correct to make a sharp distinction between the sacramental and the sacrificial aspects of the Eucharist as A. Piolanti has done.[113] For

---

108. Ibid., p. 26.
109. Ibid., p. 28.
110. A. Vonier (1955), pp. 62-126.
111. O. Casel (1999), pp. 19-27.
112. K. Rahner and A. Häussling (1968), pp. 13-33.
113. A. Piolanti (1983), pp. 323-38.

him the Eucharist as sacrifice is directed towards God to render homage and thanks for the creation, redemption and to pray for the forgiveness of sins, and the Eucharist as a sacrament is oriented towards humans, to transmit to them the fruits of the sacrifice.[114]

The sacrament of the Eucharist has both ascending and descending dimensions, for the sacrament is not only oriented towards humans so that they may get the effects of sacrifice, but also as a rite it is also an action of Christ and the Church to God the Father. As an action to God it cannot be reduced to a descending dimension, it has also an ascending dimension, for it is through it that the Church offers herself to God. Thus, it may be more correct to hold that the Eucharist being the action of Christ and his body, the Church, has a double movement, ascending and the descending. As ascending movement Christ offers himself to the Father, and the Church on her part not only through the sacramental signs of bread and wine, which are cosmic elements, offers to the Father the signs of the sacrifice of Christ, but also offers herself to the Father, together with the Head.[115]

This does not mean that the Church immolates Christ in an unbloody manner but merely makes present through the sacramental signs and Word the sacrifice of Christ, so that she may be able to offer herself to the Father. According to P.Y. Emery, the sacrifice of Christ suppresses every sacrifice from our part outside his sacrifice.[116] There is no autonomous sacrifice of the Church, for it is the Head that offers in the Body.[117] If the Church has no sacrifice outside that of Christ, then she can present to God only the sacrifice of Christ. This she does in the ritual commemoration of the death and resurrection of Jesus wherein

---

114. Ibid., p. 323.
115. E. Quarello (1970), p. 158. See also G. Bonner (1991), p. 112.
116. P.-Y. Emery (1966), p. 67. See also E. Quarello (1970), p. 166.
117. E. Quarello (1970), p. 166.

she presents before God the bread and wine, the cosmic elements. Thus, the sacrificial nature of the Eucharist has to be sought in its visible aspect and as such it has a cosmic dimension.

JESUS' COMMAND, "DO THIS IN MEMORY OF ME" AND THE SACRIFICIAL NATURE OF THE EUCHARIST

We have seen that the sacrament of the sacrifice of Christ which is celebrated in accordance with our Lord's command,[118] and is being called *sacrificium* from the time of Cyprian,[119] has become a controversial point from the time of the Protestant reformation. The recent attempt is to rediscover the sacrificial character of the Eucharist in its sacramental dimension, starting from the notion of the *memorial* itself. Scholars like Max Thurian,[120] L. Bouyer,[121] E. Quarello,[122] and J.M.R. Tillard make recourse to this term on the one hand to safeguard the centrality of the sacrifice of the cross and on the other hand to maintain the Eucharist as sacrifice.

---

118. Only in Paul and Luke we can find Jesus' command, "do this in memory of me" (I Cor 11: 23-25; Lk 22: 19). According to Max Thurian, "Its absence in Matthew and Mark is no reason for thinking that Jesus did not use it. These are liturgical formulae employed by the apostolic Church which preserved what was essential of the works of Christ. "Do this in remembrance of me" is not part of the liturgical text itself; it is a command to celebrate; it is, in liturgical parlance, a rubric, and the liturgical tradition represented by Mark and Matthew could have dispensed with it, since the regular celebration of the Eucharist was the carrying out of this command or rubric. Paul, on the other hand, concerned to give an account of the complete tradition, derived from the Lord, to the last detail, twice records the command to celebrate (I Cor 11: 24, 25), while Luke was content with a single reference (22: 19). M. Thurian (1966), p. 17.
119. G. Bonner (1991), p. 32.
120. M. Thurian (1966) and (1961).
121. L. Bouyer (1983), pp. 95-96.
122. E. Quarello (1970), p. 112; J.M.R. Tillard (1981), p. 307.

According to Tillard, the memorial helps us to transcend the old polemics[123] and to form a structural line around which all the Tridentine material can be integrated, balanced and each part set in its proper place.[124] Therefore the way to get away from the problems created by the lack of a symbolic understanding of the language of the sacrifice by the Council is a proper understanding of the memorial character of the Eucharistic sacrifice itself. The concept of memorial helps us to understand the sacrificial character of the Eucharist in the sacramental dimension of the Eucharist without putting into question the centrality of the sacrifice of the cross and without reducing the Eucharist to a subjective memorial.

In this field the contribution of Max Thurian is important for he gives a detailed analysis of the memorial from the biblical point of view and has shown that the Eucharist is the sacrifice because it is the memorial meal.[125] The Last Supper which took place in the proximity of the Passover meal, cannot be understood properly, if not in the background of the traditional liturgy of the OT,[126] and the Passover meal itself was a memorial of the liberation of Israel from Egypt.

The memorial character of the Passover meal gives a sacramental character to the Last Supper of Jesus and if Jesus' Last Supper was a Passover meal, even though there is no agreement among the scholars due to the difference in the date,[127] then we cannot overlook its sacramental character. For the Passover meal was celebrated every year in memorial of the liberation from Egypt, and such a celebration revived mystically

---

123. J.M.R. Tillard (1981), p. 307.

124. Ibid., p. 312.

125. M. Thurian (1966), pp. 7-56. See also C. Giraudo (1989b), pp. 579-81.

126. Ibid., pp. 20-26.

127. J. Jeremias (1987), pp. 15-88.

and sacramentally the events of the liberation and the exit from Egypt.[128] When the Hebrews ate such a meal they became contemporary to their ancestors and were considered to be saved with them. This is possible because in the Passover meal there takes place a type of superimposition of two ages of history, the present and the exodus from Egypt. That event became present, or better everyone became contemporary to the event.[129] In this way the words like mystery and sacrament help us to grasp how "the once and for all" historical event is made actual, operative and equally present in all times through Word and Sacrament.[130] However, if for O. Casel the ritual *anamnesis* is the ritual renewal and re-presentation of the divine act,[131] for Max Thurian it is the act given by God himself that we may become present to the divine act.

One of the meanings of memorial, according to Max Thurian, is calling God's attention through sacrifice,[132] in particular with the first fruit oblations of flour, oil and incense (Lev 2: 1-10). The memorial is that part of the sacrifice which the priests take and burn on the altar. And this memorial sacrifice proclaims the presence of God, of his faithfulness and of his works in favour of us, and is a sign toward God to remember him. It proclaims God's faithfulness and at the same time expresses a prayer to God to remember his promises.

Another aspect of the Hebrew memorial is that it not only revived liturgically the liberation from the slavery of Egypt, but also prayed to God to send the Messiah. In this way it became the sign of the eschatological liberation that was to take place on the day of the coming of the Messiah. As Max Thurian writes,

---

128. M. Thurian (1966), pp. 27-28.

129. Ibid., p. 28.

130. Ibid., p. 28-29.

131. O. Casel (1999), p. 53. See also C. Giraudo (1989b), pp. 579-81.

132. M. Thurian (1966), p. 46.

> The Jewish Passover effects the liturgical reliving of the deliverance from the Egyptian bondage, which is itself a sign of the great eschatological deliverance on the day when the Messiah shall come. So, in the paschal meal, we find a triple *anamnesis*, a triple memorial: of a past deliverance regarded as typical, of a present deliverance through the sacramental action of the paschal meal and of a coming salvation in the day of the Messiah. And, as thanks are offered for the past which has become present by the "sacrament," God is asked to accomplish His salvation by sending the Messiah. The past deliverance becomes a pledge of that which is to come, which will be perfect and definitive. Sometimes there was placed on the table a further cup for Elijah who was to precede the Messiah; the door was left ajar in order that he might not have to wait. The night of the Passover becomes the night when the Messiah is awaited, that upon which he will certainly come.[133]

Just as there is a triple *anamnesis* in the Passover meal so, too, in the Eucharistic celebration we can find a triple *anamnesis*: the memorial of the liberation from our sins by the sacrificial death of Jesus on the cross, a type of actual liberation from sins for the same Christ who liberated us from our sins is present and gives himself to us in holy communion, and the future liberation, on the day of resurrection. This is done concretely in the breaking of bread and wine. For in the words of Thurian,

> The fraction of the bread may then be taken to signify the Body of Christ *given* or *broken*. The fraction is indeed an action which represents and presents the sacrifice of the Lord, i.e. the gift of Himself to men at the Last Supper, as at each Eucharist, because of the unique gift of the cross.[134]

As Thurian writes again:

> They [some Christians] forget that the Eucharist is not a simple mental recollection or recalling of the love of God, but the

133. Ibid., p. 28.

134. M. Thurian (1961), p. 48.

> memorial of the Lord, the representation or presentation of the unique and perfect sacrifice of Christ in thanksgiving and intercession, as well as the proclamation of the death of the Lord "till he comes."[135]

Again according to Thurian,

> When it celebrates the Eucharist, the Church places on the altar the signs of the sacrifice of Christ, the bread and the wine, His Body and His Blood, as Israel placed the shewbread on the golden table as a memorial before Yahweh. The Church, when it proclaims Christ's sacrifice, accomplishes on the altar the *shewing*-forth of the sacrifice of the Son before the Father. . . .[136]

Thus, the ritual character helps us not to reduce the memorial of the death and resurrection of Jesus in a mental activity, but to consider it as the sacrifice of the Church. And according to Thurian, only in the biblical perspective of the memorial can we speak of the Eucharist as sacrifice.[137]

This ritual remembrance of his sacrificial death in the sacrament of the Eucharist should not be taken as an incentive for God to act but a recreation of a relationship. The Eucharist, then, is the ritual memorial of his sacrifice through which the participants are called to enter into a relationship with him. This is possible not through a mental activity but through a ritual. According to A.J. Gittins, the word *anamnesis* can be translated better by saying that it is the opposite of "dismember."[138] He says:

> "Remember me," in this sense, would mean "put me together again," in *relationship* with you. For remembering (*anamnesis*) is all about relationship. The *anamnesis* of the Last Supper — the act and the *remembrance* of the Last Supper — puts Jesus' sacrifice together again, not by rehearsing it or repeating it, but by an act

---

135. M. Thurian (1966), p. 114.

136. M. Thurian (1961), p. 36.

137 Ibid., p. 76.

138. A.J. Gittins (1991), p. 428.

> which "remembers" Jesus and the community, lest Jesus be forgotten because excluded from our relationships. . . .[139]

The Eucharist is, therefore, neither the re-enactment of the death of Jesus nor a mere mental remembrance of the passion and death of Jesus Christ. It is an *anamnesis in a ritual celebration through which we Christians enter into a new relationship with Jesus* who laid down his life as a loving sacrifice to the Father. When the Church in obedience to the command of the Lord celebrates the Lord's Supper and places on the altar the signs of the sacrifice of Christ, his Body and Blood, she is doing as the Israelites used to place the shewbread on the golden table as memorial before Yahweh.[140] Thus, the Eucharist being the memorial of the death and resurrection of Jesus becomes our sacrifice in which we not only plead for the benefits of the death and resurrection of Jesus for us, but also for the whole world.

The Eucharist and the Offering of Bread, Wine, Praise and Thanksgiving by the Church for herself and for the Cosmos

This heading introduces on the one hand the elements of the Eucharistic sacrifice and on the other the double functions of the Eucharist, an offering of the Body of Christ together with its Head to the Father for itself and for the cosmos.[141] The *anamnesis* of the death and resurrection of Jesus in the ritual offering of bread, wine, praise and thanksgiving, thus, form the basis of the sacrificial, sacramental and cosmic dimensions of the Eucharist. Jesus has given this memorial to the Church that she could present before the Father not only the sacrifice of the cross but also unite her

---

139. Ibid.

140. M. Thurian (1961), p. 36.

141. In this section we are slightly anticipating the central theme of our discussion of the next chapter. But we find it necessary for the fact that the offering of bread and wine by the Church as the Body of Christ in the Eucharistic sacrifice has a cosmic aspect.

self-offering to the Father with Christ her Lord. Our attempt is now to show in which way the Eucharist can be seen as the sacrifice of the Church for herself and for the cosmos.

THE OFFERING OF BREAD AND WINE AS THE CONSTITUENT PART OF THE EUCHARISTIC SACRIFICE FOR WHOLE OF CREATION

The ascending and the descending dimensions of the sacrifice and the cosmic nature of the sacrament become clear in the offering which is an integral part to the sacrifice and the Eucharist in particular. But the offering which constitutes the central aspect of sacrifice, whether material or spiritual, has become one of the controversial issues in the Catholic and Protestants reformers' understanding of the sacrifice of the Eucharist. D.N. Power, a contemporary Catholic theologian, denies this central aspect of sacrifice and the Eucharist for the fact that it is a reductionist hermeneutic that led to consider the offering as constitutive to a sacrifice.[142] He writes:

> . . . many of our difficulties, theological and cultural, spring from what can only be called a reductionist hermeneutic, whereby we blithely take it for granted that performing sacrifice means offering a gift, for whatever purpose that may be. Through this tendency to subject sacrifice to the controlling image of offering, have we in effect lost a fuller appreciation of what is signified in Christian tradition's use of this term? . . . A fuller awareness of language, of its relation to feeling, of its surplus of meaning, as well as knowledge of the complexity of the conceptual, affords a new examination of the sacrificial within Judaeo-Christian tradition, particularly in reference to its presence in eucharistic practice and doctrine. It will save us from the rather banal explanation of the Eucharist which carries us no further than the harmless observation that the Church now offers herself along with the offering of Christ.[143]

---

142. D.N. Power (1979), p. 386.

143. Ibid., pp. 386-87.

He argues again that it was the early Christian literature which wrongly identified the words *thusia* with *prosphora,* for the fact that the writers could not ignore the important place it occupied in the religious practice.[144] Nevertheless in his view the NT and the early Christian writers do not use the term *thusia* in the sense of offering but in the metaphorical or spiritual sense of "(a) the Christian life, (b) the eucharistic celebration, and (c) Christ's death."[145] He writes again:

> It is not implied, in any of the three cases, that a gift is offered to God, whether it be person, animal or thing. What is rather suggested is (a) that a life lived in obedience and faith outweighs sacrifice, (b) that because of Christ's death no sacrifices are now necessary, and the praise and thanksgiving of the redeemed people is acceptable worship, and (c) the willing witness to the Father's love which Jesus Christ gave in his death renders absurd and obsolete any further offering of sacrifice.[146]

Even though we cannot accept fully what Power holds — ". . . Many of our difficulties, theological and cultural, spring from what can only be called a reductionist hermeneutic, whereby we blithely take it for granted performing sacrifice means offering a gift, for whatever purpose that may be," — at least some of our theological difficulties with the Protestant reformers were due to our interpretation of offering Christ in the sacrifice of the Mass.[147]

---

144. Ibid., p. 387.
145. Ibid.
146. Ibid.
147. The disputed question of the Church offering Christ to the Father in the Mass is a problem yet to be solved. There is no satisfactory answer to it. The Catholic position is that we offer Christ in the Mass, and the Protestants do not accept it. According to Vagaggini, no sacrifice of the Church will be acceptable to God if the Church does not offer Christ. In the mass the Church offers Christ because without that our offering is not possible. See C. Vagaggini (1969), pp. 191-92. Some others explain this delicate problem by arguing that we have no offering outside the sacrifice

This is a clear fact. But that does not mean that many of our difficulties, theological and cultural spring from the reductionist hermeneutic whereby we blithely take it for granted that performing sacrifice means offering a gift.

Contrary to what Power holds, the offering makes an integral part of sacrifice. There is no sacrifice without some form of offering and Christian tradition has inherited the sacrificial terminology from the OT in which there is no sacrifice without some form of offering. Jesus' death as sacrifice too depends very much on the fact that it is an offering to the Father in love and obedience. His words at the Last Supper on the bread and wine show clearly that he presented his sacrificial death as an offering to the Father for the sake of humanity. Only in this sense can we understand the words of Jesus over the bread and wine: "this is my body given for you," "this is my blood shed for many." It is true that in Mark and Matthew the words over the bread do not have the phrase "for you," but that does not mean as Power holds that the words over the bread have no sacrificial meaning. Luke and Paul have clearly the phrase "for you" over the bread. Power may be making a theory based on the priority of the Petrine font over the Pauline font. But this does not make sense, for the fact is that first of all there is no consensus among the exegetes over the criteria for determining such a priority,[148] and secondly, the exegetical studies of recent years have turned upside down certain theories based on the priority of certain texts.[149] The priority of a written text need not necessarily be the most authentic vision of Jesus and the early community over a subject.

→ of Christ. So what we offer is the sacrifice of Christ, but this does not mean that we offer Christ again in the forms of bread and wine. See P.Y. Emery (1966), p. 67.

148. R.J. Daly (1981), pp. 21-27.

149. See E.C. Lucas (1995), pp. 60-66.

Again according to Power, the words of Jesus over the cup and the bread refer to a double metaphor which do not have any sense of offering, for:

> In the first place, Jesus' words recall the blood ritual of such sacrifices as the passover and the covenant. In these, the blood ritual has no implications of offering but signifies God's mercy to man. . . . In the second place, an era is also apparently assumed in which the Hebrew people put great store by offering gifts to God. This is necessary to the evocation of Jeremiah 31: 31 and Isaiah 53: 12. It introduces the second metaphor, whereby the death of Jesus is rendered meaningful by way of reference to such usage, so that the similarity of desire or purpose stands out in evident dissimilarity of means. . . . It is further apparent that in the "sacrifice" of supper, it is God who gives to man, not man to God.[150]

Even though the Passover and the covenant implied first of all God's initiative, that does not mean that the blood poured to God is not an offering. By pouring the blood on the altar humans affirm that it belongs to God and offers it to him; by pouring a part of it on the assembly the other truth is affirmed, i.e. God in making a covenant with humans gives them something that belongs to him alone, the divine life. It is this participation in God's life that is made possible through sacrifice, and still better in the sacrificial death of Jesus and in the Eucharist. Again the fact that it is God who takes the initiative and gives himself to humans in the sacrifice of the supper does not mean that the offering does not make part of the sacrifice.

The NT has inherited from the OT the sacrificial terminology and in the OT sacrifice the offering constituted the integral part of it. The usage of the word *thusia* for non- ritual purposes in the NT does not justify that the offering is not constitutive to sacrifice. According to H. Lietzmann, within the first centuries the Eucharist

---

150. D.N. Power (1979), p. 392.

was considered as sacrifice in a threefold sense and the offertory is an integral part of it, for he writes:

> Within the first three centuries the eucharist was conceived as a sacrifice in a threefold sense: first the prayers, secondly the bread and wine laid on the altar by the congregation or by the individual members of it, and thirdly the sacred action at the altar itself as an analogue of the sacrificial death of Christ. These three conceptions have survived side by side in the liturgy and been combined in various ways; out of the second has developed the independent liturgical act of the offertory procession, the so-called OFFERTORIUM, the object of which is the laying on the altar of the elements intended for the eucharist.[151]

If from the first centuries the offering was seen as part of the Eucharistic sacrifice, then we cannot accept the view of Power that the offering is not a constitutive part of the Eucharist. Jesus' command "do this in memory of me" refers to a concrete action of benediction over the bread and wine, breaking the bread, passing it, eating it, and in the same manner passing the cup and drinking from it. According to Lietzmann, the eating and drinking of the body and blood of Jesus can be identified to offering.[152] If so the celebration of the Eucharist by the early Christian communities had a sense of offering. Further, Jesus' command "do this" refers not merely to an act of benediction alone, but also to taking the bread, breaking it, passing it, and eating it and taking the cup of wine, passing it, and sharing it. Even though Jesus' words and actions at the Last Supper can be better understood in the light of his banquet with the sinners and publicans it does not mean that his Last Supper refers merely to an eschatological banquet. His words rather refer to his sacrificial self-offering to the Father for the remission of sins.

Further Power argues against Irenaeus who considers a literal offering of bread and wine as the first fruits of God's creation by

151. H. Lietzmann (1979), p. 68.

152. Ibid., p. 109.

arguing that the creation narrative of Genesis is not historical but mythical; and a historical redemption cannot be associated with a mythical creation.[153] The fact that the creation account of Genesis is a mythical narrative does not mean that bread and wine cannot be considered as the offering of the Church in the sacrifice of the Eucharist that they become the body and blood for the nourishment and the resurrection of the flesh as Irenaeus holds. The fact that God does not require our gifts does not mean that the bread and wine cannot make the constitutive act of the sacrifice of the Eucharist. It is here that Power fails to understand the differences between the offering and the sacrifice because God requires it, or because it is a means by which humans concretely acknowledge their dependence on God.[154] Thus the offering of bread and wine should not be confused with the offering of the body and blood as Cyprian held,[155] and it should not be taken to mean that once the bread and wine are changed into the body and blood the Christians offer them to God as their sacrifice. Here Power is right in what he holds.

Power considers the Eucharist as a spiritual sacrifice and due to that he upholds that the offering does not make a constitutive part of sacrifice. Even though in the footnote 9 of his article, "Words that Crack: the Uses of "Sacrifice" in Eucharistic Discourse," he affirms that according to Acquinas, "the realization of sacrifice is in the offering of bread,"[156] but he does not explain why it cannot be considered to be so. He considers the primary act of worship as praise and thanksgiving and due to this he is not able to see the

---

153. D.N. Power (1979), pp. 392-98.

154. For a detailed study on the tension between the ritual sacrifice and the spiritual sacrifice, see A. Grillo (1998), pp. 203-43.

155. D.N. Power (1979), p. 393. According to A. Gelston, the concept of the Eucharist as an offering of Christ by the priest first appears in Cyprian. A. Gelston (1991), p. 118.

156. D.N. Power (1979), p. 394.

offering as essential to the Eucharist.[157] In no way does the self-offering of the Church obscure Christ's gift to us. To hold that our offering in the Eucharist consists merely of praise and thanksgiving is again to fall into a reductionist hermeneutic against which Power wanted to argue in his article under evaluation. Jesus by making use of an existent rite, the Passover meal, used it to give himself to us, and we can give ourselves to Jesus only through a rite that commemorates his own self-giving to the Father and to us in the Eucharist. This rite is made not only of praise and thanksgiving but also of offering of bread and wine.

Any attempt to deny the constitutive value of the offering is not only to deny the sacramental character of it, but also to deny the very cosmic function of the Eucharist. The more one considers the Eucharist as a spiritual sacrifice, the more it becomes devoid of its sacramental and cosmic characters. It is in the Eucharistic bread and wine, i.e. in and through the cosmic elements, that Christ meets creation and elevates it to God the Father, and at the same time gives himself to the world.

THE EUCHARISTIC PRAYER AS THE SACRIFICE OF PRAISE AND THANKSGIVING FOR WHOLE OF CREATION

The Eucharistic sacrifice as a rite consists of a double offering, first the offering of bread and wine, secondly the offering of praise and thanksgiving. Both these offerings are integral parts of the Eucharistic celebration, and to reduce the Eucharist to one of the two is to fall into a reductionist hermeneutic. For both these rites go back to the four main actions of Jesus himself who at the Last Supper took the bread, gave thanks, broke it and distributed it. All these gestures of Jesus over the bread are not only repeated in the Eucharistic sacrifice in the offertory, canon, breaking the

157. Ibid., pp. 402-03.

bread and the communion,[158] but his action of giving thanks gave rise to the elaborate canon or *anaphora* of the Mass. Here we intend to develop this latter aspect to discover the cosmic and the sacrificial aspects of some of the early *anaphoras* in the Church.

The recent studies on the *anaphoras* have shown the Jewish antecedent to them and their bipartite structure.[159] We do not intend to continue in such a line but briefly to show that the contents of such prayers have a universal concern. It is interesting to see that the early *anaphoras* took consideration not only of the integrity of the rite, that is, the commemoration of all the main four actions of Jesus at the Last supper, but also gave thanks to God for creation and redemption and prayed for all human beings on earth. This universal character of the *anaphora* is something which is overlooked in the study of the Eucharist as sacrifice and of the origin and function of the *anaphoras* in the Church.

It is almost clear that the canon of the Mass had its immediate origin in the prayer of praise and thanksgiving Jesus himself said over the bread and wine. Given the Passover context it is also possible that Jesus thanked the Father for the universe, the land, Jerusalem, etc. The early Church following the Jewish pattern of prayer of praise and thanksgiving developed its *anaphoras* to remember and to thank God the Father for creation and redemption. For example, the tripartite structure of the Addai and Mari shows a universal concern and follows closely the structure of the *birkat ha-mazon* of the time of Jesus.[160] In its first

---

158. L. Ligier (1966), p. 499.

159. Some of the recent important studies on the analysis of the structure of the Eucharistic prayers are of C. Giraudo (1989a); E. Mazza (1984); A. Catella and G. Cavagnoli (1989).

160. L. Ligier (1966), p. 506. But C. Giraudo traces the origin of the Eucharistic prayers not so much to the *berakah* but to the *todah*. This view is criticized by Bradshaw who on the contrary holds the *berakah* as the legitimate source of the Eucharistic prayer. See P.F. Bradshaw (1991), pp. 257-60.

section it praises God-the-Trinity, the Creator and redeemer of the universe, in the second section it thanks God for all the benefits of the redemption, and in the third section it supplicates God to remember the Fathers, the assembly and all the inhabitants of the world.[161]

Even though the essential nature of the Eucharistic prayer consists in the offering of praise and thanksgiving for the redemption in Jesus Christ, it pleads for the well being of all creation. Not only is God praised and thanked for the creation and redemption in Jesus Christ but also intercessions are made for a good climate; health of the king, good crops, etc. The *anaphora* of the "Apostolic Constitutions," expresses clearly that it is God who gives nutriment to all the flesh on the earth.[162] The *anaphora* of St. Basil is still clearer when it says: "By offering you that which belongs to you and comes from your hands, we celebrate in all for all, we bless you, we give you thanks. . . ."[163] The praise and thanksgiving in the *anaphoras* are not, therefore, limited to the redemption but intercessions are made for all humanity and even for all the world. Hence in the ancient *anaphoras* the cosmos is an inseparable element of worship.[164] And according to Markos

161. L. Ligier (1966), p. 506. On the sacrificial aspect of the *anaphora* of Addai and Mari, see A. Gelston (1991), pp. 118-24.

162. See E. Mazza (1996a), p. 177. According to Marcel Metzger, the Book VIII of the *Apostolic Constitutions* can be considered as the most complete and systematic work on the *anamnesis* on the creative work of God. See M. Metzger (1998), p. 154. It mentions the whole creation starting from the invisible heavenly creatures and proceeds in the order of the chronological narration of the Gen 1. It puts the whole universe on God for its origin, preservation and mentions the elements of the cosmos such as sky, earth, day, night, light, darkness, sun, moon, the group of stars, water, air, fire, land, sea, rivers, vegetations, the seasons, and humans as the summit of the creation of God. Ibid.

163. L. Ligier (1966), p. 508; See also E. Mazza (1996a), pp. 259-60.

164. M. Vidalis (1998), p. 203.

Vidalis, it was probably from the liturgy of Jerusalem that the cosmic element entered into the Oriental *anaphoras* and was used against gnosticism.[165]

Nevertheless the *anaphoras* of Rome right from the beginning limited their field to the Church assembled around the altar, the priest and the holy people.[166] As Ligier says, even though in Rome the things are considered as God's gifts they are not object of the offering whereas in the East the creatures are considered as part of the object of the offering.[167] The Byzantine *anaphora* of St. Basil clearly states that the offering is "in all and for all." This phrase, "in all and for all" shows the universal character of the Eucharistic offering and prayers. As Ligier says, "Whatever may be, it remains that at least indirectly, through the mediation of Christ, the first fruit of creation, it is the whole creation that the Church presents to the Father with the gesture of the offering."[168] Thus, the *anamnesis* section of the *anaphora* is extended to humanity at large and even to all creation.

The *anaphora* too has a sacrificial character and our next step is to find out this sacrificial character of it. According to L. Ligier, during the fourth century both in the East and in the West a new type of prayer which requested the Father to be pleased with our sacrifice was introduced into the *anaphora*.[169] The Apostolic constitution number 39 reads:

> And we ask you to look with pity on these gifts presented before you who are without need, and to be pleased with them for the honour of your Christ, and to send on this sacrifice your Holy

165. Ibid., pp. 204-05.

166. L. Ligier (1966), p. 513.

167. Ibid., p. 514.

168. Ibid.

169. Ibid., p. 516. It is at the same time that the mention of the irrational creatures is left out in the *anaphoras*. See M. Vidalis (1998), p. 200.

> Spirit, the witness of the sufferings of Lord Jesus, so that he may manifest that this bread is the body of your Christ and that this chalice is the blood of your Christ.[170]

First of all this prayer clearly tells that the offering presented on the altar is the sacrifice which we offer to God who has no need of it, yet the prayer is made that the Holy Spirit who was the witness of Christ's passion may change the offering into the body and blood of Christ. This prayer is later on added to a number of Eucharistic prayers and is used in our times in the Roman Canon.[171] According to Ligier, this prayer could not have been inspired by the *birkat ha-mazon* because it had nothing to do with the cult, but might have been inspired by the benediction of the sacrificial service (*birkat 'avodah*) which had a sacrificial meaning.[172] For "it substituted the prayer of the priests who asked the pleasing of their victims, invoked the pleasure of God over the worship of Israel and asked the restoration of the sacrifices."[173] Again the introduction of this text might have been influenced by service of the synagogue which substituted the Temple service and was in a position to express the sacrificial value of the Eucharist. The presence of the Holy Spirit guaranteed the identity of the body and blood of the crucified Christ to that of the Eucharist.[174]

THE EUCHARIST AS THE SACRIFICE OF THE CHURCH, THE BODY OF CHRIST, FOR HERSSELF AND FOR CREATION

The following quotation from C. Vagaggini can serve as the starting point of our discussion on the cosmic dimension of the Eucharistic sacrifice, for he writes: "The Mass is the sacrament of the Passover

---

170. L. Ligier (1966), p. 516; E. Mazza (1996a), p. 175.

171. Ibid., pp. 516-17.

172. Ibid., p. 517.

173. Ibid.

174 Ibid.

sacrifice not only of Christ, but also of the Church. . . . The Church offers together with Christ the whole humanity, the whole cosmos, of which he is the responsible Head."[175] These words show that the Eucharist has a cosmic dimension for the Church as the body of Christ, and a cosmic function, for through her the whole creation is called to enter into the fullness of Christ.[176] The Church, therefore, becomes the link, the meeting point between God and the cosmos, and this takes place exactly in the Eucharist.

The Eucharist, thus, becomes the place of interaction between God and creation. But unfortunately Christian theology treats the Church and the cosmos separately. Such a treatment is not justified if we seriously take into consideration the ecclesiology of the Letter to the Ephesians. For in the words of J. Ernst,

> According to the testimony of Ephesians, Church and cosmos are by no means separate, but interrelated. The cosmos can come to fulfilment in Christ through the Church, just as conversely the Church will only attain its true pleroma when "the material and non-material cosmos has brought into its 'catholic,' totally comprehensive unity."[177]

Quoting Warnach, Ernst explains that it is through the sacramental process, that is, through baptism and the Eucharist that this important role is fulfilled.[178] When through Baptism new members are incorporated into the Church and through the Eucharist they are nourished there takes place the growth of the body toward the exalted Lord, and the consecration of the

---

175. C. Vagaggini (1969), p. 191, see also pp. 192-93.

176. J. Ernst (1968), pp. 58-60. We will discuss in detail the cosmic function of the Eucharist in the next chapter; here we limit ourselves in showing the universal dimension of the Eucharistic prayers.

177. Ibid., pp. 58-59.

178. Ibid., p. 59.

world.[179] More concretely, "In the symbol of bread, i.e. in a cosmic element, what is divine is, as it were, embodied; God in principle enters the world. That is essentially no other than a continuation of the meeting of God and the world in the incarnation."[180] And the purpose of the incarnation, that is, his descent into the world according to Ephesians 4, was to make possible the ascension of the cosmos into God. For he writes again:

> The "katabasis" takes place for the sake of the "anabasis." The entry of the divine into the mundane in the incarnation and the sacramental liturgical symbol, takes place in order to recover and bring back the world (not only the world of man but the entire creation, including the non-human creation) into the realm of God so that Christ may "fill all things." This ascent, this recovery, is perceptible in the sacrificed body of Christ, the "body of flesh" with which he has reconciled us by his death (Col 1: 22). And so in the Eucharistic sacrament the union of the divine and cosmic occurs.[181]

The mystery of incarnation becomes thus the basis for a further discussion on the sacramental and the cosmic character of the Eucharist. For Christ in his incarnation descended into our world that we might rise through him to the Father. This is what is meant in every Christian sacrifice, the descending of Christ to the world to lead the creation back to God the Father.

Conclusion

In our analysis of the sacrificial character of the Eucharist we have seen that Jesus gave the Eucharist as the memorial of his sacrificial death so that the Church could benefit from the fruits of his redemptive sacrificial death on the cross. If the Eucharist is celebrated in obedience to the command of Jesus himself, it cannot

---

179. Ibid.

180. Ibid.

181. Ibid.

be seen as a new sacrifice independent of the cross. And as sacrament of the sacrifice of Christ it is the visible sacrifice of Church, and the sacrificial and the cosmic characters of the Eucharist consist in this sacramental aspect.

When the Church in obedience to her Lord's command celebrates the Eucharist, Christ who gave himself in anticipation to the disciples at the Last Supper gives himself to the Church to make us participate in the effects of his redemptive death. Just as at the Last Supper the bread and wine stood for the body and blood of Jesus, the victim, so too, in the sacrifice of the Eucharist his body and blood stand for his sacrifice, and for the cosmos. They stand for the separation of the body and blood of the animal sacrificed, and in the case of the Eucharist the body and blood of the crucified and risen Christ himself, and for the whole creation.

The Eucharist as the memorial of the "once for all sacrifice of Christ" has ascending and descending dimensions which cannot be separated from one another. Its ascending dimension consists first in the sacrifice of the cross where Jesus offered himself to the Father and secondly, on the part of the Church, she offers herself to God the Father in union with Christ in the Holy Spirit. Its descending dimension consists first in God giving himself to us in Jesus' death, particularly the new covenant in the body and blood of Jesus to create a new family tie with him, and secondly Jesus giving himself to us in the Eucharistic body and blood. These dimensions are closely united in themselves that they should not be seen in separation from one another.

Further only a correct understanding of the sacrificial character of the Eucharist can stop the Christian theology of the Eucharist from being impoverished of its ritual and cosmic dimensions. Any attempt to deprive the Eucharist of its sacrificial character by reducing it to a meal of the kingdom, or to a sacrifice of praise and thanksgiving, turns out to be counterproductive for a deep theology of the Eucharist. For the Eucharistic body and blood cannot be reduced to a mere meal of the kingdom: they are not only the symbols through which the sacrifice of the cross is ritually commemorated, but also the means through which Christ gives himself to us and to the world till the *parousia*.

Finally Christ, by taking the mundane elements, bread and wine, willed the cosmic elements to symbolize his gift to the disciples and to the world. He continues to give himself to us and to the world each time he descends on the altar in the form of Eucharistic bread and wine. The sacramental character of the Eucharist becomes not only the means to reconcile the Catholic and the Protestant controversies on the Eucharistic sacrifice but also the means to rediscover the cosmic function of the Eucharist.

5

The Cosmic Dynamism of the Eucharist

EVEN though over the centuries the term "Cosmic Christ" and the related expressions were widely discussed in the Western Church,[1] such discussions have left almost untouched the cosmic dynamism of the Eucharist. The discussions on the cosmic Christ were limited to the cosmic role of Christ's death[2] and they ignored the fact that the Eucharist, being the sacrament of the sacrifice of the cross

---

1. For a detailed study on the history of cosmic-Christ terminology and the related bibliography see J.A. Lyons (1982), pp. 1-73. When we use the term cosmic-Christ we intend the idea expressed by J.A. Lyons that Christ is "the instrument in God's creative activity, the source and goal of all things, the bond and sustaining power of the whole creation; he is called the head and ruler of the universe; and his redemptive influence and his body are considered to extend to the limits of the created order." Ibid., pp. 2-3. Thus to refer to Christ as cosmic suggests that his redemptive activity goes beyond the human persons for he is "the Alpha and the Omega" (Rev 1: 8, and 22: 13).

2. Among the New Testament writers who stressed this cosmic function of Christ's redemption are St. Paul and St. John. In the following New Testament passages we can find some allusion to the cosmic function of Christ and his redemption: Rom 8: 19-23; Col 1: 15-20; 2: 9-10 and 15; 3: 11; Eph 1: 9-10 and 20-23; 4: 9-10; 1 Cor 8: 6; 15: 20-28; 2 Cor 5: 19; Phil 3: 21; Jn 1: 1-18; Rev 1: 8 and 17; 2: 8; 3: 14; 22: 13. St. Paul in his letters to the Romans, Colossians and Ephesians stress the redemption of the whole universe in Christ. Thus Christ redeems the whole creation in his sacrifice on the cross. See G.A. Maloney (1968), pp. 26-43. See also J.G. Gibbs (1971), pp. 466-79.

which has redeemed the whole created universe, has a cosmic function as well.[3] This cosmic function of the Eucharist, which is almost neglected by the Western Church, is one of the essential elements of the Eucharistic theology of the Eastern Church[4] which we partly anticipated in the last chapter in our discussion on the *anaphoras*.

In my opinion, this cosmic dimension of the Eucharist can be understood only against the background of the relation between creation, incarnation and redemption. The unity of these elements shows that Christ is the creator and the redeemer of this cosmos. The mystery of the incarnation and the redemption, thus, forms the basis to understand the role of Christ in the cosmos and the cosmic dimension of the Eucharist. This makes it necessary for us to analyse at least briefly the relation between creation, incarnation and redemption.

The mediation of Christ in the incarnation and redemption, thus forms the background for any discussion on the cosmic dimension of the Eucharist. This again has to be studied not only from the descending dimension of the incarnation but also from its ascending dimension, where the creator redeems the whole creation so that it can return to God and to his original plan. For our purpose we limit ourselves to the soteriology of St. Anselm in his most famous work *Cur Deus Homo*[5] and to Karl Barth's idea of

---

3. I do not intend to discuss the cosmic function of the Eucharist neither from the point of view of an ecologist nor from the view of a liberation theologian, but from the point of view of interrelation between God, humans and the cosmos in the Eucharist. For a discussion of the cosmic function of the Eucharist from the point of view of a liberation theologian see E. Balducci (1970), pp. 873-89.
4. V. Lossky (1973), pp. 110-11; I. Zizioulas (1994), pp. 10-25.
5. *Cur Deus Homo* was written by St. Anselm in 1097 in defence of the necessity of the incarnation. The tone of the work is apologetic and the main interlocutor is Boso who questions the necessity →

the relation among creation, covenant, and the fulfilment in his *Church Dogmatics,*[6] as presupposition for the true understanding of the cosmic perspective of the Eucharistic sacrifice. First we intend to see St. Anselm's theory of sin and satisfaction which made necessary the divine incarnation and redemption, and then we will turn to K. Barth to see the unity between the creation, incarnation and redemption.

St. Anselm's treatment of the redemption draws our attention mainly because his theory of soteriology, i.e. his theory of debt and satisfaction, has become the classical way of looking at the redemption in Jesus Christ. God created humans that they might live in obedience to him, but human beings in disobedience to God brought dishonour to their creator. In this way humans incurred a debt on themselves which they were in no way able to pay back to God. On the one hand God cannot forgive humans

---

→ of incarnation: Could not God forgive sins without compensation? To answer the necessity of the divine incarnation St. Anselm takes recourse to the divine satisfaction and he seems to rely on the divine retribution even though it comes from the free will and love of God. For a recent detailed study on the *Cur Deus Homo,* see the Acts of the International Anselmian Congress in *CDHA,* especially the following articles in it: G. O'Collins (1999), pp. 21-23; G.E.M. Gasper (1999), pp. 147-64; J. Houston (1999), pp. 621-39; L.L. Peterson (1999), pp. 659-72. See also A. Levasti (1929), pp. 140-60; One of the most important contemporary theologians who tried to draw inspiration from St. Anselm's work is Balthasar. See G.W. Olsen (1999), pp. 823-35; G.W. Olsen (1981), pp. 49-61. J. Moses in a recent book argues the need to make a restatement of the mystery of atonement in the light of the holistic approach to life today: "Theories of atonement which lead to an exclusive preoccupation with personal salvation must be judged, therefore, to be inadequate. There are dimensions that are personal and social, corporate and cosmic." J. Moses (1996), p. XIII.

6. K. Barth (1962), pp. 148-61; H. Küng (1981), pp. 9-96. See also H.U. von Balthasar (1985), pp. 138-42.

without atonement, for that would mean that the sinner is not subject to any law[7] and on the other that the sinner and the non sinner are equal. This made necessary the incarnation of the Word, who had created the universe *ex nihilo,* to pay back the debt to God, and to bring corrupt nature back to incorruptibility and to recreate humans in the image of God.[8] The Word alone was able to recreate the universe and to suffer for all, and to be an advocate on behalf of all in front of the Father.[9]

The redemption thus becomes the restoration of the original order of creation, and giving back to God the honour which was destroyed by sin and disobedience.[10] In Anselm, this restoration of the spoiled order has a cosmic function. For as J. Houston writes, ". . . for him it seems, debt-paying is an aspect of cosmic restoration, the restoration of the order which in all things accords with God's good will."[11] This cosmic dimension can become clear only if we treat incarnation and redemption in a wider perspective,[12] for Christ in his death reconciled the whole creation. The incarnation and the redemption, therefore, form the ways through which God restores the spoiled creatures, and this takes place in Jesus Christ, the Word made flesh, and still continues in the Church through the Eucharist.

---

7. *Cur Deus Homo* I.12.
8. See G.E.M. Gasper (1999), pp. 160-61.
9. It is true that for St. Anselm sin is dishonouring God and cannot be left unpunished. Such a view has led the critics of Anselm to consider him as a retributivist. For a theory against this attack on Anselm, see J. Houston (1999), pp. 621-39.
10. Here Anselm does not follow the Patristic Fathers who held that the ransom was paid to the devil. For him the debt is paid to God himself. Christ made satisfaction for sin and he shifted the emphasis from the ransom to satisfaction. For more details see J. Moses (1996), pp. 126-39.
11. J. Houston (1999), p. 639.
12. See J. Moses (1996), p. XIII.

In St. Anselm, however, the idea of incarnation is not coexistent with the creation, for it is only at a second stage, that is, after incurring the debt through the disobedience of the commandments of God, that incarnation and redemption become necessary. But the incarnation cannot be considered as a mere accident, that is, the result of the sin. It is K. Barth who succeeded in showing the intimate relation of creation, covenant and redemption, which we will see below. It is true that K. Barth does not treat these elements in relation to cosmos. However, his treatment of creation, incarnation and redemption, can help us to understand the divine plan in Christ for the cosmos.

If for St. Anselm incarnation and redemption were made necessary due to the inability of humans to pay back the debt to God, in K. Barth creation, reconciliation, and redemption form a single unity in the divine economy of salvation.[13] The creation, which is the first act of the Holy Trinity, not only presupposes the salvation, but is also the external basis for the covenant,[14] and the internal basis is the love of God. Creation, incarnation, and redemption, therefore, form a single reality, and none of them may be understood properly in isolation from the other two, even though their historical fulfilment takes place in different moments of history. They form the background to understand our further discussion on the cosmic dynamism of the Eucharist.

It is true that creation is neither the reconciliation, nor the fulfilment, but the condition for the covenant in Jesus Christ. As Barth holds, creation constitutes the formal condition for the covenant and the covenant is the material condition for creation.[15]

---

13. This is the procedure which we can find in his *Church Dogmatics* III.
14. K. Barth (1962), pp. 148-61; H. Küng (1981), pp. 9-96. See also H.U. von Balthasar (1985), pp 138-42.
15. Ibid., p. 151.

Creation is the external base of the covenant, and the covenant is the internal base of creation.[16] The scope of creation is to make possible the covenant of God with humans, that has its beginning, centre and fulfilment in Christ. Even though creation is not already a covenant, it is an expression, a revelation and an enforcement of the eternal will of the covenant. It is the work of the triune God and it takes place in Jesus Christ, the Logos.

The close relation between creation and covenant leads to another aspect, that is, the justification of humans in Jesus Christ, or redemption. It may be for this reason that K. Barth after treating the creation in his *Church Dogmatics* treats reconciliation, or the divine predestination in the election of Jesus Christ and the covenant. Creation becomes the necessary condition for justification. God in the free selection of us in Jesus Christ shows himself as the covenant God. He selects humans as partners of this covenant, and reveals himself as the God of covenant. Barth argues that without doubt the justification is the reaction to the sin of people, however, it is the realization of the covenant of God with humans. According to him, the centre to which everything must look forward, and from which everything must draw light is the man-God Jesus Christ.[17] Thus, Jesus Christ becomes the meeting point of the history.

Barth, thus, by calling our attention to the intimate relation between creation, covenant and fulfilment, invites us not to look at incarnation and redemption as something accidental in the economy of salvation. Such a view was also present in Duns Scotus even before Barth. For example, J.L. Gonzalez summarizes the view of Scotus:

> As a corollary of the primacy of will in God, as well as of the divine omnipotence, Scotus claimed that the incarnation was

16. Ibid.

17. H. Küng (1981), pp. 15-26.

> not simply the result of human sin, our needs of redemption, and God's foreknowledge of these facts. Rather, Christ was predestined to be incarnate as the primary object of the divine love. Thus, the incarnation is not simply the focal point in the history of humanity as it has unfolded, but also the focal point of the entire purpose of God, even apart from human sin.[18]

The same view can also be found in Karl Rahner, who holds creation and incarnation as the two closely related dimensions of God's self-communication to the world, for he writes:

> We are entirely justified in understanding creation and incarnation not as two disparate and juxtaposed acts of God "outwards" which have their origins in two separate initiatives of God. Rather in the world as it actually is we can understand creation and incarnation as two moments and two phases of the *one* process of God's self-giving and self-expression, although it is an intrinsically differentiated process.[19]

The intimate relation of creation, incarnation, and redemption forms the basis for any treatment of the cosmic role of the Eucharist. Such a role is again closely related to the cosmic role of Christ in creation and in redemption wherein the incarnation and redemption are seen as the capacity to establish a new relation with all the elements of the world through the cross.[20] As Col 1: 15-20 says:

> He is the image of the invisible God, the first born of all creation, for in him all things were created, in heaven and on earth, visible and invisible . . . all things were created through him and for him. He is before all things, and in him all things hold together. He is the Head of the body, the church; he is the beginning, the first-born from the dead, that in everything he might be pre-eminent. For in him all the fullness of God was pleased to dwell,

18. J.L. Gonzalez (1988), vol. 2, pp. 311-12.
19. K. Rahner (1992), p. 197.
20. A. Sacchi (1976), p. 240.

> and through him to reconcile to himself all things, whether on earth or in heaven, making peace by the blood of his cross.[21]

This hymn considers Christ as the firstborn of all creation,[22] the creator of all things, the sustainer of all things, the reconciler of all things. Still further as Salvatore A. Panimolle writes: "The risen Christ in fact for the author of Col 1: 19 is the living temple in which lives permanently all the fullness of the divinity and of the synthesis of the divine world with the cosmos."[23] All these functions give Christ a cosmic dimension, for he is the origin, the redeemer, and the sustainer of the cosmos.

In Christ, God renews the image of the cosmos by recapitulating the whole creation,[24] and in this manner reunites heaven and earth. And Christ fulfils this ongoing cosmic function through the Eucharist. Thus, the cosmic dimension of the Eucharist is closely related to the vision of the unity between creation, incarnation and redemption. We will see later that, when this intimate relation was lost sight of in the Western sacramental theology, the cosmic dimension disappeared from its liturgy.

After having put the emphasis on the syntagmatic chain, i.e. creation, incarnation and redemption through Anselm and K. Barth as the true background for the cosmic vision of the Eucharist, we try to discover the hidden cosmic dimension of the Eucharist through a study of four important theologians such as Maximus the Confessor (580-662), Vladimir Lossky (1903-1958), Johannes

---

21. For a detailed study on the cosmic character of Christ in this hymn see S. Lyonnet (1976), pp. 57-79; S.A. Panimolle (1976), pp. 177-205; A. Sacchi (1976), pp. 221-45.

22. The authors like S. Lyonnet, C.F.D. Moule, A. Marangon, see a cosmic role of Christ in the aspect of his firstborn character, in the creation and in the redemption. See S. Lyonnet (1969), p. 91; C.F.D. Moule (1962), pp. 69-70; A. Marangon (1976), p. 14.

23. S.A. Panimolle (1976), p. 204.

24. M. Vidalis (1998), p. 195.

Zizioulas (1931-Metropolitan of Pergamon), and Teilhard de Chardin (1881-1955). We have chosen them because in all of them, irrespective of the distance in time[25] and of different traditions,[26] we can find creation, incarnation and redemption as the basis of the cosmic role of the Eucharist. All of them treat the incarnation and the redemption from the descending and the ascending dimensions, and we will see that starting from Maximus there is a progressive thinking in them of which Teilhard can be seen as the peak point.

Maximus the Confessor and the Cosmic Liturgy

Maximus the Confessor,[27] who — according to Balthasar — can be considered as the thinker placed between the East and the

---

25. Maximus may be considered as the last of the Patristic Fathers, for according to G.A. Maloney, "Although St. John Damascene is usually considered the last of the great patristic Greek writers, it is Maximus the Confessor who marks the end of the patristic theological development." G.A. Maloney (1968), p. 167. All the other theologians mentioned are contemporary theologians.

26. Maximus, Lossky, and Zizioulas belong to the Eastern tradition and Teilhard de Chardin belongs to the Western theological tradition. Maximus is the basis of the Eastern theological thought, and in the course of our analysis we will find that both Lossky and Zizioulas follow closely the thought pattern of Maximus the Confessor. We have chosen Teilhard de Chardin, a scientist who discovered the cosmic dimension of Christ and the Eucharist in his scientific study, to show that even from the scientific point of view a cosmic dimension of the Eucharist cannot be fully ruled out. He is the first to bring together the world of the scientists with that of the mystical theologians in his treatment of Christ as the Omega point of the evolution. These are some of the reasons which called us to select these four theologians who belong to the different times and traditions to show the cosmic dynamism of the Eucharist.

27. We do not intend to give a detailed discussion of Maximus' writings and theology but we limit ourselves to his concepts of cosmic liturgy and redemption.

West,[28] gives us the starting point for our analysis of the cosmic dynamism of the Eucharist, for his cosmic unity in Jesus Christ. "As a thinker placed between the East and the West — writes Balthasar — he had intuited the Christian vision of the cosmos in all its broadness, and he did that starting clearly from the mystery of Christ."[29] Maximus' cosmic synthesis of the whole created order in Christ and his reading of the whole world in the light of the mystery of incarnation and redemption draw our attention to the cosmic dimension of the Eucharist. In the words of Maloney:

> Although he is best known for his staunch defence of the orthodox teaching on the two natures in Christ as defined in the Council of Chalcedon (451), Maximus interests modern readers more because of the cosmic dimensions of his synthesis of the whole created order, a harmonious unity in union with God through Christ.[30]

The cosmic unity in Jesus points to the intimate relation of creation, incarnation and redemption which, in my opinion, forms the basis for any treatment of the cosmic role of the Eucharist. Such a role

---

28. H.U. von Balthasar (1976), pp. 7 and 152. A similar view can be also found in Jaroslav Pelikan when he writes: "For as we know from his biography, Maximus may in some sense be classified not only as an Eastern thinker but as a Western one, having spent two decades (more or less) in the Occident, first in Proconsular Africa and then in Rome itself." J. Pelikan (1982), p. 398. See also A. Louth (1997), pp. 332-45.

29. H.U. von Balthasar (1976), p. 152. The other important Greek Patristic theologians who discussed the Cosmic Christ doctrine together with Irenaeus and Maximus, are Justin, Clement of Alexandria, Origen, Athanasius, Gregory of Nazianzen, Gregory of Nyssa, and Cyril of Alexandria. Ambrose is the only Latin patristic theologian who has discussed the Cosmic Christ doctrine. For more details on the theology of cosmic Christ in the Eastern Fathers see G.A. Maloney (1968), pp. 99-181; J.A. Lyons (1982), p. 2, footnote 2.

30. G.A. Maloney (1968), p. 168.

is again closely related to the cosmic role of Christ in the creation and in the redemption wherein incarnation and redemption are seen as the capacity to establish a new relation with all elements of the world through the cross.[31] In this way the risen Christ becomes the fullness of the divinity and of the synthesis of the divine world with the cosmos.[32] We shall see in detail the cosmic dimensions of his synthesis of the whole created order in Christ, and the transformation of the cosmos in the Eucharist.

CHRIST AND THE COSMIC UNITY

Maximus is important for our study of the cosmic function of the Eucharist because, among the Greek Fathers of the Church, he is the only one who gave a systematic synthesis of the whole created order, its harmonious unity and its union with God through Christ, showing a positive outlook on the world.[33] This positive approach comes from his faith that everything in this world is created by God and finds its fulfilment in Christ, the Logos incarnate. God is the goal of creation and it reaches back to God in Christ, the centre of the cosmos.

Following Irenaeus,[34] Maximus develops the theory that God in Christ recapitulates the whole creation which lost its harmonious unity because of sin. As Maloney writes, "He renews and develops

---

31. A. Sacchi (1976), p. 240.

32. See S.A. Panimolle (1976), p. 204.

33. H.U. von Balthasar (1976), p. 48. According to Maximus, nothing in this world is bad, only the wrong use is bad. Ibid., pp. 314 and 347.

34. In his main work entitled *Adversus Haereses,* Irenaeus following Eph 1: 10, treats the redemption as the recapitulation (*anakephalàiôsis*), of the whole universe (III. 18). Jesus in his incarnation recapitulated in his person all the creatures and gave them immortality, incorruptibility and re-established the universal harmony in his resurrection. See G. Bosio (1963), vol. 1. pp. 214-26.

the central idea found in the second century writings of St. Irenaeus on the recapitulation of the whole universe in Christ. He sees the whole world in the light of the Incarnation."[35] Maximus, thus, sees the redemption in the line of the Pauline word *anakephalàiôsis*, meaning recapitulation (Eph 1: 10) of everything in Christ. The whole creation is gathered together in Jesus Christ, the Head, and is restored to the original state.[36] Christ in his redemptive death gathers up all things under one head according to the divine plan and offers it to God. And he considers Good Friday, Holy Saturday and Easter Sunday as the three mystical days of the cosmos in which the whole cosmos is gathered together in the unity of Logos.[37] Maximus, thus, follows the line of thought of the early Greek Fathers on incarnation and the recapitulation of the whole creation in the Logos incarnate.

Behind Maximus' theory of incarnation and the cosmic redemption there lies his theory of the unity of all creation. According to him, God created the world to be a harmonious unity and Adam was destined to unite in his own being the

---

35. G.A. Maloney (1968), p. 168. Maximus adopts triple categories in his thinking. For example, the incarnation is threefold: the historical, scriptural and in man. Maximus the Confessor (1857b), p. 33. In *PG* 91,1285-88 A. Likewise the laws of the world are also threefold: the natural, written, and the law of grace. Maximus the Confessor (1857a), p. 64. In *PG* 90, 725. The restorations are threefold: moral, physical, and the powers of the soul. Maximus the Confessor (1857a), p. 13. In *PG* 90, 795A-C, and the being is also threefold: being, well-being/ill being and ever-being. Maximus the Confessor (1857b), p. 65. In *PG* 91, 1392A4-B4.

36. Maximus the Confessor (1857b), pp. 41 and 7. In *PG* 91, 1305 and 1081C; M. Vidalis (1998), p. 195; P. Christou (1982), p. 262; V. Croce and B. Valente (1982), pp. 251-52; L. Thunberg (1982), p. 290.

37. H.U. von Balthasar (1976), p. 360. On the agony of Jesus in the Gethsemane where his human and divine will at conflict, see Massimo il Confessore (1985), pp. 30ff.

different spheres of the cosmos, in order that deification might be conferred upon them, through its union with God.[38] But Adam turned away from the plan of God and "his first movement was not to God, so that his natural, inborn power to effect union of distinguished things was perverted rather to their divisions."[39] Thus Adam through his sin not only ruined the cosmos by corrupting nature but also turned the whole creation into antithetical categories.[40] The whole creation is, therefore, divided into five different antithetical categories such as the uncreated God and the created world, the sensible and the intelligible, heaven and earth, paradise and the inhabited earth, and finally, male and female.[41] Christ with his incarnation penetrated into the cosmos to heal it from within, to give it back the original unity.[42]

This cosmos which is divided into antithetical categories and is corrupted regains its primordial unity, according to Maximus,

---

38. Maximus the Confessor (1857b), p. 41. In *PG* 91, 1308. See also P. Sherwood (1955), p. 55; P. Christou (1982), p. 267.
39. P. Sherwood (1955), p. 55.
40. Maximus the Confessor (1857b), p. 41. *PG* 91, 1304D-1305C. See also G.A. Maloney (1968), pp. 276-77; V. Croce and B. Valente (1982), pp. 251-52.
41. Maximus the Confessor (1857b), p. 41. In *PG* 91, 1304D-05C.
42. According to Maximus, the Logos "reunited man in relation to the differences of sex by elevating him by the Spirit, and by liberating him from the passions of the common nature. . . . He has reunited heaven and the earth by showing it the nature of all sensible and the common thing in themselves. He has reunited the sensible beings with the invisible and has proved that the nature of the created beings is a single reality, considered from a mystical point of view. He has reunited, according to the word and the supernatural manner, the created nature with the uncreated." Maximus the Confessor (1857a), p. 48, 65-78. In *PG* 90, 436-46, 735.

in the incarnation and resurrection of the Logos.[43] Christ in his incarnation and resurrection not only unites the matter and spirit but also removes all antithetical dimensions in the cosmos. Christ in his incarnation assumed a material body and entered into the heart of the created world to heal it from within and to lead back the whole creation to God. The whole creation, therefore, finds its meaning only in relation to Christ who heals it of its *pathos* which consists of two aspects: guilt and punishment.[44] Christ took up on himself both these aspects and removed the curse that hung over us and, in his love, annihilated the guilt in us. In this manner he fulfilled the commandment for us who transgressed it, and worked out our salvation by making what was ours his own.[45] Maximus writes:

> . . . the Lord took on this condemnation of my voluntary sin, i.e. nature's passibility, corruptibility, and mortality, became sin on my account in passibility, mortality, and corruption, freely taking on my condemnation in nature though being guiltless in his own will. He did this in order to condemn my voluntary and natural sin and condemnation by driving away from nature sin, passion, corruption, and death, so that the economy of divine love toward me who had fallen through disobedience might become a general mystery (*koinon mysterion*). To save me he freely underwent my condemnation through death, through it giving me the grace of restoration to immortality.[46]

---

43. Christ abolishes the antithetical distinctions between man and women (Gal 3: 28), earth and paradise (Lk 23: 43), the earthly world and the heavenly world (Acts 1: 9-11), the sensible things and the intelligible beings (Eph 4: 10), and finally the created nature and the Uncreated Nature.

44. H.U. von Balthasar (1976), p. 273.

45. Maximus the Confessor (1857b), p. 4. In *PG* 91, 11044 B. Thus in Maximus we can find the anticipation of the theory of redemption of St. Anselm which we discussed at the beginning of this chapter as a background to the further discussion.

46. Maximus the Confessor (1857a), p. 42. This translation is taken from G.C. Berthold (1993), p. 139. These words show that even →

Thus, Christ by taking up on himself our rebellious will not only healed it and saved it from destruction but also gave back a pure will in conformity to its nature.[47] Further, he took up on himself our condemnation and gave us immortality.

According to Maximus, the work of salvation consists of three stages of re-establishment in the human nature: being, well-being and eternal being by incarnation, death on the cross and resurrection respectively.[48] In Gregory of Nazianzen, too, we can find a similar idea of recreation in Christ's death when he writes, "Nothing can equal the miracle of my salvation, a few drops of blood recreate the whole world."[49] Thus, Christ in his incarnation

---

→ for Maximus the redemption from sin is not excluded as Balthasar thought when he wrote that Maximus in opposition to St. John Damascene may be willing to follow the thinking of the medieval theologian Duns Scotus because he does not consider directly the redemption from the sins but the unification of the cosmos with himself and with God as the aim of the incarnation. H.U. von Balthasar (1976), p. 279. In Maximus, the purpose of incarnation is not only the cosmic unity but also the redemption from the sins.

47. Massimo il Confessore (1979), pp. 68-95; H.U. von Balthasar (1976), p. 277.

48. Maximus the Confessor (1857b), p. 65. In *PG* 91, 1392. According to Maximus, being is the most elementary mode of existence for rational creatures. It is a matter of potency and one is free to act either in accordance with the nature or against the nature. The well-being consists in a conscious choice of the good in which one seeks the higher mode of existence. Both these modes of existence are limited by time and finitude. The third and the highest mode of existence consists in the ever-being by God's gift in which the souls have their Sabbath, receiving rest from all motion. See B.E. Daley (1982), p. 336. See also V. Lossky (1973), p. 154.

49. Gregory of Nazianzen (1857), pp. 45, 22. In *PG* 36, 653 AB. This translation is taken from V. Lossky (1973), p. 153. On the point of cosmic renewal in the hymn of *exsultet* in the Easter Vigil see R. Cantalamessa (1999), pp. 98ff.

and redemption saves the cosmos from destruction by recreating it and giving it back a pure and incorruptible nature and will. In this way the redemption becomes the conservation, that is the continued existence of creation itself.

This cosmic redemption, in the incarnation and resurrection of Jesus, becomes the basis to understand the purpose of the cosmos itself. According to him, a true understanding of the cosmos is possible only through a proper understanding of the purpose of the incarnation of Christ and his resurrection, because

> The mystery of the Incarnation of the Word contains in itself the meaning of all the symbols and all the enigmas of Scripture, as well as the hidden meaning of all sensible and intelligible creation. But he who knows the mystery of the Cross and the Tomb, knows also the essential principle of all things. Finally, he who penetrates yet further and finds himself initiated into the mystery of the Resurrection, apprehends the end for which God created all things from the beginning.[50]

Thus for Maximus, Christ, man-God, is the solution to every cosmic enigma and by healing the cosmos from within, he restores it. And this restoration according to Maximus consists in three levels: moral regeneration, physical restoration, and the restoration of the powers of the soul.[51] Maximus, thus, considers redemption not only as recapitulation of everything in Christ but also as its conservation.[52] In Christ the cosmos regains its unity with God

---

50. Maximus the Confessor (1857a), p. 66. In *PG* 90, 1108A-B. This translation is taken from G.A. Maloney (1968), p. 276. See also G.C. Berthold (1993), p. 130.

51. Maximus the Confessor (1857b), p. 41 and 7. In *PG* 91, 1305 and 1081C; M. Vidalis (1998), p. 195; P. Christou (1982), p. 262; V. Croce and B. Valente (1982), pp. 251-52; L. Thunberg (1982), p. 290. See also B.E. Daley (1982), p. 323.

52. For more details on his theory of redemption as cosmic conservation see H.U. von Balthasar (1976), pp. 261-78. But in J.D.G. Dunn we can see Jesus' death as a propitiatory sacrifice →

and Christ in his person gathers the whole creation and offers it back to God. Just as in Christ there existed two distinct natures so, too, in the created cosmos there are two distinct elements but with a perfect unity.

HUMANS' DEIFICATION AND THE TRANSFIGURATION OF THE COSMOS IN THE SACRIFICE OF THE EUCHARIST

Humans are the only living beings who possess both matter and spirit and according to Maximus their cosmic function comes from this very fact. By virtue of this they are in a position to bring about a cosmic unity and their thinking capacity helps them to be mediators between the created things and God. But this is possible only if they gain perfect unity within themselves by overcoming the antithetical categories through the gradual growth in the

→ having the same effect not on the cosmos but on humans created in the image and likeness of God. He holds that the medieval theory that Jesus' death was a propitiatory sacrifice should not be taken to mean that by his death he took away the wrath of an angry God. Those passages in St. Paul's writings where the wrath of an angry God is mentioned have to be taken to mean a process willed by God to eliminate the destructive consequences of sin so that our spiritual nature may not be destroyed. God is the agent and what he destroys is the destructive consequences of sin in our life. J.D.G. Dunn (1991), pp. 48-53. In this way Jesus' death heals the destructive consequences of human sin and prevents the destruction of the image and likeness of God. G.W. Olsen, too, comes to a similar view of redemption in his analysis of the rehabilitation of St. Anselm's theory of the atonement by Balthasar when he writes:

> "Although God as he is in himself cannot be dishonoured, the sinner through disobedience destroys the order in himself which God has given, and in this sense dishonours God. By not holding to his place in the universe, he in a sense deranges the creation. The sinner is like a spoiled work of art, which instead of reflecting the beauty which it has received from its Creator, seems to mute whatever praise one might be inclined to render to that Creator."
>
> —G.W. Olsen (1981), p. 52.

spiritual life. For only humans who have brought self-unity within themselves can perform the God-given task of mediation between the rest of the created cosmos and its Creator.[53]

This may be because Maximus, like other Eastern Fathers, considers that *the like can be known only by the like,* for he holds that the true knowledge of the Trinity can be given to us only in the proportion that we are assimilated to the likeness of God.[54] Maximus, therefore, considers three phases of spirituality where we become like Christ.[55] The first phase consists in the *praxis,* i.e. the discipline of the disoriented nature and the removal of impediments to God's graces brought about by self-love, vices and disoriented passions. We have to overcome these things to be able to imitate Christ. The second phase consists in the *theoria physica,* whereby we recapitulate all things in the Logos, Christ, and through the contemplation of God in created things, we live according to our real nature.[56] The third phase consists in the *theoria theologica* where through the mystical contemplation of the

---

53. Here we can find how Maximus being faithful to the Eastern Tradition overcomes the dualism. In the words of Panayotis Christou:

> "True to the eastern orthodox tradition, he presents relations between the two categories of existence, the divine and the worldly, in a twofold manner, i.e. at the same time strange to each other and in close contact. In this way he could escape the danger of dualism, either philosophical or gnostic. He especially thinks of man as one who combines and mediates between the two extremes and who by beginning with the removal of his own division into male and female might unite all the other divisions in the universe and reach God as the cause of all."
>
> —P. Christou (1982), p. 262. See G.A. Maloney (1968), p. 169.

54. See G.A. Maloney (1968), p. 174.

55. Maximus the Confessor (1857b), p. 41. In *PG* 91, 1305-06. See also G.A. Maloney (1968), pp. 174-76.

56. For Maximus nature means to live according to the *λōγoi* (divine idea or intention) within each given nature. See J. van Rossum (1993), pp. 213-17.

Holy Trinity we progress farther and farther from earthly thoughts as we gradually become assimilated to God's own life. When we grow in the knowledge and love of God we become Christlike and effect unity again. This unity is again affected by the growth in the knowledge and love of God and of his creation. Thus, we first overcome the divisions within ourselves and then bring the unity in the cosmos by a life of virtue, obedience to the divine command, and contemplation of the *logoi*[57] in nature, i.e. the purpose of each creature in relation to God's finality in creation. In this way, we become Christlike, in whom there is "neither male nor female" and are able to carry out our cosmic mediation.

Having become like Christ, in turn we become agents of the cosmic transformation which was one of the purposes of the incarnation. This surely takes place in the Eucharist, in which Christ offers the participation to his divine life by giving himself to us as the object of food.[58] When we receive Christ in the Holy Eucharist we become deified and capable of performing our priestly function of making all things holy. As Maloney writes on the role of deification in Maximus:

> Deified man, in whom God lives and through whom he acts to fulfil the world, is the mediator between the disparate and disjointed world and the unity that has been achieved perfectly in the God-Man's humanity through the Incarnation. Maximus insists over and over on the intimate connection between man's deification and the transfiguration of the material cosmos. Man, permeated by grace, achieves a unity within himself which allows him to effect a cosmic unity in the material world around him.[59]

57. For a detailed study on the doctrine of *logoi* in Maximus see I.H. Dalmais (1952), pp. 244-49; L. Thunberg (1965), pp. 67-88. See also J. van Rossum (1993), pp. 213-17.
58. Massimo il Confessore (1979), p. 19.
59. G.A. Maloney (1968), pp. 177-78.

Then, like Christ, we will also become the convergence of all creation, for,

> We will be completely formed after him, bearing his image completely safe and sound; no mark of decay shall touch it in any way, and with us and through us he will encompass all creation at its midpoint, as if it were the ends of his limbs, and bind indissolubly around himself paradise and world, heaven and earth, perceptible and intelligible things, because he himself has body and sense and soul and mind as we do; and accommodating to each extremity, as to the members of a body, what is generally related to it, in the way we have described before, he divinely sums up (*anekephalaiosato*) all things in himself, revealing that all creation exists as one, like an individual person.[60]

It is through the Church that we fulfil our role as agents of the cosmic deification and transfiguration.[61] In Maximus, thus, the Church gets an important cosmic role, i.e. to be an instrument in the cosmic transfiguration.[62] "The Church," as Balthasar writes, "stands in the middle of the natural cosmos and the supernatural

---

60. Maximus the Confessor (1857b), p. 41. In *PG* 91, 1309C4-1312A15. This translation is taken from B.E. Daley (1982), pp. 329.

61. G.A. Maloney (1968), p. 181.

62. The transfiguration of the Lord is seen by the Eastern theologians as the transfiguration of the cosmos. See I.H. Dalmais (1998), pp. 49-58; C. Galeriu (1998), pp. 71-91. It is difficult to pinpoint what it means when Maximus and other Eastern theologians speak of transfiguration of the cosmos. Perhaps the words of a modern theologian in the preface to the Part I of his work on *cosmotheandric experience* can help us to understand this term even though this work is not written to explain the Eastern theology. R. Panikkar writes on the transfiguration in the following words:

    "The mystery of transfiguration may stand as the symbol of this study. Nothing is despised, nothing left over. Everything is integrated, assumed, transfigured. Nothing is postponed into

→

as a centre of light that focalises onto herself, and by making everything a symbolic sign, guarantees the glorious transfiguration of the whole cosmos."[63] In this way the material world, through the Church, not only meets the spirit,[64] but also helps in the transformation of the world into a harmonious cosmic unity. This transfiguration of the cosmos and its deification again take place in and through the Eucharist. The Eucharist becomes the place where the Church and the cosmos meet together[65] and attain the *pleroma*.

Humanity thus carries out this cosmic mediation concretely through the Church in its sacraments. For Christ, who brought unity among the disjointed creatures separated from the creator and from one another by ignorance and sin, called the Church to continue this unity. Christ's transforming activities are now continued in the cosmos through the power of the Holy Spirit in and through the Church.[66] When the living Logos is preached, and the sacraments are celebrated, Christ is encountered by the Christian faithful.[67]

The encounter of the cosmos with Christ in the Church is also made possible through the sacraments because according to

---

→ the future: the whole process is here. Nothing is pushed aside or considered unredeemable; the entire body and all of human memory is included. Transfiguration is not some hallucination of a more pleasant reality or mere escapism to a loftier plane. It is the totally integrated intuition of the seamless fabric of the entire reality: *the cosmotheandric vision*." —R. Panikkar (1993), p. 1.

63. H.U. von Balthasar (1976), p. 332.

64. G.A. Maloney (1968), p. 181.

65. J. Ernst (1968), p. 59.

66. Ibid., pp. 58-59.

67. See G.A. Maloney (1968), p. 177. See also P.M. Blowers (1993), pp. 145-49.

Maximus there is an analogy between creation and scripture, the cosmic order and the scriptural order.[68] Christ the Saviour is simultaneously incarnate in the world, in the Bible, and in the historical person of Jesus of Nazareth and he actively correlates cosmos and scripture in a grand macrocosmic plan of integration and deification.[69] On the basis of his presence the Logos binds together the cosmic order with the scriptural order and brings them to fulfilment. Such a cosmic view is the outcome of Maximus' anthropological outlook on the world, Scripture and the Church on the one hand and the unity of all creation in Christ, the Logos Incarnate,[70] and the consequence of his sacramental understanding of human existence on the other.

The *hypostatic*[71] union of the whole world and the Church in the person of Christ leads to another aspect, i.e. the elevation of every liturgy into the cosmic liturgy. Every liturgy necessarily takes place within the context of the cosmos in the Church, and for this reason Maximus considers every liturgy as a cosmic liturgy. For Christ, the foundation of the cosmos as well as the unitive principle of the cosmos, has made a union of the Church and the cosmos in his person. And the Church, being the body of Christ, becomes the instrument through which the cosmos gets into the process of its unification and recapitulation in Christ, until God will be "all in all." "Just as the Church is a 'world,' so too, the world is a cosmic Church, whose 'aisle' may be the sensible world and the 'choir' is that spiritual."[72] The soul contemplates the nature

---

68. P.M. Blowers (1993), p. 145.
69. Ibid.
70. See L. Thunberg (1982), p. 290.
71. For more details see N. Madden (1993), pp. 175-97.
72. Maximus the Confessor (1857b), p. 2. In *PG* 91, 668-69; H.U. von Balthasar (1976), p. 337-38. Josef Ernst too holds a similar view when he writes that the Church and the cosmos are by no means separated, but interrelated. J. Ernst (1968), p. 58.

as if in a Church under the guidance of the Logos and together with him penetrates into nature and begins to know the meaning of living beings. In Maximus the true knowledge becomes a liturgy,[73] that is, a holy service rendered for the redemption of the cosmos. Thus, human beings through contemplation and knowledge become the priest of the world and offer creation to God in their hearts as if on an altar.[74]

In Maximus, thus, the Church gets an important cosmic role, i.e. to be an instrument in the cosmic transfiguration. Christ has united matter and spirit in his incarnation and continues to unite the cosmos to himself in the Eucharist. We may summarize the incarnational, soteriological, and Eucharistic theology of Maximus the Confessor by borrowing the following words of M. Vidalis:

> This union once realized in the incarnation of the Word, Christ renews it in the celebration of the mystery of the new covenant that becomes the centre of the Christian life. Christ recapitulates then the creation, represented by the elements of bread and wine, which makes possible to discern the cosmic dimension of his work. He recapitulates not only human nature, but the whole cosmos. The Eucharist in its soteriological perspective takes an interior dimension, a movement towards its fulfilment. It is the sacrament of the incorporation to Christ, the High Priest, who offers the cosmos to the Father, recapitulating it through the Holy spirit and by giving it back the lost unity.[75]

The Eucharist thus makes possible the *katabasis* and the *anabasis*, i.e. the descent of Christ into the cosmos to raise it to the Father, by uniting it to his body. In every Eucharist Christ again gathers the whole creation in the form of bread and wine and offers it to the Father. Just as humans, so too the cosmos also will be transformed at the time of resurrection.

---

73. H.U. von Balthasar (1976), p. 338.
74. Ibid.
75. M. Vidalis (1998), p. 206.

The Deification of Humans and the Cosmos in the Eucharist in V. Lossky

Our next step will be to analyse the thought pattern of Vladimir Lossky, one of the most important contemporary Eastern theologians, who by following closely the thought pattern of Maximus the Confessor, brings to light the cosmic role of the Eucharist in the *deification* (*theosis*) *of humans and the cosmos*. To understand this role we should keep in mind the intimate relation that exists in the East between mysticism and theology. In the East the purpose of theology is the union with God or deification and it is for this reason that the Eastern tradition — according to Lossky — does not make any sharp distinction between mysticism and theology,[76] between humans and the cosmos. For humans are not isolated from the rest of creation and *all that they do have their effect on nature*. Here in this section we will discuss in detail this deification of humans and the cosmos in the Eucharist.

DEIFICATION OF HUMANS AND ITS COSMIC VALUE

Lossky, following the Eastern Fathers, considers the deification of humans or union with God as the supreme goal of knowledge and theology.[77] The cosmic role of humans comes from the fact that God created men and women to be in union with him and to be mediators between God and creation.

Lossky follows closely the thesis of Maximus and he considers that God created humans to unite in them *the whole of created being*

---

76. The Eastern theology can be considered mainly mystic and less argumentative just the opposite of the Western theology. For the Eastern theologians the scope of theology is to bring union with God and there can be no theology without mysticism and vice versa. V. Lossky (1973), pp. 8-9, 14. This mystical character prevails in the writings of the Orthodox theologians and makes our analysis sometimes difficult. On the mystic as new theologian see J. Pelikan (1977), pp. 254-70.

77. V. Lossky (1973), pp. 9-10.

and to grant the state of deification to the whole of creation.[78] But humans through their sin destroyed the union and became incapable of achieving such union for themselves and for the world. The Logos, the Word then had to become man in order to assume our human nature and to make possible this deification by breaking the triple barrier of sin, death and nature.[79] Thus, Christ in his incarnation has opened up the way to union with the Godhead and through him our humanity enters into union with God. Lossky quoting St. Irenaeus (*Adversus Haereses*, 3. 19.1) argues: "God made Himself man, that man might become God."[80] The descent of the divine person of Christ has made possible the ascent of human beings in the Holy Spirit, and the union of created beings with the Divinity.[81] The purpose of incarnation is, therefore, the deification of humans, and this is not limited to humans alone but to the whole of creation.

The effects of humans' deification can be transmitted to the cosmos only if there exists a close relation between both of them. Thus, Lossky, too, following Maximus considers a basic unity in the cosmos. Humans are not isolated creatures in the universe for they are intimately related to the whole of creation. This feeling of oneness with the whole cosmos is one of the characteristics of Eastern spirituality. As Lossky writes:

> Man is not a being isolated from the rest of creation; by his very nature he is bound up with the whole of the universe, and St. Paul bears witness that the whole creation awaits the future glory which will be revealed in the sons of God (Rom VIII, 18-22). This cosmic awareness has never been absent from Eastern

---

78. Ibid., pp. 109-10.

79. Ibid., p. 135.

80 V. Lossky (1985), p. 97. This same phrase is very dear to the fathers like St. Athanasius, St. Gregory of Nazianzius and St. Gregory of Nyssa and can be found in their writings. Ibid.

81. Ibid.

> spirituality, and is given expression in the theology as well as in liturgical poetry, in iconography and, perhaps above all, in the ascetical writings of the masters of the spiritual life of the Eastern Church.[82]

The logical conclusion that follows from such a feeling of oneness is that if humans are not isolated from the rest of the cosmos all that they do have their repercussion on the cosmos. In this regard even the ascetic life of a monk who is confined to his solitary cell in search of sanctification has a cosmic function. Lossky writes:

> Human nature must undergo a change; it must be more and more transfigured by grace in the way of sanctification, which has a range which is not only spiritual but also bodily — and hence cosmic. The spiritual work of a monk living in community or a hermit withdrawn from the world retains all its worth for the entire universe even though it remains hidden from the sight of all.[83]

Thus, humans in their union with God bring also the whole cosmos into union with God. Lossky writes again:

> In his way to union with God, man in no way leaves creatures aside, but gathers together in his love the whole cosmos disordered by sin, that it may at last be transfigured by grace.[84]

Humans, thus, are closely connected with the whole of creation and become the mediators between God and creation. They take the whole creation back to God in their life and worship. This close connection that exists between humans and the cosmos shows that all that we do have a wider influence. For we are not isolated from the rest of the cosmos, we are called to be priests of the world.

---

82. V. Lossky (1973), pp. 110-11.
83. Ibid., p. 18.
84. Ibid., p. 111.

THE CHURCH AND THE DEIFICATION OF THE COSMOS IN THE EUCHARIST

The cosmic function of the deification of humans which we have seen above is realized concretely in the Church through its sacraments and especially in Baptism and in the Eucharist. Through Baptism new members are incorporated to the Body of Christ, the Eucharist in its turn operates the growth of the body towards the glorious Lord and when the Church grows towards its Head, the consecration of the world also takes place.[85] Thus it is in the Church that we are deified and the Church is able to do it because all the conditions which are necessary for this deification are given to it.[86] And through us the cosmos comes in union with God or becomes deified.

The cosmos is, thus, dependent on humans and the Church for its deification and it cannot reach its fulfilment by itself. For God created the world out of nothing and made humans the link between Him and creation. The role of the Church is to make possible the participation of the creation in the fullness of the divine life. The Church stands between God and creation and makes possible its fulfilment. In this manner the Church becomes the centre of the universe where its destinies are determined.[87] As Lossky writes:

> The world was created from nothing by the sole will of God — this is its origin. It was created in order to participate in the fullness of the divine life — this is its vocation. It is called to make this union a reality in liberty, in the free harmony of the created will with the will of God — this is the mystery of the Church inherent in creation.[88]

---

85. See J. Ernst (1968), p. 59.
86. V. Lossky (1973), p. 179.
87. Ibid., p. 178.
88. Ibid., pp. 112-13.

If the Church is the centre of the universe where its destinies are determined then the universe needs to enter into the Church that it may accomplish its role. Thus the entire universe is called to enter into the Church to fulfil the vocation of deification. He writes:

> The entire universe is called to enter within the Church, to become the Church of Christ, that it may be transformed after the consummation of ages, into the eternal Kingdom of God. Created from nothing, the world finds its fulfilment in the Church, where the creation acquires an unshakable foundation in the accomplishment of its vocation.[89]

However, according to Lossky, the Church and the world do not have the same future. The world will grow old and will fall into decay whereas the Church will be constantly rejuvenated and renewed by the Holy Spirit, the source of its life.[90]

The Church is able to perform this deification of the cosmos because it is the image of the Holy Trinity and is being sanctified by the Holy Spirit.[91] He, following Irenaeus (*Adversus Haereses* 5.24), argues that it is in the Body of Christ that we have access to the Holy Spirit,[92] and again the purpose of the incarnation is that we might receive the Holy Spirit.[93] The presence of the Holy Spirit is important because he is the condition for our deification,[94] and the work of the Holy Spirit is inseparable from that of the Son.[95] Thus, according to Lossky, "our ultimate deification cannot be

---

89. Ibid., p. 113.
90. Ibid., p. 178.
91. Here Lossky argues that the Church is sanctified not by the observance of the law but through the participation of the divine nature by the Holy Spirit. This participation again takes place in the Holy Eucharist. Ibid., pp. 177 and 180.
92. Ibid., p. 177.
93. Ibid., pp. 179 and 181.
94. Ibid., pp. 179-80.
95. V. Lossky (1985), p. 103.

expressed on a Christological basis alone, but demands a Pneumatological development as well."[96]

In the Eucharist we receive not only the Body and Blood of Christ but also the Holy Spirit and our deification is the combined effort of both Christ and the Holy Spirit. When we are united to Christ we become deified by virtue of this union and we also become one with all the members of the Church who partake of the Body and Blood of Christ.[97] He writes:

> In the Church and through the sacraments our nature enters into union with the divine nature in the hypostasis of the Son, the Head of His mystical body. Our humanity becomes consubstantial with the deified humanity, united with the person of Christ; but our person has not yet attained its perfection. . . .[98]

Thus, in the Eucharist we become one with Christ and with the members of the Church, and when we become one with Christ we are able to transmit to the world the power of deification.

In this way Lossky takes further the idea started by Maximus on the role of deification. He argues that our deification, which was started in the incarnation is continued in the Eucharist and in Baptism. Here again the role of the sacrament in the deification becomes important, because it is through the sacrament of the sacrifice of Christ that humans and the cosmos are deified. Thus our deification which was started in the incarnation is not finished, on the contrary it continues through the Holy Spirit and through the sacraments in the Church. Still further in our deification we do not leave aside the creatures but we take them with us to God. Even the activities of a solitary monk confined to his cell is said to have a cosmic function, because humans in their spiritual realisation do not leave aside the creatures. As a result, when we become

---

96. Ibid.
97. V. Lossky (1973), p. 180.
98. Ibid., p. 181.

deified the cosmos too is deified for we are not isolated from the rest of creation.

The Eucharist and the Survival of the World in J.D. Zizioulas

John D. Zizioulas,[99] following closely the thought pattern of Maximus and Lossky, goes more deeper into the question of the cosmic dimension of the Eucharist by analysing the almost virtual disappearance of the cosmic dimension from Western sacramental theology. Among the contemporary theologians, and the Orthodox theologians in particular, he can be considered as the one who has clearly demonstrated the relation between the Eucharist and the continued existence of the cosmos. Following the Eastern theologians he considers the cosmic aspect of the Eucharist fundamental to the Eastern theology, an aspect according to him the Western theology lost in the development of its sacramental theology.[100] Herebelow we intend to discover some of the specific elements such as the relation of human being, the priest of the world to creation and the role of the Eucharist as the medicine of immortality for the world.

HUMAN BEING AS PRIEST OF THE WORLD

Zizioulas, like Maximus and Lossky, thinks in terms of basic unity between humans and nature. This basic unity is fundamental to the cosmic function of the Eucharist and to think in terms of duality

---

99. For this section we depend mainly on the book, I. Zizioulas (1994). I am indebted to the author for the development of the themes of this section. John D. Zizioulas is also sometimes written as Ioannes/Johannes D. Zizioulas.

100. Ibid., p. 17. According to M. Vidalis, till the fourth century even the irrational creation was mentioned in the *anaphoras*, but from the fourth century this mention of the irrational creatures have been left out in the *anaphoras*. M. Vidalis (1998), p. 200. The irrational creatures are said to praise God through humans. Ibid., p. 203.

is to lose sight of this cosmic function. He argues that while in the East the positive outlook on the world by Maximus continued, in the West the negative outlook on the world propagated by Boezio and Augustine became important and caused the cosmic function of humans to cease.[101]

Zizioulas, therefore, holds that the cosmic dimension of the Eucharist is central to the Orthodox liturgy, whereas Western liturgy lacks such a vision. According to him, when the Western Church under the influence of a philosophy of dichotomy lost its vision of unity in the creation it also lost the cosmic dimension in its sacramental theology, for he writes:

> The church gradually lost the awareness of the importance and the eternal value of material creation, which is made particularly evident in the manner of treating the sacraments, the Eucharist in particular: instead of being a benediction on the material world, the fruits of nature, and a grateful reminder of and consecration to the Creator, the Eucharist soon became in the first place a memorial of the sacrifice of Christ and an instrument of grace for the nourishment of the *soul*. The dimension of the *kosmos* disappears soon from the sacramental theology of the West, leaving the place to a soul-centred or spirit-centred vision of the world.[102]

Further, in the medieval and modern times human being's rational capacity was given more importance over nature and this again widened the gap between humans and nature. He writes: "The

101. I. Zizioulas (1994), p. 16. According to Zizioulas, the influence of the Platonist dualism and of the gnostics of the second and third centuries and the importance given to the reason made the cosmic function of the Eucharist disappear from the sacramental theology of the West. Ibid., pp. 15-18. According to Henry de Lubac, Teilhard had realized that the Western theology was too much dependent on St. Augustine and by contrast he loved to recall the way of thinking of Clement of Alexandria and of St. Irenaeus. H. de Lubac (1967), p. 120.

102. I. Zizioulas (1994), p. 17.

sacraments remained still in major part irrelevant to the material world, and the furrow between humans and nature widened still deeper."[103]

The dualistic outlook on the world and the predominance given to the rationality of the human being brought the Western Church to consider humans as separated from nature and as the only being concerned with eternity. Certainly in such a view nature became something that exists for humans and that can be exploited for their own selfish purposes.[104] Humans, thus, forgot that they are priests of the world and took an antagonistic view towards creation. As a result they lost sight of the interdependence between humans, nature and the Church.

Zizioulas considers the Eucharistic community as the place in which all dualistic views are overcome, for he writes:

> The eucharistic community with its understanding of the Eucharist as a *meal*, with its basic elements being material and not spiritual, with its long litanies and supplications in which man's everyday material and physical needs find their place, etc. constitutes a sign of a "catholic" view of existence in which no dualistic dichotomies can be accepted. Man and the world form a unity in harmony and so do the various dimensions in man's own existence.[105]

Thus, a "catholic" view of existence cannot accept a dualistic view and to think in dualistic terms is to lose sight of the basic unity and the interrelation that exists between the Church and the world. For he writes again:

> There is a constant interrelationship between the Church and the world, the world being God's creation and never ceasing to belong to him and the Church being the community which

103. Ibid.

104. We forget that we are also creatures and we cannot become the absolute measure of things. See R. Panikkar (1993), pp. 33-46.

105. J.D. Zizioulas (1970), p. 331.

> through the descent of the Holy Spirit transcends in herself the world and offers it to God in the Eucharist.[106]

The Eucharistic community is the place where the Church transcends all the divisions in her and in the world and offers the world to God. To think in terms of dualism is not only to lose sight of the catholicity of the Church but also to take on an antagonistic view of creation. A dualistic attitude of humans with regard to creation leads not only to losing sight of the catholicity of the Church but also to an utilitarian perspective which again makes us forget that we are responsible for the world.

Further, when we forget that God who created the world out of nothing made us priests of the world we take an antagonistic attitude towards creation for we are the only being capable of reasoning. And if humans can be spoken of as superior to the rest of creation it has to be seen in the perspective of their cosmic priesthood and not of their rationality as the rationalists thought. Only humans are able to enter into a relationship and to go beyond themselves, i.e. to God.[107] What is important, thus, is not the thinking capacity in us but our ability to create communion and to go beyond ourselves, that is, to God. And on account of this capacity we are called to be priests of the world and our priestly function consists in making possible the survival of the cosmos by offering the world to God in the Eucharist.[108]

Zizioulas too thinks, like Maximus, that Adam was created to bring the creation back to God. If for Maximus the sin of Adam consisted in his failure to bring the union or cosmic synthesis to make possible the deification of the cosmos, for Zizioulas the sin of Adam consisted in his failure to accomplish his function as priest of the world. Adam made himself the ultimate referent of creation

---

106. Ibid., pp. 331-32.
107. I. Zizioulas (1994), p. 9.
108. G. Mantzarides (1981), pp. 66.

and not God.[109] He argues that if Adam had acted as the priest of the world he could have made creation overcome its limits. Where Adam as priest of the world failed, Christ succeeded.[110] In this way Christ recapitulated in his person the whole creation and offered it to God. The Eucharist continues this recapitulating all of creation and offering it back to God.[111] Thus, whatever the first Adam and his descendants did not accomplish, the new Adam, Christ — and with him the Church, does accomplish in the Eucharist.

Another aspect which we can find in Zizioulas and other Eastern theologians is their belief that God created the universe out of nothing, and this universe cannot survive by itself, it can survive only in relation to God.[112] As St. Gregory of Nyssa writes:

> For nothing would remain in existence if it did not remain in the being. Moreover, the foremost and primary being is the divine being. The fact that all things remain in existence compels us to believe that this divine being exists in them.[113]

Maximus too thinks in a similar way when he speaks of three modes of existence: being, well-being and eternal being.[114] The

---

109. J.D. Zizioulas (1994), p. 66.

110. Ibid., p. 67.

111. P. McPartlan (1993), p. 132.

112. In the Eastern theologians the sense of God as the Creator is very strong and they do not separate themselves from the rest of creation. The role of the incarnation is again to re-establish the lost harmony in creation. In the West unity in creation was probably put into question due to the gnostic dualism. As a result redemption was considered to be the highest point to the extent of putting creation and incarnation to a secondary level. As we have seen in Karl Barth we need to rediscover the unity between creation, incarnation and redemption.

113. Gregory of Nyssa, *Kathchtikój* 32, as quoted by G. Mantzarides (1981), p. 63.

114. Maximus the Confessor (1857b), p. 65. In *PG* 91, 1392. See also P. Sherwood (1955), p. 67.

work of salvation consists of these three stages in which Christ successively re-establishes in nature the being through his incarnation, well-being by destroying the corruptible will in his earthly life and on the cross thereby giving an incorruptible will, and thirdly the eternal being by granting the incorruptibility of nature in the resurrection.[115]

The relation of the world to God through humans becomes, therefore, an ontological need and indispensable presupposition for the preservation of the cosmos. It is for this reason that the Eastern theologians consider humans as priests of the world, called to perform the cosmic liturgy.[116] Zizioulas even goes to the extent of saying, "Humans have to become liturgical beings before they can hope to overcome their ecological crisis."[117] The survival of creation is, thus, first made possible in the redemption and it now depends on our priestly function as the priest of creation, as those who bring back the world to its Creator. This priestly role of ours in the world is best explained by M. Vidalis in the following passage:

> The irrational creatures realize the fullness of their doxological vocation asking man who is the logos, the word, to express a rational praise to God. Man becomes the passage without whom the doxology and the thanksgiving of the cosmos towards its Creator and redeemer cannot be fulfilled. His place itself in the cosmos is changed. Man is no more the dominator of the cosmos as the OT cites of him, but is its co-operator. The cosmos makes part of him not only thanks to his created nature, but also for the communion of the same doxological experience for their Creator. Man takes the role of the priest who rents to the cosmos his voice and his conscience to give glory to God. Man then is put at the centre of the world to be the priest of the creation, the spokesman

---

115. Ibid. See also V. Lossky (1973), p. 154.

116. G. Mantzarides (1981), p. 64.

117. J. Zizioulas (1989), p. 2.

> of the universe, appointed to direct it to God in an unceasing doxology.[118]

So we become the voice of creation to thank God and make its existence possible.

Again according to Zizioulas, creation is not only destined by God to survive but also to reach its "fullness" in and through the hands of humans. We are made capable of this function firstly by our being *hypostatic* and secondly by our being *ecstatic*.[119] By being *hypostatic* we are integrated with the material world and by being *ecstatic*, that is spiritual, we are given the capacity to elevate the world to infinite possibilities by referring it to God. This we are able to do because we are created in the image and likeness of God. Humans as priests of the world take the world in their own hands and offer it to God and in this manner frees it from its limits and makes it reach its fullness.

THE EUCHARIST AS THE "MEDICINE OF IMMORTALITY" FOR THE WORLD

Everything that exists needs to pass through the hands of humans, the priests of the world, to God for its survival and this happens in the Eucharistic sacrifice.[120] This cosmic function of the Eucharist was very much present in the primitive Eucharistic prayers

---

118. M. Vidalis (1998), p. 203.

119. It is this ecstatic quality that helps humans to reach out to God and take the world to God. As G. Mantzarides writes: "An ecstatic being means one that surpasses itself and is turned toward something outside of itself. In theological language, man's ecstatic nature is indicated by his distinction as a creature 'according to the image and likeness of God.' An image does not have meaning except in relation to that which it reflects." G. Mantzarides (1981), p. 63.

120. According to Cyril of Jerusalem, the whole creation participates in the praise and the veneration of God. Cyril of Jerusalem (1857), pp. 5-6. In *PG* 33, 1113B. See also M. Vidalis (1998), p. 199. See also G. Bosio (1965), vol. 2, pp. 63-65.

formulated in the pattern of the Jewish prayers.[121] Whereas in the West the liturgy lost its cosmic sense, in the East this sense remained one of its characteristics. According to Zizioulas,[122] (a) all the primitive liturgies, especially in the East, include a sanctification of the material and of time, (b) all the liturgies of the first centuries were centred more on the elevation of creation to God in its *anaphora* and not so much on the consecration of the elements, and (c) this elevation of creation to its Creator in the *anaphora* can form not only the basis for a theology of creation but can also confer an equal centrality to humans' action as priests of creation so that the Holy Spirit may transform the offerings into the body and blood of Christ.[123]

According to Zizioulas, in the primitive Church *anaphora*[124] had to do with the priestly function of humans as the representative of creation and for this reason all the Eucharistic liturgies of the primitive Church began their Eucharistic prayers with the mention of creation, and only after that God was thanked for the redemption through Christ. The earliest Eucharistic prayers of the Church, composed in the best typology of the best liturgical tradition of the Jews, included a benediction on the fruits of the earth, to affirm the faith in the survival of creation, and not merely of human beings.[125]

Zizioulas holds that the priestly aspect of the Eucharist did not consist in the notion of sacrifice, as it was interpreted in the middle ages, but in that of offering back to God his own

---

121. See M. Vidalis (1998), pp. 195-208; M. Metzger (1998), pp. 153-63.

122. I. Zizioulas (1994), pp. 20-22.

123. Ibid., p. 21.

124. Ibid., On the primitive *anaphoras* see E. Mazza (1996a), pp. 125-369.

125. I. Zizioulas (1994), p. 14.

creation.[126] The disappearance of the creational dimension from the notion of priesthood was due to the prevalence of the notion of sacrifice.[127] The whole person is at the centre of the liturgy and this is possible only if we take seriously our material nature and hence the cosmos. This cosmic element is also clear in the prayer for the propitiation for the climate and for the abundance of crops.

We bring back the creation to God in the Eucharistic sacrifice, for when we go to the Eucharist we take with us the whole creation. Zizioulas writes:

> All the faithful who go to the liturgy carry with them the world (considered here in a very realistic manner). They do not carry only themselves with the proper relative incapacity and passions, but carry with them their relation with the natural world, with the creation.[128]

This offering of the world in the Eucharist is evident in the offertory procession in which bread, wine, oil, etc. are presented to the Bishop in "the Great Entrance," who in turn offers them to God. For, according to Zizioulas,

> . . . during the liturgy there takes place a movement, of a procession of the whole world towards the holy Table (the altar), of a world as it is and as it will be again when the eschatological splendour, the anticipated tasting of the paradise given by the Eucharist will end, and the faithful will be called once again "to live in peace" in the world.[129]

In the liturgy, thus, there takes place an experience of a movement of the whole world to God and this experience is fundamental to the Orthodox theology.

However, the world that meets in the liturgical space is the same world that is corrupted and by admitting the world to the

126. Ibid., p. 22.

127. Ibid., pp. 22-23.

128. Ibid., p. 75.

129. Ibid., pp. 75-76.

holy place its vocation is fulfilled. The world is admitted into the holy place not because it may remain as it is but because it may be administered the "medicine of immortality."[130] And when the world is accepted in the liturgy it gets sanctified and is put in relation to its Creator on whom its survival depends. In this manner the Eucharist becomes the place where the world is affirmed and at the same time negated, the place where the renewal of the whole creation takes place without destroying the old. Zizioulas writes:

> The liturgy expresses a paradox by operating the affirmation and the negation of the world, precisely by a transfiguration that does not destroy the world, a regeneration that does not create from nothing, a renewal that is not total regeneration; the paradox in the Eucharist is that makes present and visible in time and space the mystery of Christ, in which the old Adam renews himself without being destroyed, the human nature gets assumed without being changed, and man gets deified without ceasing to be human being.[131]

Such Eucharistic vision of the world helps us to overcome the dichotomy between the natural and the supernatural, the material and the spiritual. According to Zizioulas, it was the dualism which the Western theology advocated in the course of time that was

---

130. I. Zizioulas (1994), pp. 76-77. This phrase goes back to Ignatius of Antioch who was the first to consider the Eucharistic bread as the medicine of immortality (*phármakon athanasìas*), the antidote against the death, and food to live for ever in Jesus Christ. Ignatius of Antioch (1857), 20: 2. In *PG* 5, 66A. See also G. di Nola (1994), vol. 1, pp. 86-87. The Eucharist as the medicine of immortality is a theme very dear to the Fathers of the Church. St. Justin considers it as the nutriment that transforms us (*Apologia secunda* 66. In *PG* 6, 428), S. Irenaeus considers it as the means for life and immortality (*Adverses Haereses* 4.18.5), St. Cyril considers the flesh of the Lord as life-giving. For more details see D. van den Eynde (1957), pp. 115-27.

131. I. Zizioulas (1994), p. 77.

the reason for the rejection of the supernatural or for the indifference to it.[132] We need, thus, a liturgical vision of the world where we think not in terms of supernatural and natural, material and spiritual, but in terms of nature and creation as a single reality that comes from God and is offered to God. This offering of the world surely takes place in the Eucharist and in this way the Eucharist becomes the meeting place of the heavenly and the earthly world, where God is no more considered as beyond nature but in the person of the Son, the one who sits in heaven with the Father and who is invisibly present here with us.[133]

The Eucharistic vision not only helps us to overcome the dichotomy between the supernatural and the natural but also to overcome the antithesis between time and eternity. The Eucharist helps us not to consider history and time as a necessary evil but as preparatory to eternity, for in the Eucharist history meets eternity. In such a vision eternity is not considered as something that is completely in the future but already present here. Eternity includes the past, present and future and forms a single unity. Thus, it becomes the dimension in which time can find its full acceptance and sanctification provided that it is considered as the theological place for the realization of the eternal plan of God for our salvation which takes place in the Eucharistic sacrifice.[134]

The Eucharist, thus, has a cosmic function, for God created humans as priests of the world. Our role as priests of the world consists in bringing back creation to God in the Eucharistic sacrifice. In the forms of bread, wine, oil, incense, flowers, candles, etc. we offer creation back to God and make its survival possible. In the Eucharist, the whole world gives thanks to God through us. In the words of M. Vidalis,

---

132. Ibid., p. 78.

133. Ibid.

134. Ibid., p. 79.

> The whole world gives thanks to its Creator, be it with praises, be it with the offerings of oneself to the Lord. And God gives the fullness of his grace to creation by giving it the communion with divinity. In our journey towards the deification by grace we exercise the role of bearers of the cosmos and its guide.[135]

If for Maximus and Lossky the Eucharist was the means by which creation became deified, for Zizioulas it is not only the place where creation is unified and offered back to God but also the place where we exercise our role as priests of the world and in this way make its survival possible. The Eucharist thus becomes the medicine of immortality, not only for humans, but also for the whole cosmos. Such a vision requires a positive approach to the cosmos. The cosmic dimension of the Eucharist thus becomes clearer if we take into consideration the unity between creation, incarnation, and the continued deification of humans and the cosmos in and through the Eucharist. This theme is taken further by Teilhard de Chardin from a different point of view, i.e. from the point of view of scientific evolution which we will see now.

The Eucharist and the Cosmos in Pierre Teilhard de Chardin

Our analysis of the three important Eastern theologians in the last section has shown us clearly that the Eucharist, being the sacrament through which humanity and cosmos are deified, has a cosmic function. Now we will analyse a modern Western palaeontologist, Pierre Teilhard de Chardin, who sees the cosmic function of the Eucharist from a different point of view, i.e. starting from below, in the universal evolution.[136] If for Maximus, Lossky and Zizioulas the cosmic function of the Eucharist consisted in the

---

135. M. Vidalis (1998), p. 208.

136. The nature of Teilhard de Chardin's writings on the Eucharist is mostly mystical and spiritual and not strictly theological. As R. Faricy holds rightly that Teilhard de Chardin does not have a complete theology of Eucharist. R.L. Faricy (1967), p. 129. And →

deification and the transformation of the cosmos, for Teilhard de Chardin it consists in the Christification of the universe and the anticipation of the Omega Point of the universal evolution. Thus he adds a new element to the deification of the cosmos,[137] that is, the anticipation of the Omega Point of the universal evolution in the Eucharist.

THE EUCHARIST AND EVOLUTION

Teilhard holds a cosmic theology of the Eucharist which is very much related to his conception of the cosmic Christ and universal evolution.[138] The Eucharist is closely related to the growth of the world. Therefore, life in its totality, and not in its elements, becomes the focal point of his reflection on the Eucharist. Teilhard was moved by the attraction for the whole as he writes:

→ in the words of J. Fitzer, he has taken for granted a great deal of things on Eucharist. J. Fitzer (1973), p. 251. These facts show that our task is not an easy one. There is a lack of clear perspective in Teilhard de Chardin's writings on the Eucharist and we should understand his view on Eucharist mainly from his theory of universal evolution and not from the real presence of Christ in the Eucharist or from the relation of the Eucharistic sacrifice to that of the sacrifice on the cross. The principal Eucharistic passages in Teilhard's writings can be found in the following English translations of his writings: Teilhard de Chardin (1973b), pp. 157-73; Teilhard de Chardin (1974a), pp. 19-37; Teilhard de Chardin (1968), pp. 60-66; Teilhard de Chardin (1967), pp. 121-28; Teilhard de Chardin (1971), pp. 165-67. For more details see J. Fitzer (1973), p. 252, footnote 4.

137. On the transformation of the cosmos see H. de Lubac (1967), pp. 132-42. Here in this aspect Teilhard de Chardin follows the thought pattern of the Eastern Fathers which we discussed before in this chapter on the deification of the cosmos.

138. For more details on the Cosmic-Christ of Teilhard de Chardin see J.A. Lyons (1982), pp. 75-87 and 147-219; G.A. Maloney (1968), pp. 182-220; and for a more recent study on the same issue see J.-M. Maldamé (1995), pp. 162-78.

> It is the attraction of the whole that has set everything in motion in me, has animated and given organic form to everything. It is because I feel the whole and live it passionately that I believe in the primacy of being — and that I cannot admit that life meets a final check — and that I cannot look for a lesser reward than this whole itself.[139]

This whole that is purified, sublimated and made conscious becomes the focal point of his reflection. According to Teilhard de Chardin, we fail to understand the unity in the cosmos because we try to understand the whole through fragments of the whole and not by affirming the fundamental and substantial unity in the universe.[140] This makes him to analyse the relation of matter and spirit, of humans and the cosmos, and human's activity in the cosmos to Christ, the guiding principle behind the universal evolution.

Often we think only of the Spirit leading us forward, but according to Teilhard matter and Spirit are so interconnected that the Spirit cannot exist without the support of the matter and vice versa. It is the matter that sustains the Spirit. For he writes:

> Indeed, even if it is Spirit that constantly carries matter along and supports it in the ascent towards consciousness, it is matter, in return, that enables Spirit to subsist by constantly providing it with a point upon which to act, and supplying it with nourishment. . . .[141]

He writes further:

> In the system of creative union, moreover, it becomes impossible to continue crudely to contrast Spirit and matter. For those who have understood the law of "spiritualization by union," there is no longer two compartments in the universe, the spiritual and the physical: there are only two directions along one and the

139. Teilhard de Chardin (1968), p. 44.
140. Ibid., p. 52.
141. Ibid., p. 50.

> same road (the direction of pernicious pluralism, and that of beneficial unification). Every being in the world stands somewhere on the slope that rises up from the shadows towards light. In front of it, lies the effort to master simply its own nature; behind, the abandonment of effort in the physical and moral disintegration of its powers. If it goes forward, it meets the good: everything in Spirit for it. If it falls back, it meets nothing on its road but evil and matter. . . . Matter and Spirit are not opposed as two separate things, as two natures, but as two directions of evolution within the world.[142]

Christ becomes the centre of the universe through his immersion into the matter in his incarnation. He does not make his way into the world through any side-road, he penetrates into the stuff of the cosmos, pours himself into the life-blood of the universe by first dissolving himself in matter, later to be reborn from it.[143] Thus, Christ does first a "kenosis" into matter and then a co-feeling in the human agony and bliss.[144] Through this immersion into the world's womb he brings unity in creation.

Teilhard de Chardin too, like Maximus the Confessor, considers the cosmic unity in Christ as the basis for his further reflections on the Eucharist. And this cosmic and evolutionary theology of the Eucharist he derives from his intuition of the fundamental unity that exists in the cosmos in Jesus Christ. The unity of creation in Christ is the basis of his reflections on the interrelation of humans and the cosmos and of the evolution. He writes:

> . . . it is Christ who in a real and unmetaphorical sense of the word holds up the universe. So incredible a cosmic function may well be too much for our imagination, but I do not see how we could possibly avoid attributing it to the Son of Mary. The

---

142. Ibid., p. 51.
143. Ibid., p. 60.
144. Ibid., p. 62.

> Incarnate Word could not be the supernatural (hyper-physical) centre of the universe if he did not function *first* as its physical, natural, centre. Christ cannot sublimate creation in God without progressively raising it up by his influence through the successive circles of matter and spirit. That is why, in order to bring all things back to his Father, he had to make himself one with all — he had to enter into contact with every one of the zones of the created, from the lowest and most earthly to the zone that is closest to heaven.[145]

Thus, for Teilhard de Chardin, Christ's role is not limited to human persons alone, but to the whole created order. This he is able to do it because he is divine, human, and cosmic. Christ's resurrection, for Teilhard de Chardin, is a tremendous cosmic event, that is, Christ assuming his function as the universal centre.[146]

We know the difficulty which Teilhard de Chardin had to face with the Church on account of his mystical Christ-centred evolutionary theory, and for his concept of cosmic Christ. Now it seems that the Church is comparatively less perplexed with such an idea. The cosmic role of Christ's incarnation can be found in what the late Pope John Paul II in one of his Encyclicals wrote:

> The Incarnation of God the Son signifies the taking up into unity with God not only of human nature, but in his human nature, in a sense, of everything that is "flesh": the whole of humanity, the entire visible and material world. The Incarnation, then, also has a cosmic significance, a cosmic dimension. The "first born of all creation," becoming incarnate in the individual humanity of Christ, unites himself in some way with the entire reality of man, which is also "flesh" — and in this reality with all "flesh," with the whole creation.[147]

---

145. Teilhard de Chardin (1971), p. 71.

146. Teilhard de Chardin (1968), p. 63.

147. John Paul II (2005), pp. 873-74. One of the important contemporary Western theologians who thought in the line of cosmic evolution of Teilhard de Chardin without denying the centrality of Christ in the creation and in the redemption is Karl →

The Body of Christ, thus, for Teilhard de Chardin is the physical centre for humankind and material world. Christ in his incarnation plunges into the matter and by becoming one with the matter he becomes the physical centre of this universe. By this he directs the process of evolution. This cosmic function of Christ is being fulfilled today in and through the Eucharist. For, when a Christian, who has understood God's unifying energy in the Eucharist, receives Christ in the communion he speeds up the process of evolution.

THE COSMOS AS THE MATERIAL FOR THE EUCHARISTIC SACRIFICE AND HUMANS AS PRIESTS OF THE WORLD

The basic unity that exists in the cosmos through the presence of Christ in it by the incarnation leads to another aspect, that is, the abolition of the distinction between sacred and profane.[148] For Teilhard de Chardin the universe is one organic cosmos and all its parts are inextricably linked together and form a single totality, for in his words: "In a secondary and generalised sense, but in a true sense, the sacramental Species are formed by the totality of the world, and the duration of the creation is the time needed for its consecration."[149] For him matter and spirit, body and soul, by virtue of their interrelation, form the totality of the sacramental Species. The material for the sacrifice is the totality of the universe and not an isolated part of it. The world has become — according to Teilhard de Chardin — a sacrament in the incarnation and from that moment all matter is henceforth incarnate.[150]

→ Rahner. According to him, God is present in each part of the cosmos sustaining and empowering it, that this same God might bring the whole evolutive moment of creation to its completion. See K. Rahner (1988a), pp. 157-92.

148. Teilhard de Chardin (1967), p. 66.

149. Ibid., p. 126.

150. Teilhard de Chardin (1974a), pp. 24 and 26.

As a result he considers the whole world as fit for the Eucharistic offering. During the War in 1918 he wrote: "Since today, Lord, I, your priest, have neither bread nor wine nor altar, I shall spread my hands over the whole universe and take its immensity as the matter of my sacrifice."[151] Five years later in 1923, during a scientific expedition in the deserts of China, he found himself unable to celebrate the Holy Eucharist and on that occasion he wrote his work entitled: *La messe sur le monde* (*The Mass on the World*). Here too, he considers the world as the material for the Eucharistic sacrament for he writes:

> Since . . . I have neither bread, nor wine, nor altar, I will raise myself beyond these symbols, up to the pure majesty of the real itself; I, your priest, will make the whole earth my altar and on it will offer you all the labours and sufferings of the world. . . .
> I will place on my paten, O God, the harvest to be won by this renewal of labour. Into my chalice I shall pour all the sap which is to be pressed out this day from the earth's fruits.[152]

Teilhard de Chardin not only offers the whole world as his offering but also calls a divine consecration on this offering. He writes:

> Over every living thing which is to spring up, to grow, to flower, to ripen during this day say again the words: This is my Body. And over every death-force which waits in readiness to corrode, to wither, to cut down, speak again the commanding words which express the supreme mystery of faith: This is my Blood.[153]

In the words of J.A. Lyons:

> this utterance is not simply a rhapsodic devotional substitute for the liturgical rite which he was temporarily unable to perform. It indicates his true understanding of the Eucharist, which is probably best summed up in the following remark . . .

---

151. Teilhard de Chardin (1973b), p. 157.
152. Ibid., p. 19. See also J. Fitzer (1973), p. 252.
153. Teilhard de Chardin (1974a), p. 23. See also J. Fitzer (1973), p. 253.

> to adhere to Christ in the Eucharist is, inevitably and *ipso facto*, to incorporate ourselves, a little more each day, into a Christogenesis, which is none other than the universal cosmogenesis.[154]

Teilhard de Chardin, thus, offers the whole cosmos as his offering and together with it the advancement in the evolution of the earth according to the plan of God.

The interrelation of matter and spirit, body and soul lead to another aspect, that is, the universal consecration in the Eucharist. For Teilhard de Chardin the transubstantiation is not limited to bread and wine alone; it goes beyond them to the universe, for he writes:

> When the priest says the words *Hoc est corpus meum*, his words fall directly on to the bread and directly transform it into the individual reality of Christ. But the great sacramental operation does not cease at the local momentary event.[155]

The time needed for such consecration is the duration of the creation.[156] Thus, in the Eucharist the whole world is offered and there takes place a universal transubstantiation for the words of consecration fall not only upon the bread and wine but also upon the totality of joys and sufferings of human endeavour that brings further progress in the world.

The effects of the universal consecration become more concrete in the communion, for through the communion of the Blessed Eucharist Christ enters into us and through us gradually subjects the universe into his transforming power.[157] Teilhard de Chardin writes:

---

154. J.A. Lyons (1982), p. 163-64; Teilhard de Chardin (1971), p. 166.
155. Teilhard de Chardin (1967), pp. 123-25.
156. Ibid., p. 126.
157. Ibid.

> As our humanity assimilates the material world, and as the Host assimilates our humanity, the eucharistic transformation goes beyond and completes the transubstantiation of the bread of the altar. Step by step it irresistibly invades the universe.[158]

When we submit to Christ, his life is extended even to the sub-human cosmos. In such manner the Eucharist, being the expression and the manifestation of God's unifying energy applied individually to each spiritual atom of the universe, transforms the cosmos into the body of Christ.[159] And in this transformation of the universe the human endeavour gets an important role in the Eucharistic theology of Teilhard de Chardin. For, Christ continues to carry out his function in the universe through the human beings who work for a better world. Human work, therefore, gets a higher role in such relation because it is seen as the participation in the creative work of Christ to bring the fullness of Christ. In this process every human endeavour is considered to be a step forward in building up the *pleroma* of Christ and the role of the Eucharist is exactly to bring out the fullness of Christ. Through us Christ comes in contact with the material world and transfigures it once again into an offering to the Eternal Father. In this manner humans are called to be the priest of the world. For he writes:

> I seem to hear, rising up from all creatures — both those that are imprisoned in inert matter, and those too, who move and act in freedom — the universal lament: "Show your pity for us, O you priest, and, if it be in your power, give us our fulfilment by giving us our God!" Who, then, will utter, over the formless mass of the world, the words that will give it onc soul? What voice will overthrow the obstacle between God and creation which prevents this One from meeting with that other? . . .[160]

---

158. Ibid.

159. J. Fitzer (1973), p. 258.

160. Teilhard de Chardin (1973b), p. 158.

Teilhard de Chardin, thus, sees not only the whole universe as the material for the Eucharistic offering, but also every priest as priest of the world, called to offer to God the entire world.[161] Surprisingly he considers this offering of the world to God as more important for a priest than the care of the individual souls.[162]

THE CHRISTIFICATION OF THE UNIVERSE AND THE ANTICIPATION OF THE OMEGA POINT IN THE EUCHARIST

For Teilhard de Chardin the Eucharist holds the mystery to the plan of God for the universe. Through the Eucharist Christ's redemptive and unitive acts are being accomplished in the universe. The Host is primarily a fragment of matter to which through the transubstantiation, the presence of Christ extends to the human zone of the universe. In this way everything around us is Christified. This process began with the incarnation and continues through the Eucharist. He writes:

> . . . when Christ descends sacramentally into each one of his faithful it is not simply in order to commune with him; it is in order to join him, physically, a little more closely to himself and to all the rest of the faithful in the growing unity of the world. When, through the priest, Christ says, *Hoc est corpus meum*, "This is my body," the words reach out infinitely far beyond the morsel of bread over which they are pronounced: they bring the entire mystical body into being. The priestly act extends beyond the transubstantiated Host to the cosmos itself, which, century after century, is gradually being transformed by the Incarnation, itself never complete. From age to age, there is but one single mass in the world: the true Host, the total Host, is the universe which is continually being more intimately penetrated and vivified by Christ. From the most distant origin of things until their unforeseeable consummation, through the countless convulsions of boundless space, the whole of nature is slowly

---

161. Ibid., p. 173.

162. Ibid.

> and irresistibly undergoing the supreme consecration. Fundamentally — since all time and for ever — but one single thing is being made in creation: the body of Christ.[163]

The novelty of Teilhard de Chardin's theology of the Eucharist, thus, can be found mostly in his treatment of it in the context of evolution and of Christogenesis. The Eucharist and universal evolution have the same function, that is, the Christification of the universe and the anticipation of the Omega point.[164] The whole creation is in movement which consists in an upward and forward movement. And the goal of such movements is the Christogenesis which consists of three phases:

> First, the beginning, the uttering of the cosmos in the Word; second, the incarnation, when the Word became flesh or "cosmos," or when the cosmos became the "body" of the Word; and third, the *parousia*, where the "union" of the Word and the cosmos will be complete. The omega "point" is the crossing point, the final intersection of the cosmos with Christ: the *totus Christus*.[165]

He writes again:

> In reality the Eucharist belongs to an order of its own among the sacraments. It is the first of the sacraments, or rather it is the one sacrament to which all the others are related; and this for the good reason that the *axis* of the Incarnation, that is to say of creation, runs directly through the Eucharist.
>
> Consider . . . what happens when we go to communion. In the first place, and immediately, we enter personally into physiological contact, at the moment of communion, with the assimilative power of the incarnate Word. . . . All the communions of our life are, in fact, only successive instants or episodes in one single communion — in one and the same process of Christification.

---

163. Teilhard (1971), pp. 73-74.

164. E. Benz (1966), p. 225. See also J. Fitzer (1973), p. 251.

165. A. Bruggeman (1966), p. 134.

> . . . If, then, all my own communions form but one single great communion, then all the communions of all men of all times, taken as one great whole, also add up to but one single and even vaster communion, co-extensive in this case with the history of mankind. This amounts to saying that when the eucharist is considered in the complete effecting of its operation, it is simply the expression and the manifestation of God's unifying energy applied individually to each spiritual atom of the universe.
>
> To put it briefly, to adhere to Christ in the Eucharist is inevitably and *ipso facto* to incorporate ourselves a little more fully on each occasion in a Christogenesis, which itself . . . is none other than the soul of universal cosmogenesis.[166]

The incarnation is the final term of creation and it stands between the first creation and the *parousia*. This incarnation is realized in each individual through the Eucharistic mystery and, in this manner, it has the function of prolonging the incarnation till the *parousia*. Teilhard de Chardin writes:

> In fact, from the beginning of the Messianic preparation, up till the *Parousia*, passing through the historic manifestation of Jesus and the phases of growth of His Church, a single event has been developing in the world: the Incarnation, realized, in each individual, through the Eucharist. All the communions of a lifetime are one communion. All the communions of all men, now living are one communion. All communions of all men, present, past and future, are one communion.[167]

Further, through the incarnation Christ, the Divine Word has inserted himself into our material universe and has become the cosmic centre drawing all beings to a supernatural centre, the Omega point.[168] This function of drawing all beings to Christ, the

---

166. Teilhard de Chardin (1971), pp. 165-66.
167. Teilhard de Chardin (1967), p. 124.
168. G.A. Maloney (1968), p. 200; R.L. Faricy (1967), pp. 96-98.

centre, is now realized in and through the means of the Church. As Maloney writes,

> the Church, the phylum of salvation, and the material cosmos are moving to a completion that will be realized only in their convergence at the Omega Point in the *parousia*. . . . He [Christ] is the "summit" towards which both the Church and the cosmos are evolving.[169]

The function of the Eucharist, thus, for Teilhard de Chardin is not only to realize in each individual the mystery of incarnation but also to prolong the incarnation in the cosmos and to Christify the universe.[170] In such manner he considers the Eucharist as *the sacrament* of the world for through the incarnation the whole world has become permeated with the presence of Christ.

The Eucharist, thus, for Teilhard de Chardin is not only "first" among the sacraments; it is *the* sacrament, and all the others are in reference to it. This is because through the Eucharist passes directly the axis of the Incarnation, the process of Christification, and the process of Christogenesis. The Eucharist, therefore, contains the seed for cosmic transformation. When we receive the Holy Eucharist Christ comes into us and through us he extends his transforming power to the cosmos and continues the effects of his incarnation in the cosmos and anticipates the Omega point.

Through the incarnation Christ entered into nature to give it a supernatural life and lead it back to God the Father. In his incarnation he destroyed the obstacle between God and creation. In this way he put every being, every matter in a movement towards fulfilment. For Teilhard the salvation does not consist of the individual enjoyment of God, but of a collective fulfilment.[171] This collective fulfilment calls for a collective action that breaks

---

169. Ibid., p. 216, also pp. 192-93.

170. Teilhard de Chardin (1967), p. 124-25.

171. Ibid., p. 1.

all the boundaries not only of humanity but of matter and spirit. All are called to grow into completeness losing all the boundaries. This shows that everything in this cosmos is interconnected, interdependent. No one is excluded from it, and no one can survive unless everything else surrounds it.

Teilhard de Chardin's cosmic evolutionary theology of the Eucharist affirms the centrality of Christ in the cosmos and the basic unity that exists in the cosmos in Christ, the guiding principle of the cosmic evolution. The Christ of Revelation is the Omega of evolution.[172] For, Christ with his incarnation has made the world a sacrament and in this way he has overcome the distinction between the profane and the sacred. As a result the words of the consecration are not limited to the bread and wine but extend to the whole creation. In this manner the Eucharist realizes not only the mystery of incarnation but also prolongs the mystery of salvation in the cosmos and becomes the seed of the anticipation of the Omega Point of the evolution. Thus, in and through the Eucharist the world becomes Christified and anticipates the Omega point. Our task is to hasten this Omega point with our actions in building up the Body of Christ until its consummation in the Omega point, i.e., Christ, the *pleroma,* the plenitude. If Christ is Omega, then nothing should be considered to be alien to the physical building of the universe.

Conclusion

Our analysis of Maximus the Confessor, V. Lossky, J.D Zizioulas and Teilhard de Chardin has shown us that in all of them the Eucharistic sacrifice has a cosmic dimension. We may summarize our points of arrival in the following ways: firstly, in all of them the incarnation and redemption are the bases of any theory of the cosmic function of the Eucharist. Christ in his incarnation and redemption healed the world from within, recapitulated it in his

172. C.F. Mooney (1966), p. 74.

person and offered it back to God the Father. And the human role is to extend the transforming powers of Christ to the world through our own deification in Baptism and in the Eucharist. In this way Christ will be all in all. In every Eucharist we offer creation back to God and in this way fulfil the purpose of the creation.

Secondly, the Western Church in the course of time has lost this cosmic function due to its negative, dualistic outlook on the world, and on account of a lack of mystical theology. The Eastern Church, which follows closely Maximus the Confessor in its theological reflection, maintains a positive outlook on the world and considers the cosmos as an integral part of humans' worship of God. Still further, the real problem may be in the fact that the Eastern theology being mystical rather than discursive considers this cosmic function as one of the characteristics of its Eucharistic theology. By contrast, the Western sacramental theology being primarily discursive rather than mystical does not emphasize this aspect. Its emphasis is on the ethical dimension of humans and the unity in the Church. Such a vision surely does not consider the cosmos as an integral part of God's creation and of human salvation. Thus, the problem is one of outlook on the world and on the theological perspective.

Thirdly, all the above-mentioned theologians consider Christ as the centre of the cosmos. If for the Eastern theologians Christ recapitulates the creation, for Teilhard Christ is the guiding principle behind the universal evolution. All of them look at creation in its totality and consider Christ as the unifying link between God-humans-cosmos. Christ, the meeting point of God-humans-cosmos, continues to meet the world in the Eucharist, and changes the bread and wine, cosmic elements, into his body and blood for the salvation of the world. When humans as priests of the world offer the creation to God in the forms of bread and wine they not only give meaning to the world but also make possible its own survival. In this way the Eucharist becomes on the one hand the meeting place between the cosmos and its Creator, and on the other the means of its survival through its deification. The Church and the Eucharist, therefore, become the mediations for the deification or the Christification of the universe.

Fourthly, we can find a progressive discovery of the cosmic dynamism of the Eucharist from Maximus the Confessor to Teilhard de Chardin. Maximus considers the redemption as the cosmic unification in Christ by abolishing the antithetical divisions in the cosmos in the death and the resurrection of Jesus. Such a recapitulation of the cosmos in the Logos is nothing other than the conservation of the universe that continues now in the Eucharist. In Lossky the redemption fulfils itself in the deification of humans and the cosmos. We are not isolated from the rest of creation and on account of this when we become deified in Baptism and in the Eucharist, the whole cosmos becomes deified. According to Lossky, even the actions of a monk who is confined to his solitary cell are said to have a cosmic effect. Zizioulas goes a step further when he goes into the history of the Christian theology to find out the reasons for the loss of the cosmic dimension in the Western sacramental theology. He considers that the negative, dualistic outlook on the world in the West was the reason for the loss of the cosmic dimension of the Eucharist. He proposes the Eucharist as the medicine for the survival of the world. Teilhard de Chardin takes ahead this progressive discovery of the cosmic dimension of the Eucharist by bringing together the scientific theory of evolution and the Christogenesis or the Christification of the universe towards the Omega Point. Even though he followed a different approach to the question of relation between God-humans-cosmos from that of other theologians we discussed, he too came to the same conclusions, the unity of all creation in Christ and the cosmic role of the Eucharist in the transformation of the world. He has succeeded in overcoming the negative, dualistic outlook on the world and in bringing together scientific discovery and mystical theology in Christogenesis as the scope of universal evolution. The Eucharist is not only the means of prolonging the mystery of incarnation but also the seed of the anticipation of the Omega Point of evolution.

All the four theologians examined in this chapter show the intimate relation of creation, incarnation, redemption and the cosmic dynamism of the Eucharist. Christ, the unifying link between God-humans-cosmos meets again the cosmos in the sacrament of the sacrifice of Christ, and extends his love to the whole creation. In this way the Eucharist is not only the meeting point of God-humans-cosmos but also the sacrament of God's love for creation, the cosmos, of which we are called to be the priests. Christ shows his concern for the cosmos when through the Holy Spirit he descends once again on the altar and accepts the bread and wine, the cosmic elements, and changes them into his body and blood for the life of the World.

Part III
Yajña and the Eucharist in Dialogue

6

Yajña and the Eucharist
Sacrificial Creation and Sacrificial Redemption

THE cosmic dimensions of *yajña* and the Eucharist which we have analysed in the preceding chapters now call us to put them side by side to bring to light the similarities and the differences.[1] This does not mean that the Vedic vision of humans, the cosmos and the Ultimate Reality[2] are equivalent to the Christian notions of humans, the cosmos and God. They belong to different world-

---

1. We limit ourselves to comparing some of the aspects which we have treated in the preceding chapters and we do not intend to give a detailed study on the similarities and the differences of the Vedic sacrifice with the Eucharistic sacrifice. For a detailed comparison of the Vedic sacrifice with the Eucharist, see J. Thachil (1985), pp. 319-51; N. Sheth (1998), pp. 679-99 and 753-68. In our comparison of *yajña* with the Eucharist, first we will see the similarities and then in the last section of this chapter we will see the differences between them. For a recent comparative study on the East and the West, see A.N. Terrin (1999b), pp. 303-44.

2. It is overdue that we clarify the Vedic vision of God/Ultimate Reality. Here we try to do this even though it is not easy. There are different views with regard to the Vedic vision of the Ultimate Reality. One may find passages which speak about the monotheistic, polytheistic and the pantheistic views on the Ultimate Reality which is expressed sometimes as Supreme Being, or as Divine Self, or as Absolute, or as *Brahman,* or *ātman.* According to *R̥V* (1.164.6 and 46) the Ultimate Reality, the Unborn, is One which the sages call in many ways as Indra, Mitra, Varuṇa, Agni or the heavenly sunbird Garutmat, Yama, Mātariṣvan.

→

views and to different levels of the experience of the Ultimate

---

→ To understand the Vedic vision of Ultimate Reality, human being and the cosmos we need to keep in mind the following distinctions of metaphysical and phenomenal points of view. According to the Upaniṣads and the Vedāntins, from the metaphysical point of view (*pāramārthika*) the Ultimate Reality (*Brahman*) is *nirguṇa* (attributeless), and the world is unreal (*māyā*, not in the sense of illusion but as non-Absolute Principle, hence not everlasting). From the point of view of experience (*vyavahārika*) the Ultimate Reality is *Saguṇa* (*Brahman* with qualities, hence able to sympathise with the worshipper), and the world is real. This order is also turned upside down by Rāmānuja and the theistic schools who consider the *Saguṇa Brahman* or a personal God as the Ultimate Reality. In the *BG* Kṛṣṇa speaks of himself as the Supreme Being, the *Saguṇa Brahman* even as superior to the *Nirguṇa Brahman.* For instance in *BG* (13.12-17) the Highest *Brahman* is said to be dependent on God Kṛṣṇa, in 13.31 the Highest *Brahman* is identified with Kṛṣṇa, etc.

Modern Hinduism is divided into two major groups Vaiṣṇavites and Śaivites (also Śāktas who consider Śakti or Durgā as the Supreme Being). A Hindu may perform a sacrifice or worship a Supreme Being or a minor deity, who is regarded as a manifestation or reflection of the Supreme Being. For example, when a Vaiṣṇavite (those who consider Viṣṇu as the Supreme Being) worships Śiva and offers sacrifices or *pūjā* to him, he regards Śiva not as the Supreme Being, but as a minor god and ultimately a manifestation or reflection of Viṣṇu. See N. Sheth (1998), pp. 690-91. According to Dhavamony, such a view made Max Müller call the Vedic conception of the Ultimate Reality "henotheistic," because it is a middle way between the monotheism and the polytheism. M. Dhavamony (1982), p. 41.

Unlike Christianity, Hinduism has no problem in considering the deities as worthy of worship, but only the Supreme Being is considered to have the power to grant salvation. The minor gods or deities can grant only worldly rewards. According to *BG* (7.20-23), those who worship other gods go to gods but those who worship Kṛṣṇa will go to him, the Highest God. In *BG* (9.23-24) even those who worship other gods are said to worship Kṛṣṇa, →

Reality.[3] It is true that *puruṣa* is a mythical figure whereas Christ is a historical figure.[4] Hence the difficulty arises in putting them side by side. But if we accept that even though the Vedic and the Christian visions are different they are not completely unrelated world-views, then we can at least place them side by side to see that the notion of sacrifice can bring together these two visions on a common ground. In this highly difficult task[5] we can find that sacrifice plays the link between the theory of creation and redemption in Vedism and in Christianity. Hence we intend to make a comparison of the *yajña* with the Eucharist to discover both the homological convergences and differences which exist between them.

Puruṣa and Christ as the Origin, Sustainer and the Meeting Point of History

Both in the Vedas and in the NT we can find that at the basis of any reflection on creation, redemption and sacrifice there lies a divine sacrifice. The Vedas consider the creation on the cosmic plane a divine sacrifice in which *puruṣa*, the Primordial Man offers

→ for he is the recipient and the Lord of all sacrifices. But those who do not know Kṛṣṇa as the Supreme God will have to be reborn again. The verse 25 of the same chapter says: "To the gods go the gods' devotees, to the ancestors their votaries, to disembodied spirits go the worshippers of these, but those who worship Me shall come to Me."

3. For three levels of the experience of God, humans and the cosmos in general, see R. Panikkar (1993), pp. 20-77; and for the phenomenological approach to the study of the religions see A.N. Terrin (1983), pp. 53-226.

4. On this we will discuss later when we will be discussing the differences between the *yajña* and the Eucharist.

5. Our difficulty can be easily grasped from the single fact that no easy definition of Hinduism is possible, because it is not a single religion, but a fellowship of faiths, which differ widely in theory as well as in practice. See N. Sheth (1998), p. 679; see also M. Dhavamony (1982), p. 1.

himself for the sake of creation.[6] This *puruṣa* who in the Brāhmaṇas is Prajāpati, the Lord of the creatures, is said to have offered himself in sacrifice for the sake of creation, and gave sacrifice as the means for the continued existence of creation.

The *puruṣa* hymn stresses the unity of all existence in *puruṣa*: he is the origin, and the source of everything that exists, he is transcendent and immanent.[7] He is the meeting point of space and time because the past, the present and future converge in him. In this way the origin of this cosmos is not only attributed to a divine Being but is also shown as the first expression of the divine manifesting himself in the realm of experience.[8] This *puruṣa*, the Creator and the meeting point of all creation, of space and time in the words of H. Aguilar is worthy of a comparison with the self-emptying sacrifice of Jesus in Christianity. He writes, "Taken in its totality the myth of Puruṣa-Prajāpati is not unworthy of the Christian conception of the redemptive incarnation of the Logos by means of the *kenosis*, leaving out the question whether they can be homologated or not."[9]

Similarly in Christianity, Christ is the creator, sustainer, and the meeting point of all creation.[10] In the prologue of John, Christ[11] is said to be the Logos through whom everything was created (1: 3, 10). His cosmic role is clearer in Col 1: 15-19 which says:

> He is the first born of all creation, for in him all things were created, in heaven and on earth, visible and invisible . . . all

6. See pp. 40-48 of this book.
7. Ibid.
8. J. Gonda (1977), p. 95. See also pp. 40-48 of this book.
9. H. Aguilar (1976), p. 69. See also L. Malieckal (1989b), p. 84; N. Sheth (1998), p. 755-56. So far there has not been any serious attempt on the comparison of the *puruṣa* myth with the Christ-Event. For a detailed comparative study on Kṛṣṇa and Christ see I. Vempeny (1988), pp. 233-53.
10. See pp. 239-247 of this book.
11. See G. Segalla (1977), pp. 14-47.

> things were created through him and for him. He is before all things, and in him all things hold together. He is the Head of the body, the church; he is the beginning, the first-born from the dead, that in everything he might be pre-eminent.

This hymn considers Christ as the firstborn of all creation, the creator of all things, the sustainer of all things, the reconciler of all things. Christ is the synthesis of the divine world with the cosmos. He is the creator of all things, in heaven and on earth, visible and invisible, he is before all things and in him all things hold together. Christ is the meeting point of history, because he is the Alpha and the Omega (Rev 1: 8). All these functions give Christ a cosmic dimension, for he is the origin, the redeemer, and the sustainer of the cosmos. If for the Vedic person *puruṣa* stood for the symbol of the whole reality, created and non-created, transcendent and the immanent, visible and the invisible, for the Christians Christ, the Logos incarnate stands for the symbol of the whole reality.[12] In the *puruṣa* hymn too we find that all things are created from his self-sacrifice, he is the meeting point between the past and the present.

THE VEDIC SACRIFICE AS THE RITUAL REPETITION OF THE SELF-GIVING SACRIFICE OF PURUṢA AND THE EUCHARIST AS THE RITUAL MEMORIAL OF THE DEATH AND THE RESURRECTION OF JESUS CHRIST

For the Vedic person sacrifice is the first creative act and every sacrifice is a repetition of this first creative act.[13] To sacrifice is, then, to repeat the primordial self-giving sacrifice of *puruṣa*. Just as the sacrifice of *puruṣa* for the sake of creation and its ritual memorial in every sacrifice form the basis for any reflection on the Vedic sacrifice, so too, the sacrifice of Jesus on the cross and its ritual memorial in the Eucharistic sacrifice form the basis for

---

12. For Christ as the Christian symbol of all reality see R. Panikkar (2004), pp. 180-84.

13. J. Gonda (1983c), p. 8. See also pp. 40-48 of this book.

any reflection on the Christian sacrifice, the Eucharist. The Eucharistic sacrifice cannot be understood in isolation from the sacrifice of the cross.

If *yajña*, thus, forms the basis to understand the Vedic vision of human being and the cosmos, the sacrifice of Jesus on the cross and its ritual memorial in the Eucharist form the basis for understanding the Christian vision of human being, redemption, cosmos and worship. If behind the Vedic vision of ritual, human being and the cosmos, there lies the primordial life-giving event of Puruṣa-Prajāpati, behind the Christian vision of Eucharist and the sacraments there lies the Christ-Event.

Just as *puruṣa* sacrificed himself for the sake of creation, and gave the ritual sacrifice as the means to keep the creation from disintegration, so too, Christ the source of creation, gave the Eucharist as the means of life not only for the human beings but also for the whole world. In John (6: 51) Jesus says "the bread which I shall give for the life of the world is my flesh." Jesus' flesh, thus, becomes the life of the world and he continues to give this flesh when his self-giving sacrifice is ritually commemorated in the Eucharist.

When giving us the Eucharist, the sacrament of his sacrifice, Jesus asked for the *anamnesis* of his sacrificial self-giving death. As a sacrament the Eucharist is a ritual sacrifice through which the Church not only makes the *anamnesis* of his sacrificial death but also recreates a relationship between Jesus and those who remember him. The Eucharist is, therefore, the memorial of his sacrifice through which the participants are called to enter into a relationship with him. For in the words of A.J. Gittins the word *anamnesis* can be translated better by saying that it is the opposite of "dismember":

> "Remember me," in this sense, would mean "put me together again," in relationship with you. For remembering (*anamnesis*)

> is all about relationship. The *anamnesis* of the Last Supper — the act and the remembrance of the Last Supper — puts Jesus' sacrifice together again, not by rehearsing it or repeating it, but by an act which "remembers" Jesus and the community, lest Jesus be forgotten because excluded from our relationships. . . .[14]

The sacrifice becomes, therefore, an *anamnesis* through which one enters into a new relationship with the source of one's life. In the case of Vedic person this source of life is *puruṣa* and in our case it is Jesus who laid down his life as a loving sacrifice to the Father for our salvation.

SACRIFICE AS ĀTMAYAJÑA AND THE SELF-OFFERING OF THE CHURCH IN THE EUCHARIST

Just as *puruṣa* is the victim and the offerer in the Vedas, so too, Christ is the victim and the offerer in Christianity. Just as *puruṣa* allowed himself to be sacrificed for the sake of creation, so too, Christ allowed himself to be nailed to the cross for the redemption of the world. In both of them there is no distinction between the offerer and the victim, and the effects of their sacrifice is far-reaching to the whole cosmos hence not limited to humanity. There is a perfect identity between the offering and the offerer in both these cases. From this identity the theory that sacrifice is the self-offering takes origin. The external offering becomes the symbol of the internal offering, or surrender.

In the Vedas human life is a divine gift and this gift has to be repaid through the sacrifice of oneself. Our sacrifice is nothing other than our self-gift to the divinity who sacrificed himself for the sake of creation. Hence the notion that to sacrifice and to be sacrificed is essentially the same.[15] This self-sacrifice is not possible, hence the need to offer substitutes for oneself. The substitute, therefore, stands for the sacrificer, it is his prototype. The

---

14. A.J. Gittins (1991), p. 428.

15. A.K. Coomaraswamy (1941), p. 359. See 101-04 of this book.

Upaniṣads go further and consider the whole life of a human being as a sacrifice, whether one is awake or asleep one is offering a continuous sacrifice,[16] and one's final sacrifice will be one's funeral rite in which the body will be burned on the funeral pyre. In the *BG*[17] too, sacrifice is nothing other than the offering of oneself to Kṛṣṇa in *bhakti*, without any selfish motive other than the *lokasaṁgraha* (the well-being of all), the cosmic good.

---

16. See pp. 129-36 of this book.
17. It is difficult to prove the influence of the Gospel on the *BG* or vice versa though there are some similar concepts in both of them. According to De Smet, there is no serious ground to think that the *BG* has influenced the Gospel or vice versa. See R.V. de Smet (1989), p. 19. On the contrary A. Elenjimittam is of the opinion that Christianity and Hinduism were influenced by one another starting from the first century. See A. Elenjimittam (1996), pp. 84-85. He considers the *BG* as the proof of such influence. For me the *BG* cannot be taken as a proof to the mutual influence of Christianity on Hinduism or the latter on the former. A few similarities cannot give sufficient weight to the argument. Further it relies too much on the comment of St. John Chrisostom in his sermon on the Gospel of John which is as follows: "Similarly the Syrians, the Egyptians, the Indians, the Persians, the Etyopians, and other minor people have translated in their proper languages the Gospel announced by him (John) and in that way they have learned to philosophise." Ibid., p. 84. It is not possible to accept the affirmation of John Chrisostom that the Indians, the Syrians, the Egyptians, the Persians, etc. learned to philosophise by learning the Gospel according to John because most of the thirteen principal Upaniṣads were already written before 300 BCE. Secondly to hold that the *BG* was influenced by the Gospel means to hold that even the composition of it is later than that of the Gospel according to John. This view cannot be accepted: the scholars of Indian philosophy like S. Radhakrishnan and Juan Mascaró put the approximate date of the composition of the *BG* around the fifth century BCE and others around 200 BCE. Even if we accept a later date such as CE 200 (as some hold) it is difficult to prove the possession of the copy of the Gospel of John by the author of the *BG*.

→

The letter to the Hebrews presents Jesus' death as the perfect sacrifice where the oblation is nothing other than Jesus himself.[18] He offers himself to the Father in love and obedience. Like the *puruṣa,* Jesus is the priest, the victim, and the offerer. The altar is the cross. Sacrifice, in this sense, is nothing other than offering of oneself to God. Thus, Christ's sacrifice is considered to be the most perfect because in him there is no distinction between the victim and the offerer. When the Church in obedience to the command of Jesus offers the Eucharistic sacrifice, she offers herself in the form of bread and wine to God the Father. The bread and wine, which she offers to God the Father, represent not only her but also the whole creation.

→ However there are some doctrinal similarities between the Gospel according to John and the *BG.* (The following comparisons are taken from A. Elenjimittam (1996), pp. 83-84.) We find that in the Gospel of John Jesus is presented as the creator of everything (1.3) and in the *BG* Kṛṣṇa is presented as the source, origin and the creator of everything. John in 1: 10-11 says that the universe was made through Jesus but the world did not recognize him and Kṛṣṇa in 10.10-11 says that the fools do not recognize his transcendent nature and when he descends in human form they do not honour him. Again in John we find Jesus' promise of eternal life and the immortality to those who believe in him (3: 15; 8: 51). The same way Kṛṣṇa promises that those who believe in him will not die (10.31), and those who believe in him and take refuge in him will escape age and death (7.29). In John we find again Jesus' promise to love those who love him and believe in him (14: 21), so too in the *Gītā* we find Kṛṣṇa's promise to love his devotees (4.11). Finally both Jesus and Kṛṣṇa identify themselves with the way, the truth and the life (Jn 17: 3 = *BG* 9.18). We can also see many similarities between Kṛṣṇa and Jesus. Both of them are incarnations of God, and both of them at certain time of their earthly life transfigured to reveal their real identity, etc. For a detailed comparative study on Kṛṣṇa and Christ see, I. Vempeny (1988), pp. 233-53.

18. Heb 9: 11-14; 7: 27.

Agnicayana as the Ritual Reconstruction of the Dismembered Body of Prajāpati

One of the most important Vedic sacrifices, the *Agnicayana,* i.e. the building of the fire altar for the Soma sacrifice, is a sacrifice in the reverse order of the primordial sacrifice.[19] It is the ritual reconstruction of the dismembered body of Puruṣa-Prajāpati for the sake of the continuity of space and time. The bricks and the materials used in this altar building represent the whole cosmos, in space and time with all the living beings in it. When the altar is built the whole creation is brought to its primordial unity, the One which became many for the sake of the creation, and is offered back to Prajāpati from whom it had its origin. Thus, the *Agnicayana* ritual is the reconstruction of the primordial being who sacrificed himself for the sake of creation and offering back to the same being the whole cosmos. The continued existence of the cosmos is thus made possible by bringing back the cosmos to its primordial source and unity.

Similarly in Maximus the Confessor we can find that the redemption is the act through which the Logos brings unity in the cosmos which was divided into antithetical categories after sin.[20] Christ in his incarnation entered into the cosmos which had become corrupt through sin, healed it from within, abolished the antithetical divisions, recapitulated it in his person and offered it back to God the Father. The redemption thus consists in the restoration of the creation, i.e. Christ giving back the primordial unity, recapitulating the whole creation in the altar of his person. If in the Vedic sacrifice of *Agnicayana* the ritual consists in reintegrating the dispersed elements of Prajāpati, redemption in Christianity can be seen, at least according to the vision of Maximus the Confessor, as the re-integration and bringing the lost unity in

---

19. See pp. 80-88 of this book.

20. See pp. 241-253 of this book.

the creation. Christ, the Logos incarnate, healing the antithetical divisions of the cosmos, recapitulates the whole creation and offers it to God the Father.

The purpose of the incarnation is not only healing the division in creation but also to lead the whole of creation back to God. This is possible only if Christ becomes the altar of the cosmic redemption. For this reason Christ enters into the cosmos in his incarnation that it may be redeemed and brought back to God in him. In the words of Ernst:

> The "katabasis" takes place for the sake of the "anabasis." The entry of the divine into the mundane in the incarnation and the sacramental liturgical symbol, takes place in order to recover and bring back the world (not only the world of man but the entire creation, including the non-human creation) into the realm of God so that Christ may "fill all things."[21]

Just as the *Agnicayana* makes possible the reunification and the offering of the whole creation to its creator, so too, the incarnation makes the reunification and the ascension of the creation possible. This is what is meant in every Christian sacrifice, the descending of Christ to the world to lead the creation back to God the Father.

Now this recapitulation of the whole cosmos, and the offering of the cosmos take place in the Eucharist, the memorial of the death and resurrection of Jesus. As M. Vidalis writes:

> This union once realized in the incarnation of the Word, Christ renews it in the celebration of the mystery of the new covenant that becomes the centre of the Christian life. Christ recapitulates then the creation, represented by the elements of bread and wine, which makes it possible to discern the cosmic dimension of his work. He recapitulates not only human nature, but the whole cosmos.[22]

---

21. J. Ernst (1968), p. 59.
22. M. Vidalis (1998), p. 206.

Therefore, just as in the *Agnicayana* the whole cosmos rises to its primordial unity, so too, in the incarnation and in the redemption the whole creation returns to its primordial unity in Christ.

THE COSMOS AS MATERIAL FOR AGNICAYANA AND THE EUCHARIST

We have seen that the whole cosmos has come from the sacrifice of *puruṣa* and it has to be offered back to him in sacrifice. Even though this is done in every sacrifice, in the *Agnicayana* sacrifice the whole cosmos is represented through different bricks and the materials. Each brick stands for a part of the cosmos which is made of space and time in all their ramifications.

Coming to the Eucharist, Teilhard de Chardin considers the whole cosmos as the material for the Eucharistic sacrifice. For him the universe is one organic unity and all its parts are inextricably linked together and form a single totality in Christ. For, Christ in his incarnation united the matter and the spirit, the sacred and the profane, body and soul, and by virtue of their inter-relation they form the totality of the sacramental species. The material for the sacrifice is the totality of the universe and not an isolated part of it. The world has become for Teilhard a sacrament in the incarnation and from that moment all matter is henceforth incarnate, and forms the material for the sacrifice. It is for this reason that he calls upon a divine consecration on every element of the cosmos by saying:

> Over every living thing which is to spring up, to grow, to flower, to ripen during this day say again the words: This is my Body. And over every death-force waits in readiness to corrode, to wither, to cut down, speak again the commanding words which express the supreme mystery of faith: This is my Blood.[23]

Vagaggini, too, holds a similar view with regard to the offering of the whole creation in the Eucharist when he writes: "The Church offers together with Christ the whole humanity, rather the whole

23. Teilhard de Chardin (1974a), p. 23. See also pp. 271-84 of this book.

cosmos, of which he is the responsible Head."[24] The Church, therefore, becomes the meeting point of the cosmos and its creator. In the Eucharist, the cosmos is reassumed in the form of bread and wine, and is offered to God. A similar view can also be found in Zizioulas when he writes, " . . . during the liturgy there takes place a movement, a procession of the whole world towards the holy Table (the altar). . . . "[25] Thus, in the Eucharist there takes place a movement of the whole cosmos into the table of the Lord, that the Lord may offer it to God the Father. Therefore, the cosmos not only becomes an integral part of the *Agnicayana* and the Eucharist, but also the material for sacrifice.

The Vedic Sacrifice as the Means for the Existence of the Cosmos and the Survival of the World in the Eucharist

The interrelatedness of the creation to its creator is a necessary condition for the survival of the cosmos both in the Vedas and in Zizioulas. Like the Vedic person, Zizioulas too considers the sacrifice as the means for the existence of the world. The main function of the Vedic sacrifice is to maintain the cosmos in existence, for the creator has given it as the medicine for continued existence. This is possible only if we recognize the relatedness of creation to its creator and bring the creation back to the creator in sacrifice.

For the Vedic person creation out of nothing is not possible and creation is the self-sacrifice osf *puruṣa*.[26] The sacrifice is the foundation of everything, and without the sacrifice the world

---

24. C. Vagaggini (1969), p. 191.

25. I. Zizioulas (1994), pp. 75-76. See also pp. 260-71 of this book.

26. There are also passages which speak of the creation out of *vāc*, or through *tapas*, etc. But here we limit ourselves to the creation through the sacrifice of *puruṣa*. For the differences on the emphasis in the Vedic way of looking at creation and the Western way, see R. Panikkar (1966), pp. 71-98. According to Panikkar, →

will not be able to survive. Zizioulas comes to a similar view, i.e. the survival of the world, from a different view of creation, the creation out of nothing.[27] God created this world out of nothing and it cannot survive by itself, it can survive only in relation to God. This survival of the cosmos was first made possible in redemption, and it depends now on the human priestly function: the priest of creation who brings back the world to its Creator. Everything that exists needs to pass through the hands of human being, the priest of the world, to God for its survival, and this takes place in the Eucharistic sacrifice.[28] When the world is accepted into the liturgy, it gets sanctified and is put in relation to its creator on whom its survival depends. Thus, like the Vedic sacrifice, the Eucharistic sacrifice too becomes the means for the survival of the whole cosmos.

Sacrifice as the Means of Immortality in the Vedas and the Eucharist as the Medicine of Immortality in Christianity

In the Vedas the immortality is the birthright of no one, not even of the gods, for both gods and humans are born mortal.[29] It is

---

→ the Vedic person is not interested in a discussion of the beginning or the origin of everything, but about the problem of his being. Judaism and Christianity took a different view, i.e. creation out of nothing, to argue against the Greek view of creation. Ibid., pp. 80-82.

27. But for Christians the creation is out of nothing, and God who created out of nothing can cause creation to return to nothing. Hence the need to consider creation as dependent on God, and on our relation to God.

28. As Zizioulas writes: "All faithful who go to the Liturgy carry with them the world (considered here in a very realistic manner). They do not carry only themselves with the proper relative incapacity and passions, but carry with them their relation with the natural world, with the creation." I. Zizioulas (1994), p. 75.

29. See *PVE*, p. 365.

through sacrifice that both gods and humans achieve immortality. Gods achieved immortality through establishing the immortal sacred Agni, who is considered to be the priest, the conveyer of oblation to the gods, in their inner selves (*ŚB* 2.2.2.8-10, 14), or by drinking *soma* juice, the drink of immortality. Like the gods the human beings also gain immortality through sacrifice.

The yearning for the immortality in sacrifice is very clear in a verse of the *BṛUp* which is muttered by the sacrificer:

> From the unreal (*asat*) lead me to the real (*sat*) !
> From darkness lead me to light !
> From death lead me to immortality ! — 1.3.28

All these three lines of the same verse have the same theme, the immortality from death. For our text says again:

> When he says "From the unreal lead me to the real," the unreal, verily, is death, the real is immortality. "From death lead me to immortality. Make me immortal" — that is what he says.
>
> "From darkness lead me to light" — the darkness, verily, is death, the light is immortality. "From death lead me to immortality. Make me immortal" — that is what he says.
>
> "From death lead me to immortality" — there is nothing there that seems obscure.

In the *Agnicayana,* the sacrificer is made to take into himself the sacred Agni, the immortal self, before beginning the actual construction of the fire altar. In it the sacrificer constructs a divine and immortal self for himself that he may be able to overcome death. In sacrifice, especially in the *Agnicayana* ritual, actual death and disintegration are eliminated.[30] Thus, in sacrifice man is born again for a second time and those who are initiated into the study of the Vedas and the sacrifices are, therefore, called the *dvijas*, the twice born.[31] The *BG* says: "Eating of the leavings of the sacrifice,

---

30. J. Heesterman (1987b), p. 24.

31. According to *ŚB* (11.2.2.1) a man is born three times, first he is born from his mother and father, he is born a second time while

the food of immortality, they come to primeval *Brahman*. This world is not for him who performs no sacrifice; much less the other [world]" (4.31). Thus, sacrifice is considered to be the food of immortality.

Similarly, in Christianity too, the Eucharistic bread and blood are considered to be the food and the drink of immortality. The flesh and blood of Jesus as the food and drink of immortality is very strong in John 6. According to Wisdom (2: 23), God had created humans immortal, but they lost immortality because of sin. The manna could not grant immortality to the Israelites, hence Jesus gives his flesh and blood for immortality.[32] The bread which Jesus will give is the bread of eternal life (Jn 6: 27). The future tense, "the bread which I will give," according to G. Segalla, points to the Eucharistic bread.[33] Again Jesus says in Jn (6: 51): "I am the living bread which came down from heaven; if any one eats of this bread, he will live for ever; and the bread which I shall give for the life of the world is my flesh." Further in another verse Jesus says: " . . . Truly, truly I say to you, unless you eat the flesh of the Son of man and drink his blood, you have no life in you; he who eats my flesh and drinks my blood has eternal life, and I shall raise him up at the last day" (Jn 6: 53-54). These verses clearly speak that the Eucharistic bread which Jesus gives us is the bread of immortality. Jesus by giving his flesh and blood in the Eucharist unites us to himself and gives us immortality.

From the theme of the Eucharistic bread as the bread of immortality there developed the idea of the Eucharist as the medicine of immortality. Such a theme is very dear to the Fathers of the Church and Ignatius of Antioch was the first to use it with

---

→ performing the sacrifice, and a third time when he dies and they place him on the pyre.

32. G. Segalla (1976), pp. 56-57.

33. Ibid., p. 81.

regard to the Eucharist.[34] According to him, the Eucharistic bread is the medicine of immortality, the antidote against death, and food to live for ever in Jesus Christ.[35] St Justin considers it as the nutriment that transforms us (*Apol.* 66.2), St Irenaeus considers it as the means of life and immortality (*Adv. Haer* IV, 18.5), Cyril considers the flesh of the Lord as life-giving.[36] Zizioulas, too, following the tradition of the Fathers, especially of Ignatius of Antioch, considers the Eucharistic bread as the medicine of immortality.[37]

According to the *BG*, neither this world, nor the other belongs to the one who does not sacrifice, and according to Jesus, unless one eats and drinks his flesh and blood, one will not have eternal life. Sacrifice, therefore, is the means of immortality both in the Vedic Hinduism and in Christianity.

BRAHMAN AS FOOD OF LIFE AND JESUS AS THE BREAD OF LIFE

Food becomes another point of convergence between Vedic Hinduism and Christianity. Both *Brahman* and Jesus are compared to food of life[38] or bread of life in the Vedas and in John 6, respectively.

In the Vedic and in modern Hinduism food is much more than an element of nutriment, it is sacred. Food is life and the life

---

34. For the origin and the history of this phrase even before Ignatius of Antioch see L. Wehr (1987), pp. 106-11.

35. Ignatius of Antioch (1857), 20. 2. In *PG* 5, 66A. See also pp. 260-71 of this book.

36. See D. van den Eynde (1957), pp. 115-27.

37. See pp. 260-66 of this book.

38. For the passages which speak about *Brahman* as food in the Vedas, see *PVE*, pp. 224-37. For a detailed comparative study on the symbolism of food in a medieval Hindu saint and in Christianity see T. Dabre (1987), pp. 71-93, 196-244.

is food.[39] It is the synonym for *Brahman,* because it is the origin, source of continued life, and the end of everything. In the words of A.N. Terrin, it stands for a cosmic metabolism that is at the basis of everything[40] and as such becomes the subject of mystical speculation. In the words of Noel Sheth,

> In the Hindu tradition, food is a sacred symbol. It is not merely a biological necessity for life, but is mystically identified with life, with the universe and with the Supreme Reality itself. Food is therefore worthy of reverence and worship, and partaking of it is a sacred act, for it puts one in communion with the divine and with the cosmos.[41]

The importance of the food in the life of living beings made the Vedic seers consider food as sacred and the life-giving source of everything. According to *MaitrīUp* (6.13), the blessed Lord, the Supporter of all things is nothing other than food. In *Taittirīya Upaniṣad* (3.2) *Brahman* is presented as food, breath, sight, hearing, mind, word, the source of all beings, and the end to which all beings will return.[42] Thus *Brahman* as food stands for the Ultimate

---

39. A.N. Terrin (1998), p. 272. See also *PVE,* p. 225.

40. Ibid., p. 273. In the Vedas food is the first of all beings and those who worship *Brahman* as food surely obtain all the food they need; it (food) is eaten by beings and itself eats beings (*TaitUp* 2.2). Another text from the *ŚB* tells that Prajāpati, the Lord of creatures had to reproduce himself as food for there was no food at all (2.2.4.3-7). He then produced seven kinds of foods (*BṛUp* 1.5.1-3). In the above mentioned verse the writer does not say how Prajāpati produced food. The answer can be found in another text which says: "By the power of ascetic fervour *Brahman* expands and thence is food produced. From food comes life, from life mind, thence truth, the worlds and the immortality of works" (*MuṇḍUp* 1.1.8). Translation from *PVE,* p. 234.

41. N. Sheth (1998), pp. 679-80.

42. *TaitUp* (3.2) says, "Bhṛgu, the son of Varuṇa, approached his father Varuṇa and said: "Sir, instruct me about *Brahman.*" He explained to him, saying: "Food, breath, sight, hearing, mind, word." He said further: "That from which truly all beings are →

Reality from whom the whole universe had its origin and on whom the whole universe has its existence.

The sacredness of food calls that it be shared with others like the self-giving sacrifice of *puruṣa* which gave origin to this whole cosmos. To offer food to others is then not only a social but also a religious act, for by doing that one re-enacts the primordial sacrifice and shares in that highest principle through which the world subsists.[43] It may be for this reason that the Vedas raised the food sharing and the hospitality into the realm of sacrifice.[44]

Hospitality and sharing food are means to preserve food, and the one who eats alone, i.e. without sharing with others (but not in the sense of eating together) is considered to be eating sin. The *ṚV* says that he who eats alone is all sin (10.117.6) and in the *BG* too the one who cooks food for oneself is called sinful for one eats sin (3.13). Eating oneself without sharing the food with others is therefore considered a sin.[45] The deities are offered food before dining oneself and on account of this even the secular dining, outside the ritual context, gets a sacramental character.[46] Sharing

---

→ born, by which when born they live and into which finally they all return, that seek to understand; that is *Brahman*." He disciplined himself and, having disciplined himself, he realized that *Brahman* is food for from food assuredly all beings are born, by food when born do they live and into food finally they return." This translation is taken from *PVE*, pp. 232-33.

43. See *PVE*, p. 225.

44. We will see this in detail in the next chapter when we will be comparing the *pañca-mahāyajña*s with the Eucharist.

45. Even though the Vedas strongly encourage the sharing of food and praise the generous giver (*ṚV* 1.187), they do not emphasize on eating together. According to N. Sheth, in the ancient times the eating together was common, but only in the medieval times one was forbidden to eat with others except with one's family members and dependants. N. Sheth (1998), p. 680.

46. N. Sheth (1998), p. 680.

food is then to follow the life-giving self-gift of *puruṣa* who offered himself for the sake of the creation. Still further, Brahmā is said to be present in every guest, therefore, it is Brahmā who partakes of the food that is given to a guest.[47]

Just as *Brahman* is the food of life so, too, in John 6 Jesus is presented as the bread of life. Jesus, the bread of life, is the living bread descended from heaven for the salvation of the world. He is the real bread that gives life. He says "The bread which I will give is my flesh for the life of the world" (Jn 6: 51). The bread that perishes makes the person who eats it perish, whereas the bread that lasts makes the person who eats it last for ever.[48] However, the phrase "Jesus the bread of life" stands for much more than a symbolism of bread, it stands for the Person and the Word of Jesus. His body is not only the real food, but also the food that gives eternal life, hence the food of immortality as we saw earlier.

Although the Vedas give a divine role to food they do not recommend eating together. It may be because of the popular belief that the sins of those who eat together attach to others in the same row.[49] Nobody knows the secret sins of others, hence the recommendation not to eat with a person whose secret sins the other does not know. One may eat in the company of one's sons, younger brother, servants, etc. However, in the present day *pūjā*, the food-sharing becomes an important aspect.[50]

---

47. X. Irudayaraj (1978), p. 310.
48. G. Segalla (1976), p. 94.
49. X. Irudayaraj (1978), p. 310.
50. In the later Āgamic (non-Vedic) sacrifices especially in the *pūjā* the ritual food-sharing gathers an important place. Food offering to the divinity (*naivedya)* is the 13th of the 16 *upacāras* (services) of the *pūjā* and the food-sharing after the *pūjā* has become an important aspect of the contemporary Hindu worship. The sacred food which is offered in the temples and carried home to share with the family members and friends or that which is offered to the deity at home and is then shared with others is

→

From our short comparison of the *yajña* with the Eucharist we can find that just as the *puruṣa* hymn holds the key to understand the Vedic vision of creation, sacrifice, humans, cosmos, etc. so too, the Christ-Event holds the key to understand the Christian notion of redemption and the sacrifice. *Puruṣa* and Christ are said to be the creator, the sustainer, and the meeting point of history. Both of them willingly undergo a divine sacrifice for the sake of the creation. And sacrifice in Vedism and in Christianity is nothing other than the ritual memorial of this divine sacrifice for the life of the world. We will now see some major differences between these two world-views.

Differences between Yajña and the Eucharist

Just as there are several convergences between the Vedic and the Christian world-views on the divine sacrifice, so too, there are some differences. Herebelow we see some of the differences between the Vedic vision of the Ultimate Reality, humans, cosmos and sacrifice versus the Christian vision of God, humans, cosmos

---

→ called *prasāda*. It means a favour, a free gift. Hence the food offered to the deity is a gift to the deity and at the same time a counter-gift, a sign of God's favour to humans. It is meant to divinize the offerer in such a manner that the grace may visibly affect the devotees and they may experience it bodily for some time. X. Irudayaraj (1978), p. 311.

But for us Christians the Holy Communion is not a mere sharing of a sacred food. It is the body and blood of Jesus Christ through which he gives himself to us even today. Hence it is the sign of the covenant relationship with God fulfilled in the death and the resurrection of Jesus Christ. It becomes therefore the symbol of our union with Jesus Christ and our faith in him as saviour. It is advised that those Christians who want to receive the Holy Communion should be free from grave sins. Due to these reasons we cannot share the Holy Communion with the non-Christians, or to carry it home to eat it when we like as the Hindus do with their *prasāda*. In short the Eucharistic communion is much more than the Hindu *prasāda*.

and the Eucharist. We do not intend to give a detailed study on the differences between the Vedic/modern Hinduism and Christianity, rather we limit ourselves to the arguments which we have treated directly or indirectly in the preceding chapters keeping in mind that the basis for any comparative study is always the religious experience which is difficult to be observed.[51]

THE MYTHICAL YAJÑA OF PURUṢA AND THE HISTORICAL DEATH OF JESUS

One of the differences between the sacrifice of the *puruṣa* and that of Jesus is that the former is a mythical figure whereas the latter is a historical person.[52] Without denying the mythical character of *puruṣa* and the historical existence of Jesus, we would say that such distinctions cannot be stressed too far when we speak of

51. A.N. Terrin (1995b), pp. 136-61. Thus we are aware of the limitation that the observer's concept of other religions is based on what can be observed, whereas the essence of it lies in what cannot be observed. Ibid., p. 160. See also A.N. Terrin (1977), pp. 19-47.

52. The distinction between the myth and the event with regard to the history of religions is not easy to pinpoint. For, there is no myth which is not a sacred history, and no founding religious event which has no mythical or theological interpretation. When we come to Hinduism the difficulty is much greater because it does not have any official founder, and it does not consider the historical event or person as a necessary condition to express its religious beliefs and practices which are more than 4000 years old. Its conceptions of the Ultimate, humans and cosmos are different from the Western notions. Further its conception of time is cyclic and everything will return to its primordial point at the appointed time, and in such a concept of time the history also becomes an element which is subject to change. Hence not even a divine revelation is said to have a definitive value for humaniy. Therefore, we should not overemphasize the distinction between the mythical beginning and a historical beginning. Only when the historical fact is interpreted within the perspective of faith does it become a founding event, hence all the more need to base any comparative study of religions →

two different religious experiences mediated through the history and the culture in which they had their origin. In the words of Eliade, a religious historian who takes the history as the tool for his/her study finds that he/she cannot get back into the origin of the religion.[53] It may be because religion is not exclusively a historic phenomenon, and the history itself is conditioned by the socio-cultural, and religious situations.[54] Further, historic documents speak beyond what took place, hence the difficulty in distinguishing the mere fact from the interpretation.

If the myth is a sacred history, then it should not be taken as a mere invention as it came to mean before Eliade.[55] It has to be

---

→ starting from the religious experience.

The recent studies on the history of religions have demonstrated that since we are human beings, historicity is not the monopoly of any religion, or culture. But to reduce everything to history is again to fall into a reductionistic hermeneutic as some scholars of the history of religions, and dogmatics like R. Bultmann, K. Barth, etc. did. For a critique of the reductionistic hermeneutic of the history of religions, see M. Eliade (1969a), pp. 37-87. For a critique of Bultmann and Barth, see J.C. Thomas (1982), pp. 327-36. On a systematic hermeneutic on the study of religions, see A.N. Terrin (1983), pp. 42-226; A.N. Terrin (1997), pp. 19-47, 159-83; A.N. Terrin (1995b), pp. 136-61. On myth as the symbol and the metaphoric language, see T. Manickam (1998), pp. 56-65.

53. M. Eliade (1969a), p. 50. Our author argues that after a century of continuous research by the historians of religions to find the origins of the religion with the help of the historic instruments, they left such an old dream and have started to study the different phases of the various aspects of the religious life. Ibid., p. 52. Hence we too should not think that we can take too far the difference between the mythical approach and the historic approach to find the founding principles of different religions.

54. Ibid., pp. 52-53.

55. On the myth as a sacred history see Ibid., pp. 72-87.

taken as Elaide holds, "the revealer of a truth *par excellence*."[56] The cosmogonic myth of *puruṣa* can be an example for an expression for the primordial sacred history.[57] As such the myth does not express what took place at the beginning but something fabulous happened and from that this cosmos and all that exists in it had its origin.[58] Therefore, the religious experience not being exclusively a historic phenomenon should not be reduced to a historical event or person. Myths are sacred stories and they need to be treated as the first recorded history of a particular people.

SACRIFICIAL CREATION AND THE SACRIFICIAL REDEMPTION

For Vedic Hinduism the creation is through the sacrifice of *puruṣa* whereas in Christianity the redemption is through the sacrifice of Jesus. Hence their emphasis also differs. In the *puruṣa* myth the emphasis is on the totality of creation, of all that is visible and invisible in *puruṣa*, and on the sacrifice as the Ultimate principle of this cosmos. From this first creative divine sacrifice every sacrifice gets a creative function. In *ŚB* 11.2.1 man is said to be born three times, firstly he is born from his mother and father, secondly when he performs sacrifice,[59] and thirdly when he dies and is placed on the funeral pyre. What matters for a Vedic man is this second birth through the sacrifice, for only this is able to give him a lasting self. Again this new-birth in sacrifice is made evident through the *dīkṣā* (initiation into the Vedic sacrifices) wherein the sacrificer is placed in a hut and is made to sit like a foetus in the

56. Ibid., p. 73.
57. Ibid., pp. 75-76.
58. Ibid., p. 76.
59. The initiation into the Vedic study and the sacrifices (*upanayana*) itself is considered to be a second birth, wherein the teacher becomes the father of the student. It is this birth that counts, not the one from the parents. He who is not initiated thus becomes a degraded man.

womb. In the solemn sacrifices the fire is kindled through rubbing of two wooden pieces to symbolize this new birth in sacrifice. This creative dimension and the new birth in sacrifice can be seen as a new type of redemption but not in the same sense as the Eucharist.[60]

In the Eucharist the redemptive function of the divine sacrifice is stressed with particular evidence. The sacrifice of Christ is not seen as creative but redemptive in character. The Eucharist is then seen as the sacrament of his sacrifice that Christ may continue to give himself to sinful humankind till his second coming.

DIFFERENT RECIPIENTS OF YAJÑA AND THE ONLY RECEIVER

Another difference we can find between the Vedic sacrifice and the Eucharist is in the fact that the latter is offered to different gods even though these gods go towards an implicit unity. The Eucharist is offered to God the Father only. As we have seen in the *Aśvamedha* different gods are invoked and offerings are offered to them,[61] but this should not be taken to mean the worship of different independent supreme gods, hence polytheism. In the words of Radhakrishnan:

> The same God is worshipped by all. The differences of conception and approach are determined by local colouring

---

60. In Christianity it is baptism that is seen as the sacrament of new-birth, and not the Eucharist.

61. However, according to the *BG*, Kṛṣṇa is the recipient and the Lord of all the sacrifices. Even those who worship other gods in love worship him. For he says,

    "[Yet] even those who lovingly devote themselves to other gods and sacrifice to them, fulfilled with faith, do really worship Me though the rite may differ from the norm.

    For it is I who of all sacrifices am recipient and Lord, but they do not know Me as I really am, so they fall [back into the world of men]" (*BG* 9.23-24).

> and social adaptations. All manifestations belong to the same Supreme. "Viṣṇu is Śiva and Śiva is Viṣṇu and whoever thinks they are different goes to hell. He who is known as Viṣṇu is verily Rudra[62] and he who is Rudra is Brahmā." One entity functions as three gods that is Rudra, Viṣṇu and Brahmā.[63]

The different gods are considered only as the manifestations of the same Supreme God. As Prof. Terrin puts it rightly:

> The Absolute *Brahman* is not God and God is not *Brahman*. This doctrine appears in reality the most disturbing for us Westerners, Christians and non-Christians. Nevertheless we need to insist: there is a substantial difference between the *ātman/Brahman* and the gods. The gods can be many, they are the objects of cult, they are the sensible manifestations of the divine, but not yet the Absolute *Brahman*. He who knows only superficially the different names of gods and divinities in Hinduism may make a conception that in that religious world exists a varied and variegated polytheism that to us Westerners — logical and analytics — appear detestable enough.[64]

The Hindus are much more open to the divine manifestations than any other people, and on account of this they have no problem in considering different incarnations of the same Supreme God for the sake of salvation and as an object of cult. In Christianity we do not accept different incarnations. The Eucharistic sacrifice is offered only to God the Father through Christ, with Christ, in Christ and in union with the Holy Spirit.

DIFFERENT YAJÑAS AND THE ONLY SACRIFICE

Unlike Christianity, in the Vedas there are a number of sacrifices that an exact enumeration of them is a difficult task.[65] They are

---

62. Rudra is another name for Śiva.
63. S. Radhakrishnan (2004), p. 159. See also footnote 2 of this chapter on the Vedic vision of Absolute or Supreme God.
64. A.N. Terrin (1997), p. 167.
65. For detailed studies on the different classifications of sacrifice, the number and the roles of the 17 priests see G.U. Thite (1975), →

divided into obligatory and optional, daily, seasonal and occasional, domestic and solemn, etc. The domestic sacrifice can be performed by the head of the house whereas in Christianity only the duly ordained priest is able to preside over the Eucharistic sacrifice. The solemn sacrifices in Hinduism require three sacrificial fires to 16 priests.[66] *Aśvamedha*[67] and *Agnicayana* sacrifices last for years and they include many other sacrifices. The Vedic sacrifices show an advanced ritual reflection whereas in Christianity we do not find such an advanced ritual reflection, because everyhing is centred around the Eucharist. In Christianity we have only one sacrifice, the Eucharist, hence no variety.

YAJÑA AS FOOD FOR THE GODS AND EUCHARIST AS THANKSGIVING SACRIFICE

There are different motivations for which the *yajña* can be offered, and such motivations may vary from the world-maintaining activity to personal gains either spiritual or material.[68] Even the Eucharist is being offered sometimes by the faithful for spiritual and material benefits, and not always as pure thanksgiving sacrifice. But what draws our attention is the fact that the Vedas consider sacrifice as

---

→ pp. 104-90; J. Thachil (1985), pp. 132-216. In the Vedic sacrifices physical and ritual purity are important features that the *dīkṣā* (initiation ceremony for sacrifice) becomes an essential element for this purpose. Through that ceremony the sacrificer is purified and is re-born a second time. The exactitude in the performance of sacrifice is a must and there are always additional rites and verses to be performed or recited at the end of a ritual sacrifice to remedy any eventual mistake. These aspects are lacking in Christianity.

66. These priests belong to four groups. For more details see Ibid.
67. There are instances where the *Aśvamedha* lasted for three years.
68. For a detailed study on the purposes of the sacrifice in Hinduism see G.U. Thite (1975), pp. 222-38.

food for the gods,[69] and even the ordinary meals are considered to be remnants of food first offered to the gods, hence sacrificial.[70] Sacrifice, thus, becomes a way of sustaining gods through offering them gifts of food. Such a view expresses the Vedic person's vision of divine-human-cosmic interdependence.[71] As the *BG* says:

> With this shall ye sustain the gods so that the gods may sustain you [in return]. Sustaining one another [thus] ye shall achieve the highest good.
>
> For [so] sustained by sacrifice the gods will give you the food of your desire. Whoso enjoys their gift yet gives nothing [in return] is a thief, no more no less.
>
> Good men who eat the leavings of the sacrifice are freed from every taint, but evil do they eat who cook [only] for their own sakes. — 3.11-13

In sacrifices the offering to the deity can vary from an animal to vegetables, milk or clarified butter. The offering was mostly made

---

69. On the passages which speak about sacrifice as food to the gods in the Brāhmaṇas see ibid., pp. 255-56. On sacrifice as food to the gods in different religions see A.N. Terrin (1998), pp. 263-310. According to Irudayaraj, there is also a moving away from the traditional idea that *naivedyam* (food offered to the deity in the *pūjā*s) is food to the divinity to the idea that it is a means that the deity uses to divinise the offerer. See X. Irudayaraj (1978), p. 311. But such a view is not that common, but limited to some circles.
70. This aspect we will see in detail in the next chapter.
71. But this should not be taken to mean a commercial dealing as M. Dhavamony holds in his work. M. Dhavamony (1982), p. 187. Such a view does not take into consideration the religious sentiments of a people who through various rites and sacrifices express their belief in the divine-human-cosmic interdependence.

in fire,[72] at times it was completely destroyed. The Agni, the high priest of the gods was said to carry the offerings to the gods. The food left by the gods is called *ucchiṣṭa* (residue).[73] According to the *AV* (11.7), it is this residue (*ucchiṣṭa*) that holds together the earth, heaven, sea, waters, moon, wind, etc. Once the deity has partaken the food, the sacrificer, his wife/wives and the priests consume the remaining food. This partaking of the sacrificial food was considered to be an essential part of the sacrifice, for if a sacrificer did not partake of the sacrificial food he did not participate in the sacrifice.[74] However, according to *ŚB* (3.6.2.26), once upon a time the gods and men dined together, but now they are unseen.[75] This makes us think that earlier the Vedic sacrifice had a communion character, which was later lost.

But in the *pūjās* of contemporary Hinduism the oblations consist of different food materials which a devotee eats, but meat or fish are never offered. The offered food is said to be partly consumed by the deity and thus the remaining part (*ucchiṣṭa*) blessed by him.[76] When the sacrificer eats the rest of the food which is now permeated by the qualities of the deity, he gets those qualities. Thus, by eating the leavings of the deity the offerer partakes in

72. But the offerings to the water divinities are immersed in the water, to Rudra they are flung into the air, suspended from trees or buried under the earth, to the dead they are placed in the holes dug at the funeral site, etc. See N. Sheth (1998), p. 684.

73. According to a tradition a man should not eat all the food that is given to him. He should leave a portion of it that the remaining food may be given to one's wife or to one's servants. Ibid., p. 680.

74. A.B. Keith (1925), part 1, pp. 270-71; N. Sheth (1998), p. 685. But when the sacrificial meat consumption became an unusual practice among the Hindus with the influence of Buddhism, the cooked flesh of the animal sacrifice was only smelled and not eaten. Rāma is said to have smelled the cooked flesh of the *Aśvamedha,* and there is no mention of consumption.

75. See C. Malamoud (1996), p. 207.

76. N. Sheth (1998), p. 697.

the qualities of the deity and is in communion with him. The food is offered to the gods as means of sustenance.

Unlike the Vedas, in Christianity sacrifice is not considered to be food to God,[77] hence the bread and wine are not the remaining parts of God's food. They stand for the gifts of God and are offered back to God that Christ may give himself again to us by the means of them. They are transformed into the body and blood of Jesus through the descending of the Holy Spirit, and not because it is the residue.

In Hinduism there is a rich variation of foods used in sacrifice or worship. On the contrary in Christianity only unleavened bread and wine are used. Further our Eucharistic Host has become almost a symbol for food than food itself. Often it is made very thin that it melts before one gets the taste of food in the mouth. The use of the fermented *soma* juice was common in the Vedic times, but later on only in the Tāntric worship was wine used as an element of sacrifice.

However, the major difference between the Vedic notion of sacrifice and the Eucharist can be found in the Vedic understanding of it as food to the gods and the Christian notion of the Eucharist as the thanksgiving sacrifice. The very word *eucaristia* in Greek means thanksgiving. It is the thanksgiving sacrifice offered to God the Father by the Church for the salvation brought to the humanity in the death and resurrection of Jesus. The Eucharist is, thus, a thanksgiving sacrifice.

Conclusion

In our brief confrontation of the Vedic concept of sacrifice with the Eucharist, the memorial of the sacrifice of Jesus, we have found

---

77. In Israel God was supposed to smell the sweet odour of the sacrifices (Gen 8: 21), and there was a custom of placing twelve breads known as the bread of the Presence in a table in two rows of six for God (Ex 25: 30).

that there are many homological convergences and some differences between them even though the real substance of both these religions lie in what cannot be observed. In spite of the different world-views the notion of sacrifice can bring them together in some fields.

Just as the *puruṣa* myth forms the key to understand the Vedic sacrifice, the Christ-Event forms the basis for understanding the Eucharist, the Christian sacrifice. It is striking to note the importance of both these figures for understanding sacrifice in the respective religions. Just as it is difficult to understand the Vedic notion of humans, cosmos and sacrifice without understanding the *puruṣa* myth, so too, it is difficult to understand the Christian vision of humans, redemption and the Eucharist without understanding the Christ-Event. As Maximus holds, he who understands the enigma of incarnation and redemption, has understood the purpose of cosmos itself.[78] The Christ-Event, therefore holds the key to the Christian vision of humans and cosmos.

Both the *yajña* and the Eucharist recall a divine sacrifice of the creator God for the sake of his creation. Just as in Vedism *puruṣa* is considered to be the creator, the sustainer and the meeting point of time, so too, in Christianity Christ is considered to be the creator, the sustainer, and the meeting point of time and history. Both these figures undergo self-sacrifice for the sake of creation.

In Vedism sacrifice is the link between creation and immortality, and in Christianity too sacrifice is the link between the redemption and immortality. Sacrifice constitutes the link between creation and the divine being in Vedism, whereas it forms the link between the redemption and the divine being in Christianity. In either case there exists a divine sacrifice in relation to humans and the cosmos.

---

78. See pp. 239-47 of this book.

In Vedism *Brahman* is considered to be the food of life, and in Christianity Jesus is considered to be the bread of life. In the *Agnicayana* the whole cosmos forms the material for the sacrifice, and in the Eucharist the whole cosmos is gathered together under the cosmic elements of bread and wine and is offered to God. Thus, both the Vedic and the Eucharistic sacrifice have cosmic dimensions.

As regards the differences between them the most striking is the Vedic notion of sacrifice as food to the gods and the Eucharist as the thanksgiving sacrifice. Further in the Vedas the food is sacred and sharing it is to take part in the great cosmic metabolism but in Christianity such a vision is lacking. However in the Vedic sacrifice the divine-human-cosmic interdependence is much more evident than in the Christian notion of sacrifice. The Western Eucharistic theology needs to discover this interdependence from the Eastern sacramental theology and from the Vedic sacrifice.

Finally, just as every Vedic sacrifice is the ritual memorial of the sacrifice of *puruṣa,* so too, every Eucharist is the ritual memorial of the sacrificial death of Jesus for our sake, rather for the world. In my opinion the *puruṣa* myth and the Christ-Event hold the keys to understanding the respective world-views on creation, redemption and sacrifice.

7

A Comparison of the Pañca-mahāyajñas with the Eucharist

THE similarities between the Vedic sacrifices and the Eucharist which we saw in the last chapter can become clearer if we make a comparison of the *pañca-mahāyajñas*[1] (five great daily sacrifices): *devayajña* (sacrifice to gods), *pitṛyajña* (sacrifice to the ancestors), *bhūtayajña* (sacrifice to all living beings), *nṛyajña* (sacrifice to men), and the *brahmayajña* (sacrifice to *Brahman*) with the Eucharistic sacrifice. This is possible because both of them insist that the liturgical life should not be separated from the daily human life, and both of them consider the ritual sacrifice as the means to overcome the mortal condition of humans. Sacrifice helps to go beyond one's limited experience of space and time by opening a wider horizon of divine-human-cosmic relations. Thus, in this chapter we make an attempt to bring to light the similarities which exist between the *pañca-mahāyajñas* and the Eucharistic sacrifice.

The necessity of minimum ritual needed to carry out one's religious duties[2] and the possibility of everyone doing it might have helped them to survive in the course of sacrificial and ritual

---

1. We have not discussed in detail these sacrifices in the first part, for we have kept them for this chapter.

2. C. Malamoud (1977), p. 14. See also B.K. Smith (1989), p. 197. The Vedic sacrifice holds its fascination not only for its detailed and complicated elaboration of the solemn (*śrauta*) sacrifices like *Aśvamedha*, or *Agnicayana* which last for years, and for its cosmic dimension which we have seen in detail in the chapters

→

re-thinking in Hinduism. It may be due to these reasons that even though the complicated Vedic sacrifices almost vanished from the ritual practices[3] with the arrival of the temple worship and the Āgamic *pūjā*, the *pañca-mahāyajña*s survived and are still practised everyday by devout Hindus.

But before making the comparison of the *pañca-mahāyajña*s, which belongs to the domestic sacrifices and not solemn sacrifices,[4] with the Eucharistic sacrifice we should see the text and the different motives given for the performance of these five daily sacrifices. According to the earliest text the *pañca-mahāyajña*s are as follows:

→ 2 and 6 of book, but also for its capacity to adapt and modify it according to the life situation of the ordinary householder, making him this time the priest of his *pañca-mahāyajña*s. By such an act the Vedic ritualists have demonstrated that sacrifice is not a prerogative of a few kings or rich persons, but is also within the reach of everyone, and every twice-born male can be the priest of such sacrifices. As P.V. Kane writes: "Every man could not afford to celebrate the solemn *śrauta* rites prescribed in the Brāhmaṇas and Śrauta-Sūtras. But everyone could offer a fuel-stick to fire that was deemed to be the mouth of the great Gods of Heaven and thus show his reverence and devotion to them." P.V. Kane (1941), vol. 2, pp. 697-98.

3. But there is also a tendency to revive the old sacrificial system, an example of which can be seen in the 1975 *agnicayana* in Kerala in which many Western Indologists participated. See C.G. Kashikar and A. Parpola (2001), pp. 199-251; B.K. Smith (1989), pp. 200-03.

4. The *pañca-mahāyajña*s are distinguished from the solemn, costly, and occasional *śrauta* sacrifices on different grounds. They are the daily simple sacrifices (though they are given the adjective great) against the occasional, solemn and the costly *śrauta* sacrifices, and can be performed by any householder. They do not require the service of a professional priest whereas in the *śrauta* sacrifice the priests occupy a prominent role and the sacrificer's role is reduced to a passive spectator. Further in the *pañca-mahāyajña*s the sacrificer is motivated by the desire to →

> There are five great sacrifices, namely, the great ritual services: the sacrifice to all beings, sacrifice to men, sacrifice to the ancestors, sacrifice to the gods, sacrifice to *Brahman*.
>
> Day by day a man offers sustenance to creatures, that is the sacrifice to beings. Day by day a man gives hospitality to guests including, a glass of water, that is sacrifice to men. Day by day a man makes funerary offerings, including a glass of water; that is the sacrifice to the ancestors. Day by day a man makes offerings to the gods including wood for burning; that is the sacrifice to the gods. And the sacrifice to *Brahman*? The sacrifice to *Brahman* consists of sacred study. — *ŚB* 11.5.6.1-3[5]

Now the question is why one should perform these five great sacrifices daily? What are the rationales given for their daily performance? The two important motives given for their performance are as means to pay back the prenatal debts, and the expiation against the violence secured to living beings. The first motive may be the result of the idea that human life is a debt and one needs to pay back such a debt through sacrifices. For example, the *TS* (6.3.10.5) speaks that when a brāhmaṇa is born, he simultaneously acquires three debts, the study of the Vedic texts to the *ṛṣis*, the sacrifice to the gods, and the procreation to the

→ discharge his duties towards God, the creator of everything, to his ancestors who gave him life, to living beings and to men with whom he needs to live in harmony and co-operation. Here the personal interest behind the performance is less evident than the *śrauta* sacrifices which were often performed to secure some favour from the gods such as prosperity, a son, victory over the enemy, etc. Hence the intention of the *pañca-mahāyajñas* can be considered spiritually more progressive and ennobling than that of *śrauta* sacrifices. J. Thachil (1985), pp. 162-63. P.V. Kane considers the *pañca-mahāyajñas* as domestic sacrifices and for the different texts of the Gṛhya-Sūtras (rules for the domestic rituals) which speak about the *pañca-mahāyajñas*. See P.V. Kane (1941), vol. 2, pp. 696-756; J. Gonda (1980), pp. 413-40.

5. This translation is taken from *PVE*, p. 394. *TA*, 11.10 too speaks of these five sacrifices.

Fathers. Here the debt is spoken only of the brāhmaṇas, but *ŚB* (1.7.2.1-6) speaks of fourfold debts due to all. Every being by birth acquires a debt to the gods, to the sages, to the Fathers and to men. Through the five daily sacrifices one pays back these debts.[6] Then Manu adds another motivation to this debt-giving, i.e. the expiation of the sins committed by hurting or killing beings at work (Manu 3.68-71). Day by day man causes violence to the living beings and this has to be remedied by giving food to them.[7]

The purpose of the *pañca-mahāyajñas* as the expiation of the sins committed daily against the sentient beings may be the result of the later influence of Buddhism and Jainism on Vedism and the emergence of the notion of non-violence. Kane sees in the performance of the *pañca-mahāyajñas* something more than these two above-mentioned motives. According to him, the sentiments of devotion, gratitude, reverence, loving memory, kindness and tolerance seem to have been the springs that prompted the sages to emphasize the performance of these sacrifices.[8] G.P. Upadhyay too holds a similar view when he writes,

> in the earlier texts these *yajñas* signify devotion, gratitude, reverence, loving memory, kindness and toleration leading towards the general wealth of society. But the authors of our age, like Manu, transformed the conception of the *pañca-mahāyajñas* as the means of expiation of sins committed in the daily life of a householder, e.g. the killing of insects.[9]

Even though all these above-mentioned motives can be taken as legitimate reasons for the performance of the *pañca-mahāyajñas*, they are not complete without a further explanation of the idea of

6. However, only the three upper castes are given the possibility of liberation from the debts, the members of the fourth caste are again excluded from it.
7. See P.V. Kane (1941), vol. 2, p. 699.
8. Ibid., p. 698.
9. G.P. Upadhyay (1979), pp. 190-91.

the debt according to the Brāhmaṇas. It is the idea of debt that can help us to gather the real motive behind their performances, and in this attempt C. Malamoud is right when he writes that the idea of debt need to be taken from the point of view of our mortal condition.[10] Then the idea of paying the prenatal debt would mean more than a mere obligation to the gods, ancestors, to the sages, and to living beings, but primarily our natural condition as a creature, i.e. our mortal condition. The debt which is constitutive to human nature, would then mean the presence of death and the means to pay back this debt or to overcome this condition is again sacrifice. *ŚB* (3.6.2.16) says that when man is born, he is born as a debtor to death, when he sacrifices he redeems himself from death.[11] In sacrifice he pays back the debt to Yama (the god of death) and redeems himself.

According to the Vedic vision, a human person is made of five cosmic elements,[12] and at his/her cremation these elements return to their origins. The debt then can mean on the one hand

---

10. C. Malamoud (1996), pp. 100-01.

11. In sacrifice man is said to make a journey to heaven to make sure of a place for himself, but he cannot stay on there because he has not paid the final debt due to Yama, his life itself. But a part of him survives in heaven and only after his death will he be able to stay there in the world which he has ritually created. For more details see B.K. Smith (1989), pp. 104-19.

12. According to the Vedic conception, a human being is made of five cosmic elements (*pañca-mahābhūtas*), such as earth (*pṛthvī*), water (*āp*), fire (*tejas*), air (*vāyu*), and space/ether (*ākāśa*). At the cremation or dissolution of the human body all these cosmic elements return to their original condition. Thus, the dissolution takes place exactly like the cosmogonic sacrificial dispersion of *puruṣa*, in which man returns to the cosmos the cosmic elements of his body. As the *BṛUp* says: ". . . the voice of a dead man goes into fire, his breath into wind, his eye into the sun, his mind into the moon, his hearing into the quarters of heaven, his body into the earth, his soul (*ātman*) into space, the hairs of his head into plants, the hairs of his body into trees, and his blood and semen

→

that his/her body is made of different cosmic elements, and on the other his/her mortal condition, i.e. the presence of death. The prenatal debt, therefore, has to be taken not only as a duty as some would prefer to argue,[13] but as the mortal condition of humans. As C. Malamoud writes: "the material debt is an image, a particular manifestation of an inseparable debt, it means to say, definitively, of the fact that man is mortal."[14] If the prenatal debt means the mortal condition of humans, then the way to overcome it is again sacrifice, the five daily great sacrifices.

Manu says that he who does not sacrifice breathes but does not live really (3.72). The five daily sacrifices become the way to overcome the natural condition of humans and to live really by carrying out one's duties towards gods, ancestors, sages, and all living beings. The sentiments of devotion, gratitude, reverence, loving memory, kindness, and tolerance present in these sacrifices,[15] and the sacrifice as the means to overcome our mortal condition, can bring us closer to the Eucharist which is also celebrated as devotion, gratitude, loving memorial, and the Eucharistic body and blood of Jesus as the food and drink of immortality.[16] Therefore, in this chapter we make an attempt to

→ are placed in water . . ." (3.2.13). This is the final debt that we have to pay, because our body is made up of five different cosmic elements. This takes place surely at our final sacrifice, on the funeral pyre where we give as oblation our own bodies.

13. The Naiyāyikas argue that when the Vedas speak of a debt, they speak of a duty to show how positive it is to celebrate the sacrifices, and how negative it is to be neglected. C. Malamoud (1996), p. 100. But this duty also needs to be taken as something prescribed by the Vedas to overcome one's mortal condition, by faithfully fulfilling the *dharma* prescribed by the Vedas.

14. Ibid., p. 108.

15. P.V. Kane (1941), vol. 2, p. 698; G.P. Upadhyay (1979), pp. 190-91.

16. On the Eucharistic body and blood of Jesus as the food and drink of immortality see the last chapter pp. 305ff.

compare them with the Eucharistic sacrifice to understand the similarities and the differences that exist between them. Both of them are closely related to daily life and the ethical dimension of the sacrifice. They can be the best examples that liturgy cannot be separated from daily life, and sacrifice can have a wider meaning without rejecting its ritual action and character.

Devayajña and the Eucharist as Sacrifice to God the Father

Devayajña, the sacrifice to the gods, is the first of the five daily sacrifices and it can be compared to the Eucharist as the sacrifice to God the Father. *Devayajña* is offered both in the morning and in the evening.[17] A devout Hindu householder is called to begin his day with a sacrifice to gods and to bring to an end his activities with the evening sacrifice to the gods. The oblation is offered into the nuptial fire which was kindled at the marriage ceremony and with which food is cooked daily (Manu 3.67). It is performed into *agni* (the fire), which is identified with the deity Agni, the mouth of gods, the priest of the gods who takes the sacrifice to the gods.[18]

---

17. For the different texts which speak of this sacrifice see P.V. Kane (1941), vol. 2, pp. 705-40.

18. Agni's role as the mouth of the gods, as the mediator, as the brother, and as the friend is very clear in *Ṛ̥V* 1. 75. 1-4 which are as follows:

    Accept our praise resounding,
    the food beloved by the Gods,
    opening your *mouth* to consume our oblations!
    O Lord, noblest of the noble,
    wisest and best *mediator*,
    may we utter an acceptable prayer, efficacious!
    Who among men is your brother?
    Who offers you holy worship?
    Who are you, Lord? On whom dependent?
    You are of all Men the *brother*

Devayajña in its simplest form can be performed in the domestic fire by offering materials like *ghī* (clarified butter), milk, rice, grains, or even a fuel stick to the fire reciting some formula like "to god Indra offering" (*indrāya svāhā*), "to god Agni offering" (*agnaye svāhā*), etc. The *devayajña*, therefore, consists of a simple ritual with the offering of some material into the fire, followed by the recitation of certain ritual formulas[19] which even the poorest of the poor is able to perform.

As a sacrifice being performed in the fire it can be seen as part of the *agnihotras*[20] whose result may vary according to the *ŚB* from the removal of evils (2.3.1.6), freedom from death (2.3.3.7-10), and to a ship leading to the heavenly world (2.3.3.15).[21] According to Manu, the one who performs this sacrifice to the gods sustains the whole universe, moving and unmoving (3.75); because the offering correctly put into the fire reaches the sun, from the sun the rain is produced, from rain comes the food and from this the offspring (3.76). Hence the *devayajña,* one of the *pañca-mahāyajñas*, too has a cosmic dimension. To sacrifice to the gods is to ensure one's own existence and of the whole cosmos.

Just as the *devayajña* is the daily sacrifice to the gods, so too, the Eucharist is the daily sacrifice of the Church to God the Father. Another similarity between the *devayajña* and the Eucharist can be in the memorial aspect of it. *Devayajña* is not only the sacrifice *to* the gods but also *of* the gods. For, gods were the first to offer sacrifice and men imitate the gods in their sacrifice. Just as sacrifice to the gods is following the example of the gods, so too, the Eucharist is the *anamnesis* of the sacrifice of Christ, wherein the

---

→ and dear *companion*, O Lord,
the *friend* whose name we may invoke for our friends!

This translation is taken from *PVE*, p. 838. The cursive is mine.

19. P.V. Kane (1941), vol. 2, p. 705. See also J. Thachil (1985), p. 164.

20. H.W. Bodewitz (2003), pp. 191ff.

21. See G.U. Thite (1975), p. 54.

Church unites her self-offering to the sacrifice of Christ to God the Father. Just as a devout Hindu begins his day and ends it with the *devayajña*, so too, a devout Christian whenever possible begins or ends his/her day with the participation at the Eucharistic sacrifice.

But the *devayajña* is performed at home by the householder, whereas the Eucharist is celebrated in the churches by the priests. In the *devayajña* the material can be any item of the food generally eaten by the householder, such as grains, milk, clarified butter or even a piece of firewood, whereas in the Eucharist only the unleavened bread and wine are used. The recipient of *devayajña* can be any of the gods whom the sacrificer considers as his Supreme God or his favourite deity, whereas the Eucharist is offered only to God the Father.

Pitṛyajña and the Offering of the Eucharist for the Dead

The earliest mention of *pitṛyajña* (sacrifice for the dead), the second daily sacrifice that a devout Hindu is called to perform can be found in *ṚV* (10.16.10), but its exact meaning is not certain.[22] This sacrifice can be compared to the Eucharist as the sacrifice for the dead in Christianity because from the time of St. Augustine the Catholics offered it as sacrifice for the dead.[23]

The *pitṛyajña* can be performed in three ways: as *śrāddha* (by inviting a brāhmaṇa for dinner, Manu 3.82-83), *tarpaṇa* (by offering water to the Fathers, Manu 3.70 and 283), and as *baliharaṇa* (in which *bali* food is offered to the Fathers, Manu 3.91), and any one of them is enough.[24] As *tarpaṇa* it consists in offering libations of water daily to the deceased ancestors. Every devout Hindu, before

---

22. P.V. Kane (1941), vol. 2, p. 748.
23. G. Bonner (1991), pp. 104-11.
24. P.V. Kane (1941), vol. 2, p. 700.

taking a bath, takes water with both hands joined together and offers it first to the gods and then to the deceased ancestors. Only after such offerings does one proceed with his bath. These sacrifices are meant as propitiation to the ancestors, and to neglect such performances can cause their anger.

But in the *Śatapatha Brāhmaṇa* the procreation is seen as the sacrifice to the ancestors (1.7.2.4), for through the procreation human life is preserved on the earth. By that one pays the debt to the deceased ancestors and gains immortality. According to *AB* (7.13), the procreation is the means to obtain immortality, and the liberation is immediate; it is enough to see the face of the child to be liberated from one's debts to the fathers.[25]

Unlike the Hindus the Christians do not have a particular sacrifice to the dead ancestors, nor is the son considered to be the saviour of the father from hell. Yet we Catholics offer the holy sacrifice of the Eucharist in commemoration of the dead and to plead for the divine mercy on them. Rarely do Catholics conduct a burial service without the celebration of the holy sacrifice of the Eucharist. In every Eucharist the dead persons are recommended to the mercy of God and the intercession for the dead is one of the constituent elements of the Eucharistic prayer. Hence there is no holy sacrifice of the Eucharist without an intercession for the dead, and it can be seen as the Christian equivalent for the sacrifice for the dead.

However, the *pitṛyajña* cannot be fully identified with the holy sacrifice of the Eucharist because the former is not for the expiation

---

25. According to C. Malamoud, etymologically the *putra* (son), means the one who saves from hell, and makes possible for his father a life of happiness in the other world. It seems that the son takes on himself the debt of his father and in his turn transfers it to his son. And the one who has no son is said to have no world, for he will have no son to perform sacrifice for him. C. Malamoud (1996), pp. 102-04.

of the sins of the dead ancestors, but to keep good relationship with them so that the life of the living may not be in danger. The holy sacrifice of the Eucharist is also offered for the remission of the sins of the dead,[26] and to feel their presence in day-to-day life. We Catholics do pray for the dead and offer them the holy sacrifice of the Eucharist for we believe that God's love, mercy and forgiveness do not vanish with the physical death of a person.

Bhūtayajña and the Intercession for the Well-being of All in the Eucharist

Bhūtayajña (sacrifice to all living beings)[27] is another daily sacrifice which in my opinion can be seen in relation to the element of intercession for the well-being of all in the Eucharist. In both of them we can find the universal kindliness and charity.

Bhūtayajña as a rite consists of offering oblation (*bali*) to all living beings such as outcastes, dogs, birds, insects, etc. Human being is not seen in isolation from the rest of the creatures, she/he is called to be the supporter of every living being in this cosmos. It may be for this reason that one needs to share with all the living beings the food one has cooked, and only after feeding them is one supposed to eat. Thus the injunction not to eat anything without having cut-off a portion to these above-mentioned beings.[28] The householder before taking food takes some part of

---

26. For the Protestants' objections on the catholic practice of Mass for the dead see D.N. Power (1987), p. 46.

27. P.V. Kane sees in the term *vaiśva-devayajña* the sacrifice to gods, to the living beings, and to men. For he writes, "Vaiśvadeva comprises all actions from the offering into fire oblations of food up to the throwing of food to dogs and the like in the morning and the evening." P.V. Kane (1941), vol. 2, pp. 741-47. But we prefer to keep the distinction of the different sacrifices to gather their particular meanings.

28. Ibid., p. 747.

the cooked food and offers it to them.[29] He cannot throw food as he wants, it has to be put on the ground (if it is for the animals, birds and the insects) prepared by wiping it with his hands and sprinkled with water. He has to sprinkle water on it after the food is placed on the ground. According to P.V. Kane,

> These directions to give food even to outcastes, dogs and birds were the outcome of the noble sentiment of universal kindliness and charity, the idea that One Spirit pervades and illumines the meanest of creatures and binds all together.[30]

But according to Manu the purpose of this sacrifice is not so much the well-being of all the creatures, but the expiation of the sins that one committed against the creatures during the day.[31] In the *Bhagavad-Gītā* too, we find that the food eaten after giving it to others brings the remission of sins, for "Good men who eat the leavings of the sacrifice are freed from every taint, but evil are they and evil do they eat who cook [only] for themselves (3.13). By the phrase "eating the leavings of the sacrifice" what is meant is eating after feeding the living beings. This is clear from Śaṅkarācārya's translation of the same verse which is as follows: "The righteous, who eat the remnant of the sacrifice, are freed from all sins; but sin do the impious eat who cook for their own sakes."[32] The offering of food to the living beings, therefore, frees one from the sins committed daily involuntarily against the living beings.

---

29. For the action to have any sacrificial value it has to be performed before one takes food. Only then it can be seen as a sacrifice. Later on even the food given to the outcastes is included into this rite, but rarely an outcaste is given food before the householder eats, because not even the wife eats before the husband has eaten.
30. P.V. Kane (1941), vol. 2, p. 746.
31. Manu 3, 68-69.
32. Śaṅkarācārya (1995), p. 99.

The Vedas not only called for the sharing of food but also prayed for the world peace, harmony, love and happiness.[33] Just as in the Vedas we find a concern for the well-being of all, so too, in the Eucharist we can see a concern for the well-being of all. This is expressed in different ways first by interceding for the well-being of all and secondly by inviting the participants to live in charity and solidarity especially with the poor and the needy. Firstly the prayers in the Eucharist are directed to God the Father for the well-being of all, because the object of the prayer is the whole world, the living and the dead. Thus we can find a concern for the well-being of all in our intercessions. Secondly the Eucharist calls the participants who take part in the body and blood of Jesus Christ to live in solidarity and fellowship with all especially with the poor and the marginalized. Just as the *bhūtayajña* calls a devout Hindu to live in love and harmony with all the living beings, so too, the Eucharist calls a Christian to rise above his/her selfish interests and to look for the well-being of all.

The Eucharist, however, cannot be fully identified with the *bhūtayajña,* because the Eucharist is never celebrated for the

---

33. The last verse of the *ṚV* (10.191.4) says:

United your resolve, united your hearts, may your spirits be at one, that you may long together dwell in unity and concord!

Again in *AV* (3.30.1-3) we read:

Of one heart and one mind I make you, devoid of hate.

Love one another, as a cow loves the calf she has borne.

Let the son be courteous to his father, of one mind with his mother.

Let the wife speak words that are gentle and sweet to her husband.

Never may brother hate brother or sister hurt sister.

United in heart and in purpose, Commune sweetly together.

These translations are taken from *PVE,* p. 863 and p. 857 respectively.

expiation of the sins committed against the creatures. The merits of the Eucharistic sacrifice may be applied for the remission of the sins of the dead. The *bhūtayajña* is an example not to limit the communion with the human beings but to widen it to universal or cosmic level. It is this cosmic communion that is almost lacking in the Western Eucharistic theology but is present in the Eucharistic theology of the Eastern Church.

Nṛyajña and the Eucharist as the Agapic Meal

According to the Brāhmaṇas, *nṛyajña* (sacrifice to men) is another sacrifice that a householder needs to offer daily,[34] and this may be compared to the Eucharist as the fellowship meal. Sacrifice to men consists in the hospitality and the reception of the guests.[35] The gestures of hospitality,[36] friendship and love are seen as sacred actions and are put in level with the sacrifice that maintains the

34. *Nṛyajña* is also called *manuṣya-yajña*.

35. On the question who is a guest, P.V. Kane summarizes the notion of the different texts in the following words: ". . . he is called an *atithi* who belonging to a different village and intending to stay one night only arrives in the evening, that one who has already been invited for dinner is not an *atithi* properly so-called, that a person who belongs to the same village or who is a friend or fellow-student is not an *atithi*, that one has to honour guests according to one's ability, that guests are to be preferred according to the order of *varṇa*s and that among the brahmins, the Śrotriya and one who has completely mastered (at least one) recension of the Veda is to be preferred." P.V. Kane (1941), vol. 2, p. 751.

36. The *pūjā* of the modern Hinduism follows closely the various stages of the reception and the feeding of the guests in its worship. According to K. Luke, *pūjā* was originally the householder's action of welcoming guests, and later on such a treatment was transferred into the idea of welcoming god as guest. See K. Luke (1975a), pp. 351-65, especially pp. 362-63. For more details on the procedure of the *pūjā*, see also G. Bühnemann (1988), pp. 29-66, and pp. 135-82; G. Favaro (1993), pp. 47-48.

world. To share food is then to take part in the universal exchange or to the great cosmic metabolism which maintains the whole cosmos.[37]

Just as the oblation to all the living beings (*bhūtayajña*) has to be given before one takes food, so too, the guest has to be fed before the family members take food. A householder should not eat immediately after offering sacrifice to the living beings; he has to wait in front of his door for as much time as would be required for milking a cow or for a longer time as he desires, for receiving guests.[38] It is interesting to note that it is not enough to give food to the one who comes and knocks at the door, the householder should wait in front of the house to receive the guest. And in the words of Kane:

> The guest is to be shown honour by going out to meet him, by offering him water to wash his feet, by giving him a seat, by lighting a lamp before him, by giving food and lodging, by personal attendance on him, by offering him a bed and by accompanying him some distance when he departs.[39]

The *AV* (9.6) considers these various stages of the reception of the guests and feeding them as various actions performed in a sacrifice: when the host catches sight of his guests, it is as though he were witnessing a solemn sacrifice (v.3), when he offers them water, he is bringing forward the sacrificial water (v.4), the satisfaction which the guest experiences can be compared to the animal that is bound (v.6), preparing lodging for them is equal to the priests taking seat and getting ready for the sacrifice (v.7), the bed prepared for them is sacrificial grass arranged for the victim (v.8), and ointment and unguent offered to them is the sacrificial butter (v.11), the snacks given are the sacrificial cake (v.12), and the scattered rice or food particles signify the *soma*

---

37. See A.N. Terrin (1998), pp. 272ff.

38. P.V. Kane (1941), vol. 2, p. 751.

39. Ibid., p. 752.

shoots (v.14). Not only that the various stages of the reception of the guest are seen as sacrifice but also the attention and concern one shows towards the guest are seen as the sacrificial fees. For according to the Anuśāsana Parva of *Mahābhārata,* the host should give his eyes, mind and agreeable speech to the guest, he should personally attend on him and should accompany him for some distance when the guest departs, for this sacrifice demands these five fees (7.6).[40]

A possible answer to the question why the Vedas consider hospitality as a sacrifice may be in the fact that in the Indian culture a guest is sacred[41] because it is believed that Brahmā,[42] or Viṣṇu[43] or Agni himself is said to be present in every guest, and as a result said to partake the food that is given to the guest. According to the *R̥V*, Agni is the permanent guest in the house of the sacrificer (1.73.1; 5.1.9; 7.15.2). He is not only the guest but also the closest relative and the friend (*R̥V* 7.15.1). The warmth that Agni diffuses calls for warm human relationships, for a unity of hearts and minds.[44] The *R̥V* urges for the sharing of food with the needy, praises a generous giver and calls the one who eats alone a sinner (10.117). The *BG* too, calls the one who eats alone a sinner.[45] This sharing food with others is a sacrifice because it helps to preserve life, and it secures one heaven and freedom from misfortunes.[46]

---

40. See also ibid., pp. 752-53; J. Thachil (1985), p. 166.
41. Not only in Vedic India was a guest considered to be sacred but also in almost all the nomadic communities the guest was treated as sacred. See R. de Vaux (1964), pp. 20-21. However, we do not know whether in other cultures the service of the guest was considered to be one of the daily sacrifices.
42. X. Irudayaraj (1978), p. 310.
43. P.V. Kane (1941), vol. 2, p. 754.
44. *PVE,* p. 833.
45. BG 3.13. See also pp. 306-10 of this book.
46. P.V. Kane (1941), vol. 2, p. 754.

Another reason why hospitality is a sacrifice may be that the guest who stays for a night is said to destroy the accumulated sins of the householder.[47] Just as the guest destroys the sins of the householder, so too, the opposite can happen if one refuses a guest. For it is said that a despised guest transfers on to the householder the former's sins, and takes away the latter's merits.[48] Although one is invited to give food to all, even to the low castes and to the enemies,[49] one is not obliged to give cooked food to unworthy persons (those who have become *patita*,[50] fallen, degraded for grave sins, and to heretics).[51] Manu maintains that a priest who knows the real meaning of the Vedas should be given alms (3.96), and any gift to an unworthy priest is a waste (3.97).[52] Just as the hospitality to an unworthy person can be a waste of material, so too, a brāhmaṇa who neither performs asceticism,

---

47. But to receive the hospitality also has its responsibility, for the gift is said to embody the sins of the donor. In sacrifice the gift paid to the priests become a means by which the donor transfers the burden of death and impurity. Just as the victim is the surrogate for the sacrificer, so too, the gift is the surrogate for the donor, and it stands for what he must expiate. Hence the instruction not to seek for gifts, nor to accept from the one who lives an unholy life. For more details see J. Heesterman (1964), pp. 1-31; J. Parry (1986), pp. 459-61.

48. P.V. Kane (1941), vol. 2, p. 754.

49. Sāntiparva of *Mahābhārata* (146.5) says that even an enemy when he comes to one's house as a guest must be hospitably treated, because a tree does not remove its shade from one who approaches to cut it down. See also P.V. Kane (1941), vol. 2, p. 752.

50. See also pp. 104-09 of this book.

51. P.V. Kane (1941), vol. 2, p. 752. However, one may give grains to them.

52. According to W. Doniger and B.K. Smith, this refers to the brāhmaṇa who has put off the sacrificial fire. W. Doniger and B.K. Smith (1996), p. 138.

nor studies the Vedas, yet delights in receiving hospitality and gifts is said to sink with the donor into hell (Manu 4.190). Thus, the gifts and hospitality have to be offered to those who practise asceticism and study the Vedas.

Again for the Vedic person the sharing food with others is a sacrificial act because such an act is the re-enactment of the primordial life-giving self-gift of *puruṣa* for the sake of creation.[53] Similarly in Christianity the Eucharist calls us to live the self-gift of Jesus for the sake of the redemption. We can find that in the primitive Church the Eucharistic celebration was a fellowship meal which they called *agape* in memory of the sacrificial self-gift of Jesus.

Without entering into any exegetical study, we may say that according to Luke (24: 13-35) the risen Lord revealed himself to the two disciples on the way to Emmaus, when they offered hospitality to their unknown stranger.[54] The earliest form of the celebration of the Eucharist consisted in a fellowship meal where each one used to bring food and drinks to share with others before the real "breaking of bread." From Paul's first letter to the Corinthians we know that slowly abuses crept in and the apostle had to write a letter to correct them (1Cor 11: 17-22). According to the Canons of the Hyppolytus, the *agape* was not celebrated in a Church but in the house of a person who issued the invitations to the meal and met the expenses of it.[55]

The Eucharist, being the memorial of Jesus' self-emptying sacrifice on the cross, invites all those who take part in it to share

53. See also pp. 306-10 of this book.

54. In Rev (3: 26) the risen Lord presents himself as a guest standing and knocking at the door, ready to go in and dine with the one who opens the door for him. And in Gen (18: 1-16) Abraham is said to have received God at his tent and gave food to him when he welcomed the three guests, who then promised a son for Abraham from Sarah.

55. H. Lietzmann (1979), p. 161.

their lives with others. Justin Martyr, for example, used to invite the participants immediately after the Holy Communion to make a collection for the poor, needy, prisoners, foreigners who were settled among them, etc.[56] According to G. Segalla, "The sharing of Jesus, the bread of life, should be an encouragement and a commitment to share the material bread, so that nobody may suffer hunger."[57] He argues again by saying that it may be a contradiction and a scandal to participate in the Eucharistic communion if one does not realize the communion with the brethren, because Jesus is in the brethren.[58] The Eucharistic sacrifice, therefore, calls us to live the self-gift of Jesus to us in our fellowship with our brethren, especially with the poor and the needy.

Just as the hospitality and the reception of the guests are seen as one of the five daily sacrifices in Hinduism, similarly the letter to the Hebrews considers doing good to others as sacrifice. For it says: "Do not neglect to do good and to share what you have, for such sacrifices are pleasing to God" (13: 16).[59] Just as in Hinduism Brahmā, or Agni or Viṣṇu is seen as present in every guest, and partakes of the food that is given, so too, in Christianity Jesus is seen as present in every person, and all that we do to others we do to Jesus. The final judgement is presented in terms of love and solidarity towards others, for Jesus will say to the righteous,

> I was hungry and you gave me food, I was thirsty and you gave me drink, I was a stranger and you welcomed me, I was naked

---

56. Justin, Saint (1977), pp. 106-07.
57. G. Segalla (1976), p. 162.
58. Ibid.
59. Similarly in the *BG* we can read: "[Works of] sacrifice, the gift of alms, and works of penance are not to be surrendered; these must certainly be done: it is sacrifice, alms-giving, and ascetic practice that purify the wise (18.5).

> and you clothed me . . . as you did it to one of the least of these my brethren you did it unto me. — Mt. 25: 35-36, 40

The lack of love and solidarity become the reasons for the condemnation of the unrighteous, for in Mt (25: 42-45) we have the condemnation of the wicked because they did not share food, cloth, etc. with the needy and the strangers. Hence we can see a parallel between the service of the guests in Hinduism and the solidarity in Christianity. The Eucharist, the *anamnesis* of Jesus' self-emptying sacrifice cannot neglect the fellowship which Jesus showed for the poor and the needy. The sharing of Jesus, the bread of life, thus, may encourage one to share the material bread with the needy following the example of Jesus and the primitive Christian *agape*.

Brahmayajña and the Liturgy of the Word

The *brahmayajña* (sacrifice to *Brahman*), which B.K. Smith calls the "sacrifice of speech,"[60] can be seen in relation to the Liturgy of the Word. It is the last of the five great daily sacrifices to be offered by a devout Hindu householder, and it consists in the daily study of the sacred scriptures, teaching, and the recitation of the Vedas.[61]

---

60. B.K. Smith (1989), p. 197.

61. We can find some parallels between this study of the Vedas as sacrifice and the study of Torah as incense sacrifice in Judaism. For, according to R. Hayward, in Judaism the incense offering was held sometimes, especially in Ben Sira (39: 13-14), and in the Qumran community, to symbolize those who labour in Torah by studying it. The actual Torah study was sometimes compared to the incense smoke which falls into the category of a "most holy thing," and rises up at the very place in the sanctuary where God is present to meet his people (Ex 30: 36). R. Hayward (1991), pp. 4-25, and 28. According to a famous saying attributed to Simon the Righteous, "Upon three things the universe stands: upon the Torah, and upon the Temple service, and upon deeds of loving kindness" (M. Aboth 1: 2 as quoted by Hayward). Ibid., pp. 31-32. So too, for a Vedic person the five great daily →

One may recite only as much as one feels that one can afford to do with a concentrated mind. A random recitation is discouraged, rather one should start from the point where he stopped the previous day.[62] If one is not able to sit up for the recitation, one may do it lying down. At the end of the recitation one should repeat thrice the verse "Adoration to Brahmā . . . to Agni, to the Earth, to herbs, to speech, to the Lord of the speech (Bṛhaspati), I offer adoration to the great Viṣṇu."[63]

And the shortest *brahmayajña* would be *oṁ bhūr, bhuvaḥ svaḥ;*[64] the Gāyatrī verse repeated thrice[65] then at least one *ṛk*[66] verse and

---

→ sacrifices which comprise study of the Vedas (*brahmayajña*), the sacrifices to gods (*devayajña*), and the loving-kindness to the human beings and to all living beings (*nṛyajña*, *pitṛyajña* and the *bhūtayajña*) become the sacred actions on which the whole universe stands.

62 P.V. Kane (1941), vol. 2, p. 702.

63. Ibid., pp. 702-03.

64. *Bhūr bhuvaḥ svaḥ* are the three words through which Prajāpati created this universe, and they stand for the earth, atmosphere, and the sky respectively. When they are pronounced during the Vedic rituals they stand for the three worlds: earthly, the atmosphere, and the heavenly world, or existence, being and Self. (The word *bhūr* is only an exclamative word that belongs to the liturgical formulas and has no particular meaning. However, *bhūr*, *bhuḥ* and *bhuvaḥ* all come form *bhuḥ*, the root verb of existence). According to the *ŚB* the golden egg (*hiraṇyagarbha*) after having floated for a year produced Prajāpati, who then broke open this egg. And after a year he spoke three creative words such as *bhuḥ* which became this earth, *bhuvaḥ* which became the air, and *svaḥ* which became the sky (*ŚB* 11.1.6.1-3).

65. *Oṁ, tat savitur vareṇyam । bhargo devasya dhīmahi । dhiyo yo naḥ pracodayāt oṁ* (*Oṁ*, We meditate upon the glorious splendor of the Vivifier divine. May he himself illumine minds *Oṁ*!). This translation is taken from *PVE*, p. 38. The divine illumination of the mind is what one asks by the recitation of this verse in the morning.

66. *Ṛk* = one stanza or verse of a Ṛgvedic hymn.

then the verse *namo brahmane*[67] . . . repeated thrice . . . the one who knows only a portion of the Veda should recite as *brahmayajña* the Puruṣa-Sūkta (*ṚV* 10.90).[68]

Thus, in this sacrifice too, we can find a reference to the creative action of Prajāpati through the *vāc*, and the recitation of the Puruṣa-Sūkta again recalls the primordial sacrifice for the sake of creation. Even the daily recitation of the verses of the Vedas has something to do with the creative act of Prajāpati; it is to recreate the cosmos as Prajāpati did at the beginning, that the cosmos may survive.

As we have seen there is absolutely no obvious ritual here yet it is called a sacrifice. Studying, interpreting, teaching and the recitation of the sacred scriptures are seen as sacrifice to *Brahman*, the highest God of the Upaniṣads. Here it is not water, milk, butter, rice or some other material that is offered to *Brahman* but the student's intellect. The Vedas, therefore, give an important place to the daily study of the scriptures because it is only by studying the scriptures that one can understand the real nature of the ritual, its internal meaning, one's true nature in relation to *Brahman*, the knowledge of the transitory and the intransitory elements in the universe, etc. The reward of such daily study of the Vedas is so great that according to *ŚB* whoever studies the Vedic lessons day by day gains an imperishable world which is far superior to the world which one may secure by making gifts to all the priests of the world (11.5.6.3).[69]

In the Eucharist too, we can find an important role given to the reading and the interpretation of the Word of God. There is no celebration of the Eucharist without the proclamation of the Word of God, and on Sundays and solemn feast days the homily is made compulsory. The SC 7, while affirming the fourfold

67. = adoration to *Brahman*.

68. P.V. Kane (1941), vol. 2, p. 703.

69. See also ibid., p. 701.

presence of Christ in the celebration of the sacraments, says that it is Christ who speaks to the assembly through the Liturgy of the Word. Hence it is Christ who reveals himself to the assembly gathered together for the celebration of the sacrament. The reading, interpreting and studying of the Word of God form an integral part of the holy sacrifice of the Eucharist. The rite of reading the Word of God in the Liturgy helps us to understand the mystery of salvation and thereby it prepares us for the sacrifice of the Altar.

Conclusion

From our above comparison we have seen that the *pañca-mahāyajña*s and the Eucharist constitute the central Hindu and the Christian sacrifice respectively. Just as the *pañca-mahāyajña*s are the five great daily sacrifices of a devout Hindu, so too, the Eucharist is the great daily sacrifice of the devout Christians. All the five sacrifices such as the sacrifice to the gods, to all living beings, to men, to ancestors and to *Brahman* can be seen in the single Christian sacrifice, that is, in the Eucharist. Again the Eucharist is not only our daily sacrifice to God the Father, but also the source for our Christian life and universal concern. In it we not only intercede for the dead but also pray for the whole world; the whole cosmos becomes the object of our prayer.

Both the *pañca-mahāyajña*s and the Eucharist express beautifully the vertical and the horizontal dimensions of human life in Hinduism and in Christianity respectively. The *pañca-mahāyajña*s can help us to relate the former to daily life and to discover the unity between the Eucharist and life, between the ritual handling and the actual living, between the ministerial priesthood and the common priesthood of every baptised person.

In our attempt at a comparison on the basis of the convergences and differences we have also seen that some elements cannot be fully compared with one another. The *pañca-mahāyajña*s do not belong to the *Śrauta* sacrifices (solemn sacrifices which can be celebrated only by a professional priest), and as such they can be performed by anybody especially by any householder. But the Eucharist can be celebrated only under the presidency of an ordained priest and not by lay people. Further, the Eucharist is celebrated in the churches and rarely at home.

*Pañca-mahāyajña*s are an inspiration not to reduce the worship and the participation in the Eucharistic sacrifice, to a weekly, not to speak of yearly, attendance to fulfil an obligation, and to take seriously the personal daily study of the Bible, prayers for the well-being of all, and the need for the creation of a family spirituality based on daily family rites. The *pañca-mahāyajña*s are the best examples that the liturgy should not be isolated from the domestic life of Christians, and an encouragement to rethink the liturgical celebrations not only from the point of view of active participation but also from the point of a family spirituality based on domestic rites. On the other hand, the Eucharist can help Hindus not to consider sacrifice as food to the gods or as propitiation to the dead ancestors, but as a homage, or thanksgiving for their love, and to plead for the divine mercy on them. Both the *pañca-mahāyajña*s and the Eucharist express beautifully the vertical and the horizontal dimensions of human life in Hinduism and in Christianity respectively, and can be seen as complementary.

Conclusion

YAJÑA and the Eucharist — two profound, powerful religious experiences belonging to two different anthropological and theological visions as we have seen in the preceding chapters — hold the keys to the Vedic and Christian concepts on the interrelation between the Absolute/God, humans and the cosmos. An experience of this interrelation can be considered a vital element not only in Vedism but also in the Eucharistic theology. They express not only our fundamental religious experience, but also our consciousness of being related to nature.

In the beginning my intention was to make a comparison of the two different anthropological and theological world-views, i.e. the Vedic and Eucharistic views on sacrifice. But as I proceeded the work showed the complexity of these two world-views and made me look more deeply into them. As a result I went further ahead of what was initially decided upon.

Sacrifice as religious experience has a vital importance both in Vedism and in Christianity. Both *yajña* and the Eucharist have cosmic dimensions, for they stand for the divine-human-cosmic relations, and our search for totality.

Our research has shown us that *yajña* and the Eucharist are two fundamental modalities of expressing the human religious consciousness, our search for an all-comprehensive vision. This all-comprehensive vision can help us to discover the convergence between sacrifice and the cosmos. For, the profound relation at the theological level between creation and the redemption is given by sacrifice. If the Vedic sacrifice can be taken as the best example for creation through sacrifice, the sacrifice of the cross is the best example for redemption through sacrifice. Between the creation and the redemption there exists a divine sacrifice both in Vedism and in Christianity. Just as the myth of Puruṣa-Prajāpati expressed the intuitive experience of unity between the Absolute, humans and the cosmos, so too, the sacrifice of the cross expresses the relation between creation and redemption and the unity between God, humans and the world. Creation is in view of the redemption, and Christ, the Creator offers himself in sacrifice for the sake of his creation. The Eucharistic sacrifice, being the ritual memorial of this sacrifice which redeemed the whole cosmos, acquires a cosmic dimension as well. Now let us look at the thematic steps in our work, so as to bring to memory some of its salient points.

Our research has shown that sacrifice is a complex universal phenomenon which has really many-sided and multifaceted religious connotations. It means different things to different cultures. Although the term sacrifice cannot be easily reduced to a single theory acceptable to all the primitive religions of the world, *the most obvious character is in its cosmic dimension, i.e. in the world-maintaining aspect*. It is the symbol through which primitive humanity expressed its relation to the Absolute/God and fulfilled its responsibility for the continued existence of the world. *This is a profound religious symbol which expresses not only our relation to the Absolute/God but also our consciousness of being responsible for the continued existence of this cosmos.*

This world-maintaining function is foremost in the Vedic sacrifice, for sacrifice is seen as the beginning and basis of all reality. This cosmos had its origin in the self-emptying sacrifice of *puruṣa,* and thanks to the continued sacrifice this cosmos remains in existence. Creation on the cosmic plane is the self-sacrifice of the Creator who offers himself as the offering. This *puruṣa* who offers himself is "this all" and the meeting point of space and time. And the cosmic order (*ṛta*) is nothing other than the sacrificial order, for this universe rests neither on gods nor on any other ground, but on sacrifice.

The continued existence of the cosmos depends, thus, on the cosmic regeneration, and the main functions of *Aśvamedha* and *Agnicayana* are this cosmic regeneration and the ritual construction of the continuity of space and time. In the *Agnicayana* this whole cosmos is ritually reconstructed and is offered back to its creator so that it may continue to exist. To sacrifice is then to make possible one's own existence and that of the whole cosmos. Sacrifice is the *highest act of giving* that one can make in his life. This cosmic good becomes the motive for sacrifice.

The Vedic sacrifice, however, has also a personal dimension. For the Vedic person, if the sacrifice on the cosmic plane maintains the cosmos in existence, on the personal level it creates an immortal self for the sacrificer. Therefore, a person is considered to be born three times, first from one's parents, secondly when one performs sacrifice, and thirdly when one is placed over the funeral pyre which is seen as the last sacrifice (*ŚB* 11.2.1). One who does not undergo the initiation which leads to second birth in sacrifice is, then, considered to be without an immortal self. It is the second birth, in sacrifice, that gives us an immortal self. Even the gods are said to have attained immortality in sacrifice (*TS* 1.6.10.2). Sacrifice is the soul of beings and of gods (*ŚB* 14.3.2.1).

The Vedic sacrifice has its fascination not only for its cosmic dimension, but also for the ongoing rethinking of it in the Upaniṣads and in the *BG*. In the Upaniṣads it is subordinated to the notion of knowledge, and it is subordinated to *bhakti* in the *BG*. Thus, sacrifice gets a new vision in the Upaniṣads and in the *BG* but without losing its cosmic character. For the mystics of the Upaniṣads there takes place a continuous cosmic sacrifice, and the whole human life of one devoted to the acquisition of the knowledge revealing the identity between the Cosmic self and the individual self is a sacrifice. Whether awake or asleep such a person is offering a continuous sacrifice to the inner self which abides within (*KauṣUp* 2.5). In such manner one's whole life is an ongoing sacrifice: procreation, initiation, study of the Vedas, married life, death, etc. are all raised to the realm of sacrifice. We perform this enduring sacrifice with our body, to the Self-dwelling within.

The *BG* takes this spiritualization and interiorization of the Vedic sacrifice further by introducing the notion of *bhakti*. On the one hand *bhakti* purifies the intention behind the performance of sacrifice, and, on the other, it makes sacrifice a loving action without neglecting the cosmic dimension. Sacrifice is the law of life and neither this world nor the other belongs to the one who does not offer sacrifice. But it has to be performed without any selfish desire: the only motive behind its performance should be the cosmic welfare, the *lokasaṁgraha*. In sacrifice humans are, therefore, called to imitate God Kṛṣṇa who acts without any selfish desire, but for the well-being of all. In this way the *BG* advocates the cosmic welfare in the performance of sacrifice.

After clarifying the cosmic function of the Vedic sacrifice in chapters two and three, in the fourth chapter our attempt was to discover the hidden cosmic dimension in the Eucharist in the sacramental order. Just as the Vedic sacrifice has a descending (sacrifice of *puruṣa*) and an ascending dimension (the creation returning to its source in sacrifice), so too, the sacrifice of the cross implies a descending and an ascending dimension. The incarnation of Christ was to make possible the ascension of the creation to God. These descending and ascending dimensions imply a hidden cosmic dimension as well. For the Eucharist, as the sacrament of the sacrifice of the cross which redeemed the whole cosmos, on the one hand reveals God's plan for the cosmos, and on the other it plays a role of mediation between God and creation.

In the fifth chapter we brought to light the cosmic dynamism of the Eucharistic sacrifice through a study of four theologians.

All of them recognize that the Church, as a mediator between God and creation, has a cosmic role to play, and she fulfils this role in the Eucharistic sacrifice. The Church, when she offers the cosmic elements of bread and wine, offers the whole cosmos to God. These cosmic elements become the means by which Jesus descends to this world to consecrate it and extend his presence to the whole cosmos. Thus, the Church as the body of Christ leads the whole creation back to God in the Eucharist.

However, for Teilhard de Chardin the Eucharist has a wider role for it is not only the means through which the mystery of incarnation is prolonged, but also the means for the Christification of the universe or the actualization of the Omega Point of universal evolution. The scope of the Eucharist is, therefore, to bring about the Omega Point.

In chapter six we made an attempt to compare *yajña* with the Eucharist so as to bring to light the convergences and differences. Of course, there is no one-to-one similarity between them but a certain circularity of ideas which helps us to understand the religious experience of Vedism and Christianity. In our comparison of the *yajña* with the Eucharist we saw that there are several points of convergence in spite of their different anthropological and religious experiences. We have seen that just as the myth of Puruṣa-Prajāpati holds the key to understanding the Vedic vision of sacrifice, so too, the Christ-Event forms the key to understanding the Eucharistic sacrifice.

The seventh chapter can be considered not only as a type of synthesis of the whole thesis, but also the merging together of different perspectives in which we conducted our research. In it the phenomenological, comparative, theological and the liturgical methods merge together and form a synthesis showing the richness these methods can give when they are used together. Just as the *pañca-mahāyajña*s are the best examples that the liturgical life should not be separated from the daily life, so too, the Eucharist calls us not to isolate liturgical celebrations from ordinary life. *Pañca-*

mahāyajñas and the Eucharist can help us to go beyond our limited experience of space and time by opening a wider horizon of divine-human-cosmic relationship. In this way we showed that the *pañca-mahāyajñas* and the Eucharist have many aspects in common and hence can be considered complementary. Thus, our procedure was to demonstrate the relation between the *yajña*/Eucharist and the cosmos. Both of them are more than a personal affair, they express a religious consciousness of being related to the cosmos.

In our research we have found that Vedism and Christianity represent two different anthropological and theological patterns of expressing their basic religious experiences. They can be considered as moving in a binary code,[1] and their complementary character depends precisely on this binary approach. Vedism on the one hand moves on a vision of totality, and a lived experience of the unity between the Absolute-humans-cosmos, whereas Christianity moves on the track of a historic divine redemption, the experience of God in history, the love of neighbour as its distinguishing mark, etc.

The fast move towards a global epistemology, the rewriting of the world in more "holistic" terms through a more intense intersection of matter and spirit, immanence and transcendence,[2] which take place in the contemporary world, call Hinduism and Christianity to join hands against growing secularization. Thus, in the contemporary world when the distance between religions is becoming reduced due to growing dialogue, the task of the phenomenologists and theologians for the coming century will be to discover this complementarity and the interconnection between Hinduism and Christianity. The time has come that Hinduism and Christianity, which have remained in watertight compartments and looked at each other with suspicion, make an attempt to overcome the differences through sincere dialogue and look at

1. A.N. Terrin (1999b), p. 304.
2. Ibid.

each other with trust and respect. In this, as we have seen, the concept of sacrifice can be of help to bring them to some extent closer. The Vedic concern for the cosmos and the Christian concern for the love of one's neighbour can then be complementary rather than antithetic anthropological and theological approaches. In all these matters the religious experience needs to have the upper hand and not the positivistic, dualistic, and analytic approach. When the religious experience is given the upper hand in religious dialogue then the religions will come closer and their distances will diminish. This will be the task of theology for the century.

Glossary

Adam : The first man created by God. According to Jewish and Christian creation narrative, God formed Adam from the clay in God's own image and likeness and breathed into his nostrils the breath of life. The name Adam also stands for humankind. Eve was the first woman and wife of Adam.

Adhvaryu : One of the four types of priests at solemn sacrifices whose duty is the practical execution of various rites.

Aditi : The cosmic goddess of space, heaven and earth in their unlimited characters, liberty, the cosmic cow.

Agape : The Greek word for the love of God for humanity and for the love which ought to characterize Christians, brotherly or spiritual love of one Christian for another, unselfish love, fellowship meal.

Agni : One of the important Vedic gods, the sacred or the sacrificial fire, the priest or mediator between the gods and men, the mouth of gods (for all sacrifices are performed in fire); the fire of the stomach, the digestive faculty.

Agnicayana : Arranging or preparing the sacred sacrificial fire altar in the form of a bird.

Agnihotra : An oblation to Agni, daily fire sacrifice performed morning and evening by the householder. It consists in offering milk, grains, or fuel stick into the fire reciting the name of the god to whom it is offered.

Agniṣṭoma : Praising of Agni, name of a sacrificial rite technically of one day, but in practice extending over several days in spring. One of the forms of the *Soma* sacrifice, and the basic type of the *Jyotiṣṭoma*.

Ahiṁsā : Non-violence, not to kill, a fundamental virtue of Hindus, Buddhists and Jains.

Āhuti : Offering, any solemn rite accompanied with oblations, calling, invoking.

Akṣara : Imperishable, undecaying, *oṁ*, *Brahman*.

Amṛtatva : Immortality.

Anabasis : Ascent, going up. See also *katabasis*.

Anafora/anaphora : A Greek word meaning: to bring, to lift up, to offer. It is the central part of the Eucharistic prayers.

Anamnesis : A Greek word meaning: memorial, calling to mind, reminding, remembrance. It is one of the parts of the Eucharistic prayers.

Aṅga : Body, a limb or member of the body, a division or department (of anything), the mind.

Anna : Food (in general), boiled rice, food as representing the lowest form in which the Supreme Soul is manifested, *Brahman* as represented by food.

Anuvāka : Subdivision of the Vedas, section, recitation.

Āp (*āpaḥ*) : Water, the celestial and earthly waters, the origin of all realities.

Apsaras : The lovers of *gandharva*s found in the paradise of Indra, the dancers of gods, beautiful young women.

*Āraṇyaka*s : The third layer of the Vedas which contain the books of the forest. They contain the symbolic interpretations of the Vedic sacrifices.

Āryan : It literally means "the noble". A group of people who migrated from Iran to the northern parts of India around the beginning of the second millennium BCE

Asura : Spiritual, incorporeal, divine, an evil spirit, a demon, a general name for the enemies of the *deva*s (gods) and not of men. A group of the offspring of Prajāpati, and the others being the *deva*s.

Aśva : Horse, the symbol of luminous deity, particularly the sun, the natural symbol for power.

Aśvamedha : The horse sacrifice performed by a victorious king, to regenerate his kingdom. It is the most important and costly Vedic sacrifice which lasts for more than a year.

Atirātra : Prepared or performed over-night, one of the *Soma* sacrifices that has to be performed before *Agniṣṭoma*, an optional part of the *Jyotiṣṭoma* sacrifice.

Ātman : The Self, the soul, the substratum of life, which is identical with *Brahman* in the Upaniṣads. It also refers to the whole person.

Ātmayajña : Self-sacrifice, the offering of oneself as sacrifice.

Autonomic : Self governing, spontaneous.

Avatāra : Descent (of a God in a human or animal form for a particular redemptive work), incarnation. There are ten incarnations of Lord Viṣṇu. They are Matsya (fish), Kūrma (the tortoise), Varāha (the boar), Narasiṁha (man-lion), Vāmana (the dwarf), Paraśurāma (Rāma with the axe), Rāma, Kṛṣṇa, Buddha, and Kalki at the end of the world. Kalki will be the tenth and the last incarnation of Viṣṇu to destroy the wicked and to liberate the world from its enemies.

Bali : The ball of rice offered to living beings as part of the daily sacrifice to them, any propitiatory offering, tribute, offering.

Bandha : Bond, relation.

Bandhu : Relation, kinship (especially on the mother's side), husband, relative, connection.

Bhagavad-Gītā : Also written as *Bhagavadgītā*. It is a compound noun which means "song by the Lord." It is the most important, the most influential and the best known of all the Hindu sacred scriptures. It is the only Smṛti text raised to the status of the Śruti. It is found in the 6th book (chapters 23-40) of the Bhīṣma Parva of the *Mahābhārata*. The authorship of the *BG* is attributed to Vyāsa, the legendary author of *Mahābhārata*. Its composition is considered between 500 BCE to CE 200.

Bhakti : Love, ardent love and devotion for a personal God.

Bhūr : An exclamative word that belongs to the liturgical formulas and as such it has no particular meaning. It is the first of the three words through which Prajāpati created the universe (*bhūr, bhuvaḥ, svaḥ*), the name of one of the mystical worlds.

Bhūta : That which exists, all living beings, a lower spirit.

Bhūtayajña : One of the five great daily sacrifices which consists in offering food (*bali*) to the living beings (the low castes, animals, birds, insects, etc.).

Bhuvaḥ : The name of one of the mystical worlds.

Birkat ha-mazon : Prayer/grace before and after the Jewish family meal.

Body of Christ (the) : The Church, the Christian community; the consecrated bread that has become the body of Christ during the Eucharist.

Brahmā : The Creator God of the *Trimūrti* (Trinity).

Brahmacarya : The stage of student life that lasted till the 25th year and during that time the student was supposed to stay with the master and learn from him self-discipline, the scriptures and other sciences necessary for life. It is a time of celibacy and one was supposed to live with *Brahman.*

Brahman : The Supreme God or the Absolute according to the Upaniṣadic thinkers, prayer. One of the main four priests of the solemn sacrifice whose function is to observe the ritual performance and to offer rectifying oblations or verses in case of ritual mistakes. He is, therefore, called the physician of the sacrifice.

Brāhmaṇas : The second layer of the Vedas, the liturgical texts which deal with the Vedic sacrifices.

Brahmayajña : Sacrifice to *Brahman,* one of the five daily sacrifices which consists in studying and teaching the Vedas.

Brāhmaṇa : The first of the four castes from which came priests and teachers.

Cāturmāsya : Seasonal sacrifice that is performed every four months, i.e. at the beginning of the three seasons (the Spring, the Rainy, and the Autumn).

Civitas : City, polis.

Cosmos : Universe.

Covenant : A bilateral agreement, contract between God/ Yahweh and the Israelites. It is God's self-commitment, his faithfulness to his people or their representatives. It implies that Yahweh is God of Israel and Israel is the people of Yahweh.

Daiva : Divine.

Dakṣa : A son of Brahmā counted among the 7 Identified also as one of the Prajāpatis.

Dakṣiṇā : Sacrificial fee, metaphorically it means oblations given to the gods.

Darbha/Kuśa : The most imposrtant sacred sacrificial grass for the Hindus.

Deicide : The killing or killer of a God.

Devas : Gods, celestial beings, a group of the offspring of Prajāpati, partial manifestation of *Brahman.*

Devatā : Divinity.

Devayajña : Sacrifice to gods, one of the five daily sacrifices.

Dharma : Religious and moral duties, law, social custom, that which keeps together, movement, dynamism.

Dīkṣā : Initiation, consecration, initiation of the sacrificer.

Diś : Quarters, space.

Do ut des : Theory of mutual exchange.

Eastern/Orthodox Churches : See Western theology/Church.

Epiclesis : The invocation of the Holy Spirit to descend over the gifts of bread and wine to transform them into the body and blood of Jesus Christ in the celebration of the Eucharist.

Eucharist : (Holy Eucharist). Literally it means thanksgiving (from the Greek). It is the Christian worship instituted by Jesus Christ during his Last Supper with his disciples. As Christian worship it has different characteristics: sacrifice, sacrament, ritual meal, thanksgiving, spiritual sacrifice, memorial of the passion, death and resurrection of Jesus Christ, etc. It is also called the Lord's Supper, (Holy) Mass, the Breaking of the Bread, the sacrifice of the Holy Mass, the sacrament of the Holy Communion, etc. It is one of the seven sacraments in the Catholic and Orthodox Churches.

Ex nihilo : Out of nothing. According to Jewish and Christian understanding, God created the world without need of pre-existing material.

Gāyatrī mantra : General morning prayer/hymn which consists of twenty four syllables. One of the most sacred verses of the *Ṛgveda* (3.62.10).

Gṛhastha : The second stage in the life of a man, after the *brahmacarya*, that begins with marriage.

Gṛhya-Sūtras : Collection of laws for the social, domestic and ritual activities.

Guṇa : Quality, the three qualities or fundamental constituents of the *prakṛti* (nature) such as *sattva, rajas,* and *tamas*. All human beings possess these three qualities. The predominance of one or other quality explains the character of a person.

Haviṣ : An oblation that is offered into the fire.

Hilasterion : Propitiation/expiation.

Hiraṇyagarbha : Literally it means the golden womb (*hiraṇya* = gold; *garbha* = womb). Golden egg, golden germ. According to the *Ṛgveda* (10.121) it means Brahmā who was said to be born out of the seed deposited in the waters. The seed became a golden egg from which Brahmā the creator was born.

Hotṛ : One of the four groups of priests at the solemn sacrifices whose duty is to recite the chants or *mantra*s (sacred verses or formulas).

Hypostatic union : The union of divine and human natures in Christ.

Indra : One of the important Vedic gods to whom are dedicated many hymns of the *Ṛgveda*. He is said to have killed Vṛtra, the demon of the draught, and liberated the water.

Iṣṭi : "Seeking," "going after," desire, wish, an oblation consisting of butter, fruits, etc. opposed to the *Soma* and animal sacrifice. It is performed by sacrificer and his wife with the help of four priests. The full moon sacrifice is the pattern or archetype of all *iṣṭi*s.

Iṣṭaka : Bricks, specially those used in the construction of the fire altar.

Jāmi : Related like brother and sister, consanguinity, uniformity, repetition, tautology, daughter-in-law, a near female relative, excessive resemblance.

Jāti dharma : Caste duty, duty pertaining to one's caste by birth.

Jyotiṣṭoma : One of the *Soma* sacrifices, considered as the type of a whole class of sacrificial ceremonies.

Ka : The first consonant of the alphabet, interrogative pronoun, who, what, which, name of Prajāpati, of Viṣṇu, of Dakṣa, of Yama.

Kāli : A Goddess, an epithet of Pārvatī (Śiva's wife), blackness, ink.

Karman : Work, action (originally sacred action, sacrifice), the effects of an action which binds the soul to the circle of rebirth.

Katabasis : Descent, going down. See also *anabasis*.

Kimpuruṣa : Defective man, inhabitants of the forest or the spirits of the forest, monkey.

Kṛṣṇa : Literally it means black, dark blue, one of the incarnations of Viṣṇu, in the *Mahābhārata* he is presented as a great hero and teacher, the charioteer of Arjuna (in the Mahābhārata war), he is also called Vāsudeva sand by many other names.

Kṣatriya : The caste of the warriors and kings.

Kula dharma : Duty towards one's family. Protection of one's family members.

Last Supper : The Last Supper of Jesus Christ with his disciples the night before he was crucified. It was during this supper that he established the sacrament of the Eucharist. See Eucharist

Liturgy :The official worship of the Christians or the official church prayer.

Logos : This is a Greek term for "word" or utterance. In the Christian theology it stands for "the pre-existent Christ, the Word, the mediator of creation now incarnate."

Loka : A world, a division of the universe. There are different worlds such as: *Brahmaloka* (the world of Brahmā), *Svargaloka* (the world of Indra, paradise), *Pitṛloka* (the world of the ancestors), *Yamaloka* (the world of the Yama, the Lord and judge of the dead), etc. *triloka* (three worlds) = sky, earth and the atmosphere.

Lokasaṁgrhu (*Lokasaṅgraha*) : Cosmic welfare, propitiation of humankind.

LXX : It is pronounced as Septuagint (seventy). It stands for the classic Greek version of the OT, traditionally said to have been translated by 70 or 72 Jewish scholars at the request of Ptolemy II.

Mahābhiṣeka : Great consecration, the royal consecration.

Mahiṣi : The first wife of the king who is made to lie down with the dead horse in the *Aśvamedha*.

Manas : The mind, heart, intellect, the inner organ which is the seat of thinking, one of the main constituents of man.

Manna : Bread from heaven. A substance said to have been the Israelites' main food during their 40 years of journey in the wilderness. When the people grumbled at the lack of food in the desert God gave them "bread from heaven" (manna) and this provision did not cease until they crossed into Cannan and ate the food of that land.

*Mantra*s : Formulas, stanzas, verses with magical power.

Manu : "Man," the law giver and the ancestor from whom the human race had its continuation after the universal flood, the first man to offer sacrifice.

Manusmṛti (*Mānava Dharma Śāstra or Manu*) : The laws of Manu, that is, a collection of laws for day-to-day life based on the Vedas.

Mass (Holy Mass) : See Eucharist.

Meal of the Kingdom : Salvation, the heavenly banquet.

Messiah : The Christ, the anointed, the servant of the Lord, the saviour.

Mīmāṁsā : One of the six classical systems of Indian philosophy which gives the rules for the interpretation of the Vedic texts.

Mishnah : The first written summary of the Oral Law. It also stands for the "recitation" or "recapitulation" of the Oral Torah.

Mithuna : A couple, a fertile couple.

Mitra : A Vedic god associated with Varuṇa, a friend, a companion, united in friendship, relation between the king and his subjects.

*Muhūrtta*s : An hour like division of time that consists of 48 minutes.

Nābhi : Navel, centre and birth place, home, origin, friend, affinity, relationship.

Nisan : A month of Jewish calendar. The Jewish ecclesiastical year begins with Nisan (March-April) and the civil year with Tishri (September-October). The Passover feast begins on the eve of the 14th of Nisan and continues for a week.

Niṣkāma-karma (*Naiṣkarmya*) : Desireless action, an action performed as duty and not for any selfish motive, the renunciation in action because the fruits of all actions belong to God, the real agent of action.

Nṛyajña (*Manuṣyajña*) : Sacrifice to human beings which consists in giving hospitality to the guests.

Oṁ (auṁ) : The sacred syllable uttered as a holy exclamation at the beginning and end of a reading of the Vedas, or previous to the commencement of a prayer or sacred work. It can mean "yes," "amen," "so it be."

Omega : The last letter of the Greek alphabet. It is written as Ω/ω. It stands for the final stage, the fulfilment, the end. In the writings of Teilhard de Chardin it stands for the final stage of evolution. Alpha and Omega = beginning and end.

Ontonomic : Governed by reality or being, metaphysically.

Pāda : Four, foot, the fourth part of a poem, a measure, a division.

Pañca-mahāyajña : The five great daily sacrifices (*pañca* = five; *mahā* = great; *yajña* = sacrifice).

Parama : Highest, supreme.

Pāriplava : Revolving legends of

gods or great kings which are recited during the period in which the horse for the *Aśvamedha* is left to wander.

Parousia/Parusia : The Second Coming of Jesus Christ in judgement at the end of the world.

Passover : Literally it means passing over. It is one of the most important Jewish feasts in memory of the liberation of the Israelites from the slavery in Egypt. See also Nisan.

Paśu : Sacrificial animal, animals in general, a soul in bondage and in impurity.

Pathos : Disease, suffering.

Patita : Fallen, degraded, fallen morally, out-caste. (*Patita sāvitrīka* = one who is deprived of the Savitṛ, a man of the first three castes whose initiation has been unduly performed or omitted.)

Pauline font : Antiochene institution narrative of the Eucharist found in Paul and Luke.

Petrine font : Palestinian institution narrative of the Eucharist found in Matthew and Mark.

Phālguna : The eleventh month of the Hindu calendar (February-March).

Pitṛyajña : Sacrifice to the deceased ancestors which consists in offering water, food, etc.

Pleroma : Fullness, plenitude.

Polis : Ancient Greek city-state.

Prajāpati : The Lord of creation or procreation (*prajā* = procreation, offspring, father; *pati* = lord, husband), the god presiding over creation, *puruṣa*, an epithet of Brahmā, of Viṣṇu, of Śiva.

Prakṛti : Nature, primary matter; in Sāṁkhya one of the two fundamental principles of the universe.

Prāṇa : The vital breath, life, breath of life that holds together the body.

Prasāda : Divine grace, benevolence, divine gift (the food shared among the devotees after it is being offered to a divinity).

Pratimā : Image, counterpart, likeness, resemblance, similitude, a statue.

Prāyaścitta : Penitence, the penitence performed to extinguish the acquired demerits, rites performed to remedy any possible mistakes or omissions in the ritual performance of the sacrifice.

Preta : Literally it means "gone," "departed." The intermediary state of a soul after the death of a person before he is ritually united to his ancestors. At this stage the spirits can turnout to be hostile if they are not propitiated with the correct performance of funeral rites.

Prosphera : Offering (in Greek).

Protestant Church : In the sixteenth century the Western Church got divided into Roman Catholicism and Protestant/ Reformation Churches. The Protestant Reformation was initiated in Germany by Martin Luther (1483-1546) in 1517. The Protestant word comes from the protest that in 1529 the German Lutheran states waged against an anti-Lutheran resolution of an imperial Diet at Speier. See also Western theology/ Church.

Pṛthak : Extreme differentiation, — total independency (opposite of *jāmi*).

Pūjā : Worship, reverence, adoration, honour with homage, respect. It has become the main form of worship in the contemporary day Hinduism.

Puruṣa : Man, the primordial cosmic man, male being, the soul, the Supreme Being, the primordial man from whose self-dismemberment this universe and everything in it had its origin, identified with Prajāpati. In the Sāṁkhya philosophy the opposite of *prakṛti*.

Puruṣamedha : The human sacrifice.

Puruṣārtha : The goals of human life which are fourfold: *dharma* (righteousness), *artha* (material or economic well-being), *kāma* (satisfaction of the sentiments, pleasure), and *mokṣa* (liberation or salvation).

Puruṣa-Sūkta : The hymn of *puruṣa* in *ṚV* (10.90).

Pūtīka : A kind of herb, a species of plant serving as substitute for *soma* plant (perhaps *Guliandina Bonduc*).

Rajas : One of the three *guṇa*s gathered by the soul in relation to the *prakṛti*. It is the principle of activity, passion, restlessness, etc. in a person.

Rājasūya : The consecration of a king.

Rākṣasa : Demon, the evil spirit who disturbs the sacrifices.

*Ṛṣi*s : The ancient Vedic seers who are supposed to have received directly the Vedic scriptures from the divinity. The title is recognized mainly as the authors of the Vedas.

Ṛta : The cosmic order which maintains the equilibrium in the universe.

Ṛtu : A pre-determined time, a fixed time or period for an action, especially for sacrifice, and for periodical acts of cult, a subdivision of a year, a season.

Rudra : One of the Vedic gods who is considered to be the god of thunder. He is said to send rain and fertilize the earth. He may also send flood. He is said to be the only one who will survive the cosmic flood at the end of times and is identified with Śiva.

Rūpa : Form, figure, shape, appearance, essence, natural state of condition, nature, characteristic.

Sacrificium visibile : Visible sacrifice.

Sāman : Songs of glorification or composition according to a meter to be sung at the sacrifices; also refers to Sāmavedic hymms.

Saṁhitā : Collection of hymns, the oldest layer of the Vedas.

Saṁskāras : Sacraments, consecration, sanctification, making perfect, refining, polishing.

Sanhedrin : The highest tribunal of the Jews both before and at the time of Jesus.

Saṁnyāsa : The last and the final stage of a man when one completely renounces this world and family relations for the pursuit of spiritual values and liberation.

Sarva : Complete, totality, all.

Sat : Being, *Brahman,* lasting, enduring, existing, wise, venerable, honest.

Śatapatha Brāhmaṇa : One of the most important *Brāhmaṇa*s that deals with the Vedic sacrifices. It contains all the important liturgical formulas to be recited at the performance of sacrifice.

Sattva : The highest of the three *guṇa*s. The aspect of goodness, brightness, purity, etc. in a being.

Satya(m) : True, genuine, real, honest, truthful, successful, valid.

Savitṛ : The Sun god, giver of life, the symbol of Supreme God.

Śiva : One of the *Trimūrti* (Hindu Trinity). He is one of the most important gods of the modern Hinduism (the Supreme God of Śaivites or Śaivas).

Skambha : Support, pillar, cosmic pillar.

Smṛti : Remembrance, recollection, memory, calling to mind, what was delivered by human authors such as law, traditions, canon, rule of law, law-book, etc. These texts, laws and scriptures do not have any absolute or binding value of the Vedas.

Ṣoḍaśopacāra pūjā : *Pūjā* (worship) with sixteen elements. *Pūjā* with five elements is known as *pañcopacāra pūjā*.

Soma : Name of a drink extracted from the *soma* plant (said to be the climbing plant *Sarcostema viminalis* or *Asciepias acida*). The stalks of *soma* were pressed between the stones by the priests, purified in a strainer and made to ferment before being offered to the gods. The drink was first offered to the gods and then it was drunk by the priests and the sacrificer. This drink was supposed to give immortality to the drinker. This rite corresponds to the *Haoma* ritual of the Iranian Avesta. *Soma* is also identified with the moon.

Śraddhā : Faith, an indispensable element in sacrifice. Without faith the offerings to the gods are useless, and the sacrifice performed with faith lasts for ever.

Śrāddha : A supplementary funerary rite celebrated in honour of the deceased.

Śrauta-Sūtra : A collection of *sūtra*s based on the sacred tradition or on the Vedic texts which were composed to describe or to clarify the sacrificial institution contained in the Brāhmaṇas.

Śruti : The act of "hearing" or that which is heard — the Vedic Revelation. The Vedas are said to be *apauruṣeya*, that is without a human authorship for they were heard by the sages who again transmitted them orally for centuries. Hence they are called *Śruti*.

Status Questionis : The present state of the question/topic under discussion.

Stoma(s) (*Ṣṭoma*) : The way of recitation of a hymn, a praise, *soma* libation.

Stotra : Praise, a hymn of praise.

Śūdras : The members of the fourth caste who were mainly servants and the workers.

Sukṛtaḥ : Good actions, sacrifice, heaven.

Sūkta : The Vedic hymn, distinct from *ṛk*, that is, a single verse, a hymn of praise.

Sūtra : Literally it means "thread," and later on it meant the different written compositions in the aphoristic style. They are composed to illustrate the laws related to the sacrificial rites of the head of the family, or his duties towards the community, etc. or of any field of study.

Svarga : Heaven, the paradise of Indra.

Svayamātṛṇṇa bricks : The three naturally perforated stones used in the *Agnicayana* to represent the three spaces: sky, earth and atmosphere.

Svāhā : An exclamation or ritual invocation pronounced when one offers the oblation to gods. It is the unchangeable part of all the rituals while the oblations are offered to gods.

Synagogue : Jewish house of prayer, worship, centre for study of the scripture, meeting place, etc. Important decisions were also taken in this place. Unlike the temple, it was located in all parts of the land. Sacrifices were offered only in the temple.

Synoptics : The Gospels of Matthew, Mark and Luke which have a common structure and some parallel passages. The Gospel of John has its own structure.

Tabernacle : The receptacle in which the consecrated Hosts for Holy Communion are reserved in churches and chapels. Originally the "Tent" in Judaism where the Tablets of the Law of Moses were kept. Place of divine presence.

Tamas : The lowest of the three *guṇas*. It represents darkness, selfishness, lawlessness, laziness, etc.

Tapas : Heat, ardour, the heat generated by the ascetical practice, one of the means by which Prajāpati created this universe.

Targum : The paraphrastic Aramaic translations of the Jewish Bible for the sake of people who could not follow Hebrew.

Tejas : Energy, splendour, vital power, spirit, efficacy, beauty.

Theology : Etymologically it means "talk" or "discourse" (*logos*) about "God" (*theos*). It is the critical and methodical reflection on faith. It is the science of faith.

Thusia : Sacrifice.

Todah : Thanksgiving, praise. See also Zebah Todah.

Torah : The Law books of the Jewish Bible. It stands for the first five books of the OT (the Pentateuch).

Trinity : It is the Christian understanding of God. Christians believe that in the Godhead there are three persons: the Father, the Son, and the Holy Spirit. They are different from one another but not separate entities (therefore no tritheism). God is one and three. It stands for the Being of God as communion of three persons, a model for human existence. To be is to be related, to be in communion. Being is thus relationship, and God is the fullness of this relationship. However, often God and Father are used as synonyms.

Triṣṭubh : The poetic meter consisting of forty-eight syllables.

Udgātar (Udgātṛ) : One of the four main priests of the sacrifice, whose duty is to chant the hymns of the *Sāmaveda*.

Ukthya : One of the *Soma* sacrifices, libation at the morning and midday sacrifice, name of a liturgical ceremony forming part of the *Jyotiṣṭoma*.

Upanayana : Initiation into the study of Vedas and sacrifice; the saered thread ceremony.

Upaniṣads : They contain philosophical and theological reflections on *Brahman*, creation, man, liberation, etc. and form the fourth and last layer of the Vedas. Their exact number is not clear, and only 13 of them are taken as canonical ones, which belong to a period before the birth of Buddhism. *Upa* + *ni* + *ṣad* = to understand, to sit near the feet of a master, or "to put together," "to relate." Hence, it is the secret doctrine that a disciple learnt by listening to the master, the sage.

Vāc (*vāk*) : Word, sound, language, the personified Word, the supreme principle of the creation, Sarasvatī.

Vaiśyas : The members of the third caste, whose main occupations were trade and agriculture.

Vanaspati : The Lord of the forests, the sacrificial post (*yūpa*), the protector of trees.

Vānaprastha : The third stage in the life of a man when one retires to the forest for meditation and prayer.

Varṇa : It literally means "colour." It is used to denote the four-castes system of the Hindu society (brāhmaṇas, kṣatriyas, vaiśyas and śūdras). This last group was probably made of aborigines of the place conquered by the Āryan in their invasion of northern India. Originally society was divided into different castes according to the occupation but later on it became a symbol of the social status, and hence a rigid social stratification.

Varuṇa : A Vedic god who lost importance later on. He is

supposed to be the god who keeps the *dharma*, the right behaviour, the law.

Vāyu : One of the Vedic gods associated with Indra, wind, the breath of *puruṣa*, the life breath, one of the five constitutive elements of living beings.

Vedas : They are the most important Hindu scriptures (Śruti), and are four in number, such as: *R̥gveda*, *Sāmaveda*, *Yajurveda* and *Atharvaveda*. The *R̥V* consists of 10,552 stanzas, and is considered to be the Veda of praise. The *Sāmaveda* has 1,875 stanzas and is called the Veda of the sacred hymns, because most of them are hymns from the *R̥V* re-elaborated to satisfy the liturgical needs. The *YV* has 1975 stanzas (some of them are in prose) and is called the Veda of Yajus, i.e. the manual for Adhvaryu priest with necessary instructions for the celebration of sacrifice. The *AV* consists of 5,987 stanzas (some of them are in prose) and is called the Veda of the Atharvan, or the science of the magical formulas. Again the Vedas are divided into four layers: Saṁhitās, Brāhmaṇas, Āraṇyakas and Upaniṣads. In all, they consist of nearly 20,389 stanzas and a number of them are repetitions. (Veda literally means knowledge, the knowledge of the supreme truth).

Virāja : The cosmic power identified with Prajāpati, Indra, Agni, the first uncreated emanation of the Supreme (R. Panikkar), as a verb it means to reign, to rule, to excel.

Viṣṇu : One of the *Trimūrti* (Trinity). He is the preserver of the universe and incarnates when there is a special redemptive function to be accomplished.

Viśvakarman : The divine architect of the universe, the supreme creative power of knowledge.

Vivasvat : The splendour, an epithet of the Sun, one of the Adityas, the father of Manu Vaivasvata.

Vr̥tra : The person who represents chaos, the demonic power of impediment, the demon of darkness and of the drought who took control of the clouds that no rain could fall on earth, the demon whom god Indra killed to liberate the water.

Western theology/Church : Church:Theology held by the Western i.e. the Latin Catholic Church. As Christianity spread to different regions of the Roman Empire there also came up simultaneously different centres. One of the important centres was Rome which, being the place of martyrdom of Peter, the leader of the apostles, became for later history the most important centre of Christianity. Around the eleventh century (1054) there occurred a schism in Christianity between the (Orthodox) East and the Latin West. Later on in the sixteenth century the Western Church got divided into Roman Catholicism and Protestant/ Reformation Churches. Each Church has its own spirituality, theology and administrative structure.

YHWH/Yahweh : YHWH is the often used Jewish name for God. Scholars added vowels between the letters (consonants) and read it as Yahweh, thus making it possible to pronounce.

Yajamāna : Sacrificer, the patron of the sacrifice who bears all the expenses and on whose favour sacrifice is performed.

Yajña : Sacrifice, offering oblation, worship, devotion, praise.

Yama : The Lord and judge of the dead, the first man to die and the one who leads the dead to the world of the dead.

Yoni : Womb, female reproductive organ. In sacrifice it is compared to *vedī* (altar).

Yuga : One of the great epochs of time within a *kalpa* (a *kalpa* = a day of Brahmā or 1000 *yuga*s, i.e. a period of 4,320 millions of years of mortal beings, equal to the duration of a universe). The *yuga*s are four: Satya, Tretā, Dvāpara, and Kali Yuga, the Present one.

Yūpa : Sacrificial post to which the victim is tied. It is also identified with the cosmic tree, an intermediary between the divine and the earthly worlds.

Zebah todah : Sacrifice of praise or sacrifice with praise. (*zebah* = slaughter, sacrifice).

Bibliography

Vedic Sacrifice and the Religious Anthropology

Agrawala, V.S., 1962, *Sparks from the Vedic Fire*. Varanasi: The Chowkambha Sanskrit Series.

Aguilar, H., 1976, *The Sacrifice in the Ṛgveda: Doctrinal Aspects*. Varanasi: Bharatiya Vidya Prakashan.

Anand, S., 1986, "Advaita or Agape: An Ancient Holistic Vision for Modern Fragmented Man." *Vidyajyoti* 50: pp. 7-30.

———, 2002, "Purusa-Yajna: Self-giving as the Mystery of Being." *Third Millennium* 5: 2. pp. 24-44.

Apte, V.M., 1958, "Vedic Rituals." In *The Cultural Heritage of India*. vol. 1, Calcutta: The Ramakrishna Mission Institute of Culture, reprint, pp. 234-63 [1937].

Aurobindo, Sri, 1967, *Key to Vedic Symbolism*. Compiled by M.P. Pundit, Pondicherry: Sri Aurobindo Ashram Trust.

———, 1971, *Hymns to the Mystic Fire*. Pondicherry: Sri Aurobindo Ashram Trust.

———, 1974, *Essays on the Gita*. Pondicherry: Sri Aurobindo Ashram Trust [1950].

Baaren, T.P. van, 1964, "Theoretical Speculations on Sacrifice." *Numen* 11, pp. 1-12.

Bailey, G.M. and I.K. Watson (eds.), 1992, *Bhakti Studies*. New Delhi: Sterling Publishers.

Banerjee, S., 1981, "Prajāpati in the Brāhmaṇas." *Vishvesvaranand Indological Journal* 19, pp. 14-19.

Beers, W., 1992, *Women and Sacrifice: Male Narcissism and the Psychology of Religion*. Detroit: Wayne State University Press.

Bergman, J., 1987, "Religio-Phenomenological Reflections on the Multi-Level Process of Giving to the Gods." In *GGPU*, pp. 31-42.

Bhargava, P.L., 1979, "Names and Epithets of Kṛṣṇa in the Bhagavad-Gītā." *Indologica Taurinensia* 7, pp. 93-96.

Bhattacharji, S., 1983, "Rise of Prajāpati in the Brāhmaṇas." *Annals of the Bhandarkar Oriental Research Institute* 64, pp. 205-13.

Bhattacharyya, N.N., 1996, *Ancient Indian Rituals and Their Social Contents.* New Delhi: Manohar Publishers [1975].

Bianchi, U., 1960, *Teogonie e cosmogonie.* Rome: Studium (Universale Studium 69).

———, 1986, *Problemi di storia delle religioni.* Rome: Studium (Nuova Universale Studium 48).

Biardeau, M. and C. Malamoud (eds.), 1976, *Le sacrifice dans l'Inde ancienne.* Paris: PUF (Bibliotèque de l'École pratique des hautes études, section des sciences religieusés 74).

Bodewitz, H.W., 1973, *Jaiminīya Brāhmaṇa 1.1-65.* Translation and commentary with a study of Agnihotra and Prāṇāgnihotra. Leiden: E.J. Brill.

———, 1990, *The Jyotiṣṭoma Ritual: Jaiminīya Brāhmaṇa 1,66-364.* Introduction, translation and commentary. Leiden: E.J. Brill (Orientalia Rheno-Traiectina 34).

———, 2003, *Daily Evening and Morning Offering (Agnihotra) according to the Brāhmaṇas.* Delhi: Motilal Banarsidass [1976].

Bolle, K.W., 1983-84, "A World of Sacrifice." *HR* 23, pp. 37-63.

Bonaccorso, G., 1994, "Le azioni simboliche alla luce della fenomenologia religiosa." In *Amen vestrum. Miscellanea di studi liturgico-pastorali in onore di P. Pelagio Visentin O.S.B.,* A. Catella (ed.). Padua: Messaggero-Abbazia di S. Giustina (Caro Salutis Cardo. Studi 9), pp. 105-32.

———, 1998, "Il sacrificio come rito o come evento? Un problema aperto in René Girard." In *SEER,* pp. 181-202.

Bonfante, G., 1959, "Macrocosmo e microcosmo nel mito indo-europeo." *Die Sprache* 5, pp. 1-8.

Brekke, T., 1998, "Contradiction and the Merit of Giving in Indian Religions." *Numen* 45, pp. 287-320.

Brereton, J.P, 1986, "Tat Tvam Asi' in Context." *ZDMG* 136, pp. 98-109.

Brown, W.N., 1931, "The Sources and Nature of Puruṣa in the Puruṣasūkta (*Rig Veda* 10.90)." *JAOS* 51, pp. 108-18.

———, 1942, "The Creation Myth of the Rig Veda." *JAOS* 62, pp. 85-98.

———, 1965, "Theories of Creation in the Rig Veda." *JAOS* 85, pp. 23-34.

———, 1968, "Agni, Sun, Sacrifice, and Vāc: A Sacerdotal Ode by Dīrghatamas (Rig Veda 1.164)." *JAOS* 88, pp. 199-218.

Bühnemann, G., 1988, *Pūjā: A Study in Smārta Ritual.* Vienna: Institute for Indology, University of Vienna.

Burkert, W., 1962, "Caesar und Romulus-Quirinus." *Historia* 11, pp. 356-376.

———, 1966, "Greek Tragedy and Sacrificial Ritual." *Greek, Roman and Byzantine Studies* 7, pp. 87-121.

———, 1981, *Homo Necans. Antropologia del sacrificio cruento nella Grecia antica.* Turin: Boringhieri.

———, 1987, "Offerings in Perspective: Surrender, Distribution, Exchange." In *GGPU*, pp. 43-50.

———, 1991, *Mito e rituale in Grecia. Struttura e Storia.* Rome-Bari: Laterza (Biblioteca Universale Laterza 348).

Canobbio, G. (ed.), 1993, *Dio, mondo e natura nelle religioni orientali.* Atti del convegno ATI, Brescia, 2-22 giugno 1991. Padua: Messaggero.

Casa, C. Della (ed.), 1976, *Upaniṣad.* Turin: UTET.

———, 1970, "Sukr̥tam in Taittirīya Upaniṣad II, 7." *Archivio glottologico italiano* 55, pp. 47-51.

———, 1973, "Di alcune caratteristiche delle Upaniṣad piú antiche." *Indologica Taurinensia* 1, pp. 33-46.

———, 1979, "On the Transition of Vedic Sacrificial Lore." *Indo-Iranian Journal* 21, pp. 181-88.

Chakrabarti, S.C., 1989, "A Study of the Pāriplava." *Indo-Iranian Journal* 32, pp. 255-67.

Chakraborti, H., 1973, *Asceticism in Ancient India: in Brahmanical, Buddhist, Jaina and Ajivika Societies, from the Earliest Times to the Period of Śaṅkarācārya.* Calcutta: Punthi Pusthak.

Chelhold, J., 1955, *Le sacrifice chez les Arabes. Richerches sur l'évolution, la nature et la fonction des rites sacrificiels en Arabie Occidentale.* Paris: Presses Universitaires de France.

Chilton, B., See next section.

Clooney, F.X., 1985, "Sacrifice and its Spiritualization in the Christian and Hindu Traditions: A Study in Comparative Theology." *Harvard Theological Review* 78, pp 361-80.

———, 1985-86, "Jaimini's Contribution to the Theory of Sacrifice as the Experience of Transcendence." *HR* 25, pp. 199-212.

Colombo, A., 1998, "Panorama bibliografica sul tema del sacrificio." In *SEER*, pp. 71-110.

———, 1999, *Il sacrificio in René Girard. Dalla violenza al dono*. Brescia: Morcelliana.

Condren, M.T., 1997, "Mercy not Sacrifice: Toward a Celtic Theology." *Feminist Theology* 15, pp. 31-54.

Converse, H.S., 1974-75, "The Agnicayana Rite: Indigenous Origin?" *HR* 14, pp. 81-95.

Coomaraswamy, A.K., 1941, "Ātmayajña: Self-Sacrifice." *Harvard Journal of Asiatic Studies* 6, pp. 358-98.

———, 1946, "R̥gveda 10.90.1: aty atiṣṭhad daśāṅgulam." *JAOS* 66, pp. 145-61.

Coppet, D. de (ed.), 1992, *Understanding Rituals*. London: Routledge.

D'Onofrio, C., 1953-54, "Le 'nozze sacre' della regina col cavallo nel rito dell'Açvamedha." *Studi e materiali di storia delle religioni* 24-25, pp. 133-62.

D'Sa, F.X., 1980, "Dharma as Delight in Cosmic Welfare: A Study of Dharma in the Gita." *Bible Bhashyam* 6, pp. 335-57.

———, 1999, "Lokasangraha: The Welfare of the Whole World. A Hindu Vision of a World Order." *Jnanadeepa: Pune Journal of Religious Studies* 2, pp. 47-59.

Dabre, T., 1987, *God Experience of Tukaram: A Study in Religious Symbolism*. Pune: Jnanadeepa Vidyapeeth.

Dasgupta, S.N., 1957, *A History of Indian Philosophy*. 2 vols., Cambridge: Cambridge University Press.

Deodikar, S.G., 1992, *Upaniṣads and Early Buddhism*. Delhi: Eastern Book Linkers.

Detienne, M., 1975, *I giardini di Adone. I miti della seduzione erotica*. Turin: Einaudi.

———, 1981, *Dioniso e la pantera profumata*. Rome-Bari: Laterza (Biblioteca di cultura moderna 843).

Deussen, P., 1906, *The Religion and Philosophy of India: The Philosophy of the Upanishads*. Edinburgh: Clark.

Dhavamony, M., 1971, *Love of God according to Śaiva Siddhānta: A Study in the Mysticism and Theology of Śaivism*. Oxford: Clarendon Press.

———, 1982, *Classical Hinduism*. Rome: Università Gregoriana Editrice (Documenta Missionalia 15).

Doniger, W. and B.K. Smith (trans.), 1996, *Le leggi di Manu*. Milan: Adelphi (Biblioteca Orientale 3).

Dumont, P.-E., 1927, *L'Aśvamedha. Description du sacrifice solennel du cheval dans le culte védique d'après les textes du Yujurveda blanc*. Paris: Geuthner.

Edgerton, F., 1929, "The Upaniṣads: What Do They Seek and Why." *JAOS* 49, pp. 97-121.

———, 1942, "Dominant Ideas in the Formation of Indian Culture." *JAOS* 62, pp. 151-56.

———, (ed.), 1952, *The Bhagavad Gītā. Translated and Interpreted*. vol. 1. *Text and Translation*. vol. 2. *Interpretation and Arnold's Translation*. Cambridge-Massachusetts: Harvard University Press.

Eggeling, J. (ed.), 1966, *Śatapatha Brāhmaṇa*. Delhi: Motilal Banarsidass (SBE vols. 12, 26, 41, 43, 44).

Elenjimittam, A., 1996, *Mukti. La liberazione nella filosofia indiana*. Milan: Mursia (Biblioteca Esoterica 28).

Eliade, M., 1959a, *Cosmos and History: The Myth of the Eternal Return*. New York: Harper Torchbooks.

———, 1959b, *The Sacred and the Profane: The Nature of Religion*. New York & London: A Harvest/HBJ Book.

———, 1961, *Images and Symbols: Studies in Religious Symbolism*. New York: Sheed and Ward.

———, 1969a, *The Quest: History and Meaning in Religion*. Chicago and London: The University of Chicago Press.

———, 1969b, *Yoga: Immortality and Freedom*. Princeton: Princeton University Press.

———, 1975, *Myth and Reality*. New York and London: Harper & Row.

———, 1979a, *A History of Religious Ideas*. vol.1. *From the Stone Age to the Eleusinian Mysteries*. London: Collins.

———, 1979b, *Patterns in Comparative Religion*. London: Sheed and Ward.

Englund, G., 1987, "Gifts to the Gods — A Necessity for the Preservation of Cosmos and Life. Theory and Practice." In *GGPU*, pp. 57-66.

Evans-Pritchard, E.E., 1956, *The Nuer Religion*. Oxford: Clarendon Press.

———, 1980, *Theories of Primitive Religion*. Oxford: Clarendon Press [1965].

Ewing, A.H., 1901, "The Hindu Conception of the Functions of Breath. A Study in Early Hindu Psycho-Physics." *JAOS* 22, pp. 249-308.

Favaro, G., 1993, "Contesto e significato della *pūjā* quotidiana nel mondo religioso-culturale indū." In *Dio, mondo e natura nelle religioni orientali,* G. Canobbio (ed.). Padua: Messaggero, pp. 31-66.

Fontenrose, J., 1966, *The Ritual Theory of Myth.* Berkeley-Los Angeles: University of California Press.

Frazer, J., 1996, *The Golden Bough: A Study in Magic and Religion.* Abridged edition. London: Penguin Books [1922].

Girard, R., 1986, *Violence and the Sacred.* Baltimore and London: The John Hopkins University Press.

———, 1987, *Things Hidden since the Foundation of the World.* Research undertaken in collaboration with Jean-Michel Oughourlian and Guy Lefort. Stanford, California: Stanford University Press.

———, 1989, *The Scapegoat.* Baltimore: The Johns Hopkins University Press.

Gispert-Sauch, G., 1977, *Bliss in the Upanishads: An Analytical Study on the Origin and Growth of the Vedic Concept of Ananda.* New Delhi: Oriental Publishers.

———, 1988, "An Inquiry into the Upanishadic Prayer 'From the Unreal Lead Me to the Real . . .'" In *Dialogue in Action: Essays in Honour of Johannes Aagaard,* L. Thumberg, et al. (eds.). New Delhi: Prajna Publication, pp. 179-213.

Goman, T.G. and R.S. Laura, 1972, "A Logical Treatment of some Upaniṣadic Puzzles and Changing Conceptions of Sacrifice." *Numen* 19, pp. 52-67.

Gonda, J., 1956, "Ancient Indian Kingship from the Religious Point of View." *Numen* 3, pp. 36-71, 122-55.

———, 1957, "Ancient Indian Kingship from the Religious Point of View." *Numen* 4, pp. 24-58, 127-64.

———, 1964, "Gifts and Giving in the Ṛgveda." *Vishvesvaranand Indological Journal* 2, pp. 9-30.

———, 1977, "Vedic Cosmogony and Viṣṇuite Bhakti." *Indologica Taurinensia* 5, pp. 5-111.

———, 1979, "Upanayana." *Indologica Taurinensia* 7, pp. 253-59.

———, 1980, *Vedic Ritual. The Non-Solemn Rites.* Leiden: E.J. Brill.

———, 1982, "All, Universe and Totality in the Śatapatha Brāhmaṇa." *Journal of the Oriental Institute* 32, pp. 1-17.

———, 1982-83, "The Popular Prajāpati." *HR* 22, pp. 129-49.

———, 1983a, "The Creator and His Spirit (Manas and Prajāpati)." *WZKS* 27, pp. 5-42.

———, 1983b, "The Redundant and the Deficient in Vedic Ritual." *Vishvesvaranand Indological Journal* 21, pp. 1-34.

———, 1983c, "Vedic Gods and Sacrifice." *Numen* 30, pp. 1-34.

———, 1985, *Change and Continuity in Indian Religion*. Delhi: Munshiram Manoharlal [1965].

———, 1993, *Aspects of Early Viṣṇuism*. Delhi: Motilal Banarsidass [1954].

———, 1996, *Viṣṇuism and Śivaism: A Comparison*. Delhi: Munshiram Manoharlal [1970].

Griffith, R.T.H. (ed.), 1971, *The Hymns of the Ṛgveda*. Varanasi: Chowkamba Sanskrit Series Office [1926].

Griffiths, B., 1985, *The Cosmic Revelation: The Hindu Way to God*. Bangalore: ATC.

Grottanelli, C., 1980, "Cosmogonia e sacrificio, I. Problemi delle cosmogonie 'rituali' nel Ṛg Veda e nel Vicino Oriente antico." *Studi storico religiosi* 4, pp. 207-35.

———, 1981, "Cosmogonia e sacrificio, II. Death as the Supreme God's Beloved Son and the Origin Myth of Human Sacrifice." *Studi storico religiosi* 5, pp. 173-96.

———, 1993, "Uccidere, donare, mangiare: problematiche attuali del sacrificio antico." In *Sacrificio e società nel mondo antico*, C. Grottanelli and N.F. Parise (eds.). Rome-Bari: Laterza (Biblioteca Universale Laterza 388), pp. 3-53.

———, 1999, *Il Sacrificio*. Rome-Bari: Laterza (Biblioteca Essenziale Laterza 24).

——— et al., 1984, "Sacrificio, organizazzione del cosmo, dinamica sociale, Premessa: spartizione e società." *Studi storici* 25, pp. 829-33.

Hacker, P., 1963, "Śraddhā." *WZKS* 7, pp. 151-89.

Hatt, G., 1951, "The Corn Mother in America and Indonesia." *Anthropos* 46, pp. 853-914.

Hecht, R., 1982, "Studies on Sacrifice, 1970-80." *Religious Studies Review* 8, pp. 253-59.

Heesterman, J.C., 1959, "Reflections on the Significance of the Dakṣiṇā." *Indo-Iranian Journal* 3, pp. 241-58.

———, 1964, "Brahmin, Ritual and Renouncer." *WZKS* 8, pp. 1-31.

———, 1987a, "Self Sacrifice in Vedic Ritual." In *Gilgul. Essays on Transformation, Revolution and Permanence in the History of Religions*, S. Shaked, et al. (eds.). Leiden: E.J. Brill, pp. 91-106.

———, 1987b, "The Case of the Severed Head." *WZKS* 11, pp. 22-43.

———, 1993, *The Broken World of Sacrifice: An Essay in Ancient Indian Ritual*. Chicago: The University of Chicago Press.

———, 2001, "Other People's Fire." In *AGNI*, vol. 2, pp. 76-94.

Hendel, R.S. See next section.

Heusch, L. de, 1985, *Sacrifice in Africa: A Structuralist Approach*. Bloomington: Indiana University Press.

Hiltebeitel, A., 1984-85, "The Two Kr̥ṣṇas on One Chariot: Upaniṣadic Imagery and Epic Mythology." *HR* 24, pp. 1-26.

Hiriyanna, M., 1958, *Outlines of Indian Philosophy*. London: George Allen & Unwin [1932].

Hubert, H. and M. Mauss, 1981, *Sacrifice: Its Nature and Function*. Chicago: University of Chicago Press, Midway Reprint [1898].

Hulmes, E., 1991, "The Semantics of Sacrifice." In *SRDE*, pp. 265-81.

Hultgård, A., 1987, "The Burnt-Offering in Early Jewish Religion: Sources, Practices and Purposes." In *GGPU*, pp. 83-91.

Hume, R.E., 1949, *The Thirteen Principal Upanishads*. Madras: Oxford University Press [1921].

Irudayaraj, X., 1978, "Hindu Communion-Sacrifice." *Vidyajyoti* 42, pp. 305-15.

James, E.O., 1971, *Origins of Sacrifice: A Study in Comparative Religion*. London: Kennikat Press [1933].

Jamison, S.W., 1996, *Sacrificed Wife/Sacrificer's Wife: Women, Ritual, and Hospitality in Ancient India*. New York: Oxford University Press.

Jay, N., 1992, *Throughout Your Generations Forever: Sacrifice, Religion and Paternity*. Chicago: University of Chicago Press.

Jensen, A.E., 1963, *Myth and Cult among Primitive Peoples*. Chicago: University of Chicago Press, reprint.

Josephus, F., 1966a, *The Jewish War. Books IV-VII*. With an English tr. H. St. Thackeray. London-Massachusetts: William Heinemann Ltd.-Harvard University Press.

———, 1966b, *The Life. Against Apion.* With an English translation by H. St. Thackeray. London-Massachusetts: William Heinemann Ltd.-Harvard University Press.

Joshi, J.R. 1972, "Prajapati in Vedic Mythology and Ritual." *Annals of the Bhandarkar Oriental Research Institute* 53, pp. 101-25.

Kaelber, W.O., 1975-76, "Tapas, Birth, and Spiritual Rebirth in the Veda." *HR* 15, pp. 343-86.

———, 1978-79, "The 'Dramatic' Element in Brahmanic Initiation Symbols of Death, Danger and Difficult Passage." *HR* 18, pp. 54-76.

Kane, P.V., 1941, *History of Dharmaśāstra*. 5 vols., Poona: Bhandarkar Oriental Research Institute.

Kashikar, C.G. and A. Parpola, 2001, "Śrauta Traditions in Recent Times." In *AGNI*, vol. 2, pp. 199-251.

Keith, A.B., 1925, *The Religion and Philosophy of the Veda and Upanishads.* Parts 1 & 2. Cambridge-Massachusetts: Harvard University Press.

———, (tr.), 1976, *The Veda of the Black Yajus School Entitled Taittirīya Saṁhitā.* Parts 1&2, Translated from the original prose. Delhi: Motilal Banarsidass, reprint.

King, U., 1980, "Who is the Ideal Karmayogin? The Meaning of the Hindu Religious Symbol." *Religion* 10, pp. 41-59.

Kirk, G.S., 1972, "Aetiology, Ritual, Charter: Three Equivocal Terms in the Study of Myths." *Yale Classical Studies* 22, pp. 83-102.

———, 1978, *Myth: Its Meaning and Functions in Ancient and Other Cultures.* Cambridge: Cambridge University Press.

———, 1993, *La natura dei miti greci.* Rome-Bari: Laterza (Biblioteca Universale Laterza 116).

Kitagawa, J. and C.H. Long, 1969, *Myths and Symbols: Studies in Honor of Mircea Eliade.* Chicago: University of Chicago Press.

Knipe, D.M., 1972-73, "One Fire, Three Fires, Five Fires: Vedic Symbols in Transition." *HR* 12, pp. 28-41.

Kramrisch, S., 1962-63, "The Triple Structure of Creation in the Ṛgveda." *HR* 2, pp. 140-75, 256-85.

Kuiper, F.B.J., 1970-71, "Cosmogony and Conception: A Query." *HR* 10, pp. 91-138.

———, 1975-76, "The Basic Concept of Vedic Religion." *HR* 15, pp. 107-20.

———, 1983, *Ancient Indian Cosmogony.* New Delhi: Vikas.

Kulkarni, R.P, 1997, *Layout for Different Sacrifices according to Different Śrauta-Sūtras.* Ujjain: Maharshi Sandipani Rashtriya Veda Vidya Pratishthan.

Lang, B. (ed.), 1985, *Anthropological Approaches to the Old Testament.* Philadelphia-London: Fortress Press-SPCK (Issues in Religion and Theology 8).

Lanithottam, G., 1993, "The Bhagavadgita's Teaching on 'Disinterested Action.'" *Claretianum* 33, pp. 295-352.

Leach, E., 1976, "The Logic of Sacrifice." In *Anthropological Approaches to the Old Testament.* Edited with an Introduction by Bernhard Lang. Philadelphia-London: Fortress Press-SPCK (Issues in Religion and Theology 8), 1985, pp. 136-50.

Leach, E.R., 1977, *Rethinking Anthropology.* London: University of London, The Athlone Press [1961].

———, 1981, *Cultura e comunicazione. La logica della connessione simbolica. Un'introduzione all'uso dell'analisi strutturale nell' antropologia sociale.* Milan: Franco Angeli.

Lévi, S., 1898, *La doctrine du sacrifice dans les Brahmanas.* Paris: Ernest Lerous.

Lewis, G., 1980, *Day of Shining Red: an Essay on Understanding Ritual.* Cambridge: University Press.

Lincoln, B., 1975-76. "The Indo-European Myth of Creation." *HR* 15, pp. 121-45.

———, 1983, *Diventare Dea. I riti di iniziazione femminile.* Milan: Edizioni di Communità (Saggi di cultura contemporanea 145).

———, 1984, "Sacrificio e creazione, macellai e filosofi." *Studi Storici* 25, pp. 859-74.

———, 1986, *Myth, Cosmos and Society.* Cambridge-Massachusetts: Harvard University Press.

Linders, T. and G. Nordquist (eds.), 1987, See *GGPU.*

Linders, T., 1987, "Gods, Gifts, Society." In *GGPU,* pp. 115-22.

Lüders, H., 1959, *Varuṇa und das Ṛta.* Göttingen: Vandenhoeck und Ruprecht.

Luke, K., 1975a, "Pūjā: Its Origin and Significance." *Jeevadhara* 5, pp. 345-65.

———, 1975b, Yajña, the Essence of Ancient Aryan Cult." *The Living Word* 81, pp. 233-59.

———, 1980, "Righteousness, Dharma." *Bible Bhashyam* 6, pp. 311-34.

Macdonell, A.A., 1995, *Vedic Mythology*. Delhi: Motilal Banarsidass [1898].

Magi, G., 1998, *Il dharma del sacrificio del mondo. Il Pūrvamīmāṁsa Sūtra di Jaimini (Libro primo)*. Rimini: Panozzo Editore/THEUT.

Malamoud, C., 1977, *Le "Svādhyāya." Récitation personnele du Veda. Taittirīya-Āraṇyaka livre II, Texte traduit et commenté.* Paris: Bocard.

———, 1992, "Brothers and Sisters in Brahmanic India." In *Understanding Rituals*, D. de Coppet (ed.). London: Routledge, pp. 37-51.

———, 1996, *Cooking the World: Ritual and Thought in Ancient India.* Delhi: Oxford University Press.

Malieckal, L., 1984. "Symbolism in Hindu Worship." *Journal of Dharma* 9, pp. 261-73.

———, 1989a, "Sacrifice: Core of Vedic Religion and Christianity." *Journal of Dharma* 14, pp. 313-28.

———, 1989b, *Yajña and Eucharist: An Inter-Religious Approach to the Theology of Sacrifice.* Bangalore: Dharmaram Publications.

———, 1997. "Sacrifice in Hinduism." *Word and Worship* 30, pp. 39-52.

Malina, B.J., 1996, "Mediterranean Sacrifice: Dimensions of Domestic and Political Religion." *Biblical Theology Bullettin* 26, pp. 26-44.

Manickam, T., 1998, "Myths: A Missiological Understanding." *Third Millennium: Indian Journal of Evangelization* 1, pp. 56-65.

Mascaró, J. (ed.), 1980, *The Bhagavad Gita.* Middlesex: Penguin Books, 19th reprint [1962].

Mehra, B.S., 1994, *Śrauta Sacrifices in the Atharva-Veda.* Delhi: Sanjay Prakashan.

Molé, M., 1963, *Culte, mythe et cosmologic dans l'Iran ancient. Le probléme zoroastrien et la tradition mazdénne.* Paris: PUF.

Monier-Williams, M., 1970, *A Sanskrit–English Dictionary. Etymologically and Philologically Arranged with Special Reference to Cognate Indo-European Language.* Delhi: Motilal Banarsidass [1899].

Montesi, G., 1953-54, "Il valore cosmico dell'Aurora nel pensiero mitologico del Rig Veda." *Studi e materiali di storia delle religioni* 24-25, pp. 111-32.

Müller, M.F. (ed.), 1965, *Upanishads*. Delhi: Motilal Banarsidass (SBE vols. 1 & 15), reprint.

Nola, A.M. di., 1973, "Sacrificio e offerta." In *Enciclopedia delle religioni.* vol. 5., Florence: Vallecchi, cols. 649-78.

O'Flaherty, W.D., 1973, *Asceticism and Eroticism in the Mythology of Śiva.* London: Oxford University Press.

Olivelle, P., 1975, "A Definition of World Renunciation." *WZKS* 19, pp. 75-83.

———, 1976, "Odes of Renunciation." *WZKS* 20, pp. 91-100.

Otto, R., 1976, *Mysticism East and West: A Comparative Analysis of the Nature of Mysticism.* New York: Macmillan Publishing Co., Inc., Fourth printing [1932].

Ottosson, M., 1987, "Sacrifice and Sacred Meals in Ancient Israel." In *GGPU*, pp. 133-36.

Padel, F., 2000, *The Sacrifice of Human Being: British Rule and the Konds of Orissa.* Delhi: Oxford University Press [1995].

Pandey, R.B, 1998, *Hindu Samskaras: Socio-Religious Study of the Hindu Sacraments.* Delhi: Motilal Banarsidass [1969].

Panikkar, R., 1966, *Māyā e Apocalisse. L'incontro dell'induismo e del cristianesimo.* Rome: Abete (Studi Contemporanei 2).

———, 1975, *Spiritualità indú. Lineamenti.* Brescia: Morcelliana.

———, 1977a, "Maṇ as a Ritual Being." *Chicago Studies* 16, pp. 5-28.

———, 1977b, See *PVE*.

———, 1993, *The Cosmotheandric Experience: Emerging Religious Consciousness.* Maryknoll, New York: Orbis Books.

———, 2004, *Christophany: The Fullness of Man.* Maryknoll, New York: Orbis Books.

Parry, J., 1986, "The Gift, the Indian Gift and 'the Indian Gift.'" *Man* 21, pp. 453-73.

Pattison, G., 1991, "The Conscious and the Unconscious Sacrifice: Kierkegaard on Art, Suffering and Religion." In *SRDE*, pp. 205-17.

Penner, H., 1985, "Language, Ritual and Meaning." *Numen* 32, pp. 1-16.

Philip, T.V., 1980, "Krishna Mohan Banerjea and Arian Witness to Christ: Jesus Christ the True Prajapati." *The Indian Journal of Theology* 29, pp. 74-81.

Piano, S., 1993, "Macrocosmo-microcosmo. Il concetto di *ṛta* e di *dharma* nell'induismo antico." In *Dio, mondo e natura nelle religioni orientali*, G. Canobbio (ed.). Padua: Messaggero, pp. 7-22.

Potdar, K.R., 1953, *Sacrifice in the Ṛgveda: Its Nature and Influence, Origin and Growth*. Bombay: Bharatiya Vidya Bhavan.

———, (ed.), 1970, *Myth and Law among the Indo-Europeans: Studies in Indo-European Comparative Mythology*. Berkeley: University of California Press.

———, 1975-76, "Remus et Frater." *HR* 15, pp. 146-57.

Radhakrishnan, S., 1923, *Indian Philosophy*. 2 vols., London: George Allen and Unwin.

———, 1957, *History of Philosophy Eastern and Western*. vol. 1, London: George Allen & Unwin.

———, (ed.), 1989, *Principal Upanishads*. Madras: Oxford University Press [1953].

———, (ed.), 2004, *The Bhagavadgītā with an Introductory Essay, Sanskrit Text, English Translation and Notes*. New Delhi: HarperCollins/ The India Today Group, 20th Impression [1948].

Radhakrishnan, S. and H. Bhattacharyya (eds.), 1958. *Cultural Heritage of India*. 4 vols., Calcutta: The Ramakrishna Mission Institute of Culture, reprint [1937].

Rayan, S., 1990, "The Earth is the Lord's." *Vidyajyoti* 54, pp. 113-32.

Reddy, V.M., 1991, *The Vedic Epiphany*. vols. 1-2, Hyderabad: Institute of Human Study.

———, 1996, *The Vedic Epiphany*. vol. 3, Hyderabad: Institute of Human Study.

Renou, L., 1952, "Études védiques — 2 le mot Virāj." *Journal Asiatique* 240, pp. 133-54.

Ricoeur, P., 1977a, *Ermeneutica filosofica ed ermeneutica biblica*. Brescia: Paidcia (Studi Biblici 43).

———, 1977b, *Il conflitto delle interpretazioni*. Milan: Jaca Book (Di fronte e attraverso 209).

Roberts, J.J.M., 1976, "Myth versus History: Relaying the Comparative Foundations." *CBQ* 38, pp. 1-13.

Sankaracarya, 1975, *The Bṛhadāraṇyaka Upaniṣad, with a Commentary*. Calcutta: Advaita Ashrama.

———, (ed.), 1995, *The Bhagavad Gita.* Madras: Samata Books, 8th reprint [1897].

Santini, C., 1993, "Il lessico della spartizione nel sacrificio Romano." In *Sacrificio e società nel mondo antico,* C. Grottanelli and N.F. Parise (eds.). Rome-Bari: Laterza, pp. 292-302.

Sastri, K.B., 2001, "Agnicayana in the Mīmāṁsa." Ed. by J.A. Santucci, in *AGNI,* vol. 2, pp. 178-98.

Schayer, S., 1935, "A Note on the Old Russian Variant of Purushasukta." *Archiv Orientálni* 7, pp. 319-23.

Scheid, J., 1993, "La spartizione sacrificale a Roma." In *Sacrificio e società nel mondo antico,* C. Grottanelli and N.F. Parise (eds.). Rome-Bari: Laterza, pp. 267-92.

Schneider, M., 1969, "Le basi storiche della simbologia musicale." *Conoscenza religiosa* 3, pp. 267-302.

Scott, D.C., 1980, "Hindu and Christian Bhakti: A Common Human Response to the Sacred." *The Indian Journal of Theology* 29, pp. 12-32.

Segal, R.A. (ed.), 1998, *The Myth and Ritual Theory: An Anthology.* Oxford-Malden: Blackwell.

Selman, M.J., 1995, "Sacrifice in the Ancient Near East." In *BSSB,* pp. 88-104.

Selvanayagam, I., 1996, *Vedic Sacrifice: Challenge and Response.* New Delhi: Manohar.

Shastri, D.R., 1963, *Origin and Development of the Rituals of Ancestor Worship in India.* Calcutta: Bookland Private.

Shelton, J., 1988, *As the Romans Did: A Sourcebook in Roman Social History.* Oxford: Oxford University Press.

Sheth, N., 1998, "Hindu Parallels to Eucharist, I-II." *Vidyajyoti* 62, pp. 679-99, 753-68.

Silburn, L., 1955, *Instant et cause. Le discontinu dans la pensée philosophique de l'Inde.* Paris: Librairie Philosophique Vrin.

Smet, R.V. de, 1982, "Fleeting Time and Sacrificially Produced Continuity in Vedic Brahmanism and in Early Christianity." *Indian Theological Studies* 19, pp. 119-44.

———, 1989, "Gītā/Gospel Convergencies." *Sevartham* 14, pp. 13-19.

Smith, B.K., 1984-85, "Gods and Men in Vedic Ritualism: Towards a Hierarchy of Resemblance." *HR* 24, pp. 291-307.

———, 1985a, "Sacrifice and Being; Prajāpati's Cosmic Emission and its Consequences." *Numen* 32, pp. 71-87.

———, 1985b, "The Unity of Ritual: The Place of the Domestic Sacrifice in Vedic Ritualism." *Indo-Iranian Journal* 28, pp. 79-96.

———, 1989, *Reflections on Resemblance, Ritual and Religion*. New York-Oxford: Oxford University Press.

———, 1994, *Classifying the Universe: the Ancient Indian "Varna" System and the Origins of Caste*. New York: Oxford University Press.

Smith, B.K. and W. Doniger, 1989, "Sacrifice and Substitution: Ritual Mystification and Mythical Demystification." *Numen* 36, pp. 189-224.

Smith, J.Z., 1972-73, "When the Bough Breaks." *HR* 12, pp. 342-71.

———, 1980-81, "The Bare Facts of Ritual." *HR* 20, pp. 112-27.

Smith, W.R., 1894, *Lectures on the Religion of the Semites: The Fundamental Institutions*. Edinburgh: Black.

Soares-Prabhu, G.M., 1980, "The Dharma of Jesus: An Interpretation of the Sermon on the Mount." *Bible Bhashyam* 6, pp. 358-81.

Somayajipad, C.V. et al., 2001, "Recent Nambudiri Performances of Agniṣṭoma and Agnicayana." In *AGNI*, vol. 2, pp. 252-55.

Sperber, D., 1978, *Simbolismo ripensato*. Milan: Ferltrinelli.

———, 1984, *Il sapere degli antropologi*. Milan: Feltrinelli.

Staal, F., 1979, "The Meaninglessness of Ritual." *Numen* 26, pp. 2-22.

———, 1996, *Ritual and Mantras: Rules without Meaning*. Delhi: Motilal Banarsidass.

———, 2001, See *AGNI*.

Strenski, I., 1996, "Between Theory and Speciality: Sacrifice in the 90s." *Religious Studies Review* 22, pp. 10-26.

Stutley, M. and J. Stutley (eds.), 1980, *Dizionario dell 'induismo*. Rome: Ubaldini [1977].

Teasdale, W., 1990, "Nature Mysticism as the Basis of Eco-Spirituality." *Jeevadhara* 20, pp. 390-404.

Terrin, A.N., 1983, *Spiegare o comprendere la religione? Le scienze della religione a confronto*. Padua: Messaggero Abbazia di S. Giustina.

———, 1993, *New Age. La religiosità del postmoderno.* Bologna: Dehoniane.

———, 1995a, *Il sacro off limits. L'esperienza religiosa e il suo travaglio.* Bologna: Dehoniane.

———, 1995b, "L'esperienza religiosa parametro per la storia comparata delle religioni e per l'esercizio del dialogo ecumenico." *Studia Patavina* 42, pp. 136-61.

———, 1997, *Il respiro religioso dell'Oriente. Luoghi d'incontro con il cristianesimo.* Bologna: Dehoniane.

———, 1998, "Il pasto sacrificale nella storia comparata delle religioni." In *SEER*, pp. 263-310.

———, 1999a, *Il rito. Antropologia e fenomenologia della ritualità.* Brescia: Morcelliana.

———, 1999b, L'Oriente come l'altra anima dell"Occidente." *Hermeneutica: Annuario di filosofia e teologia* (Nuova Serie), pp. 303-44.

Thachil, J., 1985, *The Vedic and the Christian Concept of Sacrifice.* Alwaye (Kerala): Pontifical Institute of Theology and Philosophy.

———, 1989, "The Theology of Religions and Sacrifice." *Journal of Dharma* 14, pp. 329-42.

Thibaut, G. (ed.), 1966a, *Vedānta Sūtras, with Rāmānuja's Śrībhāṣya.* Delhi: Motilal Banarsidass (SBE 48), reprint.

———, (ed.), 1966b, *Vedānta Sūtras, with the commentary of Śaṅkarācārya.* Delhi: Motilal Banarsidass (SBE 34), reprint.

Thite, G.U., 1975, *Sacrifice in the Brāhmaṇa Texts.* Poona: University of Poona.

Tilak, B.G., 1975, *Gita-rahasya.* Poona: J.S. and B.S. Tilak.

Tsuji, N., 2001, "The Agnicayana Section of Matirāyaṇī-Saṁhitā with Special Reference to the Mānava Śrautasūtra." In *AGNI*, vol. 2, pp. 135-60.

Turcan, R., 1980, "Le sacrifice mithriaque: innovations de sens et de modalités." In *Le sacrifice dans l'antiquité*, J. Rudhardt and O. Reverdin (eds.). Vandoeuvres-Genéve: Fondation Hardt, pp. 341-80.

Turner, V., 1976-77, "Sacrifice as Quintessential Process: Prophylaxis or Abandonment?" *HR* 16, pp. 189-215.

Tylor, E.B., 1913, *The Primitive Culture.* 2 vols., London: University Press.

Upadhyay, G.P., 1979, *Brāhmaṇas in Ancient India: A Study in the Role of the Brāhmaṇa Class from c. 200 BC to c. AD 500.* New Delhi: Munshiram Manoharlal Publishers.

Vadakethala, F., 1977, "A Yoga for Liberation: Ramanuja's Approach." *Journal of Dharma* 2, pp. 35-52.

Van der Leeuw, G., 1975, *Fenomenologia della religione.* Turin: Universale scientifica Boringhieri, triple volume.

Vasu, S.C., 2000, *The Daily Practice of the Hindus Containing the Morning and Midday Duties.* Delhi: Munshiram Manoharlal [1918].

Vempeny, I., 1988, *Kṛṣṇa and Christ in the Light of some of the Fundamental Concepts and Themes of the Bhagavad Gītā and the New Testament.* Anand: Gujarat Sahitya Prakash.

Vernant, J.-P., 1980, "Théorie générale du sacrifice et mise à mort dans la θυσια grecque." In *Le sacrifice dans l'antiquité,* J. Rudhardt and O. Reverdin (eds.). Vandoeuvres-Genéve: Fondation Hardt, 1-39.

Verpoorten, J.-M., 1977, "Unité et distinction dans les speculations rituelles védiques." *Archiv für Begriffsgeschichte* 21, pp. 59-85.

Versnel, H.S., 1980, "Self Sacrifice, Compensation and the Anonymous Gods." In *Le sacrifice dans l'antiquité,* J. Rudhardt and O. Reverdin (eds.). Vandoeuvres-Genéve: Fondation Hardt, pp. 135-94.

Vesci, U. M., 1992, *Heat and Sacrifice in the Vedas.* Delhi: Motilal Banarsidass [1985].

Whaling, F., 1980, "The Bhagavad Gītā. Contradiction, Apparent Contradiction or Synthesis?" *Irish Theological Quarterly* (New Series) 47, pp. 167-82.

Wheelock, W.T., 1985, "Patterns of Mantra Use in a Vedic Ritual." *Numen* 32, pp. 169-93.

White, D.G., 1988-89, "Dogs Die." *HR* 28, pp. 283-303.

Widengren, G., 1984, *Fenomenologia della religione.* Bologna: Dehoniane [1968].

Zaehner, R.C. (ed.), 1969, *The Bhagavad Gītā with a Commentary Based on the Original Sources.* Oxford: Clarendon Press.

———, 1972, "Learning from Other Faiths. 1. Hinduism." *The Expository Times* 83, pp. 164-68.

Studies on Theology and the Eucharistic Sacrifice

Alexander, T.D., 1995, "The Passover Sacrifice." In *BSSB*, pp. 1-24.

Alfrink, J., 1959. "Biblical Background to the Eucharist as a Sacrificial Meal." *Irish Theological Quarterly* 26, pp. 290-302.

Anderson, G.A., 1987, *Sacrifices and Offerings in Ancient Israel: Studies in their Social and Political Importance*, Atlanta-Georgia: Scholars Press (Harvard Semitic Monographs 41).

Antwi, D.J., 1991, "Did Jesus Consider His Death to be an Atoning Sacrifice?" *Interpretation* 14, pp. 17-28.

Ashby, G., 1988, *Sacrifice: Its Nature and Purpose.* London: SCM Press.

Associazione Biblica Italiana, 1976, See *CRSP*.

Augustine, Saint, 1981, *The City of God, Books VIII-XIV. Writings of Saint Augustine*. vol. 7, Washington: The Catholic University of American Press (The Fathers of the Church vol. 14), Third printing [1952].

Balducci, E., 1970, "L'Eucaristia, progetto di un mondo nuovo." *Testimonianze* 13, pp. 873-89.

Balthasar, H.U. von, 1976, *Liturgia cosmica. L'immagine dell'universo in Massimo il Confessore*. Rome: Editrice A.V.E. [1961].

———, 1985. *La teologia di Karl Barth.* Milan: Jaca Book (Già e non ancora 117) [1976].

Barrett, C.K., 1954-55, "The Lamb of God." *New Testament Studies* 1, pp. 210-18.

———, 1960, *The Gospel according to St. John.* London: SPCK.

Barth, K., 1962, *Church Dogmatics. A Selection.* With an Introduction by H. Gollwitzr, New York: Harper Torchbooks.

Beckwith, R.T and M.J. Selman (eds.), 1995, See *BSSB*.

Beckwith, R.T., 1995a, "Sacrifice in the World of the New Testament." In *BSSB*, 105-10.

———, 1995b, "The Death of Christ as a Sacrifice in the Teaching of Paul and Hebrews." In *BSSB*, 130-35.

Behm, J., 1968, "Δ υω." In *Grande lessico del Nuovo Testamento.* vol. 4, F. Montagnini, et al. (eds.). Brescia: Paideia, cols. 625-58.

Benz, E., 1966, *Evolution and Christian Hope.* New York: Garden City.

Bergant, D., 1995, "An Anthropological Approach to Biblical Interpretation: The Passover Supper in Exodus 12: 1-20 as a Case Study." *Semeia* 67, pp. 43-71.

Berthold, G.C., 1993, "Levels of Scriptural Meaning in Maximus the Confessor." In *CFGA*, pp. 129-44.

Blair, J.L., 1963, "The Relation of the Incarnation to the Atonement." *Scottish Journal of Theology* 10, pp. 68-77.

Blowers, P.M., 1993, "The Analogy of Scripture and Cosmos in Maximus the Confessor." In *CFGA*, pp. 145-49.

———, 1997, "Realized Eschatology in Maximus the Confessor, *Ad Thalassium* 22." In *AOCF*, pp. 258-63.

Bonner, G., 1991, "The Doctrine of Sacrifice: Augustine and the Latin Patristic Tradition." In *SRDE*, pp. 101-17.

Bosio, G., 1963, *Iniziazione ai Padri.* vol. 1. *La Chiesa primitiva negli scritti dei Padri anteniceni.* Turin: Società Editrice Internazionale.

———, 1965, *Iniziazione ai Padri.* vol. 2. *La dottrina della Chiesa negli scritti dei Padri postniceni.* Turin: Società Editrice Internazionale.

Bouyer, L., 1983, *Eucaristia. Teologia e spiritualità della preghiera eucaristica.* Leumann (Turin): Elle Di Ci.

Bradshaw, P.F., 1991, "Zebah Todah and the Origins of the Eucharist." *Ecclesia Orans* 8, pp. 245-60.

Bravo, F., 1967, *Christ in the Thought of Teilhard de Chardin.* Notre Dam & London: University of Notre Dam Press.

Brown, D.J., 1987, "The Eucharist as Sacrifice." *The Reformed World* 39, pp. 706-11.

Brown, R.E., 1966, *The Gospel according to John I-XII. Introduction, Translation and Notes.* New York: The Anchor Bible Doubleday (The Anchor Bible 29).

Bruggeman, A., 1966, "The Cosmic Christ: Some Recent Interpretations." *The Indian Journal of Theology* 15, pp. 130-42.

Cahill, J., 1976, "The Johannine *Logos* as Center." *CBQ* 38, pp. 54-72.

Cantalamessa, R., 1999, *Il mistero pasquale.* Milan: Ancora [1985].

Casel, O., 1999, *The Mystery of Christian Worship*. New York: Herder & Herder [1932].

Catella, A. and G. Cavagnoli, 1989., *Le preghiere eucaristiche. Analisi dei contenuti e indicazioni catechistiche.* Milan: Paoline.

Catella, A., 1998, "Valutazioni circa il rapporto tra sacificio e liturgia cristiana." In *SEER*, pp. 311-29.

Cavagnoli, G., 1998, "Il rapporto tra sacrificio e liturgia cristiana: alcune testimonianze patristico-litrugiche." In *SEER*, pp. 331-54.

Ceresa-Gastaldo, A. (ed.), See Massimo il Confessore.

Chapman, M.E., 1992, "Sacrament and Sacrifice in the Theology of the Mass according to Luther, 1513-1526." *One in Christ* 28, pp. 248-66.

Chauvet, L-M., 1988, *Linguaggio e simbolo. Saggio sui sacramenti.* Leumann (Turin): Elle Di Ci [1979].

———, 1990, *Simbolo e sacramento. Una rilettura sacramentale dell'esistenza cristiana.* Leumann (Turin): Elle Di Ci [1987].

———, 1998, "La Messa come sacrificio nel Medievo e nel Concilio di Trento: pratiche e teorie." In *SEER*, pp. 19-51.

Chester, A.N., 1991, "Hebrews: the Final Sacrifice." In *SRDE*, pp. 57-72.

Chetany, J., 1978, *The Future of Man According to Teilhard de Chardin and Aurobindo Ghose.* New Delhi: Oriental Publishers.

Chilton, B., 1992, *The Temple of Jesus. His Sacrificial Program within a Cultural History of Sacrifice*. Pennsylvania: Pennsylvania State University Press.

———, 1994, *A Feast of Meanings: Eucharistic Theologies from Jesus through Johannine Circles.* Leiden: E.J. Brill.

———, 1997, "Sacrificial Mimesis." *Religion* 27, pp. 225-30.

Christou, P., 1982, "Maximus Confessor on the Infinity of Man." In *MCAS*, pp. 261-71.

Chupungco, A.J., 1977, *The Cosmic Elements of Christian Passover.* Rome: Anselmiana (Analecta Liturgica 3).

Collins, A.Y., 1996, *Cosmology and Eschatology in Jewish and Christian Apocalypticism*. Leiden: E.J. Brill.

Collins, J.J., 1977-78, "Cosmos and Salvation: Jewish Wisdom and Apocalyptic in the Hellenistic Age." *HR* 17, pp. 121-42.

Colombo, G., 1988, "Per il trattato sull'Eucaristia." *Teologia* 13, pp. 95-131.

———, 1989, "Per il trattato sull'Eucaristia." *Teologia* 14, pp. 105-37.

Cooke, B., 1960, "Synoptic Presentation of the Eucharist as Covenant Sacrifice." *Theological Studies* 21, pp. 1-44.

Courtman, N.B., 1995, "Sacrifice in the Psalms." In *BSSB,* pp. 41-58.

Croee, V. and B. Valente, 1982, "Provvidenza e pedagogia divina nella storia." In *MCAS,* pp. 247-59.

Cyril of Jerusalem, 1857, *Catecheses Mystagogicae V.* In *PG,* 33.

Dacquino, P., 1971, "Il sacerdozio della Nuova Alleanza alla luce del sacrificio eucaristico." *Rivista Liturgica* 19, pp. 137-63.

———, 1976, "Cristo capo del corpo che è la Chiesa (Col. 1,18)." In *CRSP,* pp. 131-75.

Daley, B.E., 1982, "Apokatastasis and 'Honorable Silence,' in the Eschatology of Maximus the Confessor." In *MCAS,* pp. 309-39.

Dalferth, I.U., 1991, "Christ Died for Us: Reflections on the Sacrificial Language of Salvation." In *SRDE,* pp. 299-325.

Dalmais, I.-H., 1952, "La théorie des 'logoi' des créatures chez S. Maxime le confesseur." *Revue des sciences philosophiques et thélogiques* 36, pp. 244-49.

———, 1998, "Retentissements cosmiques de la transfiguration du Christ dans la tradition Hiérosolymito-Arménienne de Vardavar." In *LCCS,* pp. 49-58.

Daly, R.J., 1977, "The Soteriological Significance of the Sacrifice of Isaac." *CBQ* 39, pp. 45-75.

———, 1978a, "The New Testament Concept of Christian Sacrificial Activity." *Biblical Theology Bulletin* 8, pp. 99-107.

———, 1978b, *The Origins of the Christian Doctrine of Sacrifice.* London-Darton: Longman & Todd.

———, 1981, "The Eucharist and Redemption: The Last Supper and Jesus' Understanding of His Death." *Biblical Theology Bulletin* 11, pp. 21-27.

———, 1990, "The Power of Sacrifice in Ancient Judaism and Christianity." *Journal of Ritual Studies* 4, pp. 91-131.

———, 1997, "Is Christianity Sacrificial or Antisacrificial?" *Religion* 27, pp. 231-43.

Donghi, A., 1988, "Celebrazione liturgica e realtà create." *Rassegna di teologia* 29, pp. 558-79.

Dragas, G.D., 1991, "St. Athanasius on Christ's Sacrifice." In *SRDE,* pp. 73-100.

Duff, P.B., 1997, "The Sacrificial Character of Earliest Christianity: A Response to Robert J. Daly's 'Is Christianity Sacrificial or Antisacrificial?." *Religion* 27, pp. 245-48.

Dunn, J.D.G., 1991, "Paul's Understanding of the Death of Jesus as Sacrifice." In *SRDE*, pp. 35-56.

Emery, P.-Y., 1966, "L'eucharistie: sacrifice du Christ et de l'Eglise." *Verbum Caro* 77, pp. 65-72.

Ernst, J., 1968, "The Significance of Christ's Eucharistic Body for the Unity of Church and Cosmos." *Concilium* 4, pp. 55-60.

Eynde, D. van den, 1957, "L'eucaristia in S. Ignazio, S. Giustino e S. Ireneo." In *Il mistero eucaristico. Il mistero dell'altare nel pensiero e nella vita della Chiesa*, A. Piolanti (ed.). Rome: Descalée & Ci — Edizioni Pontefici, pp. 115-27.

Faricy, R.L., 1967, *Teilhard de Chardin's Theology of the Christian in the World*. New York: Sheed & Ward.

———, 1970, "Christ, Cosmos and Eucharist." *The Bible Today* 48, pp. 3304-11.

———, 1971, "Christ, Creation and Baptism." *The Bible Today* 56, pp. 486-91.

———, 1976, *Building God's World*. Denville, New Jersey: Dimension Books.

Ferraris, F., 1982, "L'Eucaristia, missione della Chiesa e costruzione del mondo." *Rivista di Pastorale Liturgica* 111, pp. 42-45.

Fiedler, P., 1974, "Peccato e perdono nel cristianesimo." *Concilium* 10, pp. 1440-49.

Fink, P.E., 1985, "Living the Sacrifice of Christ." *Worship* 59, pp. 133-48.

Fitzer, J., 1973, "Teilhard's Eucharist: A Reflection." *Theological Studies* 34, pp. 251-64.

Fitzpatrick, P.J., 1991, "On Eucharistic Sacrifice in the Middle Ages." In *SRDE*, pp. 129-56.

Füglister, N., 1976, *Il valore salvifico della Pasqua*. Brescia: Paideia.

Galeriu, C., 1998, "La Transfiguration du Christ — Transfiguration de la Nature (de la Création)." In *LCCS*, pp. 71-91.

Galzignato, M., 1984, "La messa come sacrificio 'espiatorio propiziatorio" in Lutero. Alcune osservazioni metodologiche per una sua esatta comprensione." *Studi ecumenici* 2, pp. 211-31.

Gasper, G.E.M., 1999, "Anselm's *Cur Deus Homo* and Athanasius' *De Incarnatione*: Some Questions of Comparison." In *CDHA*, pp. 147-64.

Gelston, A., 1991, "Sacrifice in the Early East Syrian Eucharistic Tradition." In *SRDE*, pp. 118-25.

Gerken, A., 1977, *Teologia dell'eucaristia*. Alba: Paoline.

Gese, H., 1981, "The Origins of the Lord's Supper." In *Essays on Biblical Theology*, Helmut Gese (ed.). Minneapolis: Augsburg, pp. 117-40.

Gibbs, J.G., 1971, "Pauline Cosmic Christology and Ecological Crisis." *JBL* 90, pp. 466-79.

Gibellini, R., 1968, *La discussione su Teilhard de Chardin*. Brescia: Queriniana (Giornale di teologia 25).

Gilbert, P. et al. (ed), 1999, See *CDHA*.

Girard, R., See in previous section.

Giraudo, C., 1989a, *La struttura letteraria della preghiera eucaristica. Saggio sulla genesi letteraria di una forma (tôdâ veterotestamentaria — berakâ giudaica — anafora cristiana)*. Rome: Editrice Pontificio Istituto Biblico (Analecta Biblica 92) [1981].

———, 1989b. *Eucaristia per la Chiesa: prospettive teologiche sull'eucaristia a partire dalla "lex orandi."* Brescia-Rome: Morcelliana-Gregorian University Press (Aloisiana 22).

Gittins, A.J., 1991, "Sacrifice, Violence, and the Eucharist." *Worship* 65, pp. 420-35.

Gonzalez, J.L., 1988, *A History of Christian Thought: From Augustine to the Eve of the Reformation*. vol. 2, Nashville: Abingdon Press.

Gray, D.P., 1969, *The One and the Many: Teilhard de Chardin's Vision of Unity*. London: Burns and Oates.

Gregory of Nazianzen, 1857. *In sanctum Pascha*, XLV. In *PG*, 36.

Grillo, A., 1995, *Teologia fondamentale e liturgia. Il rapporto tra immediatezza e mediazione nella riflessione teologica*. Padua: Messaggero-Abbazia di S. Giustina (Caro Salutis Cardo. Studi 10).

Grillo, A., 1998, "Differenza e antitesi tra sacrificio spirituale e sacrificio rituale. Modernità, irrilevanza del rito e incompresensione della libertà." In *SEER*, pp. 203-43.

Hanson, A., 1988, "The Eucharist as Sacrifice." *Questions Liturgiques* 69, pp. 155-61.

Hayward, R., 1991, "Sacrifice and World Order: Some Observations on Ben Sira's Attitude to the Temple Service." In *SRDE,* pp. 22-34.

Head, P.M., 1995, "The Self-Offering and Death of Christ as Sacrifice in the Gospels and in the Acts of the Apostles." In *BSSB,* pp. 111-29.

Heinzer, F. and C. Schönborn (eds.), 1982, See *MCAS*.

Hendel, R.S., 1989, Sacrifice as a Cultural System: The Ritual Symbolism of Exodus 24:3-8." *ZAW* 101, pp. 366-90.

Houston, J., 1999, "Was the Anselm of *Cur Deus Homo* a Retributivist?" In *CDHA,* pp. 621-39.

Howard, J.K., 1967, "Passover and Eucharist in the Fourth Gospel." *Scottish Journal of Theology* 20, pp. 329-37.

Howell, C., 1965, "Sacrifice and Sacrament." *The Way* 5, pp. 126-33.

Ignatius of Antioch, 1857, *Epistolae ad Ephesies,* 20: 2, In *PG,* 5.

Irenaeus Episcopus, 1857, *Prolegomena, Adversus etc.,* In *PG,* 7.

James, E.O. See in previous section.

Jay, N., 1988, "Sacrifice, Descent and the Patriarchs." *VT* 38, pp. 52-70.

Jenson, P.P., 1995, "The Levitical Sacrificial System." In *BSSB,* pp. 25-40.

Jeremias, J., 1972, "This is My Body. . ." *Expository Times* 83, pp. 196-203.

———, 1987, *The Eucharistic Words of Jesus*. London: SCM Press, 7th impression [1966].

John Paul II, Pope, 2005, *Dominum et Vivificantem.* In Pope John Paul II, *Encyclicals.* Trivandrum: CIPH.

Jones, D.R., 1991, "Sacrifice and Holiness." In *SRDE,* pp. 9-21.

Justin the Martyr, 1857, *Apologia Prima et Secunda.* In *PG,* 6.

Justin, Saint, 1977, *The First Apology. The Second Apology.* In *The Writings of St. Justin Martyr.* Washington: The Catholic University of American Press (The Fathers of the Church, vol. 6) [1948].

Kelly, G., 1985, "Eucharistic Sacrifice in the Council of Trent." *The Irish Theological Quarterly* 51, pp. 268-88.

King, U., 1981, *Towards a New Mysticism: Teilhard de Chardin and Eastern Religions.* New York: The Seabury Press.

Koester, C.R., 1995, *Symbolism in the Fourth Gospel: Meaning, Mystery, Community*. Minneapolis: Fortress Press.

Kopciowski, E., 1987, "Stabilirò la mia Alleanza come Alleanza perenne." *Studi Ecumenici* 5, pp. 193-208.

Küng, H., 1981, *Justification: The Doctrine of Karl Barth and a Catholic Reflection.* London: Burns & Oates [1964].

Lafont, G., 1998, "Sacrificio e rito: background antropologico e teologico di una rimozione." In *SEER*, pp. 53-67.

Lattey, C., 1941, "The Prophets and Sacrifice: A Study in Biblical Relativity." *The Journal of Theological Studies* 42, pp. 155-65.

Léon-Dufour, X., 1987, *Sharing the Eucharistic Bread: The Witness of the New Testament.* New York/Mahwah: Paulist Press [1982].

Levasti, A., 1929, *Sant'Anselmo. Vita e pensiero.* Bari: G. Laterza e Figli.

Levenson, J.D., 1993, *The Death and Resurrection of the Beloved Son: The Transformation of Child Sacrifice in Judaism and Christianity.* New Haven: Yale University Press.

Lietzmann, H., 1979, *Mass and Lord's Supper: A Study in the History of the Liturgy.* Leiden: E.J. Brill [1926].

Ligier, L., 1966, "Dalla Cena di Gesú all'anafora della Chiesa." *Rivista Liturgica* 53, pp. 480-521.

———, 1973, "The Origins of the Eucharistic Prayer: From the Last Supper to the Eucharist." *Studia Liturgica* 9, pp. 161-85.

Livingstone, E.A. (ed.), 1993, See *CFGA*.

———, (ed.), 1997, See *AOCF*.

Lossky, V., 1973, *The Mystical Theology of the Eastern Church.* Cambridge & London: James Clark & Co., reprint [1944].

Lossky, V., 1985, *In the Image and Likeness of God.* New York: St. Vladimir's Seminary Press [1967].

Louth, A., 1993, "St. Denys the Areopagite and St. Maximus the Confessor: a Question of Influence." In *CFGA*, pp. 166-74.

———, 1997, "St. Maximus the Confessor between East and West." In *AOCF*, pp. 332-45.

Lubac, H. de. 1967, *The Religion of Teilhard de Chardin.* London: Collins.

———, 1968, *Teilhard Explained.* New York: Paulist Press Deus Books.

Lucas, E.C., 1995, "Sacrifice in the Prophets." In *BSSB*, pp. 59-74.

Lyonnet, S. and L. Sabourin, 1970, *Sin, Redemption, and Sacrifice. A Biblical and Patristic Study.* Rome: P.I.B. (Anelecta Biblica 48).

Lyonnet, S., 1969, *Annotationes in Epistulam ad Colossenses.* (Ad usum privatum auditorium). Rome: P.I.B.

———, 1976, "Il Ruolo cosmico di Cristo in Col. 1,15ss, alla luce del ruolo cosmico della Tora nel giudaismo." In *CRSP*, pp. 57-79.

Lyons, J.A., 1982, *The Cosmic Christ in Origen and Teilhard de Chardin: A Comparative Study*. Oxford: Oxford University Press.

Madden, N., 1993, "Composite Hypostasis in Maximus Confessor." In *CFGA*, pp. 175-97.

Maldamé, J.M., 1995, *Cristo e il cosmo. Influenza della cosmologia moderna sulla teologia*. Cinisello Balsamo (Milan): San Paolo (Prospettive teologiche 15).

Malieckal, L., See in previous section.

Maloney, G.A., 1968, *The Cosmic Christ from Paul to Teilhard*. New York: Sheed & Ward.

Mantzarides, G., 1981, "The Divine Liturgy and the World." *The Greek Orthodox Theological Review* 26, pp. 62-70.

Marangon, A., 1976, "Rapporti fra cosmo e storia della salvezza in alcuni momenti della tradizione anticotestamentaria." In *CRSP*, pp. 13-35.

Marsili, S., 1973, "Offerta-sacrificio nella preghiera eucaristica." *Notitiae* 9, pp. 231-37.

Masi, R., 1966, "Teologia delle realtà materiali alla luce del mistero eucaristico." In *Studi eucaristici*. Atti della settimana internazionale di alti studi teologici e storici, Orvieto 21-26 settembre, 1964. Orvietto: Comitato Esecut. Centr., pp. 173-200.

Massimo il Confessore, 1979, *Umanità e divinità di Cristo. Traduzione, introduzione e note*, A. Ceresa-Gastaldo (ed.). Rome: Città Nuova Editrice.

———, 1985, *Meditazioni sull'agonia di Gesú. Traduzione, introduzione e note*, A. Ceresa-Gastaldo (ed.). Rome: Città Nuova Editrice.

Mattam, J. and J. Kavunkal (eds.), 1998, *Ecological Concerns: An Indian Christian Response*. The 20th Annual Meeting of the Indian Theological Association, Aluva 26-30 April 1997. Bangalore: N.B.C.L.C.

Maximus the Confessor, 1857a, *Capita charitate; Capita teologica et oeconomicae; Liber asceticus; Quaestiones ad Thalassium; Questionis et dubia*. In *PG*, p. 90.

———, 1857b, *Ambigua; Mystagogia* 2. In *PG*, 91.

Mazza E., 1984, *Le odierne preghiere eucaristiche*, 1-2. Bologna: Dehoniane.

——— (ed.), 1996a, *Segno di unità. Le piú antiche eucaristie delle chiese.* Magnano (Biella): Edizioni Qiqajon-Comunità di Bose.

———, E., 1996b, *La celebrazione eucaristica. Genesi del rito e sviluppo dell'interpretazione.* Cinisello Balsamo (Milan): San Paolo.

McHugh, J.F., 1991, "The Sacrifice of the Mass at the Council of Trent." In *SRDE*, pp. 157-81.

McNamara, K., 1969, "Eucharist, Church and World." *Furrow* 20, pp. 4-17.

McPartlan, P., 1993, *The Eucharist Makes the Church: Henri de Lubac and John Zizioulas in Dialogue.* Edinburgh: T&T Clark.

Mello, A., 1987, "Questa é la nuova alleanza nel mio sangue: tesi sull'unità dell'antica e della nuova Alleanza," *Studi ecumenici* 5, pp. 209-20.

Metzger, M., 1998, "Liturgie et cosmos dans les Constituions Apostoliques." In *LCCS*, pp. 153-63.

Milgrom, J., 1977, "Concerning Jeremiah's Repudiation of Sacrifice." *ZAW* 89, pp. 273-75.

Mooney, C.F., 1966, *Teilhard de Chardin and the Mystery of Christ.* New York: Harper & Row.

Moses, J., 1996, *The Sacrifice of God: A Holistic Theory of Atonement.* Norwich: The Canterbury Press.

Moule, C.F.D., 1962, *The Epistles to the Colossians and to Philemon.* Cambridge: The Cambridge Greek Testament Commentary.

Neuner, J. and J. Dupuis (eds.), 1992, *The Christian Faith in the Doctrinal Documents of the Catholic Church.* Bangalore: TPI.

Nola, G. di, 1994, *Monumenta eucaristica: la testimonianza dei Padri nella Chiesa.* vol. 1, Rome: Dehoniane.

North, R., 1985, "Violence and the Bible: The Girard Connection." *CBQ* 47, pp. 1-27.

O'Collins, G., 1999, "*Cur Deus Homo* in the Context of Modern Christology and Soteriology." In *CDHA*, pp. 21-23.

Olsen, G.W, 1981, "Hans Urs von Balthasar and the Rehabilitation of St. Anselm's Doctrine of the Atonement." *Scottish Journal of Theology* 34, pp. 49-61.

———, 1999, "St. Anselm's Place in Hans Urs von Balthasar's History of Soteriology." In *CDHA*, pp. 823-35.

Ormea, F., 1968, *Teilhard de Chardin. Guida al pensiero scientifico e religioso.* vol. 1, Florence: Vallecchi (Mezzo Secolo 18).

Ottolini, E.V., 1998, "Ultima Cena-Croce-Eucaristia: la dimensione sacrificale." In *SEER,* pp. 355-449.

Panimolle, S.A., 1976, "L'inabitazione del ΠΛΗΡΩΜΑ nel Cristo (Col. 1,19)." In *CRSP,* pp. 178-205.

———, 1977, "La dottrina eucaristica nel racconto giovanneo della moltiplicazione dei pani (Gv 6,1-15." In *Segni e Sacramenti nel vangelo di Giovanni,* P.R. Tragan (ed.). Rome: Editrice Anselmiana (Studia Anselmiana 66), pp. 73-88.

Paretsky, A., 1990, "Proleptic Recapitulation: Passover, Eucharist and God's Saving Acts." *New Blackfriars* 71, pp. 541-47.

Pelikan, J., 1977, *The Spirit of Eastern Christendom (600-1700).* Chicago: The University of Chicago Press.

———, 1982, "The Place of Maximus Confessor in the History of Christian Thought." In *MCAS,* pp. 387-402.

Penrose, M.R., 1978, "Cosmic Dimensions of the Eucharist." *Review for Religious* 37, pp. 433-41.

Perry, J.M., 1993, "The Evolution of the Johannine Eucharist." *New Testament Studies* 39, pp. 22-35.

Pesch, R., 1977, "The Last Supper and Jesus' Understanding of His Death." *Bible Bhashyam* 3, pp. 58-75.

———, 1978, *Das Abendmahl und Jesu Todesverstänis.* Freiburg: Herder.

Peterson, L. L., 1999, "St. Anslem on Justice, Retribution and the Divine Will." In *CDHA,* pp. 659-72.

Philo Judaeus, See C.D. Yonge.

Piolanti, A. (ed.), 1957, *Il mistero eucaristico. Il mistero dell'altare nel pensiero e nella vita della Chiesa.* Rome: Descalée & Ci — Edizioni Pontefici.

———, 1983, "Ultime prospettive sul sacrificio della messa." *Divinitas* 27, pp. 323-38.

Power, D.N., 1979, "Words that Crack: the Uses of 'Sacrifice' in Eucharistic Discourse." *Worship* 53, pp. 386-404.

———, 1987, *The Sacrifice We Offer. The Tridentine Dogma and Its Reinterpretation.* Edinburgh: T&T Clark Limited.

Praseed, G., 2002, "The Cosmic Dimension of Yajña and Eucharist. Part 1 & 2." *Samanvaya: A Bilingual Journal for the Study of World Religions from Varanasi* 3:1, pp. 45-56; 3:2, pp. 56-73.

———, 2006a, "Violence and its Collective Scapegoating: An Analysis of René Girard's Theory of Scapegoat Mechanism." In *Wounded History: Religion, Conflict, Psyche and Social Healing,* John Chathanatt and Manindra N. Thakur (eds.). Delhi: Media House, pp. 269-86.

———, 2006b, "The Eucharist and the Cosmos in Pierre Teilhard de Chardin." *Vidyajyoti* 70, pp. 903-13.

Quarello, E., 1965, "Per una chiarificazione della realtà del sacrificio." *Salesianum* 27, pp. 355-80.

———, 1970, *Il sacrificio di Cristo e della sua Chiesa. Rassegna e riflessioni su posizioni recenti.* Brescia: Queriniana (Giornale di teologia 39).

Rad, G. von, 1965, *Old Testament Theology.* vol. 2, London: SCM Press.

Rahner, K., 1988a, "Christology within an Evolutionary View of the World." In *Theological Investigations.* vol. 5, London-Darton: Longman & Todd, pp. 157-92 [1966].

———, 1992, *Foundations of Christian Faith: An Introduction to the Idea of Christianity.* New York: Crossroad, reprint.

Rahner, K. and A. Häussling, 1968, *The Celebration of the Eucharist.* London: Burns & Oates.

Ravens, D.A.S., 1986, "St. Luke and Atonement." *Expository Times* 97, pp. 291-94.

Ricoeur, P., See in previous section.

Rideau, E., 1967, *Teilhard de Chardin: A Guide to His Thought.* London: Collins.

Rossum, J. van, 1993, "The λόγοι of Creation and the Divine "Energies" in Maximus the Confessor and in Gregory Palamas." In *CFGA,* pp. 213-17.

Sacchi, A., 1976, "La riconciliazione universale (Col. 1,20)." In *CRSP,* pp. 221-45.

Schnackenburg, R., 1977, *Il Vangelo di Giovanni.* 2 vols., Brescia: Paideia.

Schneiders, S., 1977, "Symbolism and the Sacramental Principle in the Fourth Gospel." In *Segni e sacramenti nel vangelo di Giovanni,* P.R. Tragan (ed.). Rome: Editrice Anselmiana (Studia Anselmiana 66), pp. 221-35.

Schreurs, N., 1997, "Rehabilitation of Atonement? Recent Developments in the British Theology of Atonement." *Brijdragen, Tijdschrift voor Filosofie en Theologie* 58, pp. 242-63.

Schulz, H.-J., 1982-83, "Patterns of Offering and Sacrifice." *Studia Liturgica* 15, pp. 34-48.

Schürmann, H., 1968, "Jesus' Words in the Light of His Actions at the Last Supper." *Concilium* 4, pp. 61-67.

———, 1983, *Gesú di fronte alla propria morte. Riflessioni esegetiche e prospettiva.* Brescia: Morcelliana.

Segalla, G., 1965, "Fate questo in memoria di me." *Parole di vita* 10, pp. 81-90.

Segalla, G., 1976, *Gesú pane del cielo per la vita del mondo. Cristologia ed eucaristia in Giovanni.* Padua: Messaggero (Conoscere il Vangelo 6).

———, 1977, "Segno giovanneo e sacramenti." In *Segni e sacramenti nel vangelo di Giovanni,* P.R. Tragan (ed.). Rome: Editrice Anselmiana (Studia Anselmiana 66), pp. 17-44.

———, 1997, "Il prologo di Giovanni (1, 1-18) nell'orizzonte culturale dei suoi lettori." *Teologia* 22, pp. 14-47, see also *Ricerche storico-bibliche* 10 (1998), pp. 251-78.

———, 1999, "Ritualità cristologica ed esperienza spirituale nel Vangelo secondo Giovanni." In *Mistica e ritualità. Mondi inconciliabili?,* G. Bonaccorso (ed.). Padua: Messaggero-Abbazia di S. Giustina (Caro Salutis Cardo. Contributi 16), pp. 237-73. See also *Teologia* 23 (1998), pp. 330-62.

Sequeri, P., 1989, "Dare la vita ed essere sacrificato." *Teologia* 14, pp. 143-53.

Sherwood, P., 1955, *The Earlier Ambigua of Saint Maximus the Confessor and the Refutation of Origenism.* Rome: Pontificium Institutem S. Anselmi.

Snaith, N.H. 1957, "Sacrifices in the Old Testament." *VT* 7, pp. 308-17.

———, 1965, "Sin Offering and the Guilt Offering." *VT* 15, pp. 73-80.

Stevenson, K.W., 1989, "Eucharistic Sacrifice — An Insoluble Liturgical Problem?" *Scottish Journal of Theology* 42, pp. 469-92.

Sykes, S.W. (ed.), 1991a, See *SRDE.*

———, 1991b, "Outline of a Theology of Sacrifice." In *SRDE,* pp. 282-98.

Teilhard de Chardin, 1967, *Le Milieu Divin: An Essay on the Interior Life.* London and Glasgow: Collins Fontana Books, Sixth impression [1957].

———, 1968, *Science and Christ.* London: Collins [1955].

———, 1971, *Christianity and Evolution*. New York and London: A Harvest/HBJ Book [1969].

———, 1973a, *The Future of Man*. London and Glasgow: Collins Fontana Books, Fourth impression.

———, 1973b, *The Prayer of the Universe*. Selected from the *Writings in Time of War*. London and Glasgow: Collins Fontana Books.

———, 1974a, *The Hymn of the Universe*. London: Fontana Religious Books, Fourth impression.

———, 1974b, *Let Me Explain*. Texts selected and arranged by Jean-Pierre Demoulin, London and Glasgow: Collins Fontana Books, Second impression.

———, 1978, *The Heart of Matter*. London: Collins.

Terrin, A.N., See in previous section.

Thachil, J., See in previous section.

Thoma, C., 1978, "Struttura e contenuto della liturgia cristiana." *Concilium* 10, pp. 1419-25.

Thomas, J.C., 1982, "Faith and History: a Critique of Recent Dogmatics." *Religious Studies* 18, pp. 327-36.

Thunberg, L., 1965, *Microcosm and Mediator: The Theological Anthropology of Maximus the Confessor*. Copenhagen: Lund.

———, 1982, "Symbol and Mystery in St. Maximus the Confessor with Particular Reference to the Doctrine of Eucharistic Presence." In *MCAS*, pp. 285-308.

Thurian, M., 1961, *The Eucharistic Memorial*. Part 2. *The New Testament*. London: Lutterworth Press (Ecumenical Studies in Worship 8).

———, 1966, *The Eucharistic Memorial*. Part 1. *The Old Testament*. London: Lutterworth Press (Ecumenical Studies in Worship 7), Third Impression.

Tillard, J.M.R., 1981, "Sacrificial Terminology and the Eucharist." *One in Christ* 17, pp. 306-23.

Triacca, A.M. and A. Pistoia (eds.), 1998, See *LCCS*.

Ubbiali, S. (ed.), 1998a, See *SEER*.

———, 1998b, "Teologia del Sacrificio." In *SEER*, pp. 451-81.

Vagaggini, C., 1958, *Il senso teologico della liturgia*. Rome: Paoline.

———, 1969, "La messa sacramento del sacrificio pasquale di Cristo e della Chiesa." *Rivista Liturgica* 56, pp. 179-93.

Vanhoye, A., 1992, "(Mt 26,28) Il sangue dell'alleanza nel Nuovo Testamento." *Civiltà cattolica* 143, pp. 118-32.

Vaux, R. de, 1964, *Le istituzioni dell'Antico Testamento.* Casale, Turin: Marietti.

Vidalis, M., 1998, "Louange et Récréation du Cosmos dans la Priére Eucharistique." In *LCCS,* pp. 195-208.

Vonier, A., 1955, *La chiave della dottrina eucaristica.* Milan: Paoline [1925].

Warnach, V., 1968, "Symbol and Reality in the Eucharist." *Concilium* 4, pp. 43-53.

Wehr, L., 1987, *Arznei dur Unsterblichkeit: die Eucharistie bei Ignatius von Antiochien und im Johannesevangelium,* Münster: Aschendorff.

Wenham, G.J., 1995, "The Theology of the Old Testament Sacrifice." In *BSSB,* pp. 75-87.

Whiteley, D.E.H., 1957, "St. Paul's Thought on the Atonement." *Journal of Theological Studies* (New series) 8, pp. 240-55.

Yonge, C.D. (tr.), 1993, *The Works of Philo.* New updated edition, complete and unabridged in one volume. Massachusetts: Hendrickson.

Young, F.M., 1979, *The Use of Sacrificial Ideas in Greek Christian Writers from the New Testament to John Chrysostom.* Cambridge-Massachusetts: The Philadelphia Patristic Foundation (Patristic Monograph Series 5).

Zan, R. de, 1991, "[Mt 26, 28] Sangue versato in remissione dei peccati." *Rivista Liturgica* 78, pp. 582-87.

Zizioulas, I., 1994, *Il creato come eucaristia. Approccio teologico al problema dell'ecologia*. Magnano (Biella): Edizioni Qiqajon — Comunità di Bose (Spiritualità Orientale) [1992].

———, 1996, *Eucaristia e regno di Dio*. Magnano (Biella): Edizioni Qiqajon — Comunità di Bose (Spiritualità Orientale) [1994].

Zizioulas, J.D., 1970, "The Eucharistic Community and the Catholicity of the Church." *One in Christ* 6, pp. 314-37.

———, 1989, "Preserving God's Creation: Three Lectures on Theology and Ecology 1-2." *King's Theological Review* 12, pp. 1-5; 41-45.

———, 1990, "Preserving God's Creation: Three Lectures on Theology and Ecology 3." *King's Theological Review* 13, pp. 1-5.

Index